FAIRY TAIL

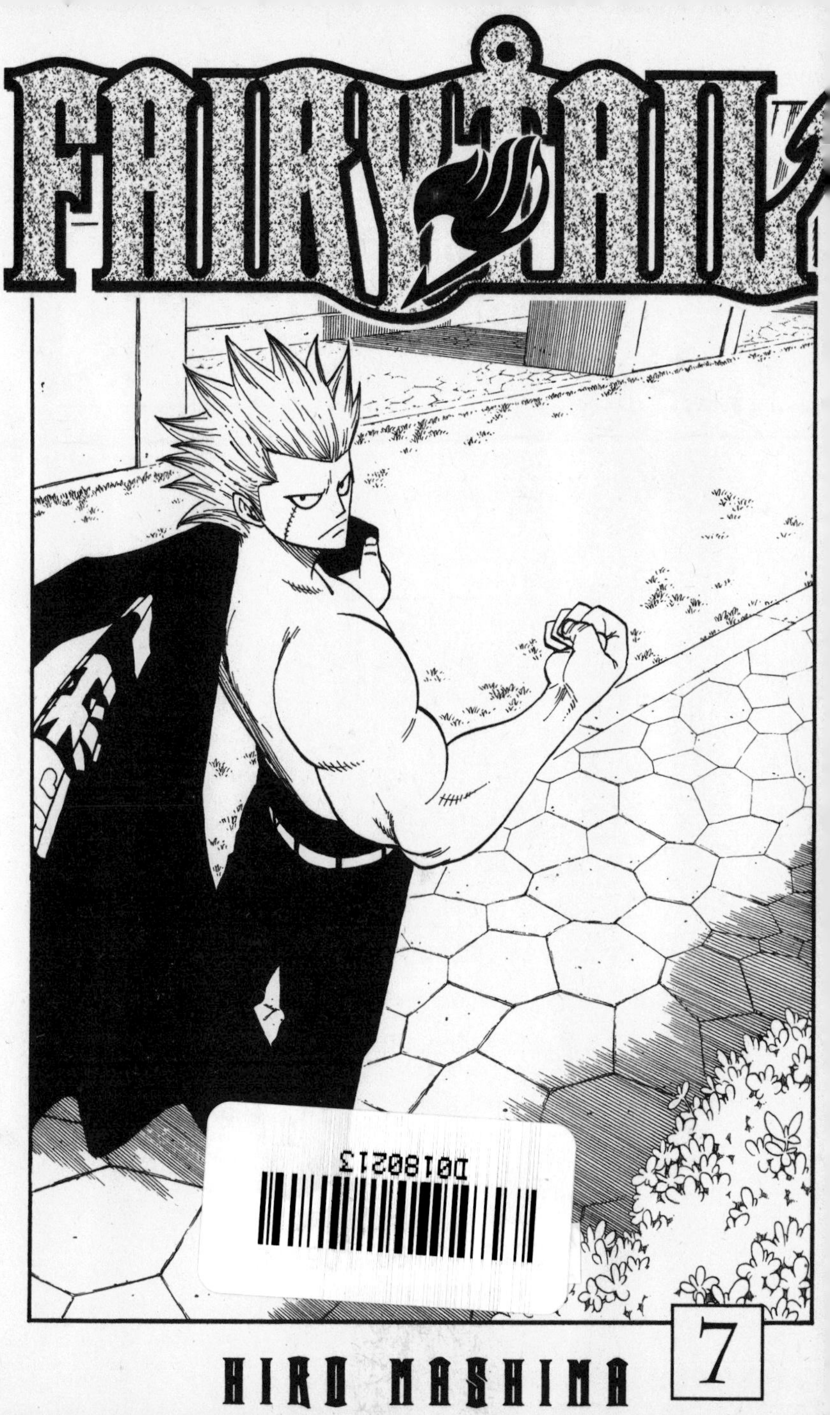

7

HIRO MASHIMA

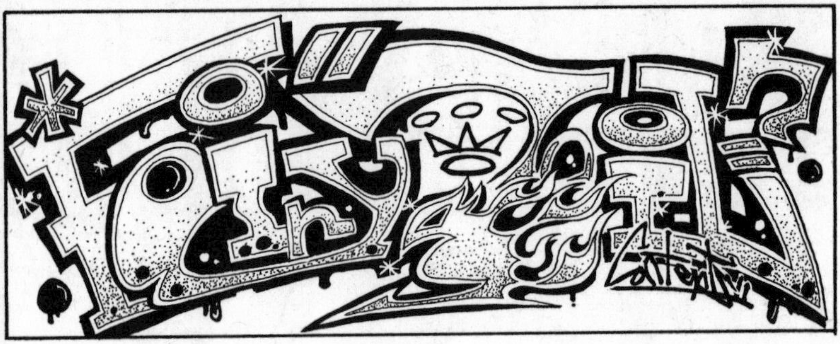
Contents

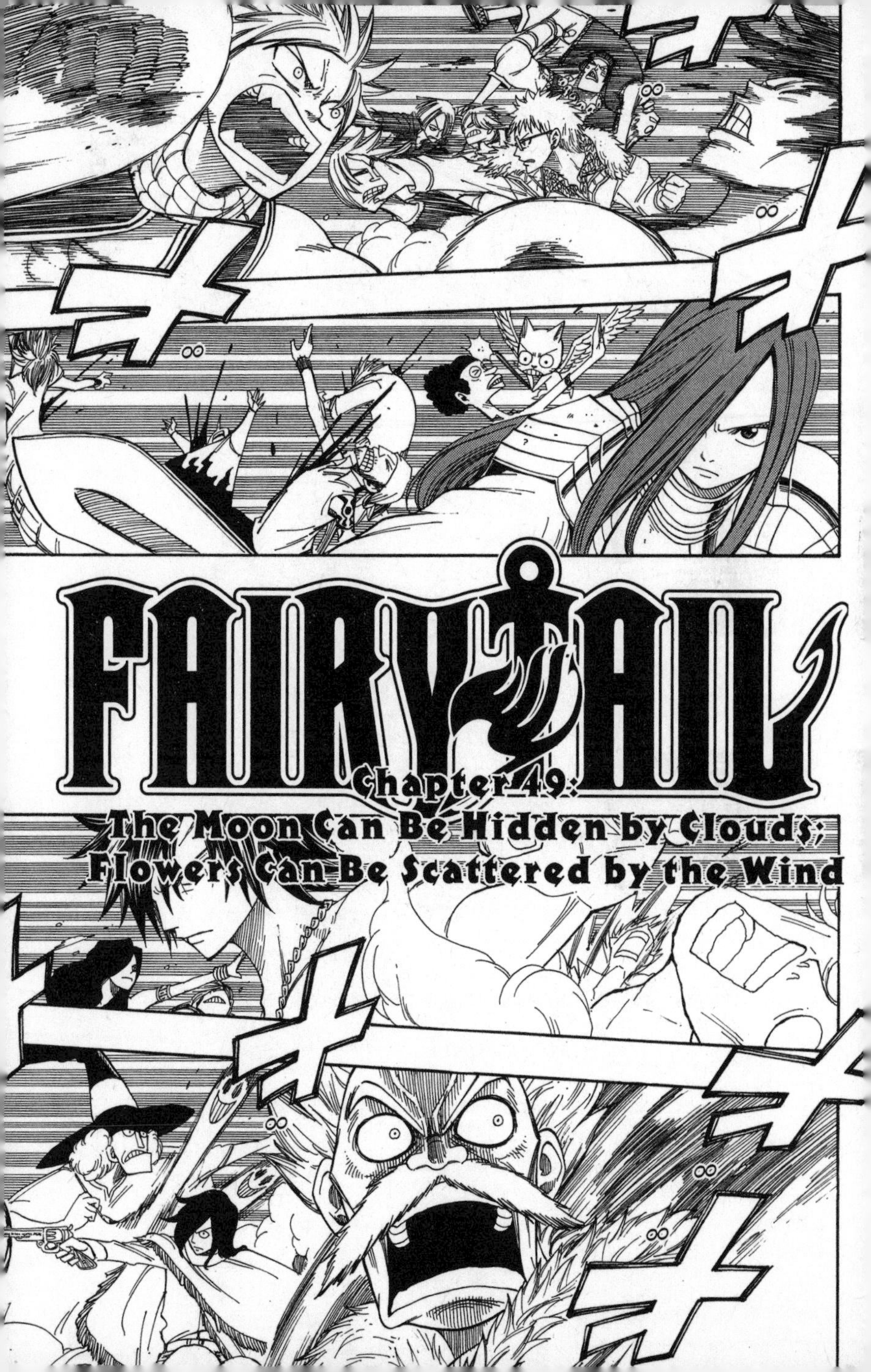
FAIRY TAIL
Chapter 49:
The Moon Can Be Hidden by Clouds;
Flowers Can Be Scattered by the Wind

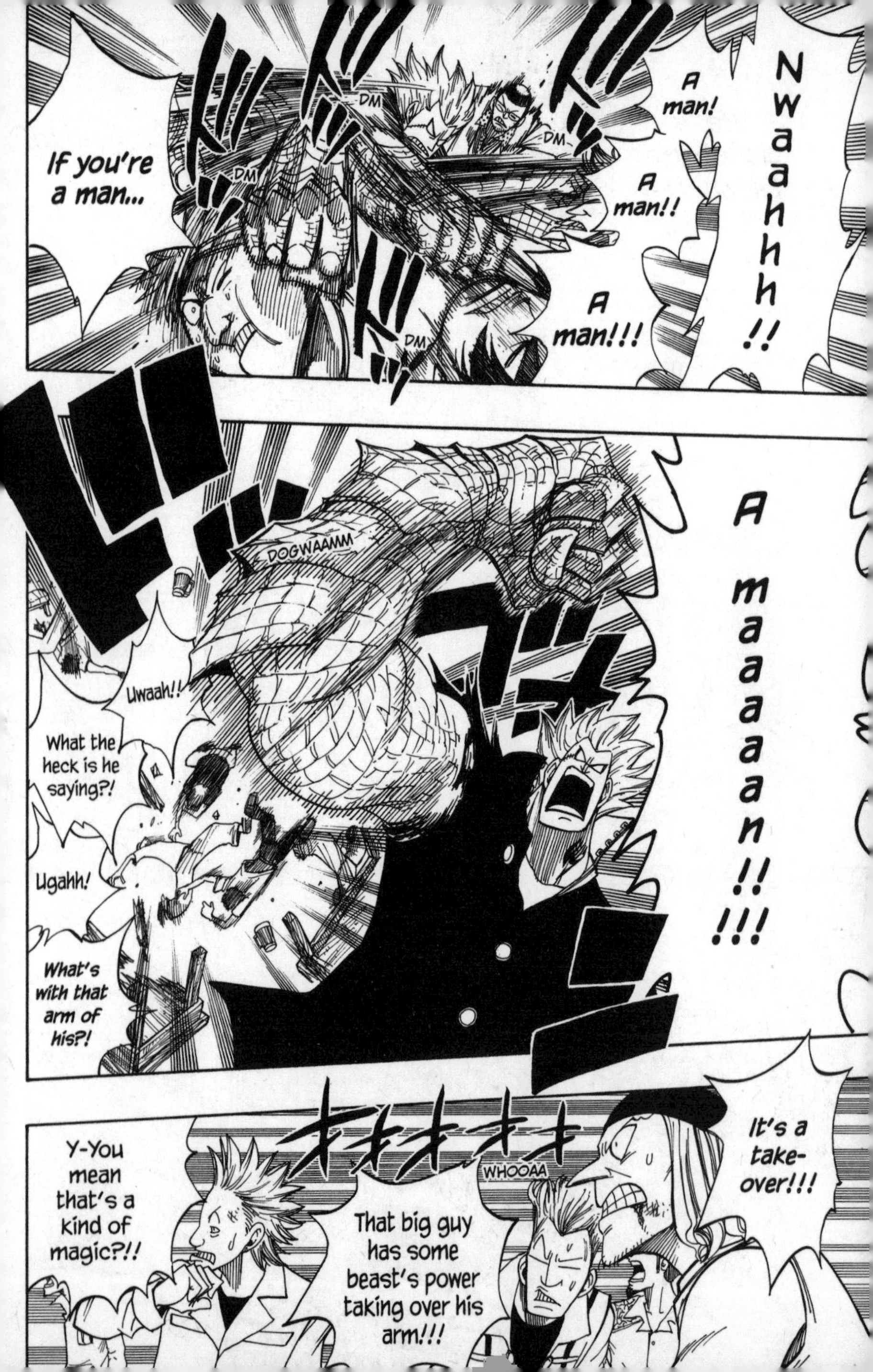
Nwaahhh!!
A man!
A man!!
A man!!!
DM
DM
DM
DM
If you're a man...
A maaaaaan!!!!!
DOGWAAMM
Uwaah!!
What the heck is he saying?!
Ugahh!
What's with that arm of his?!
It's a take-over!!!
WHOOAA
That big guy has some beast's power taking over his arm!!!
Y-You mean that's a kind of magic?!!

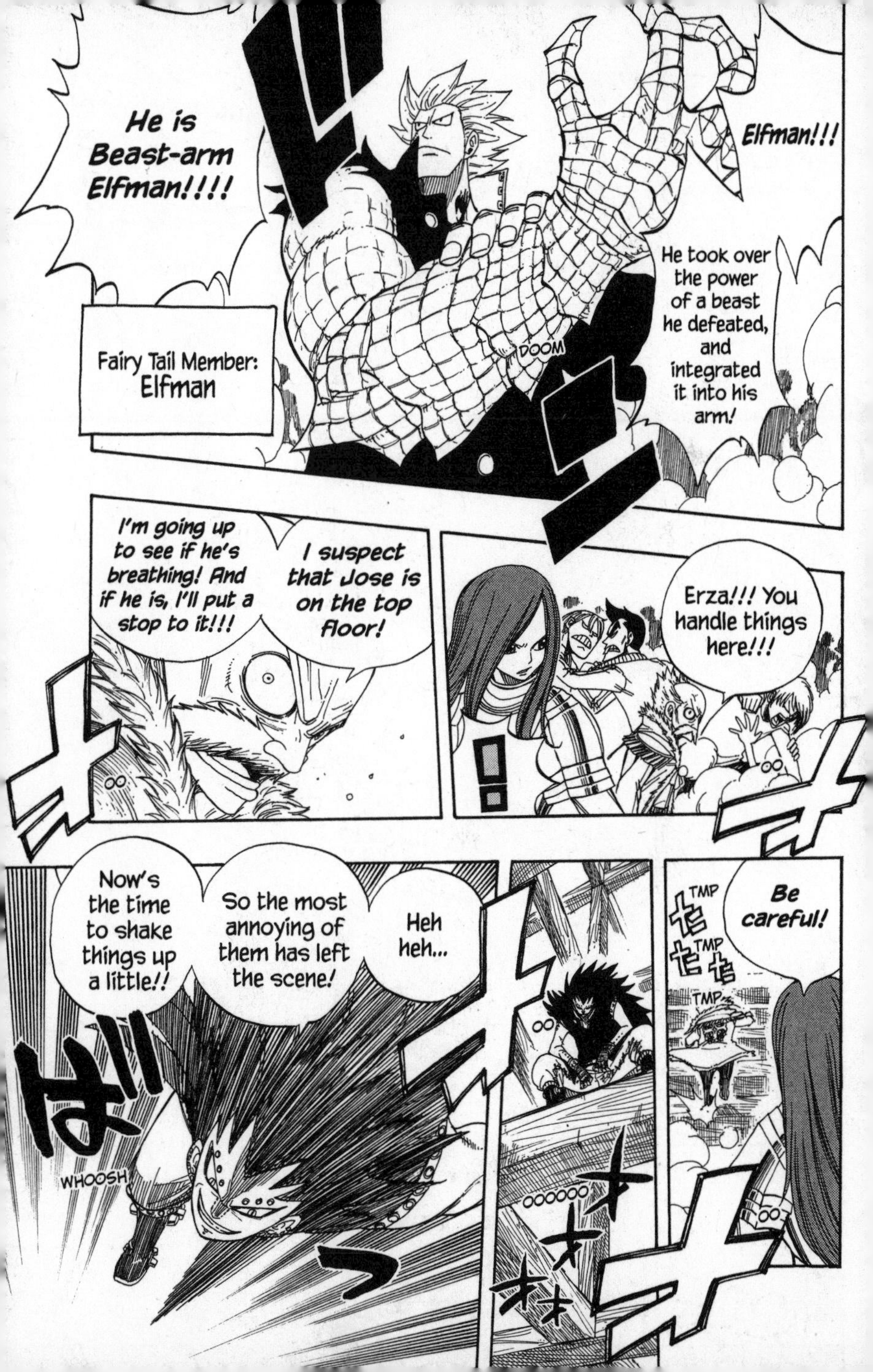
Elfman!!!
He took over the power of a beast he defeated, and integrated it into his arm!
He is Beast-arm Elfman!!!!
DOOM
Fairy Tail Member: Elfman
Erza!!! You handle things here!!!
I suspect that Jose is on the top floor!
I'm going up to see if he's breathing! And if he is, I'll put a stop to it!!!
Be careful!
TMP
TMP
TMP
Heh heh...
So the most annoying of them has left the scene!
Now's the time to shake things up a little!!
WHOOSH

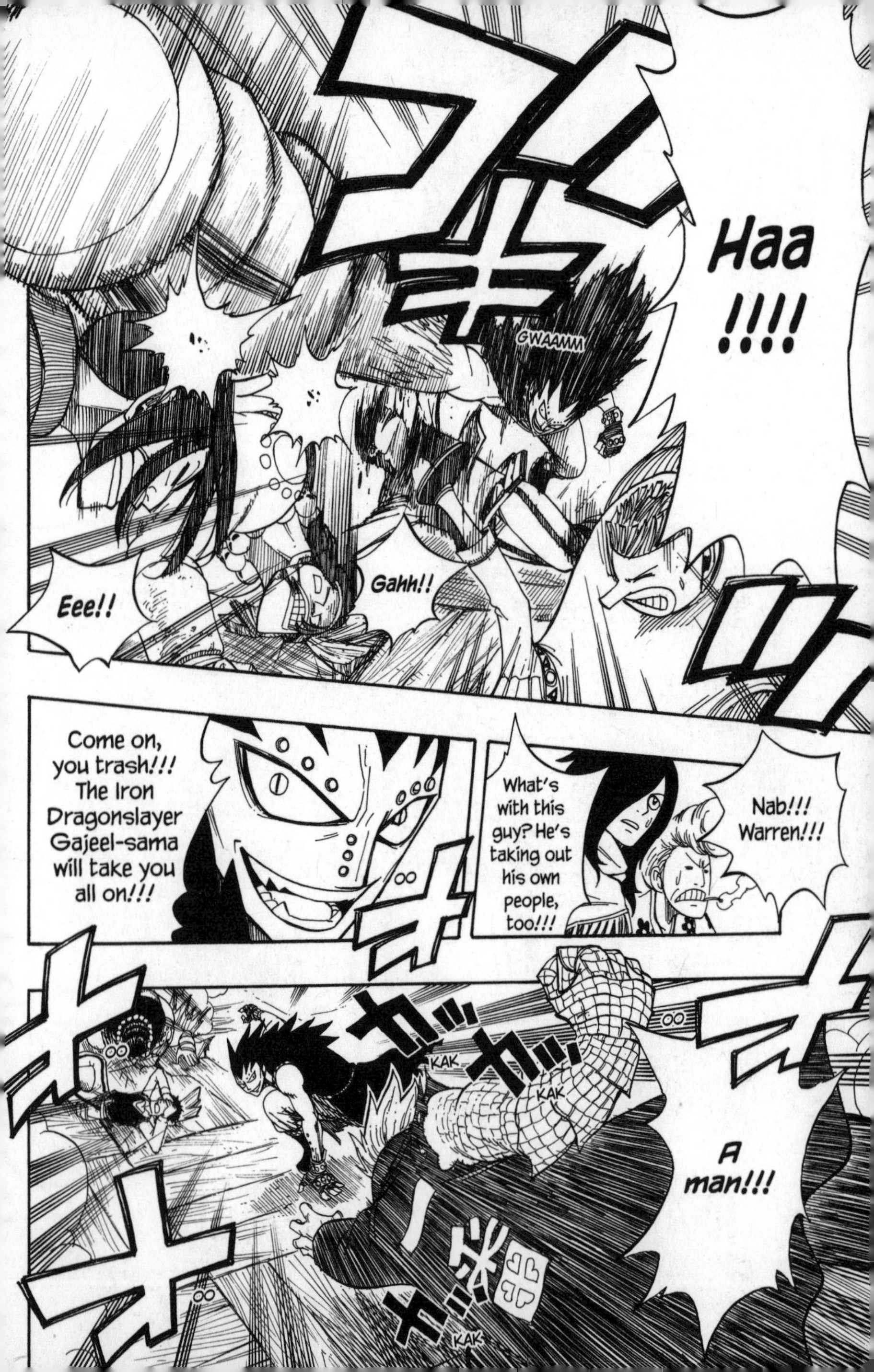
Haa!!!!
GWAAMM
Gahh!!
Eee!!
Nab!!! Warren!!!
What's with this guy? He's taking out his own people, too!!!
Come on, you trash!!! The Iron Dragonslayer Gajeel-sama will take you all on!!!
A man!!!
KAK
KAK
KAK

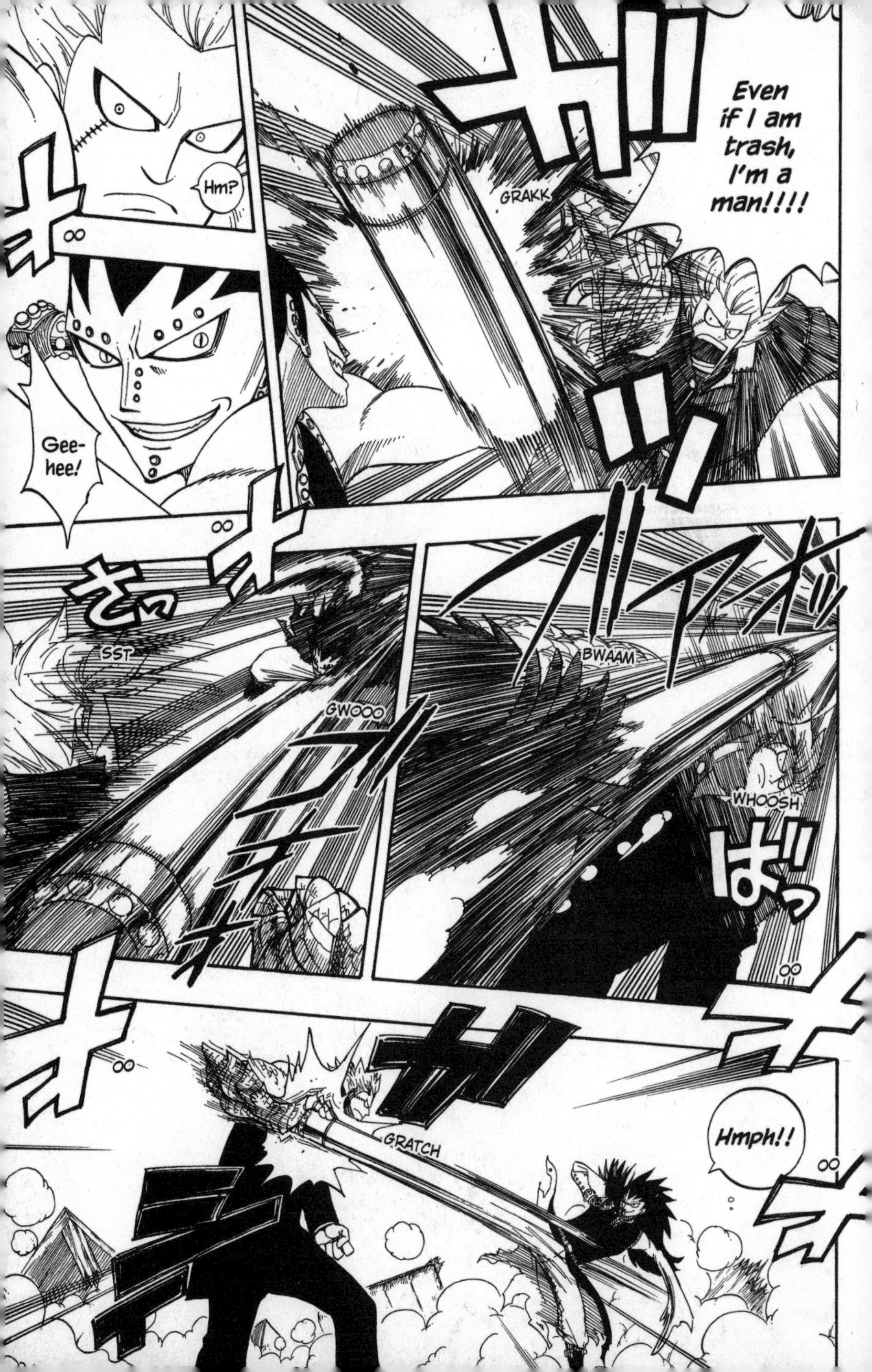
Even if I am trash, I'm a man!!!!
GRAKK
Hm?
Gee-hee!
BWAAM
WHOOSH
ばっ
SST
GWOOO
GRATCH
Hmph!!

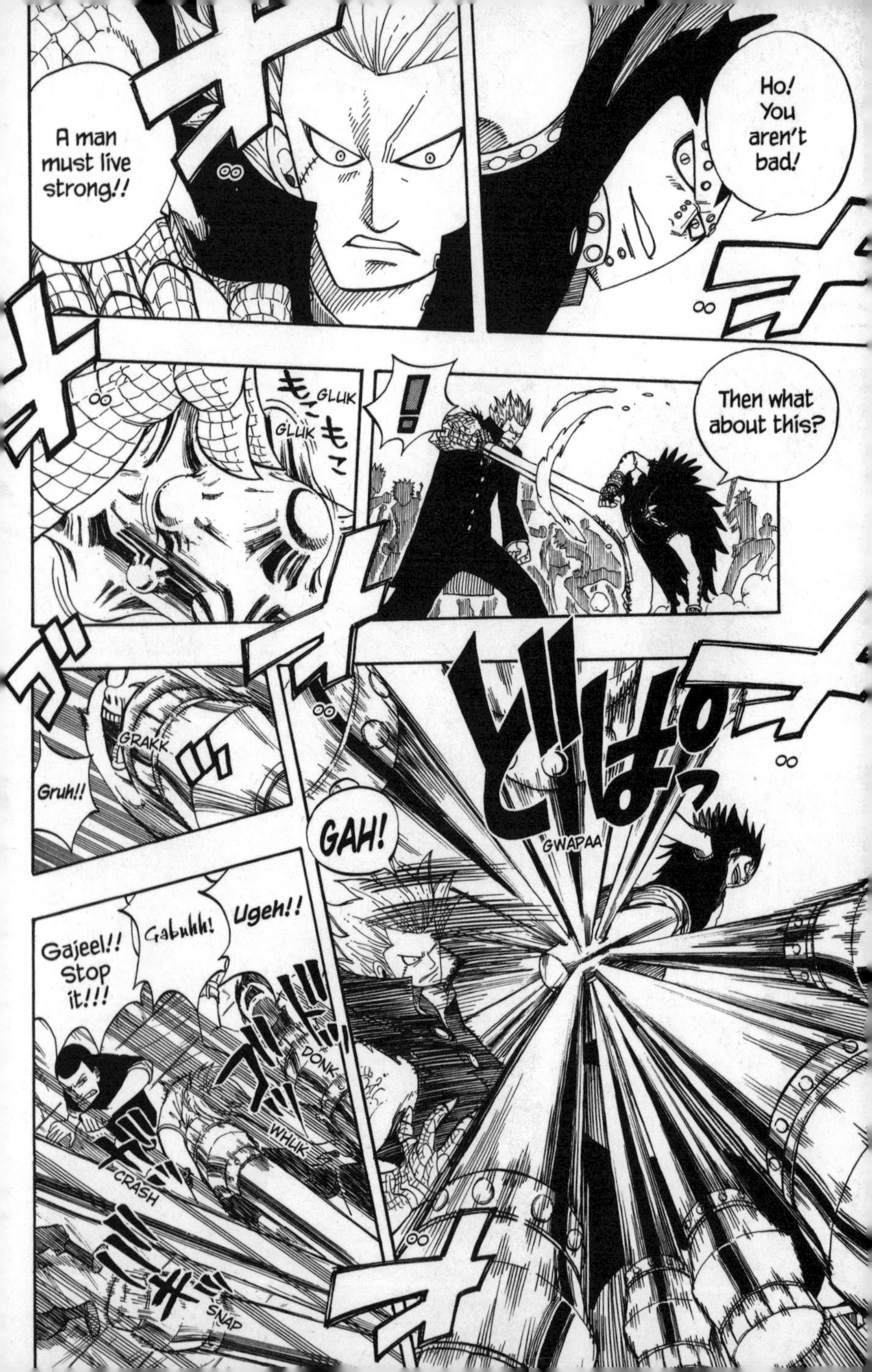
Ho! You aren't bad!
A man must live strong!!
Then what about this?
!
もこ GLUK
GLUK もこ
GAH!
GWAPAA
GRAKK
Gruh!!
Ugeh!!
Gabuhh!
Gajeel!! Stop it!!!
DONK
WHUK
CRASH
SNAP

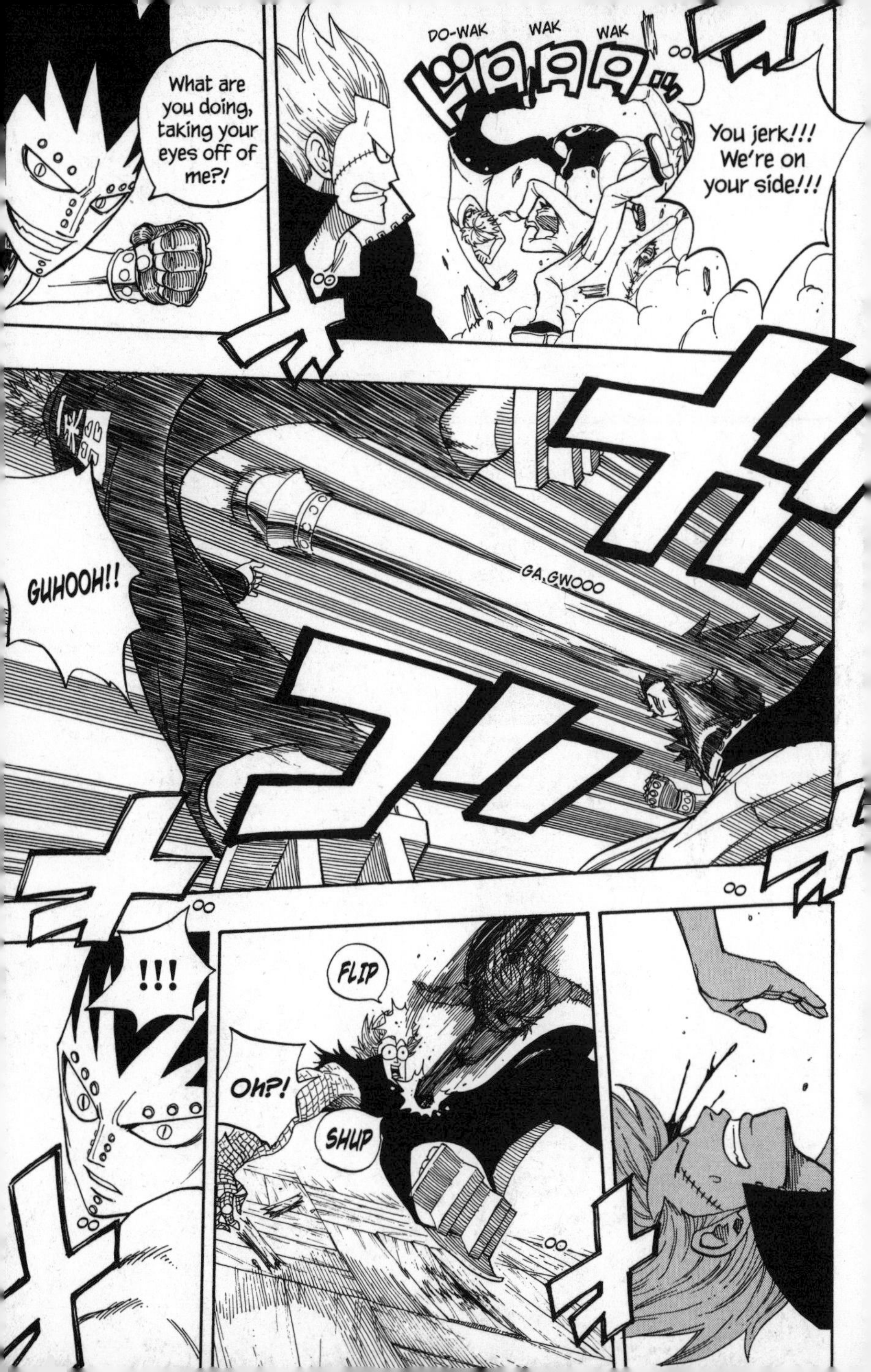
DO-WAK
WAK
WAK
You jerk!!! We're on your side!!!
What are you doing, taking your eyes off of me?!
GA GWOOO
GUHOOH!!
FLIP
Oh?!
SHUP
!!!

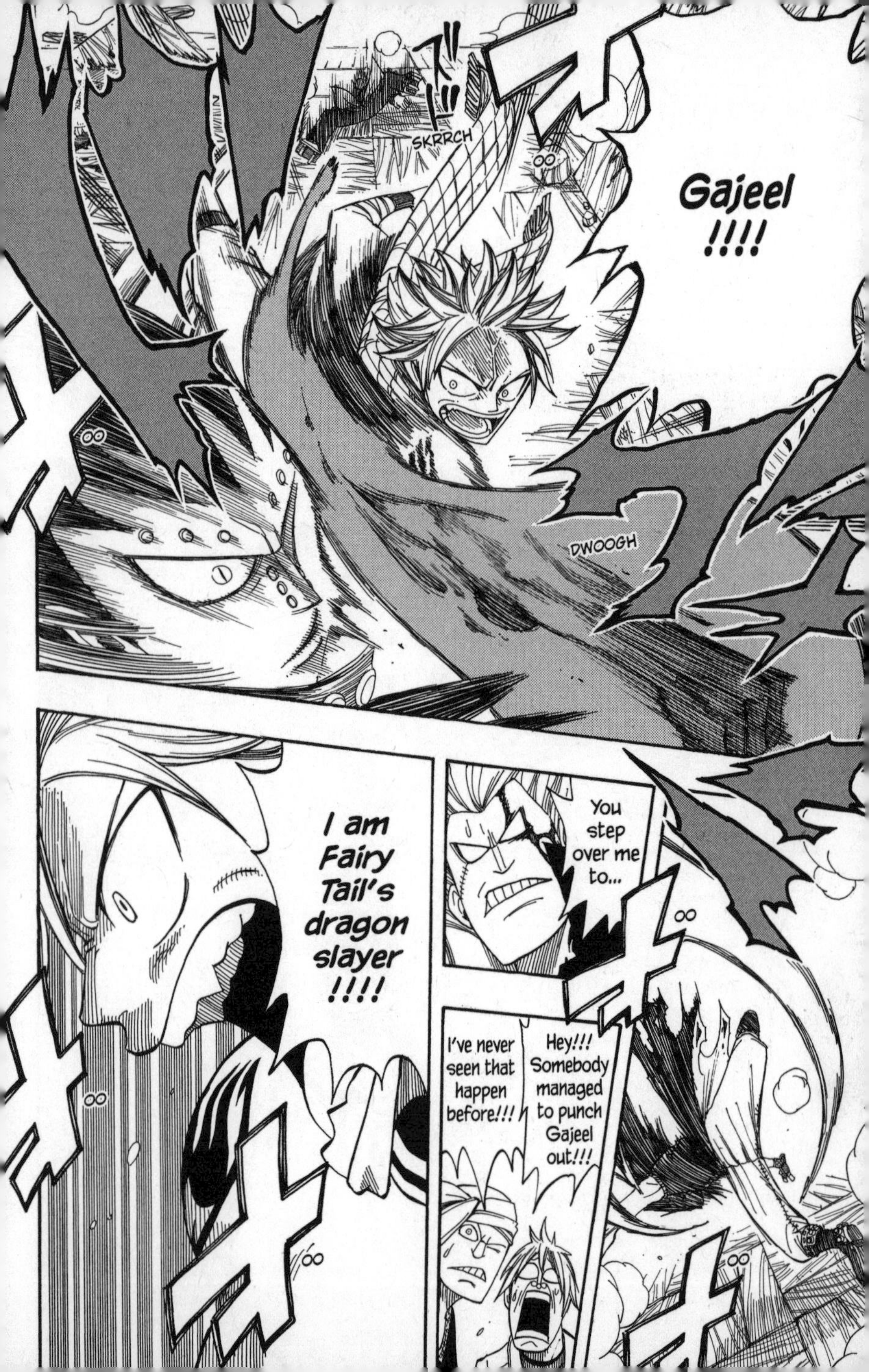
Gajeel
!!!!
SKRRCH
DWOOGH
You step over me to...
Hey!!! Somebody managed to punch Gajeel out!!!
I've never seen that happen before!!!
I am Fairy Tail's dragon slayer
!!!!

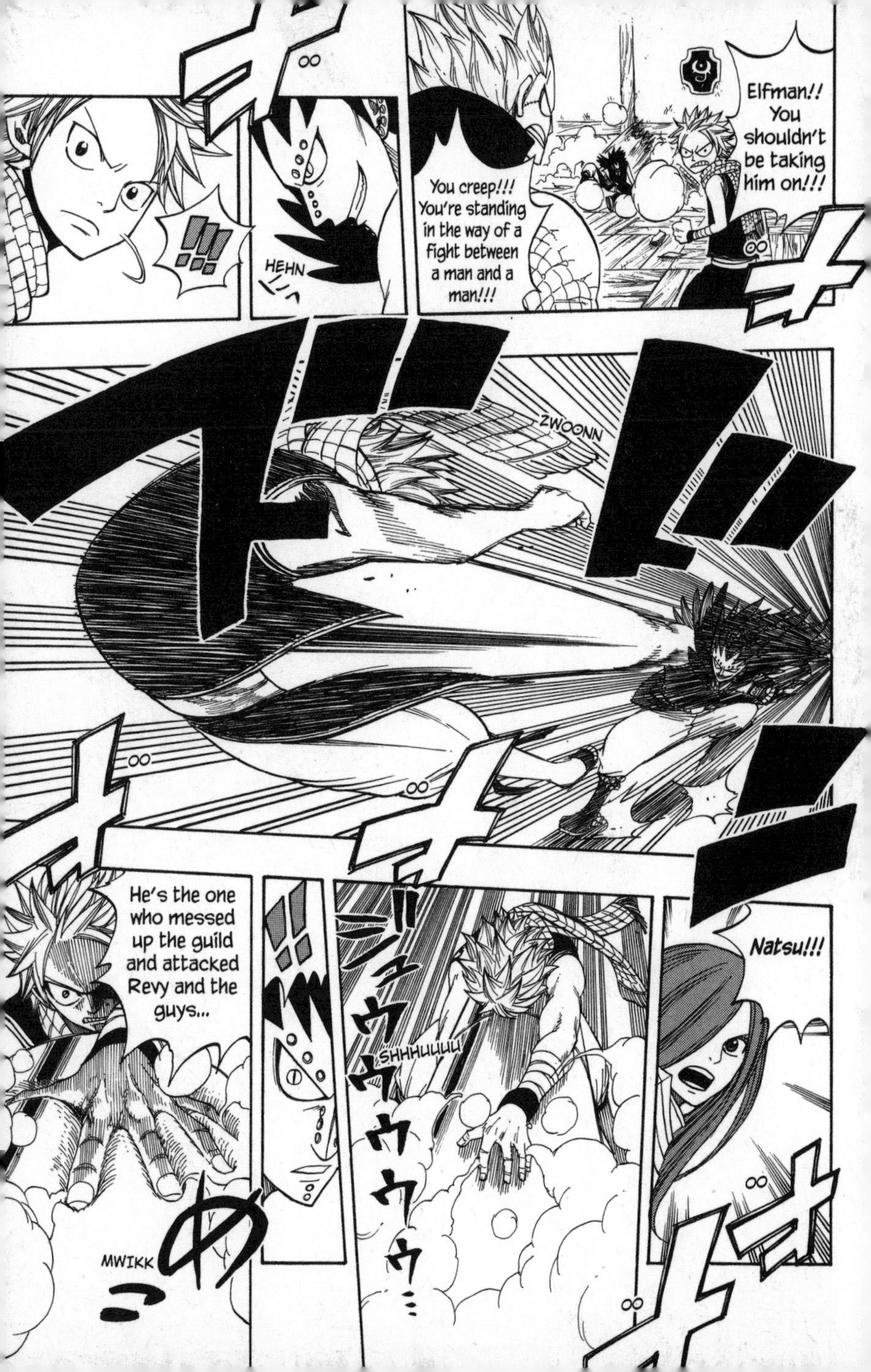
Elfman!! You shouldn't be taking him on!!!
You creep!!! You're standing in the way of a fight between a man and a man!!!
HEHN
ZWOONN
Natsu!!!
SHHHUUUU
He's the one who messed up the guild and attacked Revy and the guys...
MWIKK

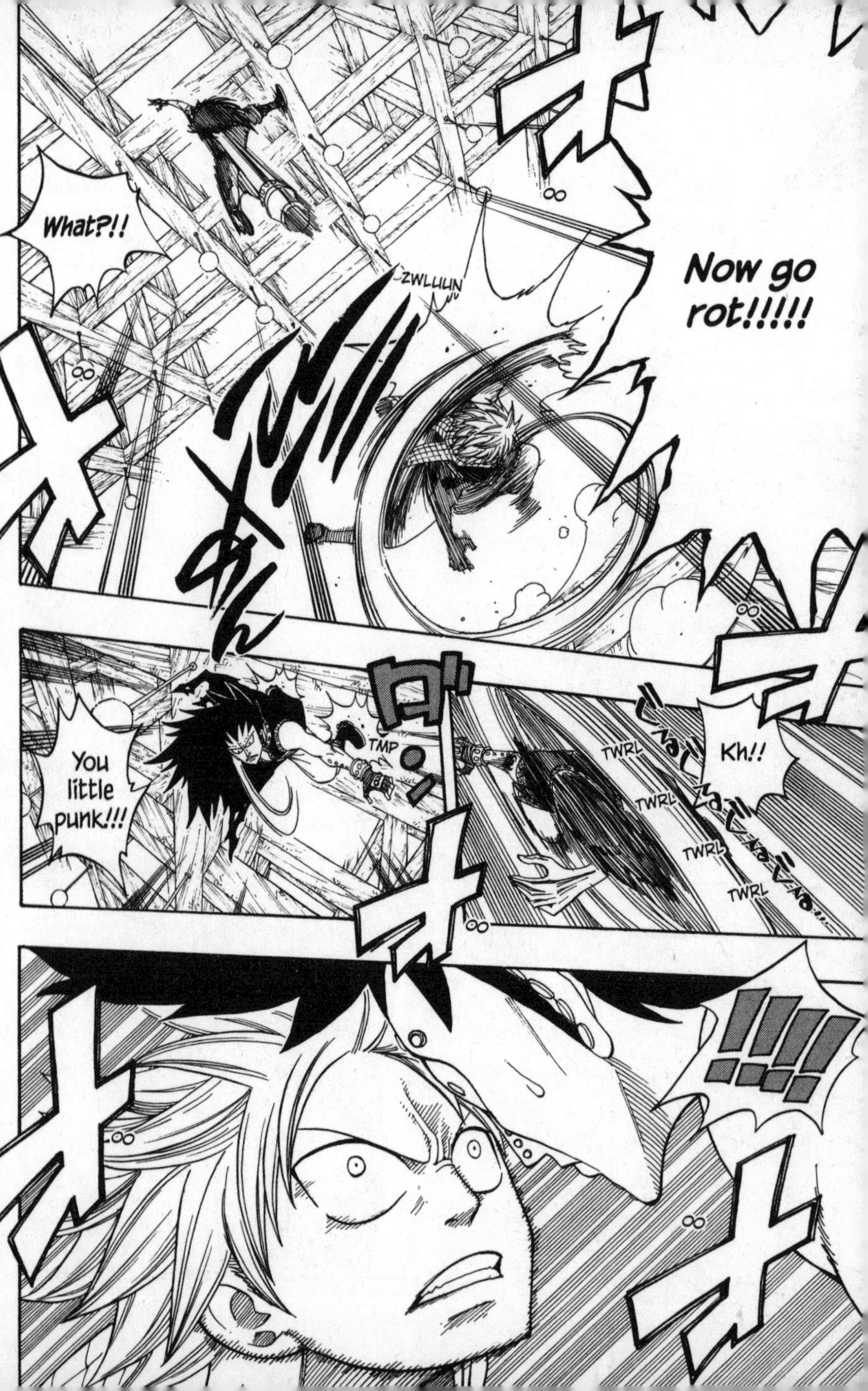
Now go rot!!!!!
ZWLUUN
What?!!
Kh!!
TWRL
TWRL
TWRL
TWRL
TMP
You little punk!!!

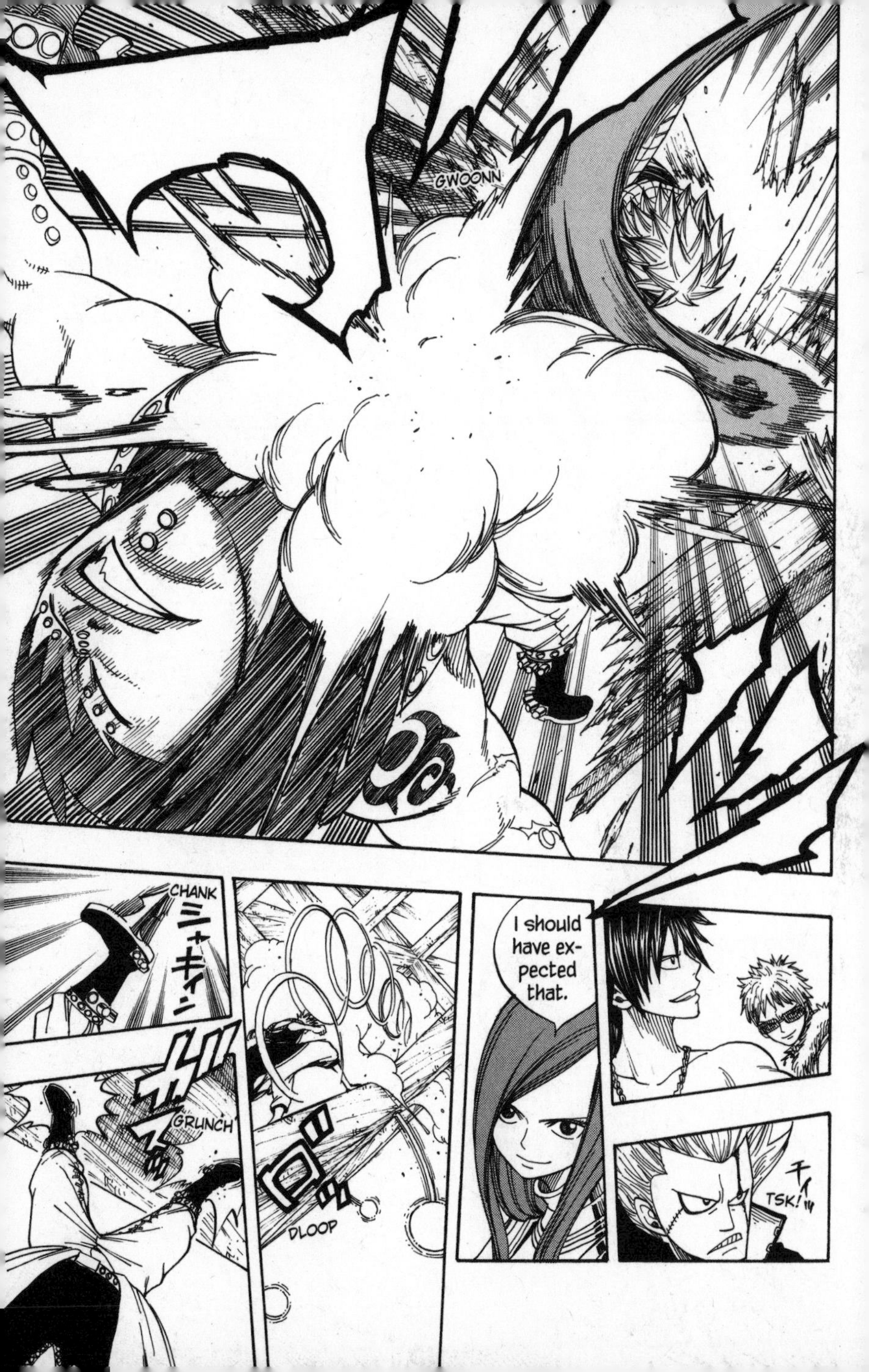
GWOONN
チィ
TSK!
I should have expected that.
DLOOP
CHANK
シャキィン
GRUNCH

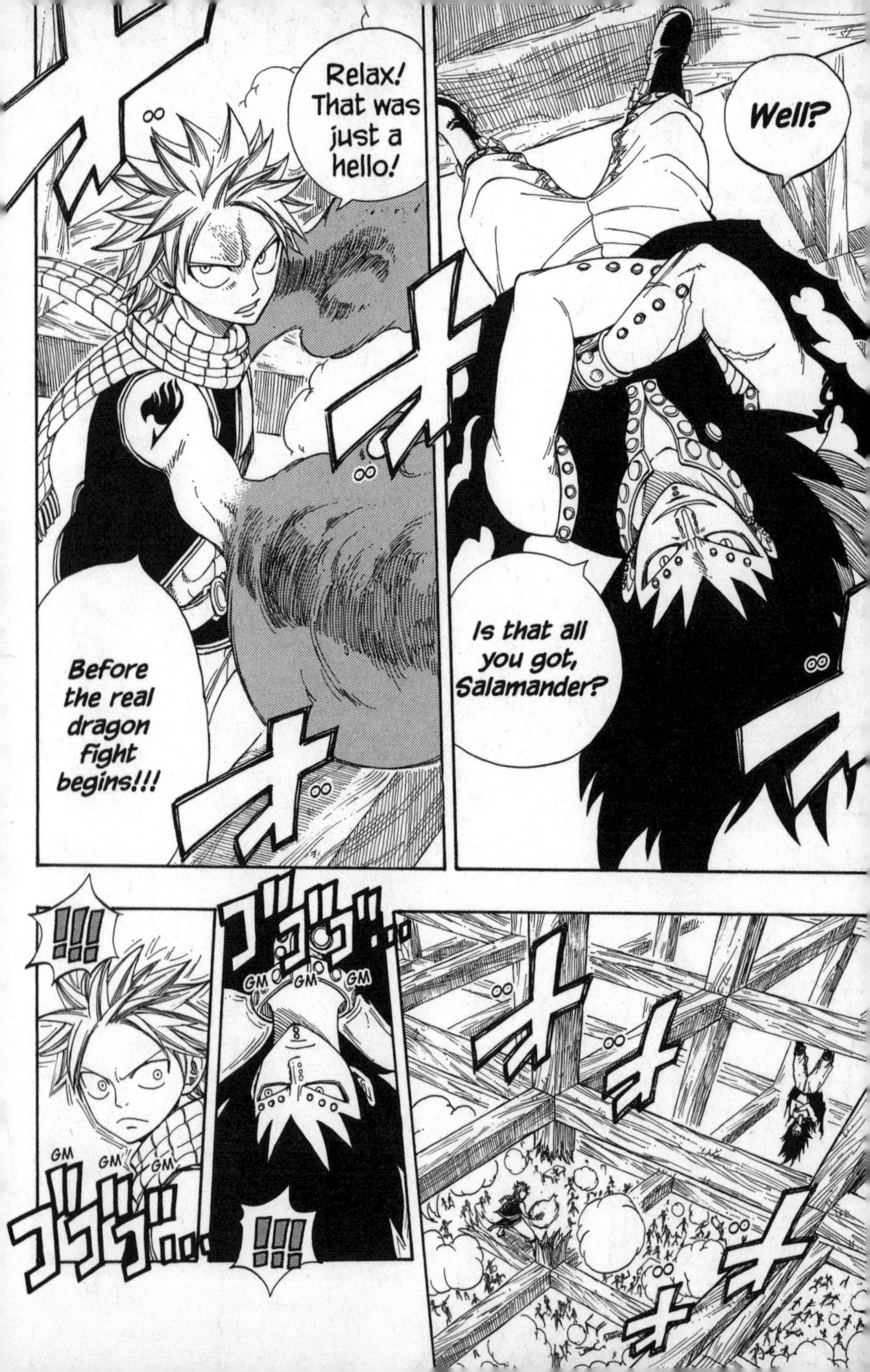
Well?
Is that all you got, Salamander?
Relax! That was just a hello!
Before the real dragon fight begins!!!
GM GM GM
!!!
!!!
GM GM GM

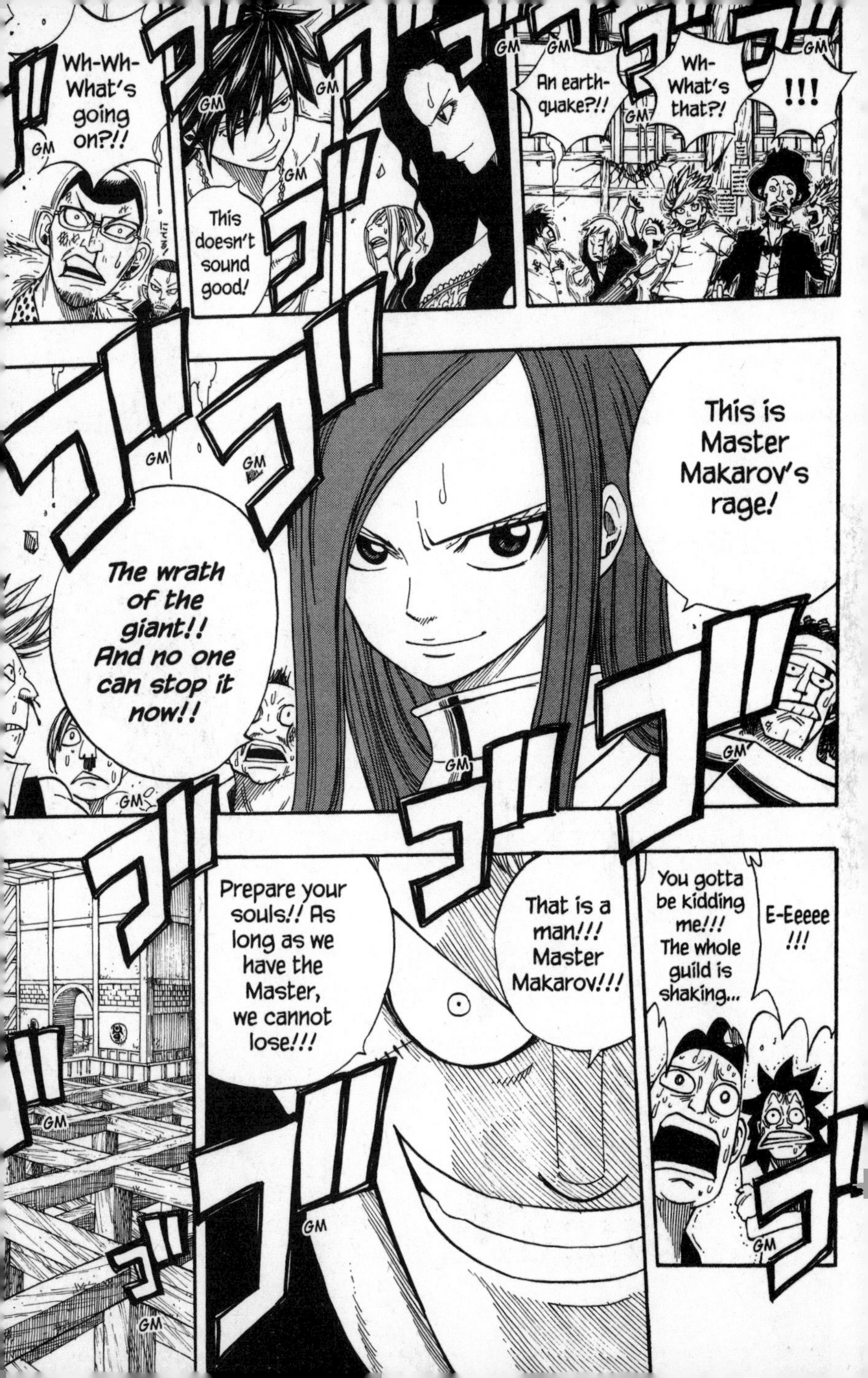
GM
!!!
Wh-What's that?!
An earthquake?!!
GM
This doesn't sound good!
GM
Wh-Wh-What's going on?!!
GM
This is Master Makarov's rage!
GM
The wrath of the giant!! And no one can stop it now!!
GM
E-Eeeee!!!
You gotta be kidding me!!! The whole guild is shaking...
GM
That is a man!!! Master Makarov!!!
Prepare your souls!! As long as we have the Master, we cannot lose!!!
GM
GM

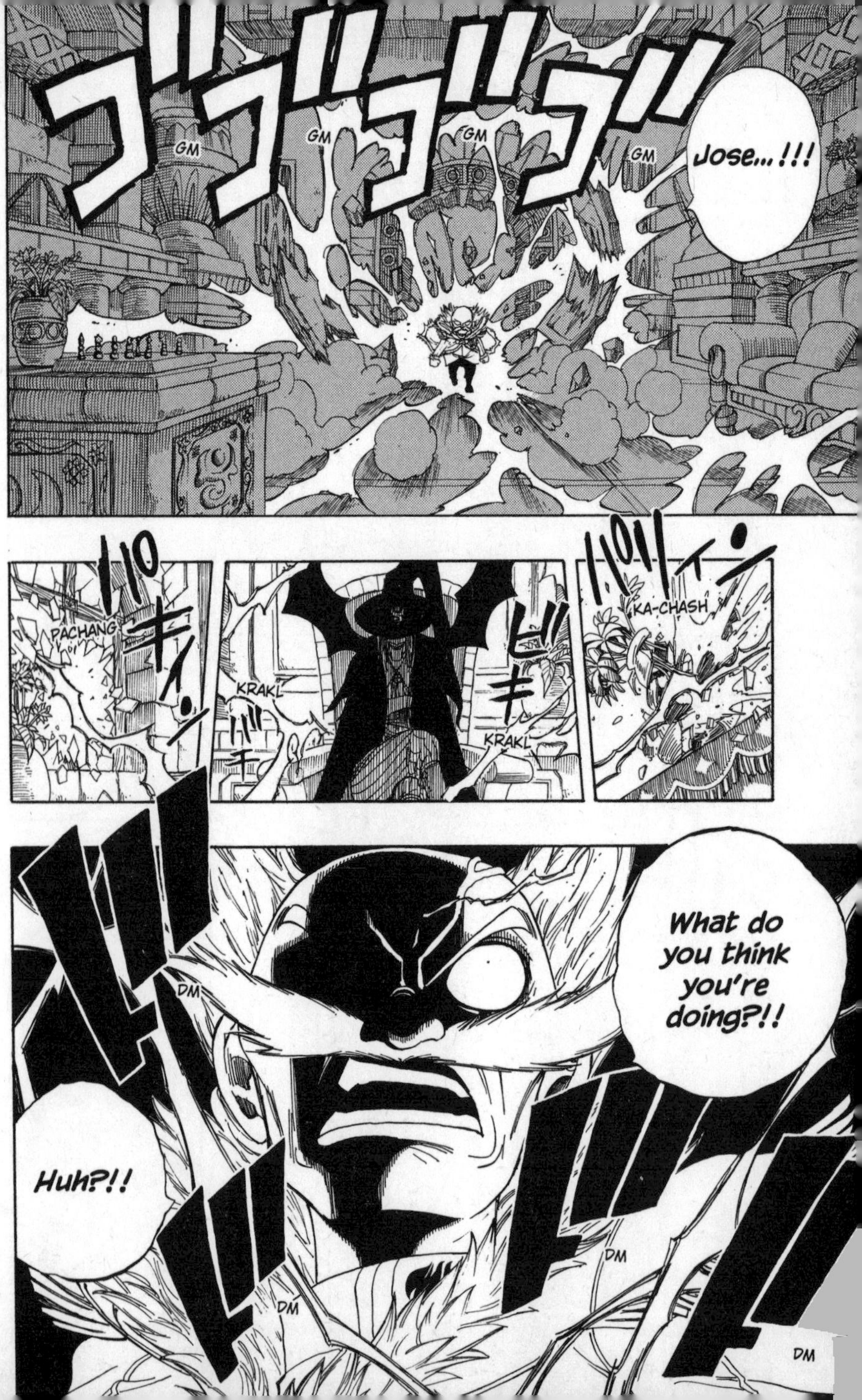
Jose...!!!
GM
GM
GM
GM
KA-CHASH
KRAKL
KRAKL
PACHANG
What do you think you're doing?!!
DM
Huh?!!
DM
DM
DM

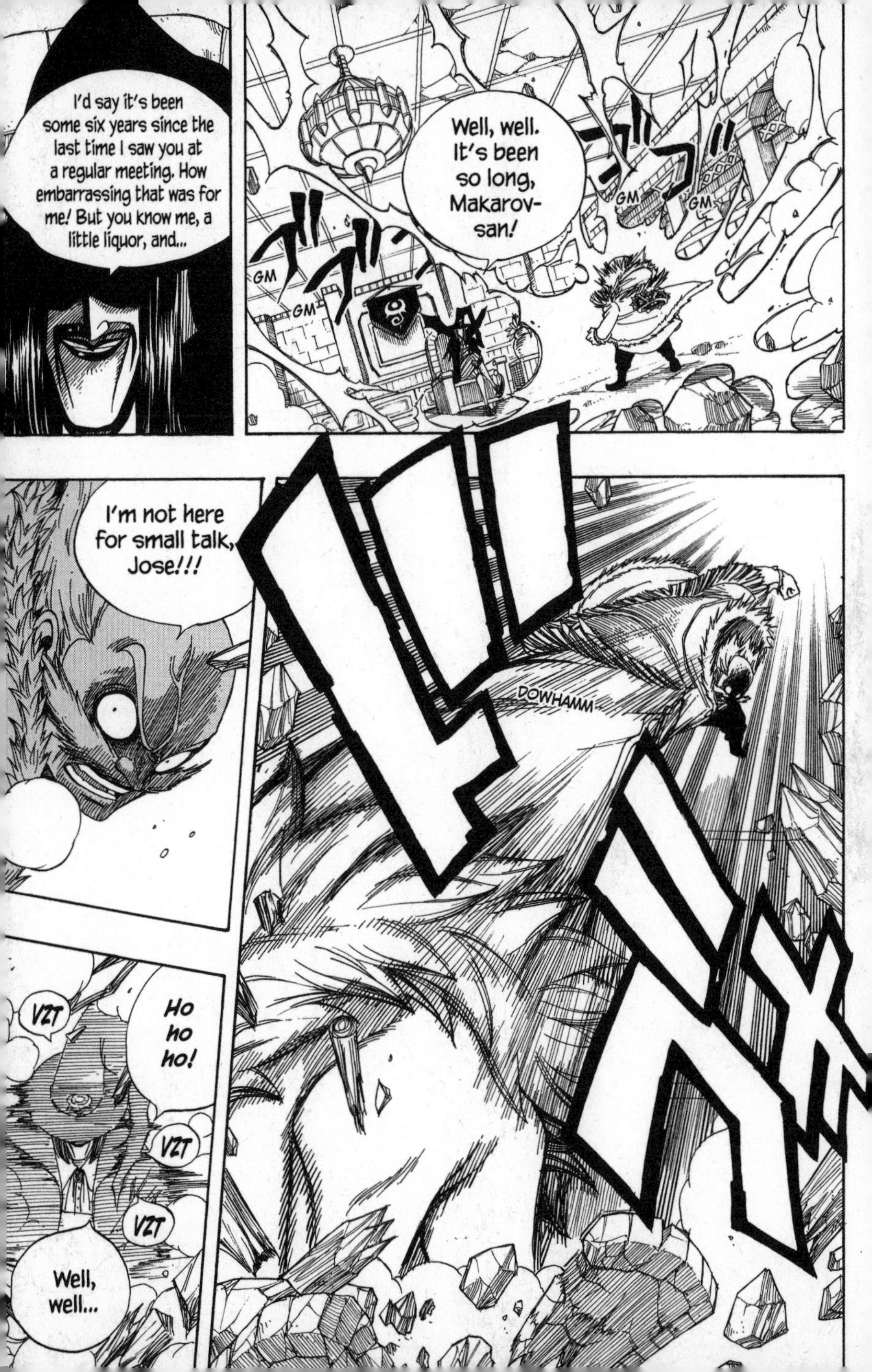
Well, well. It's been so long, Makarov-san!
GM
GM
GM
GM
I'd say it's been some six years since the last time I saw you at a regular meeting. How embarrassing that was for me! But you know me, a little liquor, and...
DOWHAMM
I'm not here for small talk, Jose!!!
VZT
Ho ho ho!
VZT
VZT
Well, well...

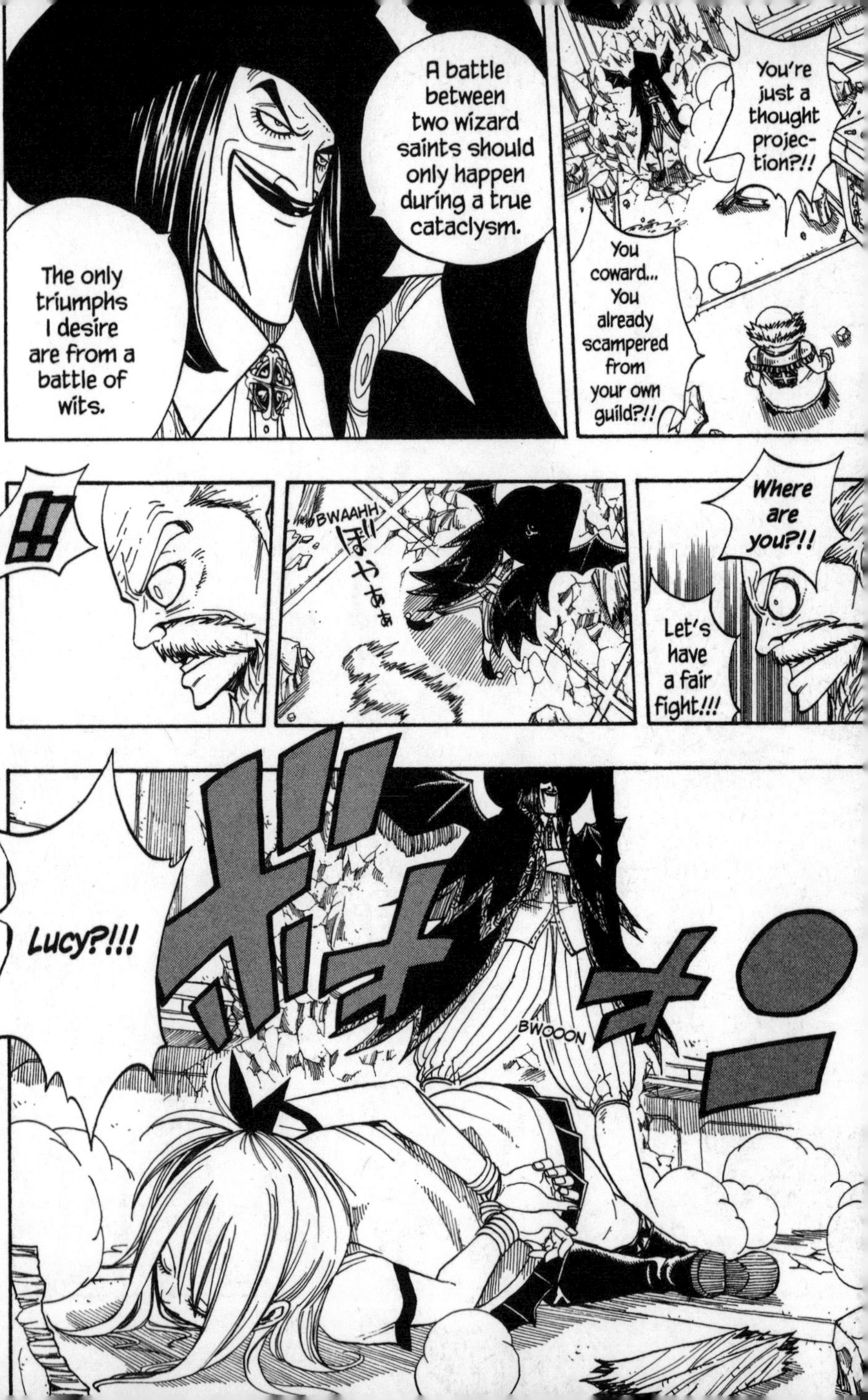
You're just a thought projec-tion?!!
You coward... You already scampered from your own guild?!!
A battle between two wizard saints should only happen during a true cataclysm.
The only triumphs I desire are from a battle of wits.
Where are you?!!
Let's have a fair fight!!!
BWAAHH
ぼやぁぁ
!!
Lucy?!!!
BWOOON

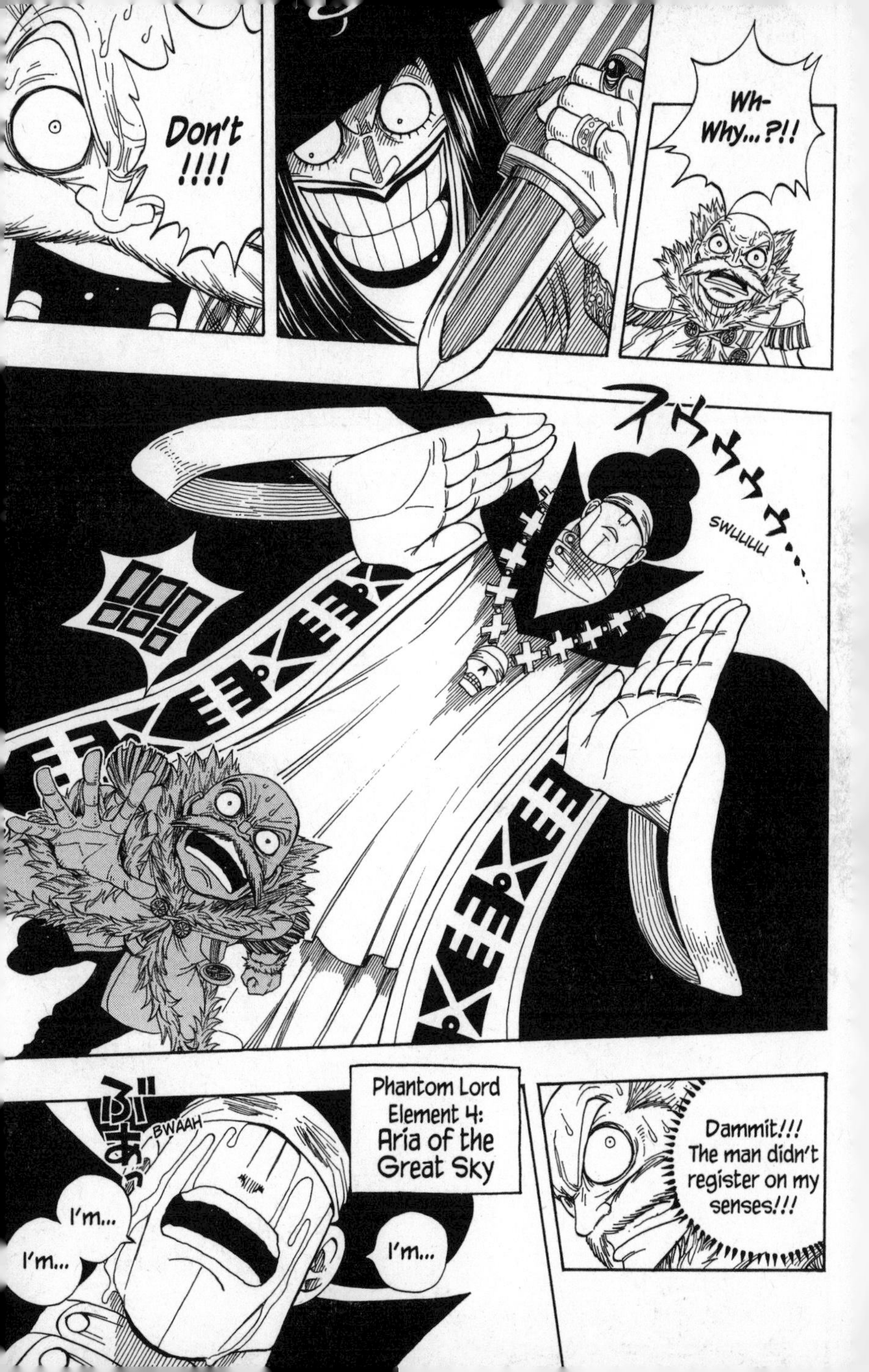
Wh- Why...?!!
Don't !!!!
SWUUUU
!!!!!
Dammit!!! The man didn't register on my senses!!!
Phantom Lord Element 4: Aria of the Great Sky
ぶあっ
BWAAH
I'm...
I'm...
I'm...

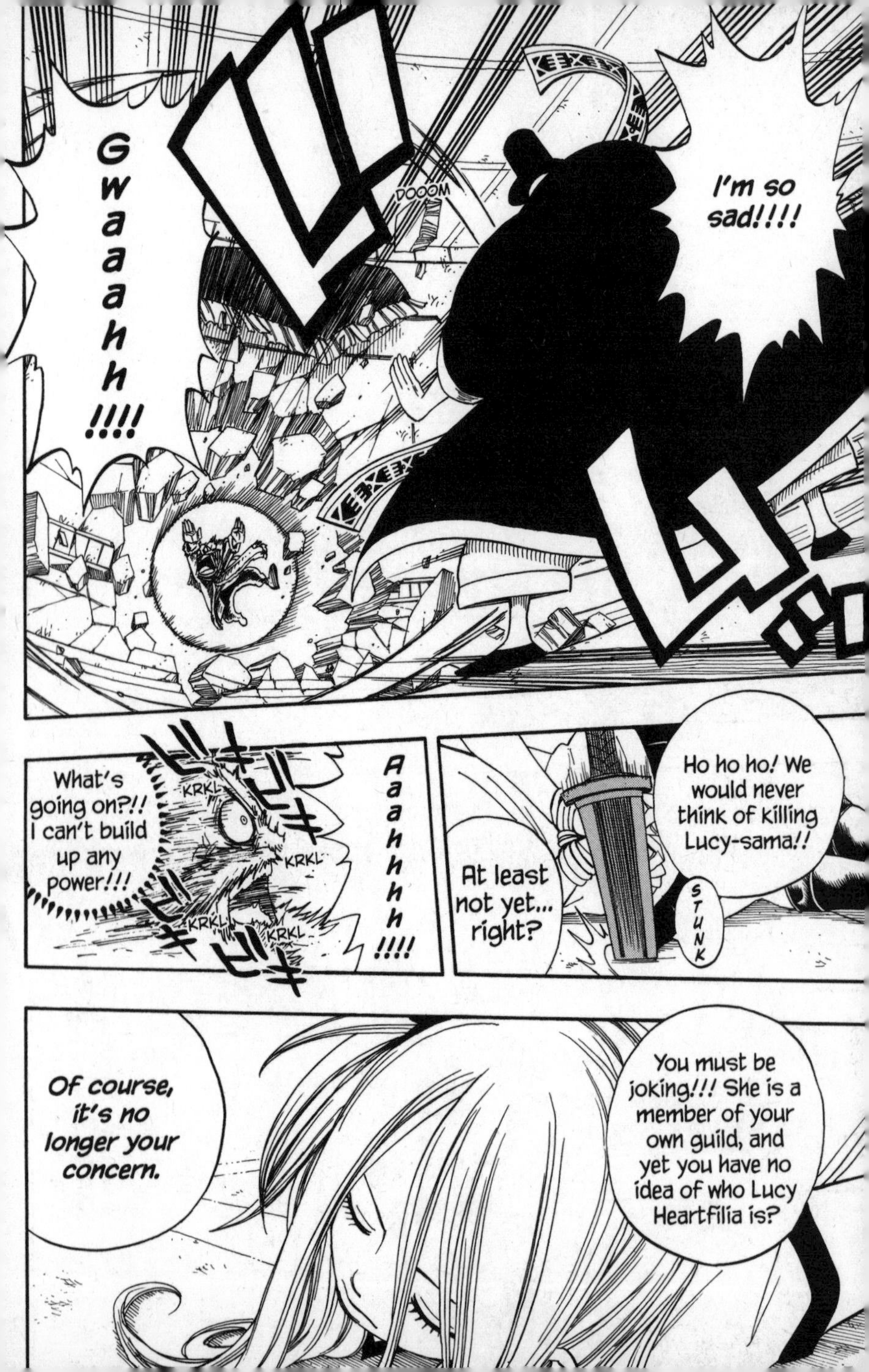
I'm so sad!!!!
DOOOM
Gwaaaahh!!!!
Ho ho ho! We would never think of killing Lucy-sama!!
STUNK
At least not yet... right?
Aaahhhhh!!!!
KRKL
What's going on?!! I can't build up any power!!!
KRKL
KRKL
KRKL
You must be joking!!! She is a member of your own guild, and yet you have no idea of who Lucy Heartfilia is?
Of course, it's no longer your concern.

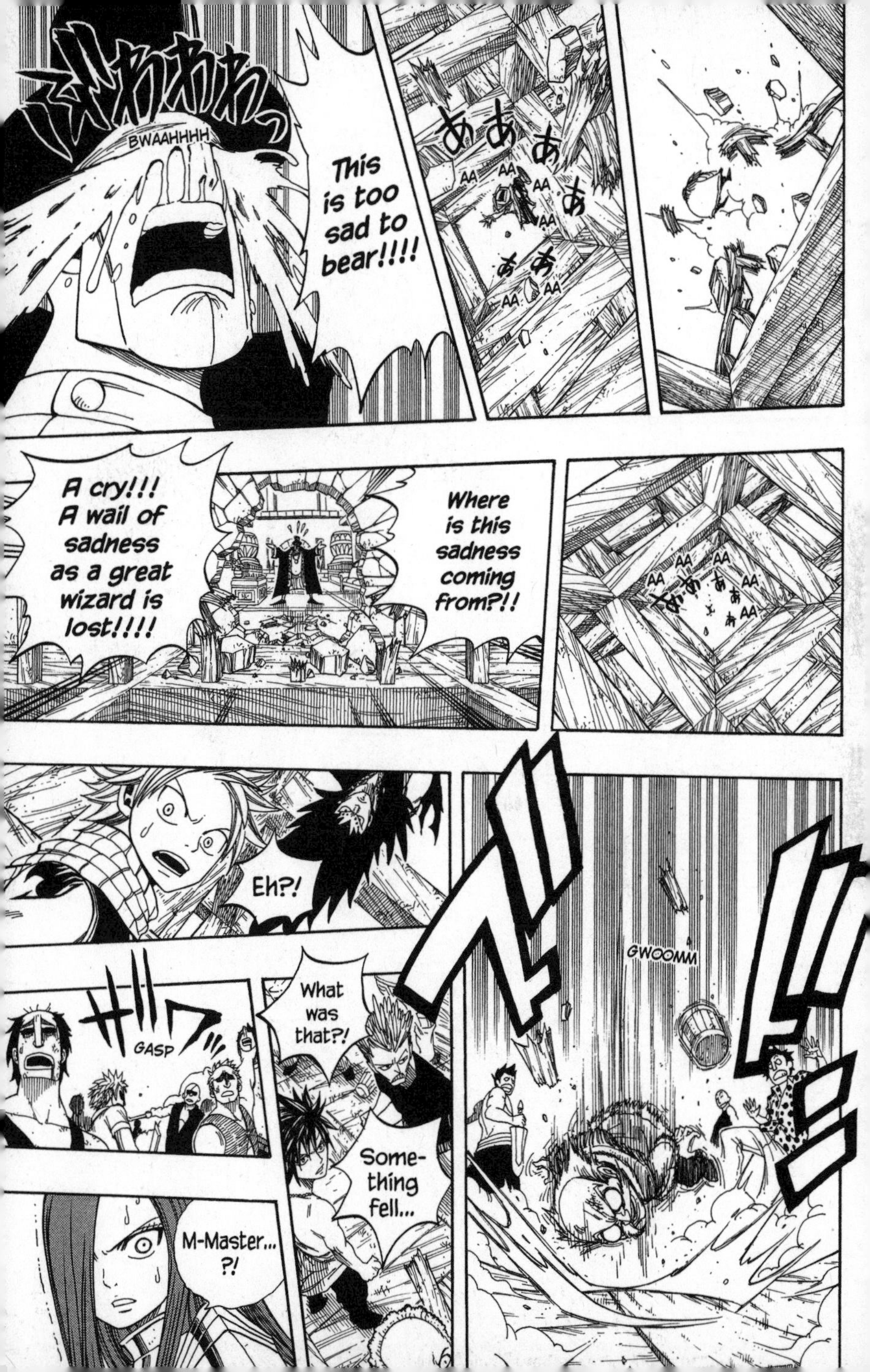
AA AA AA AA AA AA
BWAAHHHH
This is too sad to bear!!!!
AA AA AA AA AA
Where is this sadness coming from?!!
A cry!!! A wail of sadness as a great wizard is lost!!!!
GWOOMM
Eh?!
What was that?!
Some-thing fell...
GASP
M-Master...?!

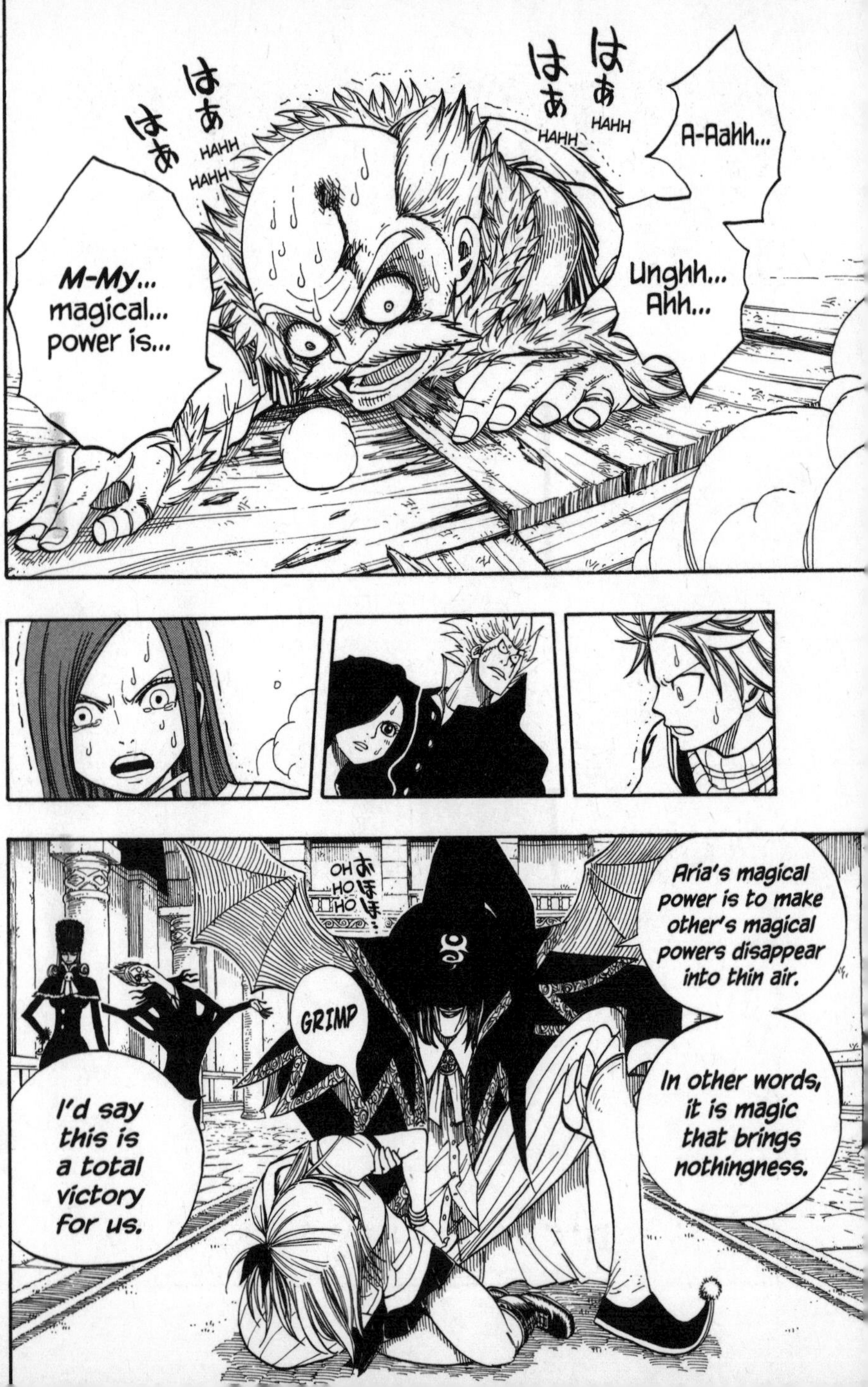
A-Aahh...
はぁはぁ
HAHH
HAHH
Unghh... Ahh...
はぁはぁ
HAHH
HAHH
M-My... magical... power is...
Aria's magical power is to make other's magical powers disappear into thin air.
In other words, it is magic that brings nothingness.
おほほ…
OH HO HO
GRIMP
I'd say this is a total victory for us.

FAIRY TAIL

50

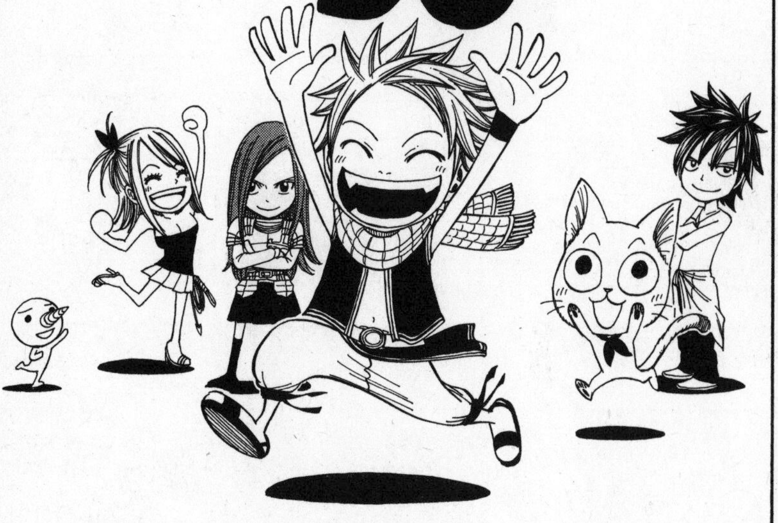

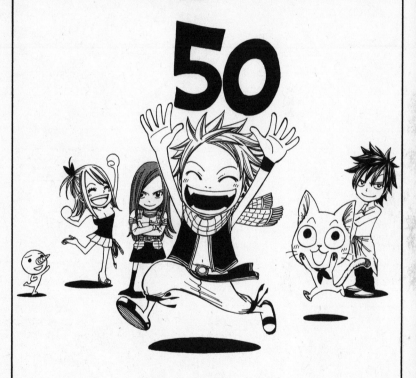

Chapter 50: Lucy Heartfilia

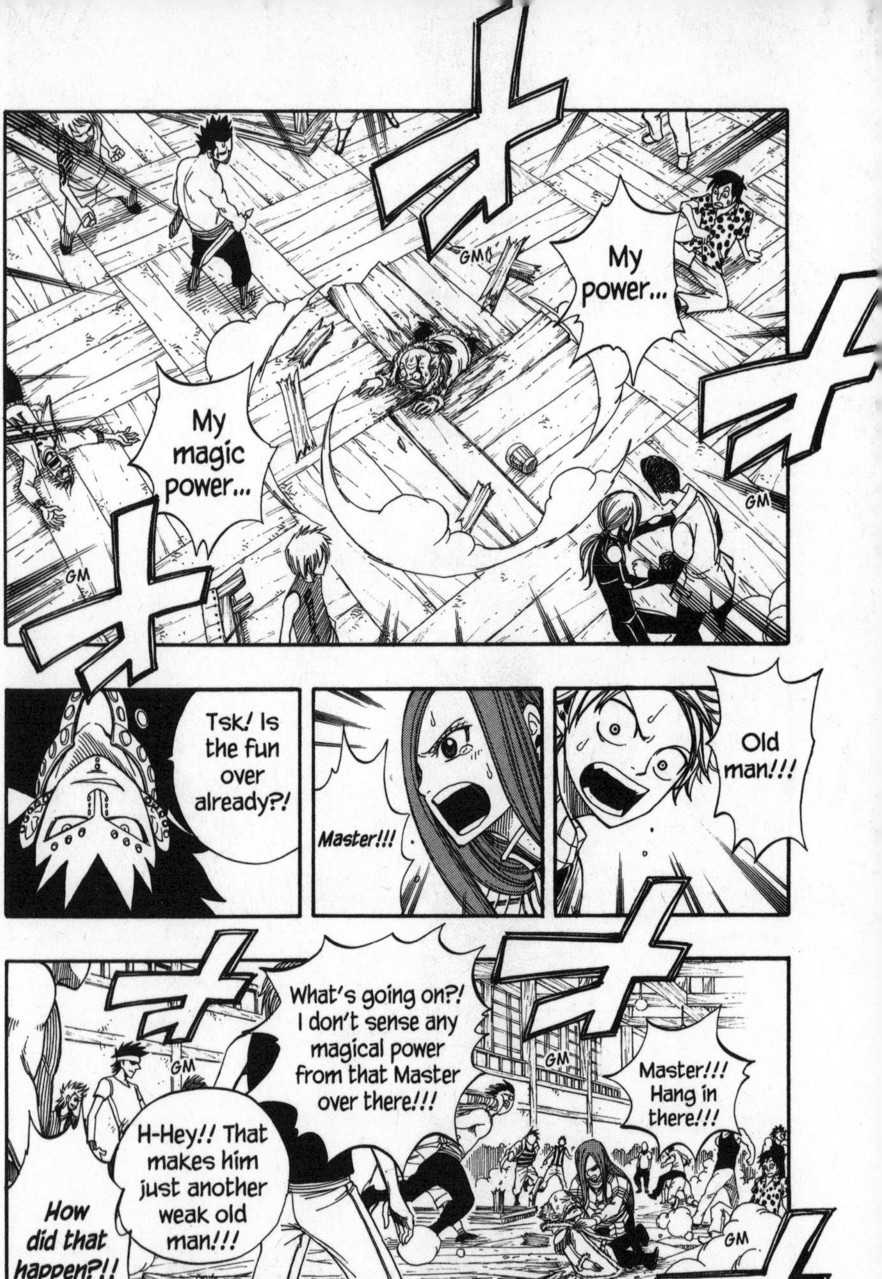
GM
My power...
GM
My magic power...
GM
Old man!!!
Master!!!
Tsk! Is the fun over already?!
Master!!! Hang in there!!!
GM
What's going on?! I don't sense any magical power from that Master over there!!!
GM
GM
H-Hey!! That makes him just another weak old man!!!
How did that happen?!!

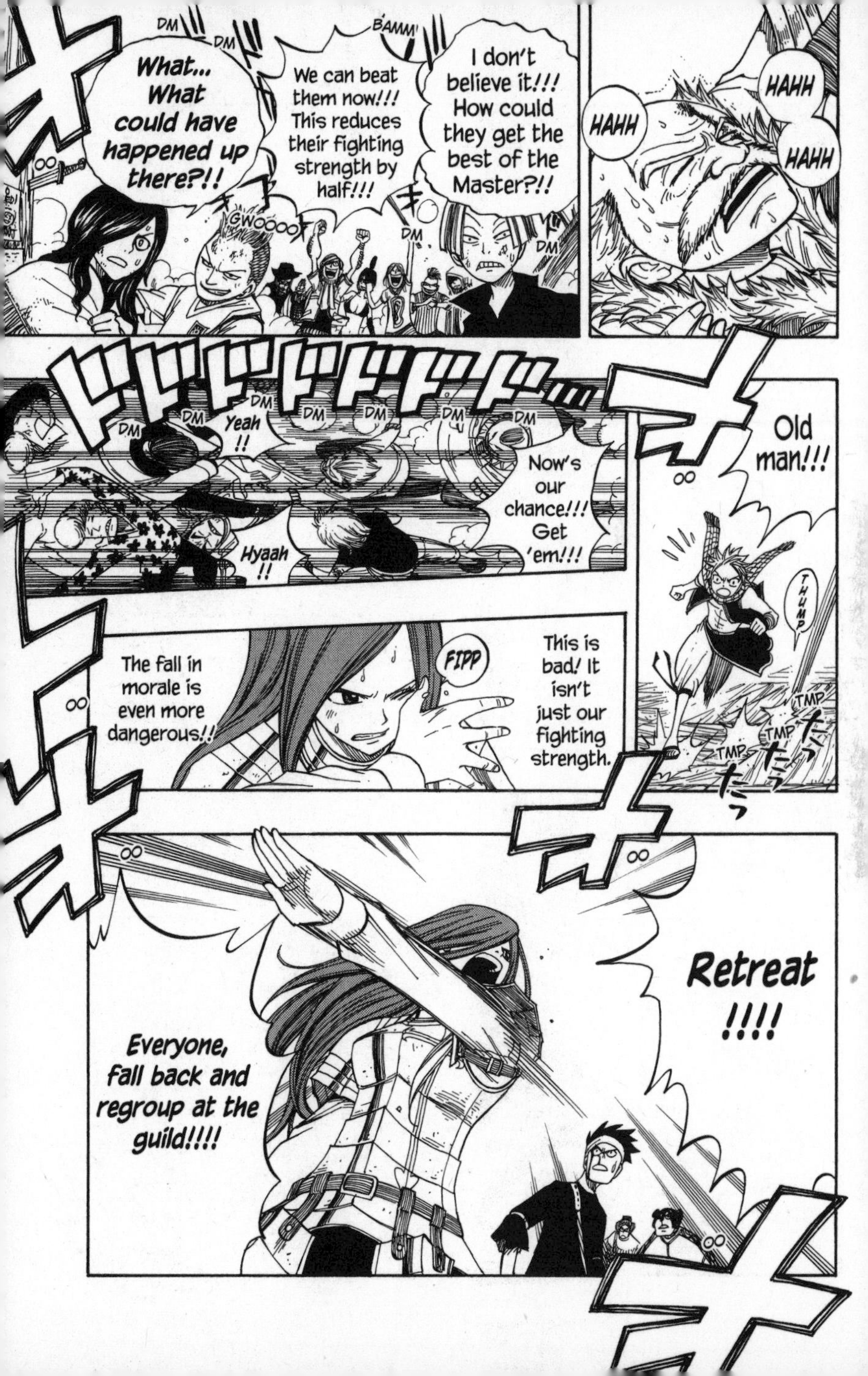
HAHH
HAHH
HAHH
I don't believe it!!! How could they get the best of the Master?!!
BAMM
We can beat them now!!! This reduces their fighting strength by half!!!
DM DM
What... What could have happened up there?!!
GWOOOO
DM
DM
Old man!!!
THUMP
TMP
TMP
TMP
DM DM DM DM DM DM
Now's our chance!!! Get 'em!!!
Yeah!!
Hyaah!!
This is bad! It isn't just our fighting strength.
FIPP
The fall in morale is even more dangerous!!
Retreat!!!!
Everyone, fall back and regroup at the guild!!!!

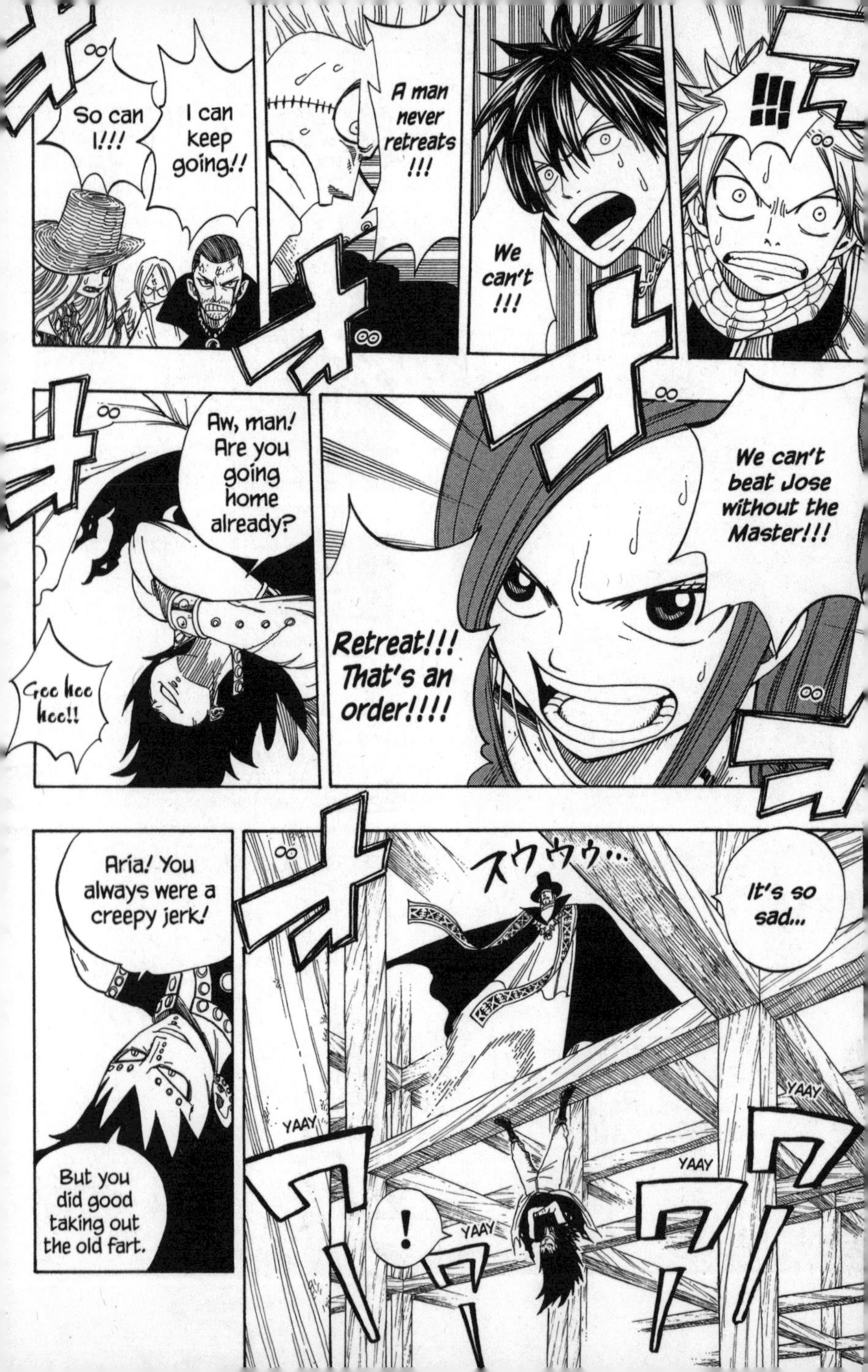
!!!
We can't !!!
A man never retreats !!!
I can keep going!!
So can I!!!
We can't beat Jose without the Master!!!
Retreat!!! That's an order!!!!
Aw, man! Are you going home already?
Gee hee hee!!
スウウウ…
It's so sad...
YAAY
YAAY
YAAY
YAAY
!
Aria! You always were a creepy jerk!
But you did good taking out the old fart.

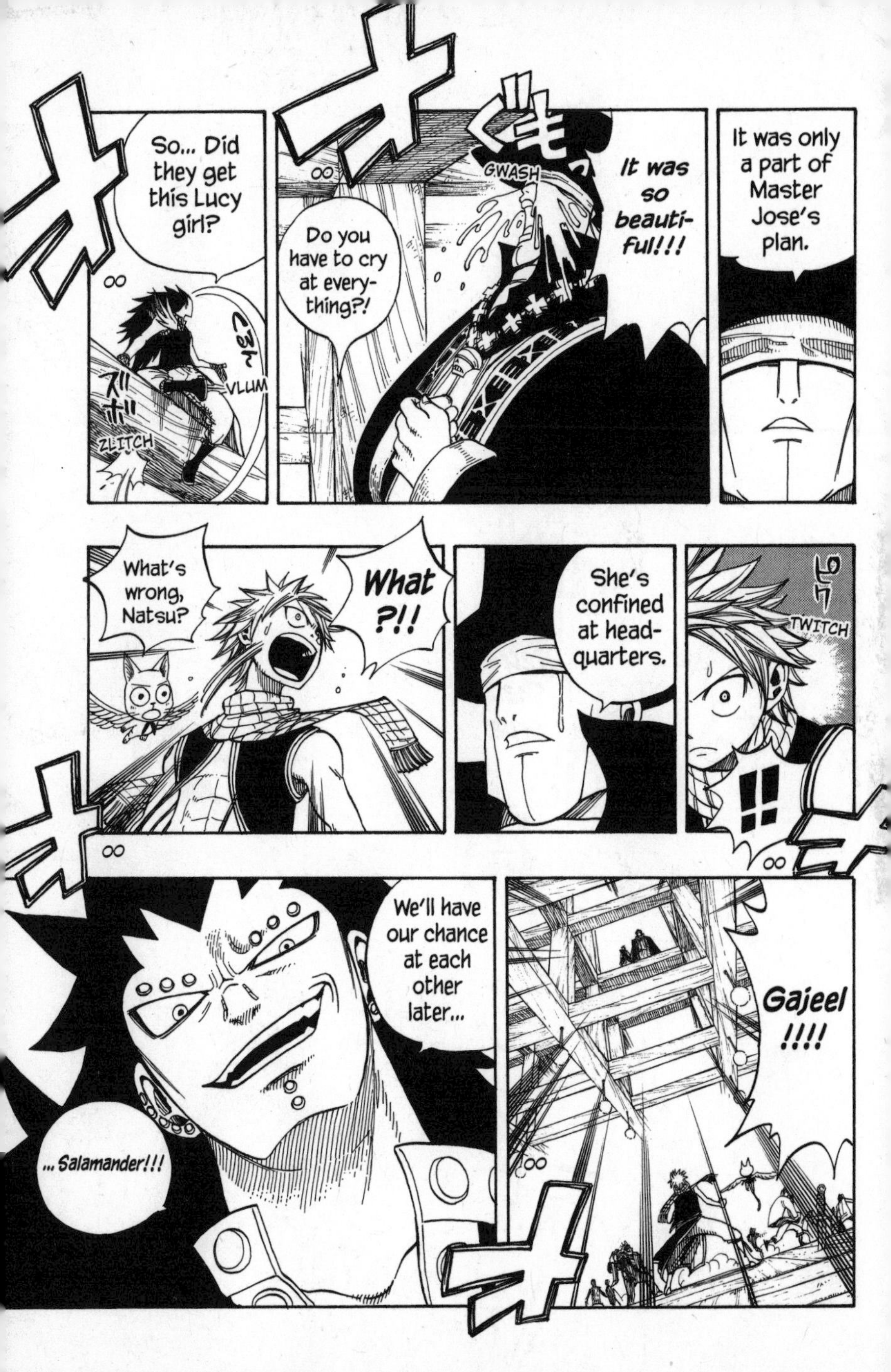
It was only a part of Master Jose's plan.
It was so beauti-ful!!!
GWASH
Do you have to cry at every-thing?!
So... Did they get this Lucy girl?
VLUM
ZLITCH
TWITCH
!!
She's confined at head-quarters.
What ?!!
What's wrong, Natsu?
Gajeel !!!!
We'll have our chance at each other later...
... Salamander!!!

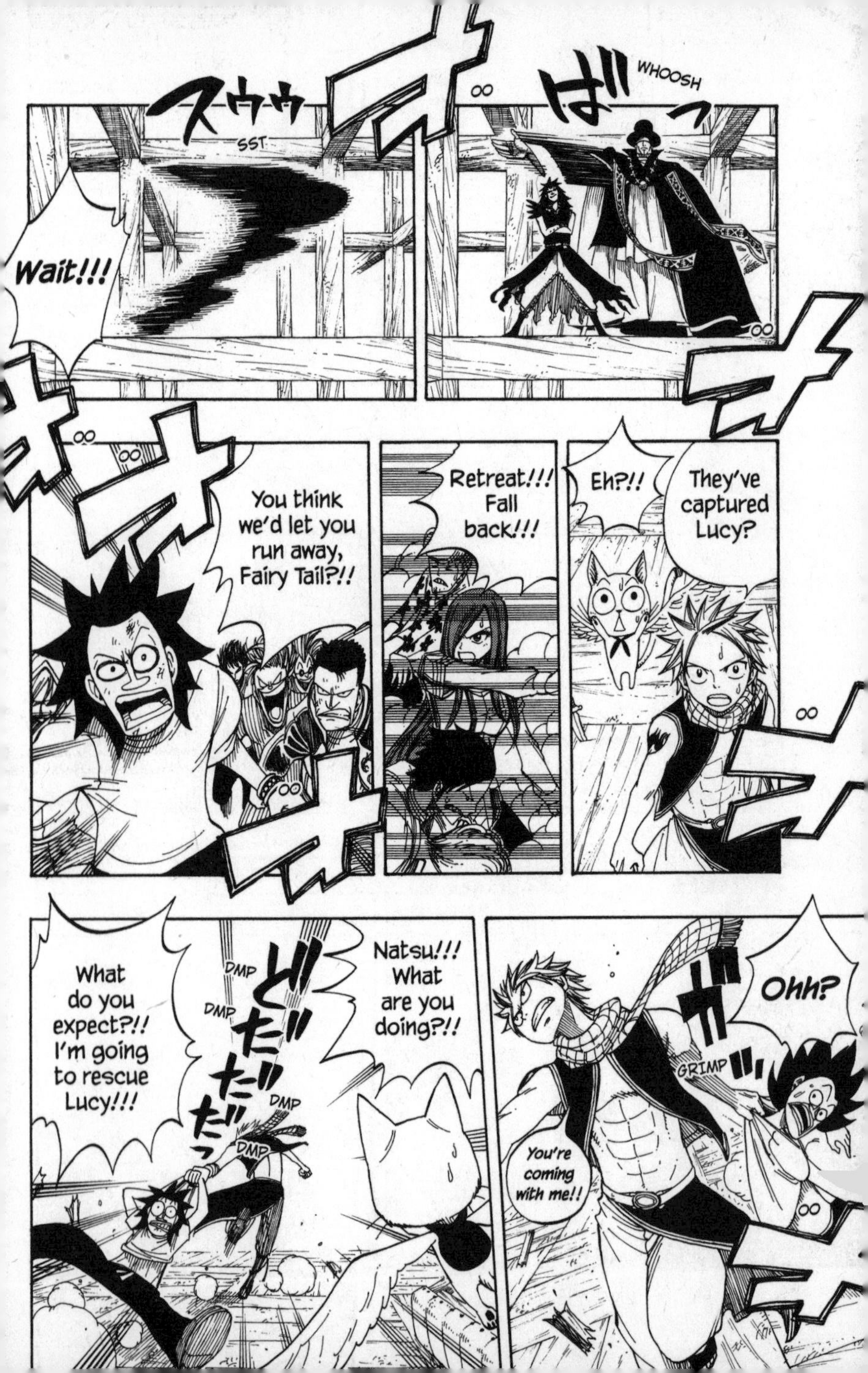

ばっ
WHOOSH
スゥゥ
SST
Wait!!!
They've captured Lucy?
Eh?!!
Retreat!!! Fall back!!!
You think we'd let you run away, Fairy Tail?!!
Ohh?
GRIMP
You're coming with me!!
Natsu!!! What are you doing?!!
DMP
DMP
DMP
DMP
What do you expect?!! I'm going to rescue Lucy!!!

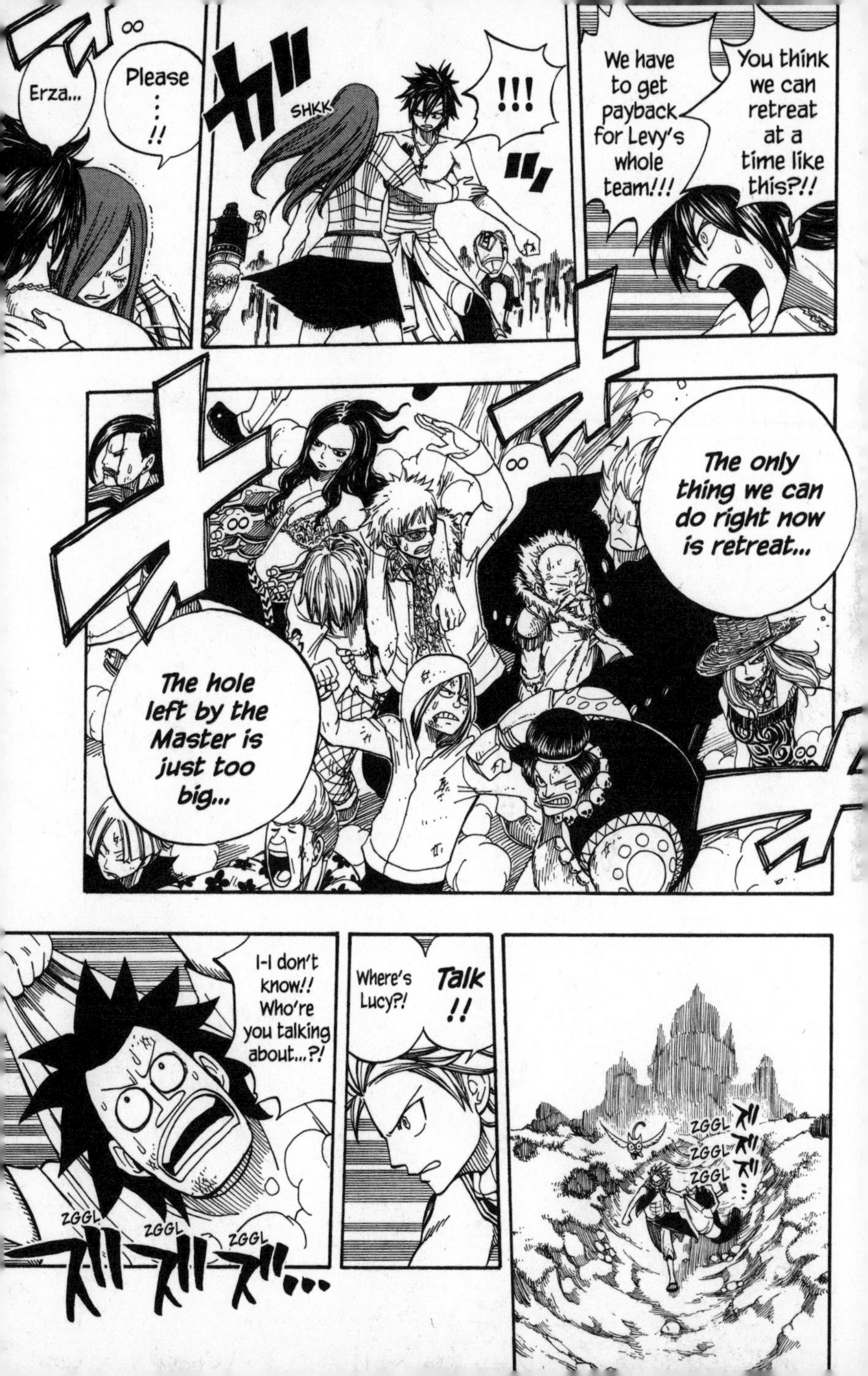
You think we can retreat at a time like this?!!
We have to get payback for Levy's whole team!!!
!!!
SHKK
Please ...!!
Erza...
The only thing we can do right now is retreat...
The hole left by the Master is just too big...
ZGGL
ZGGL
ZGGL
Talk !!
Where's Lucy?!
I-I don't know!! Who're you talking about...?!
ZGGL
ZGGL
ZGGL

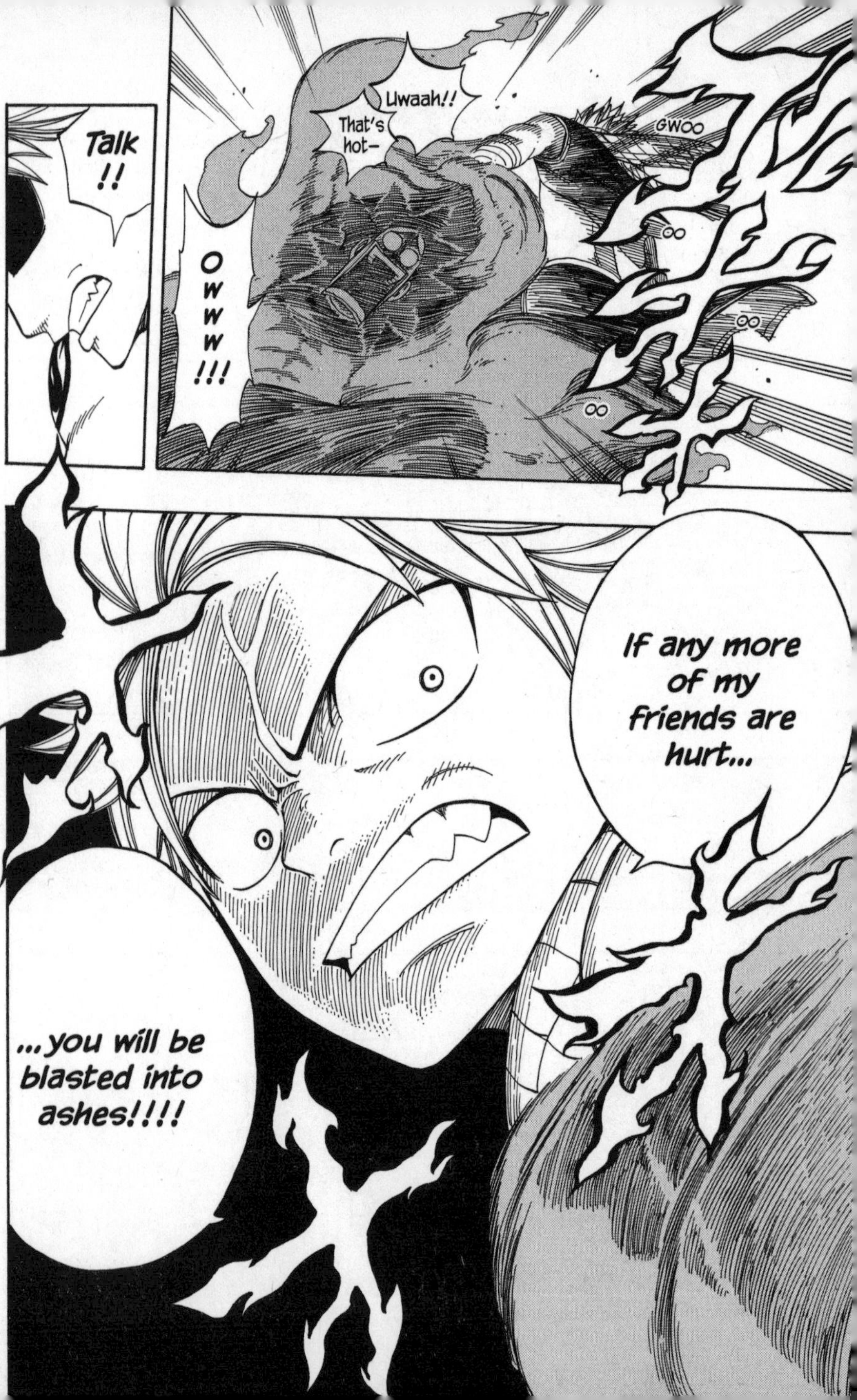
GWOO
Uwaah!!
That's hot-
OWWW!!!
Talk !!
If any more of my friends are hurt...
...you will be blasted into ashes!!!!

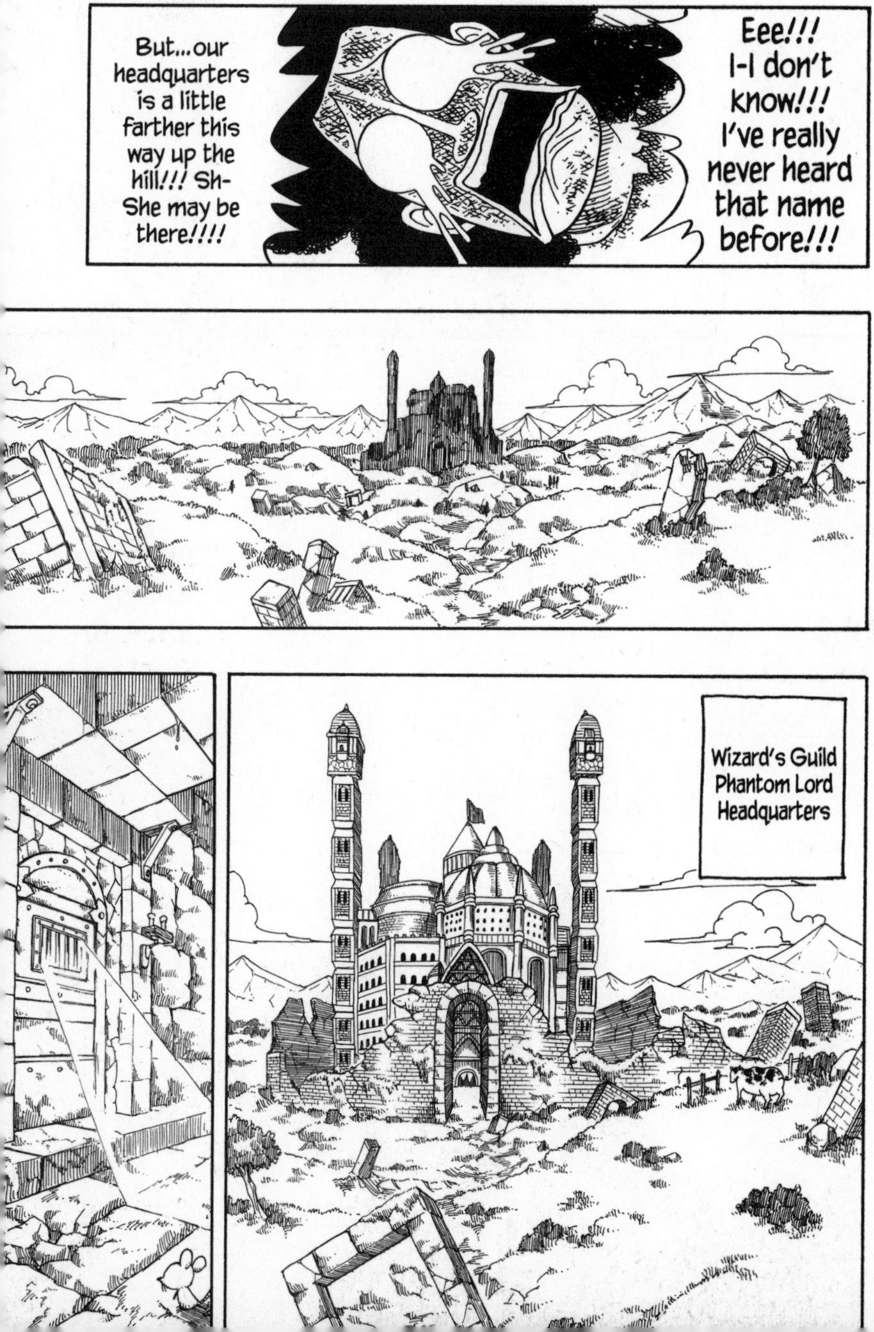
Eee!!! I-I don't know!!! I've really never heard that name before!!!
But...our headquarters is a little farther this way up the hill!!! Sh-She may be there!!!!
Wizard's Guild Phantom Lord Headquarters

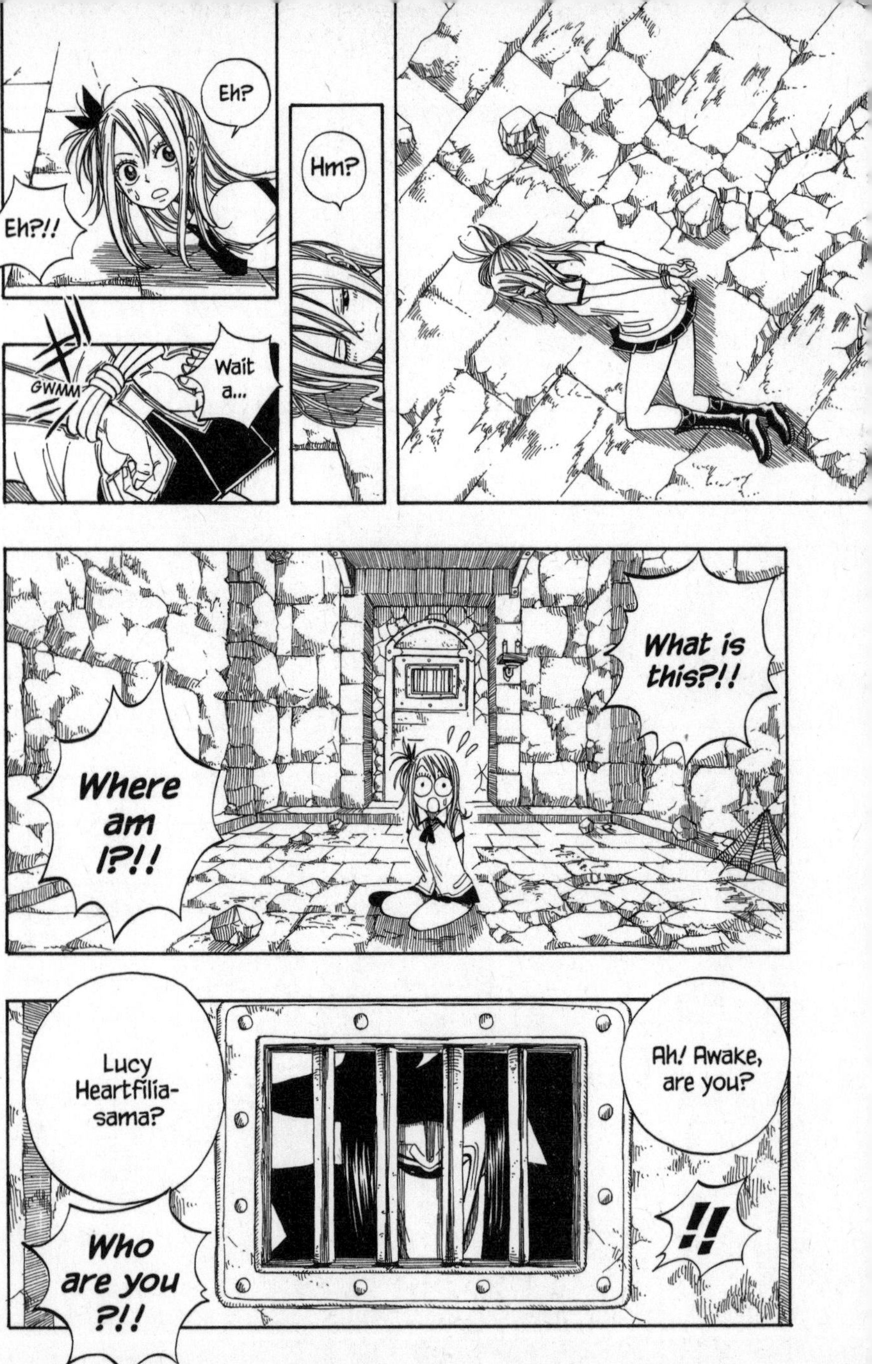
Hm?
Eh?
Eh?!!
GWMM
Wait a...
What is this?!!
Where am I?!!
Ah! Awake, are you?
!!
Lucy Heartfilia-sama?
Who are you ?!!

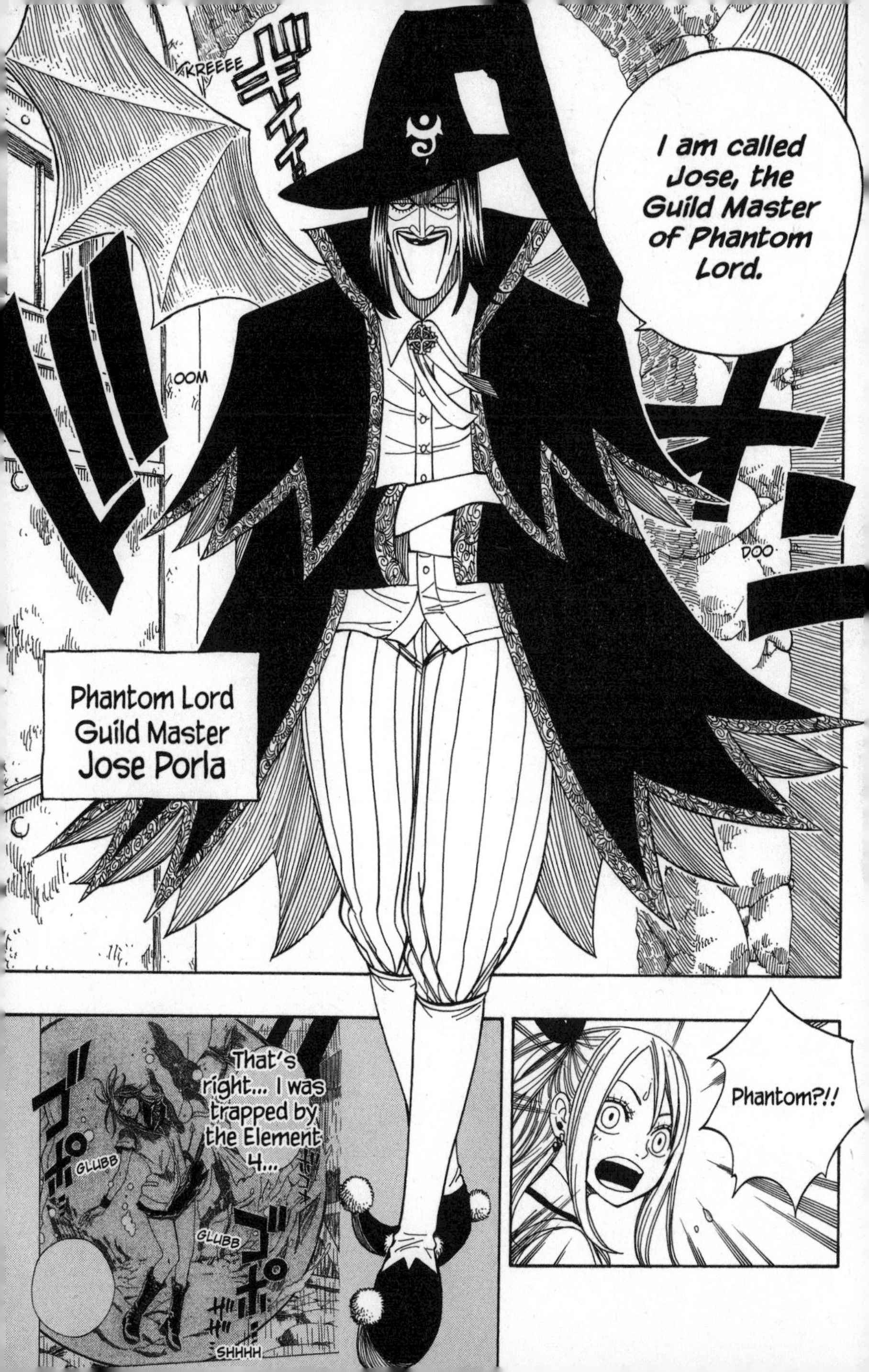
I am called Jose, the Guild Master of Phantom Lord.
KREEEE
DOO
OOM
Phantom Lord Guild Master Jose Porla
Phantom?!!
That's right... I was trapped by the Element 4...
GLUBB
GLUBB
SHHHH

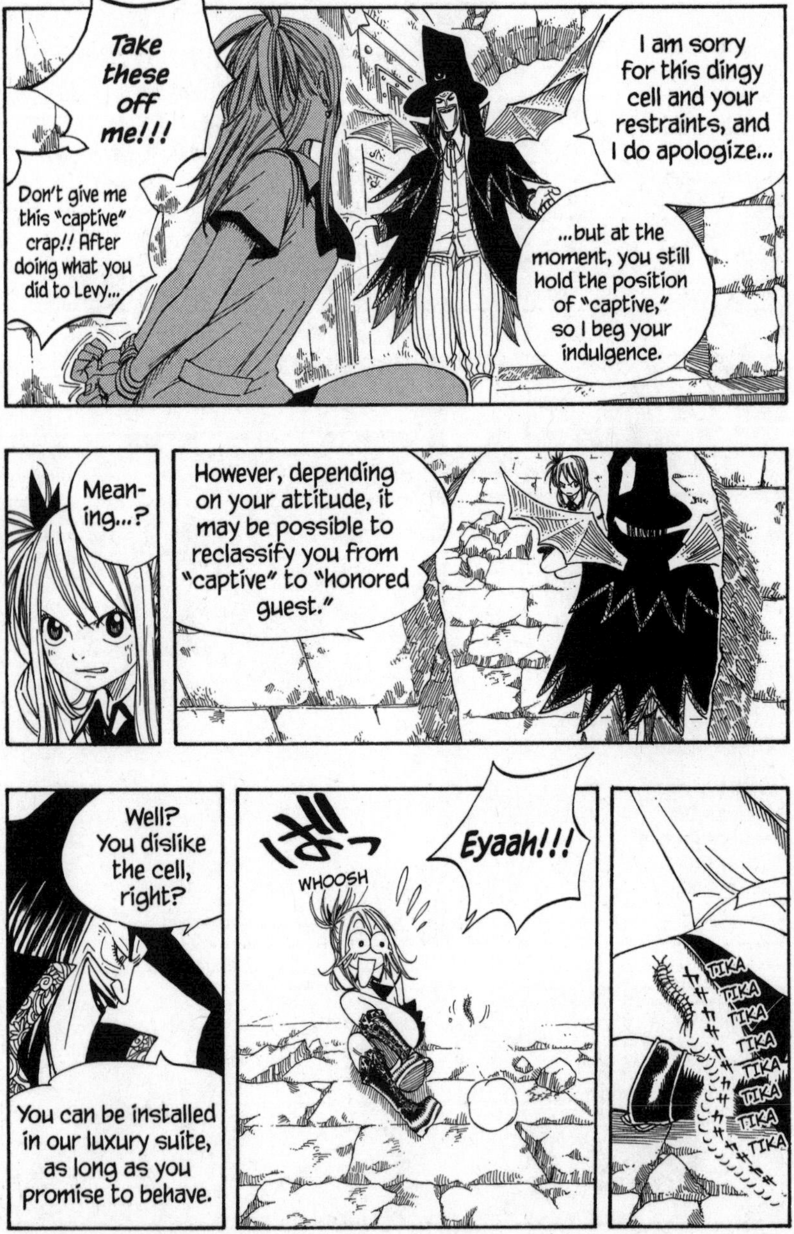
I am sorry for this dingy cell and your restraints, and I do apologize...
...but at the moment, you still hold the position of "captive," so I beg your indulgence.
Take these off me!!!
Don't give me this "captive" crap!! After doing what you did to Levy...
However, depending on your attitude, it may be possible to reclassify you from "captive" to "honored guest."
Meaning...?
TIKA TIKA TIKA TIKA TIKA TIKA TIKA TIKA
Eyaah!!!
WHOOSH
Well? You dislike the cell, right?
You can be installed in our luxury suite, as long as you promise to behave.

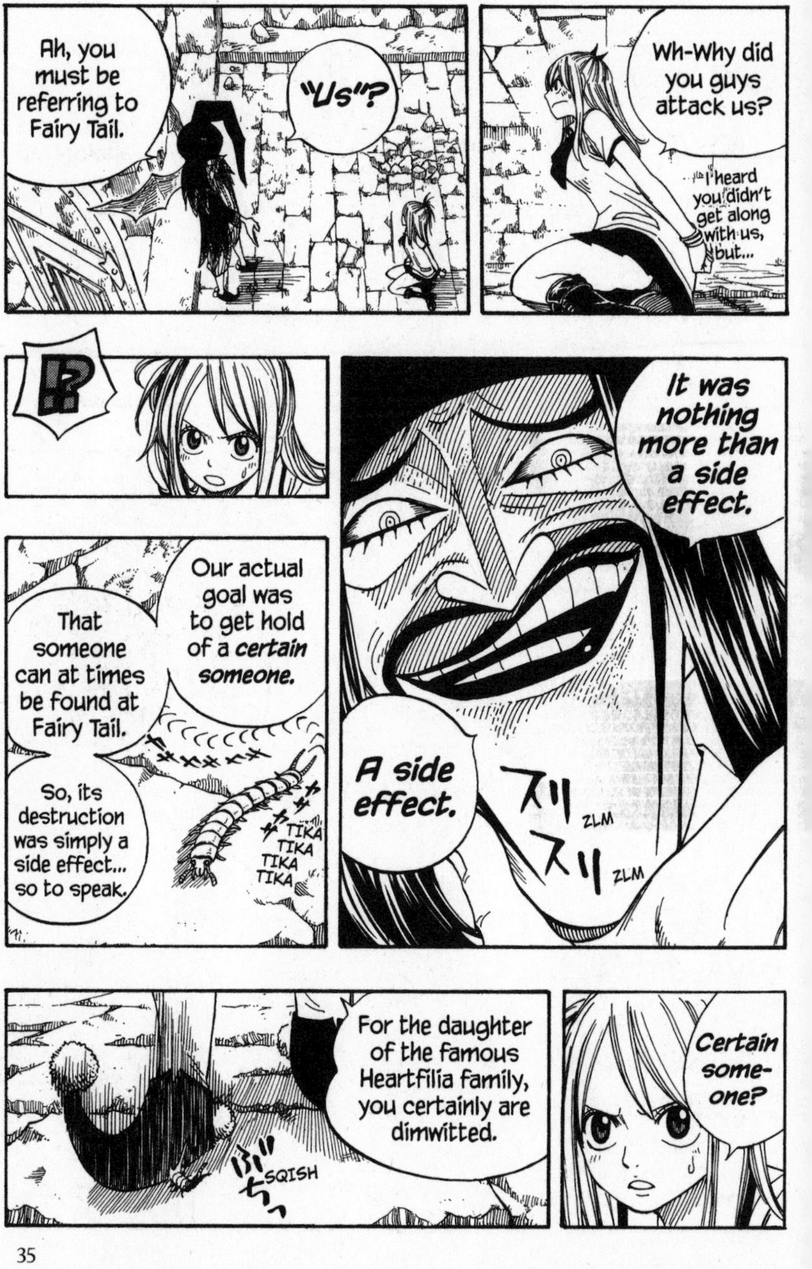
Wh-Why did you guys attack us?
I heard you didn't get along with us, but...
"Us"?
Ah, you must be referring to Fairy Tail.
It was nothing more than a side effect.
A side effect.
スリ ZLM
スリ ZLM
!?
Our actual goal was to get hold of a *certain someone.*
That someone can at times be found at Fairy Tail.
So, its destruction was simply a side effect... so to speak.
TIKA TIKA TIKA TIKA
Certain some-one?
For the daughter of the famous Heartfilia family, you certainly are dimwitted.
SQISH

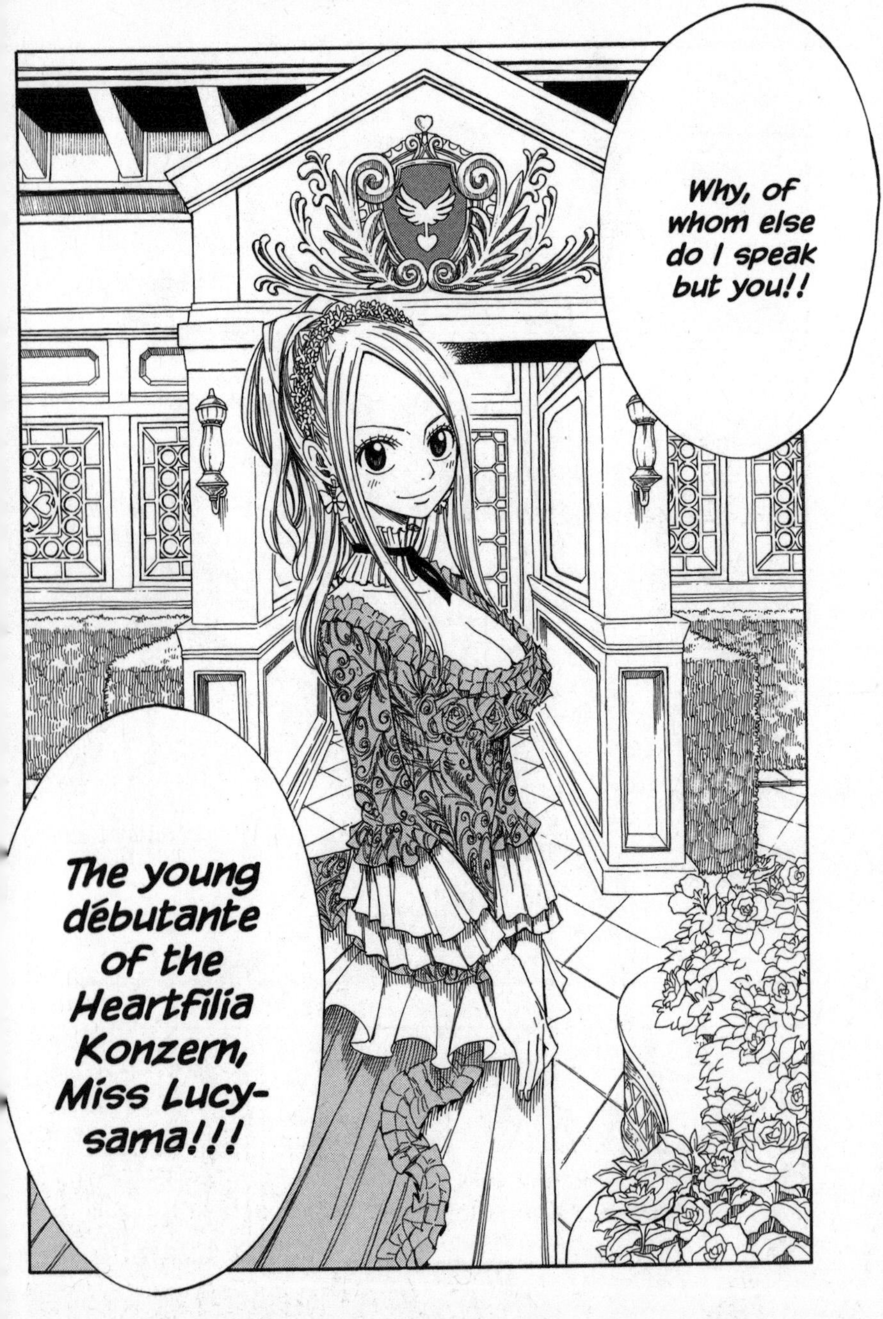
Why, of whom else do I speak but you!!
The young débutante of the Heartfilia Konzern, Miss Lucy-sama!!!

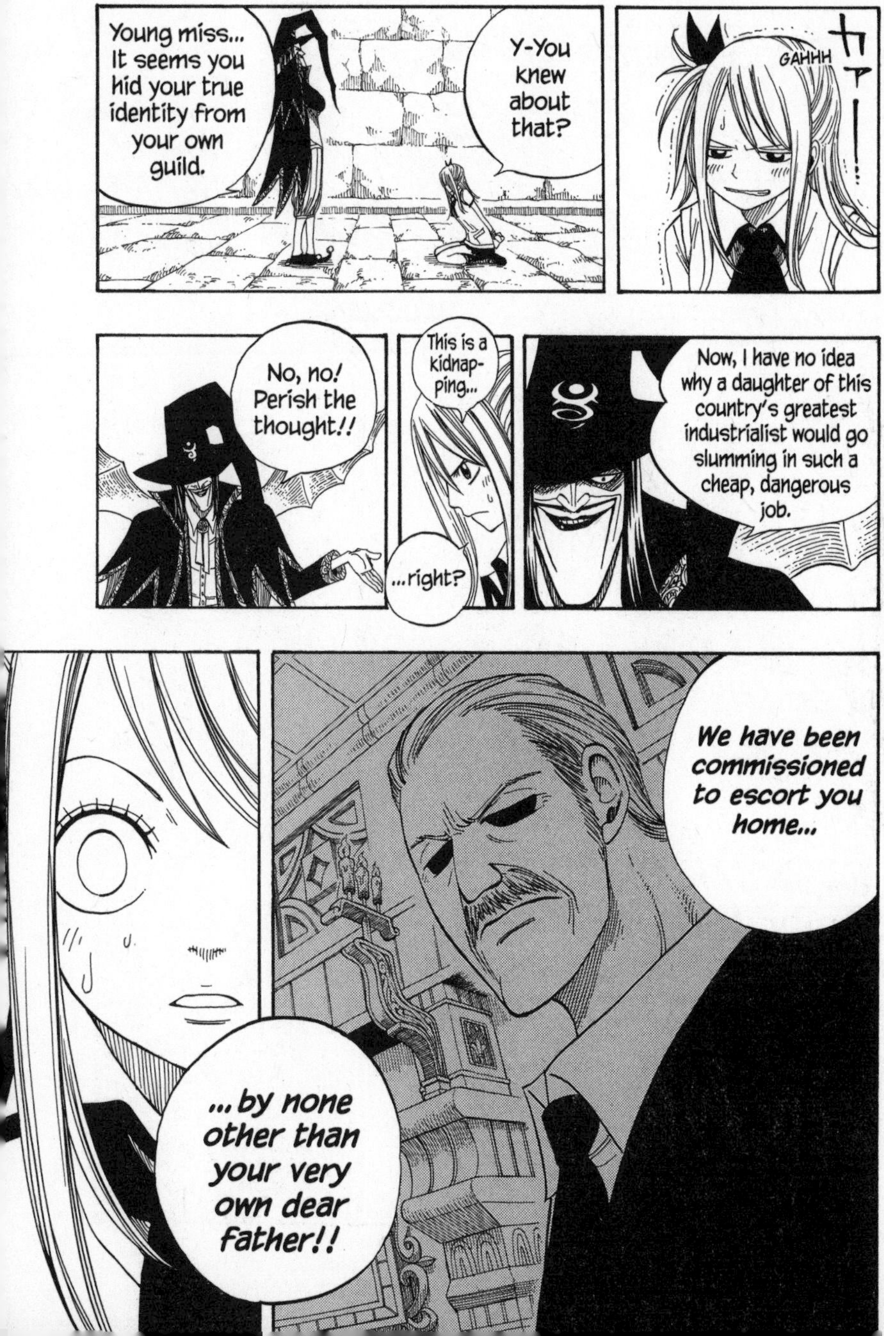
GAHHH
ガァー!!
Young miss... It seems you hid your true identity from your own guild.
Y-You knew about that?
Now, I have no idea why a daughter of this country's greatest industrialist would go slumming in such a cheap, dangerous job.
This is a kidnapping...
...right?
No, no! Perish the thought!!
We have been commissioned to escort you home...
...by none other than your very own dear father!!

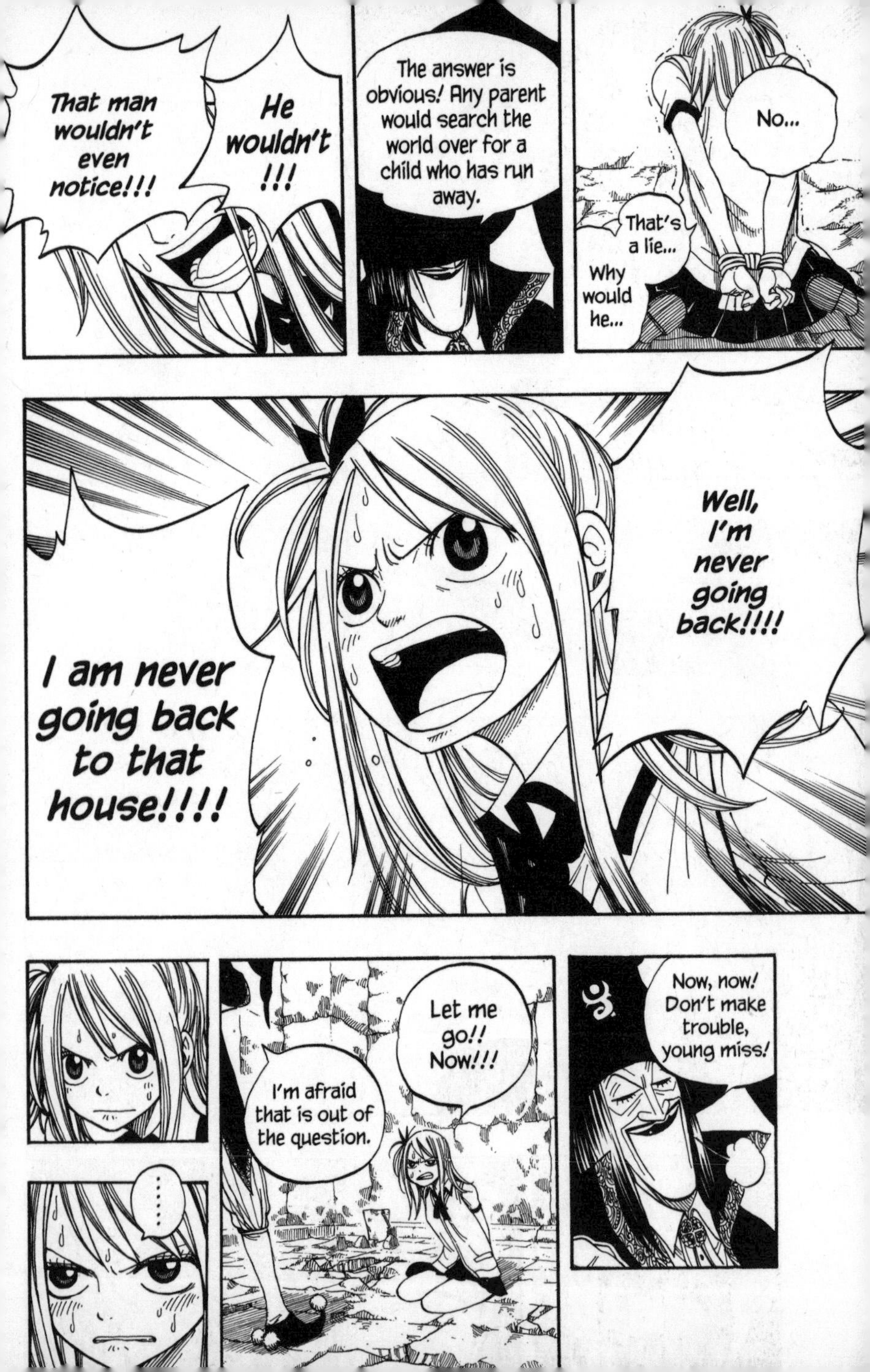
No...
That's a lie...
Why would he...
The answer is obvious! Any parent would search the world over for a child who has run away.
He wouldn't!!!
That man wouldn't even notice!!!
Well, I'm never going back!!!!
I am never going back to that house!!!!
Now, now! Don't make trouble, young miss!
Let me go!! Now!!!
I'm afraid that is out of the question.
......

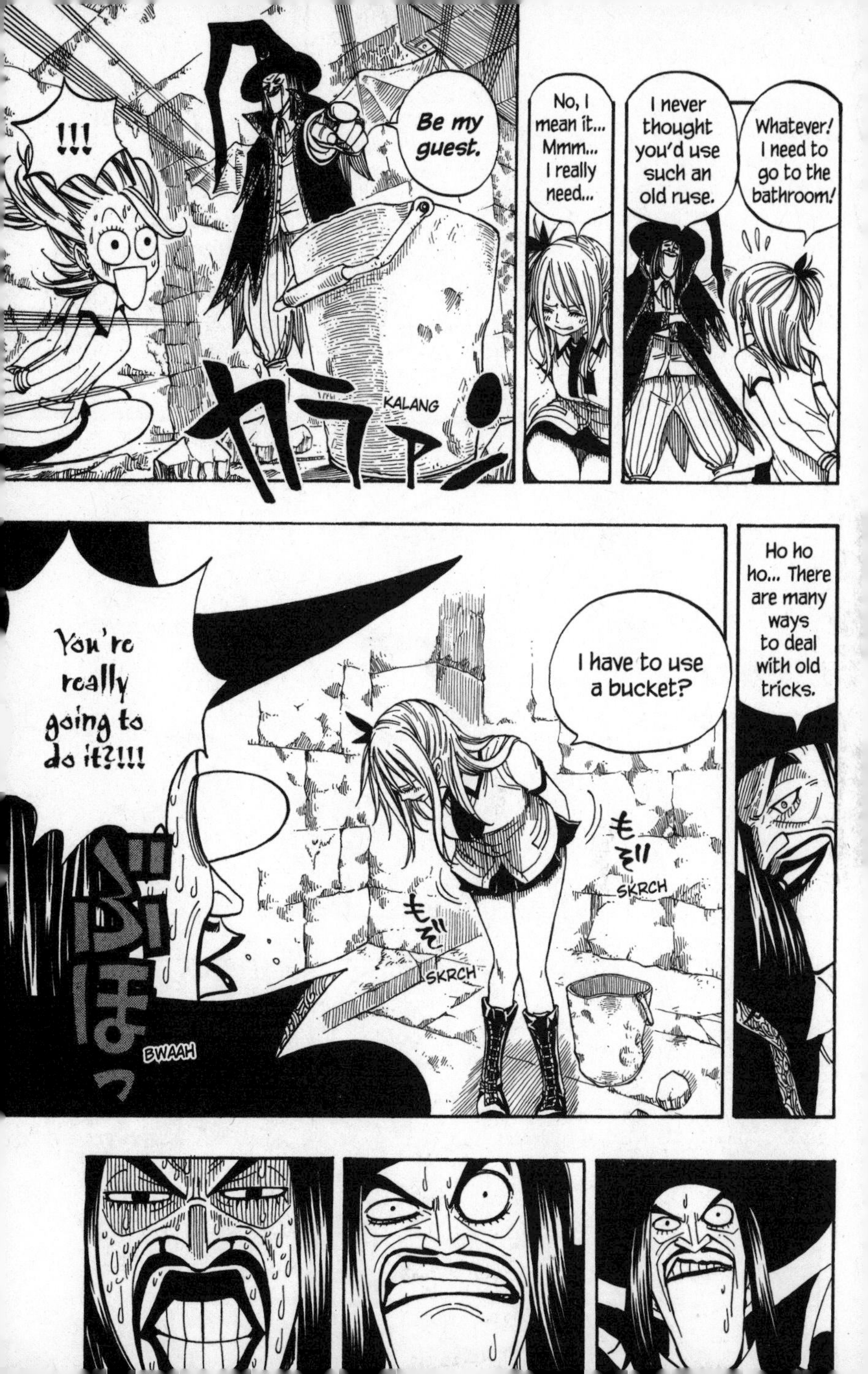

Whatever! I need to go to the bathroom!
I never thought you'd use such an old ruse.
No, I mean it... Mmm... I really need...
Be my guest.
!!!
KALANG
Ho ho ho... There are many ways to deal with old tricks.
I have to use a bucket?
SKRCH
SKRCH
You're really going to do it?!!!
BWAAH

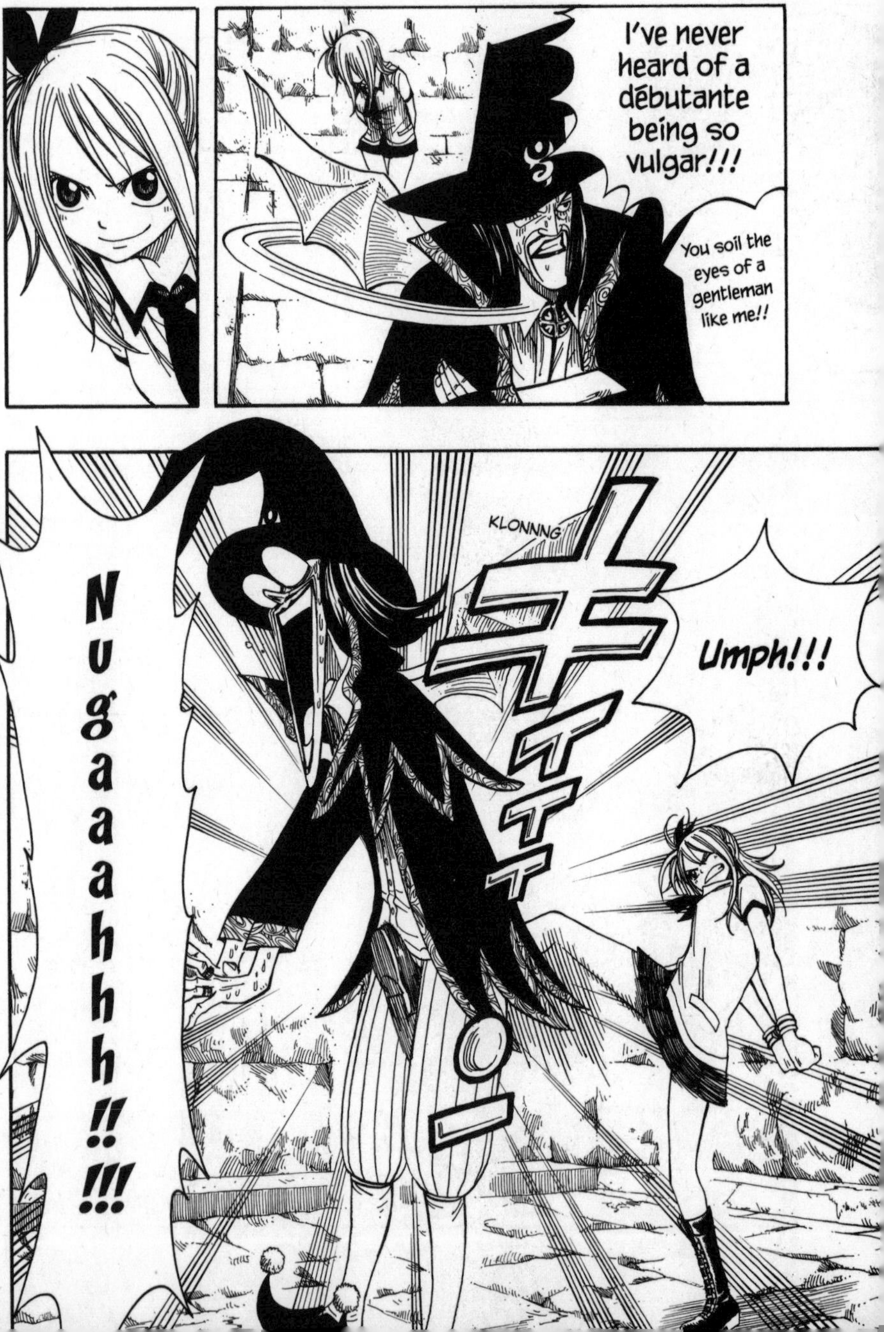
I've never heard of a débutante being so vulgar!!!
You soil the eyes of a gentleman like me!!
Umph!!!
KLONNNG
Nugaaahhh!!!!!

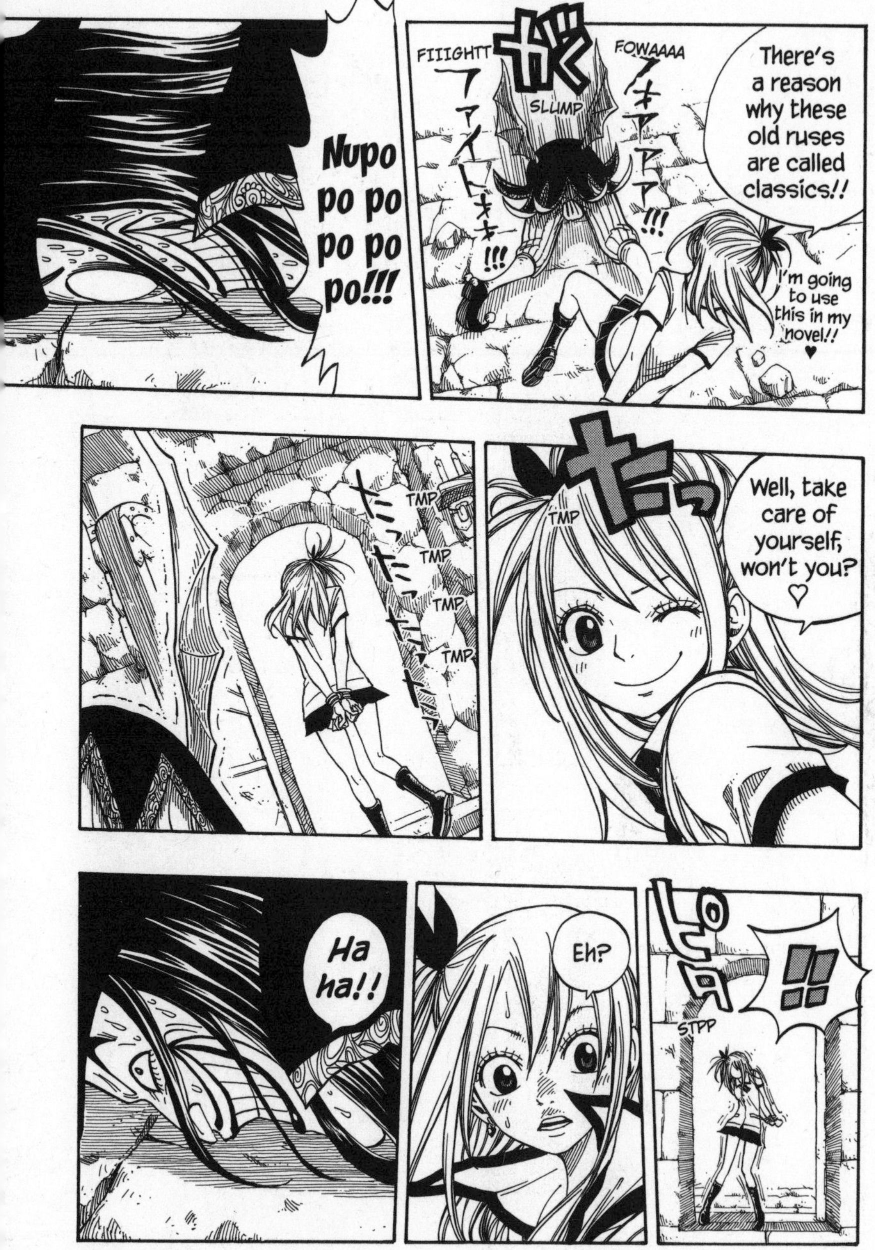
There's a reason why these old ruses are called classics!!
FOWAAAA
FIIIGHTT
SLUMP
I'm going to use this in my novel!! ♥
Nupo po po po po po!!!
Well, take care of yourself, won't you? ♡
TMP
TMP
TMP
TMP
TMP
!!
STPP
Eh?
Ha ha!!

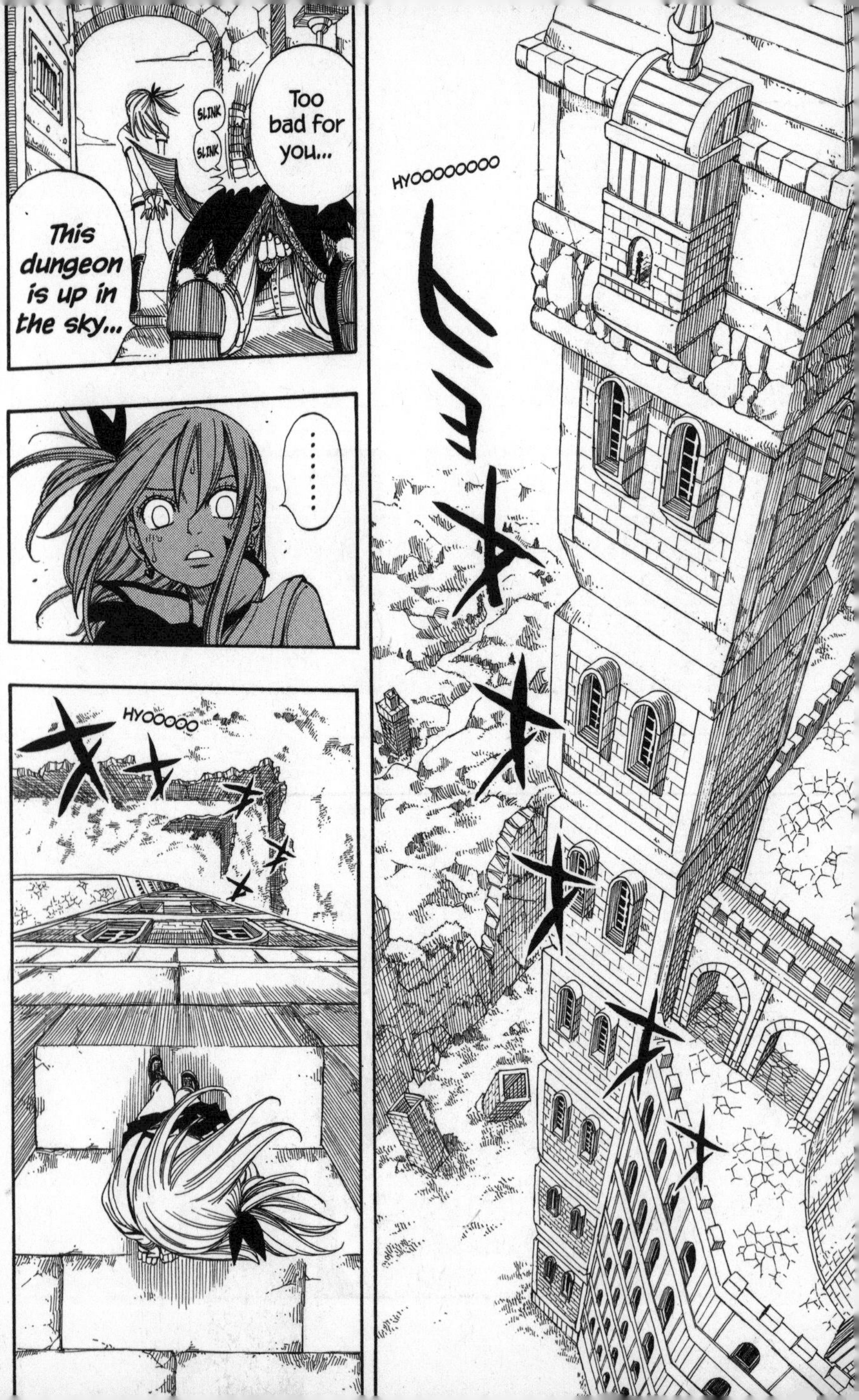
HYOOOOOOOO
Too bad for you...
SLINK
SLINK
This dungeon is up in the sky...
......
HYOOOOO

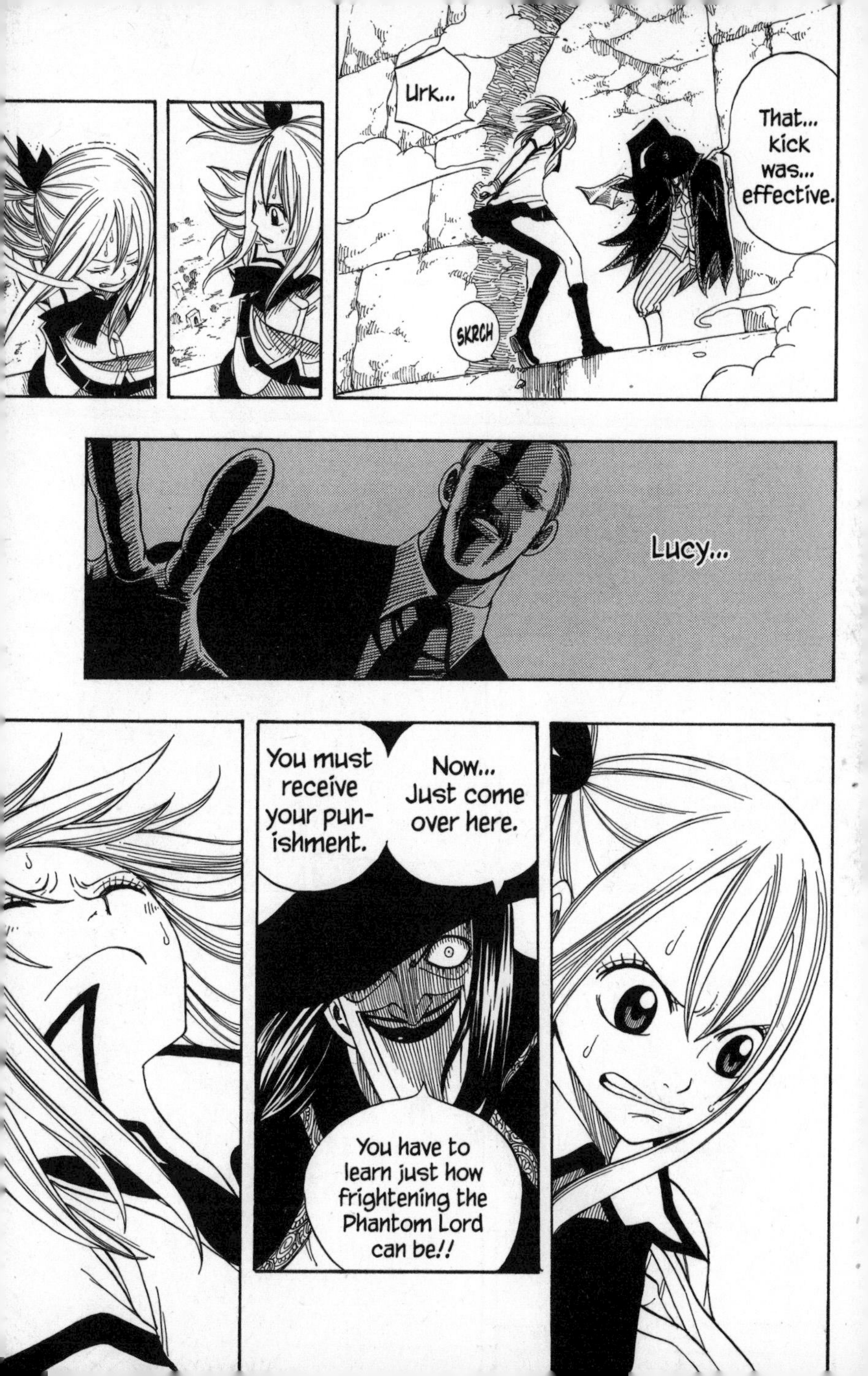
That... kick was... effective.
Urk...
SKRCH
Lucy...
Now... Just come over here.
You must receive your punishment.
You have to learn just how frightening the Phantom Lord can be!!

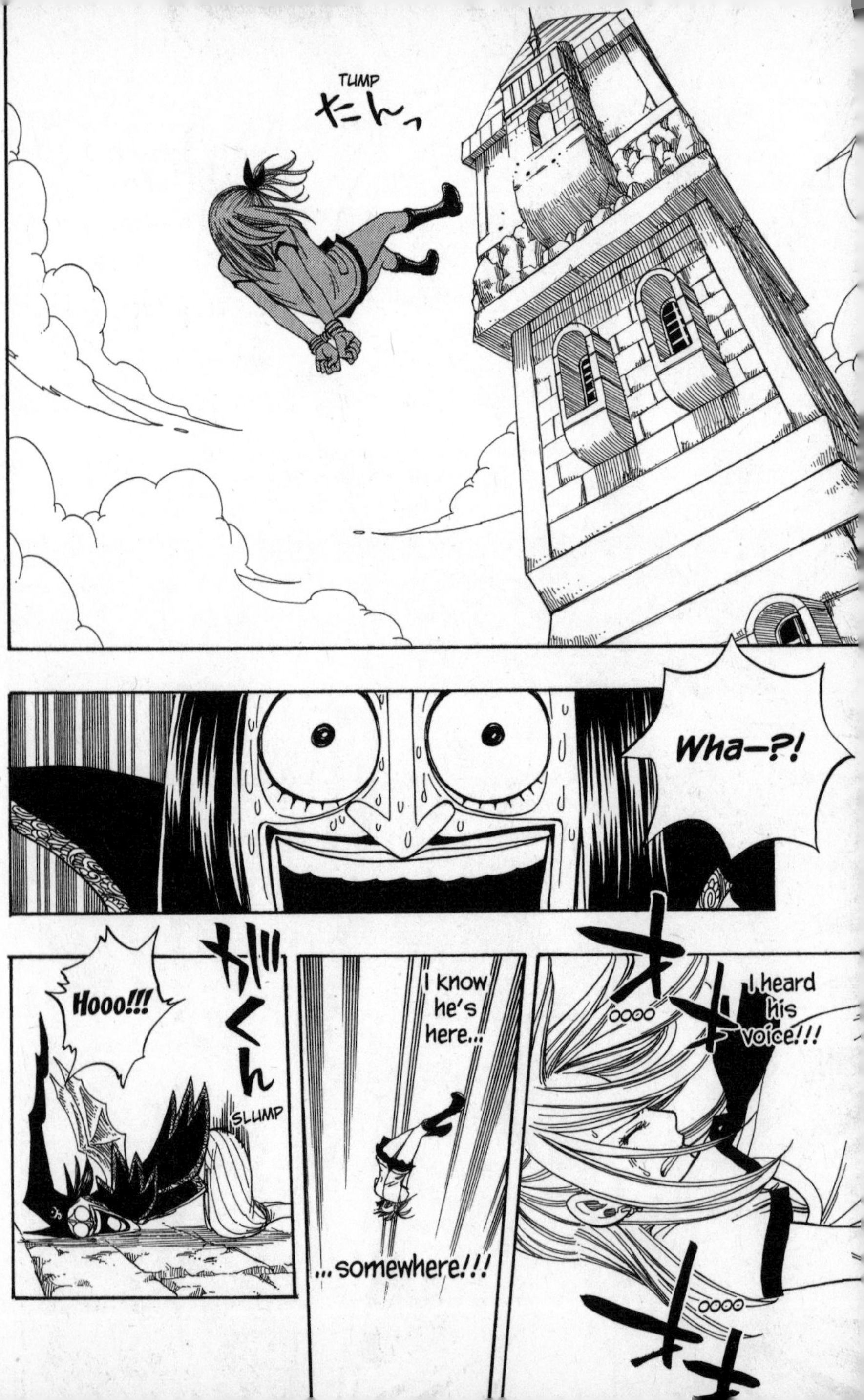
TUMP
たんっ
Wha-?!
I heard his voice!!!
oooo
oooo
I know he's here...
...somewhere!!!
Hooo!!!
がくん
SLUMP

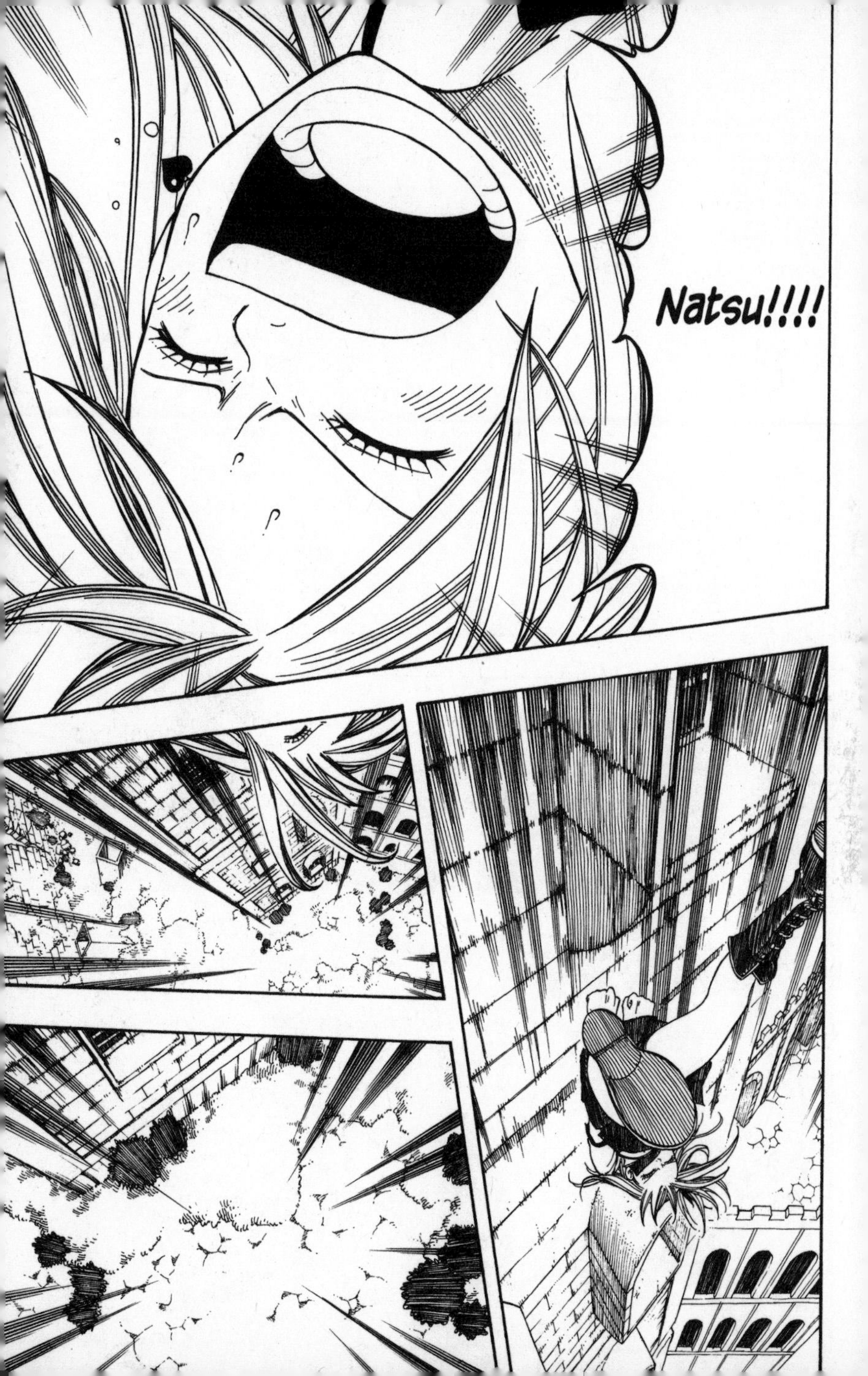
Natsu!!!!

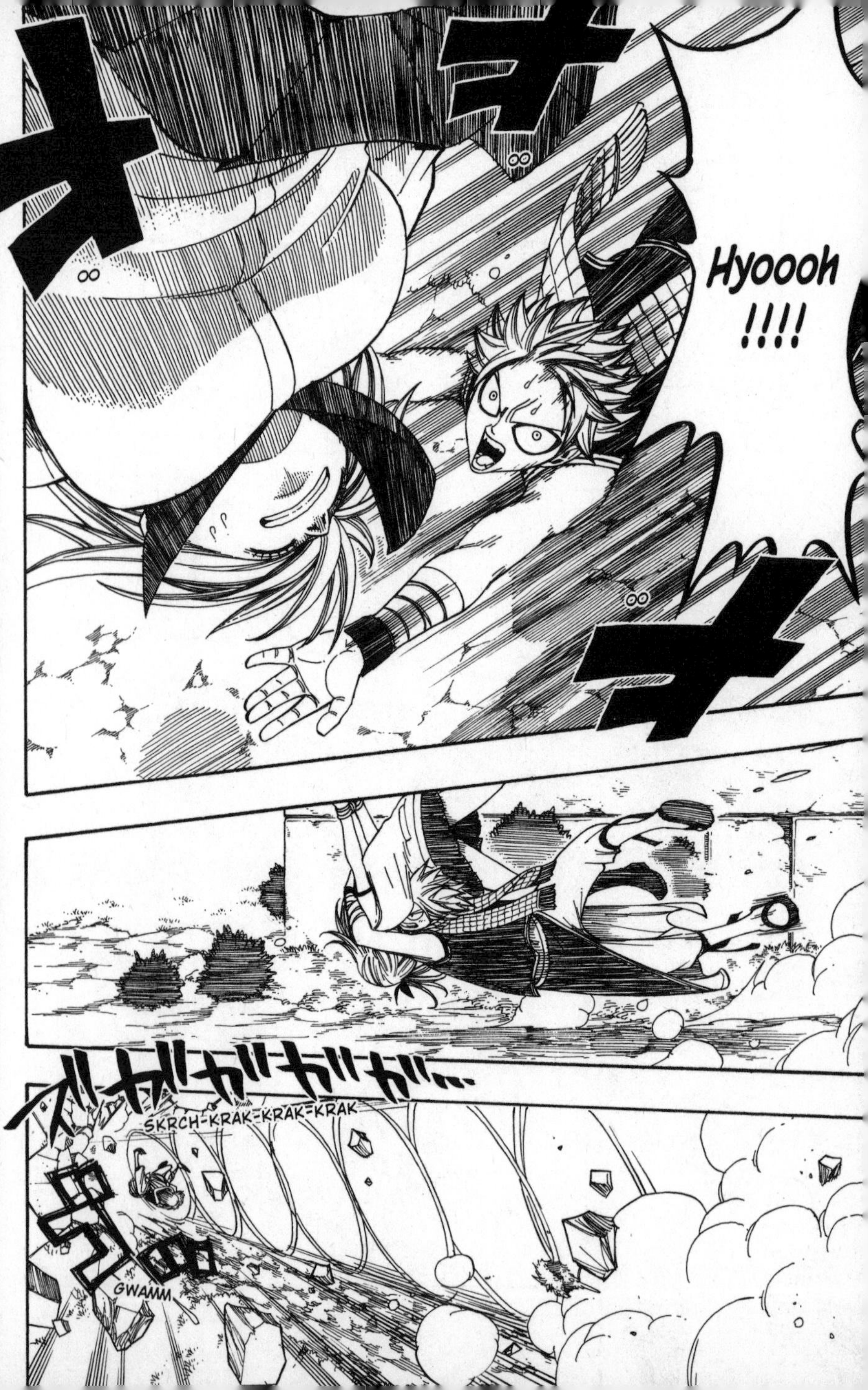
Hyoooh !!!!
SKRCH-KRAK-KRAK-KRAK
GWAMM

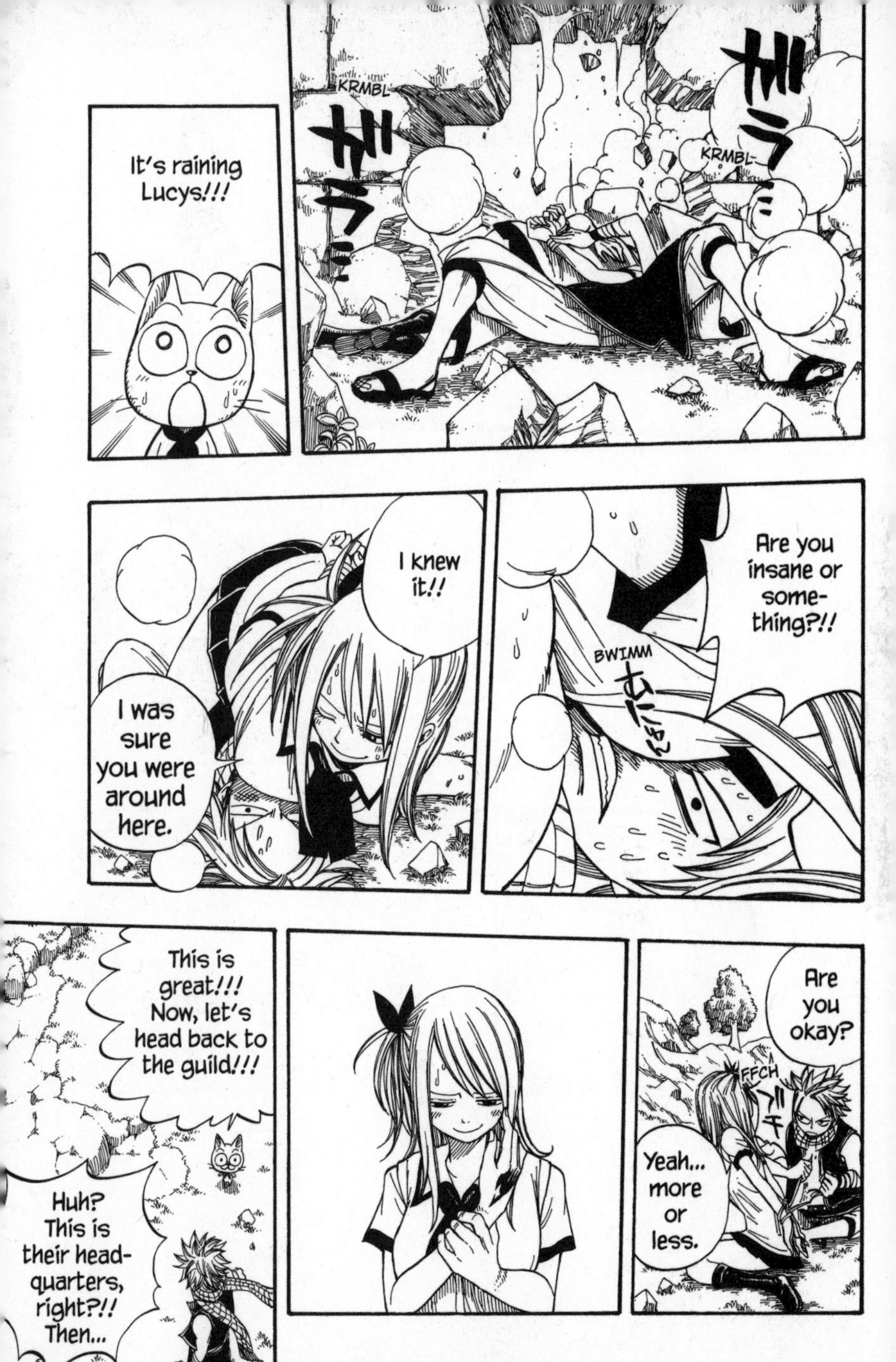
KRMBL
KRMBL
It's raining Lucys!!!
Are you insane or some-thing?!!
BWIMM
I knew it!!
I was sure you were around here.
Are you okay?
FFCH
Yeah... more or less.
This is great!!! Now, let's head back to the guild!!!
Huh? This is their head-quarters, right?!! Then...

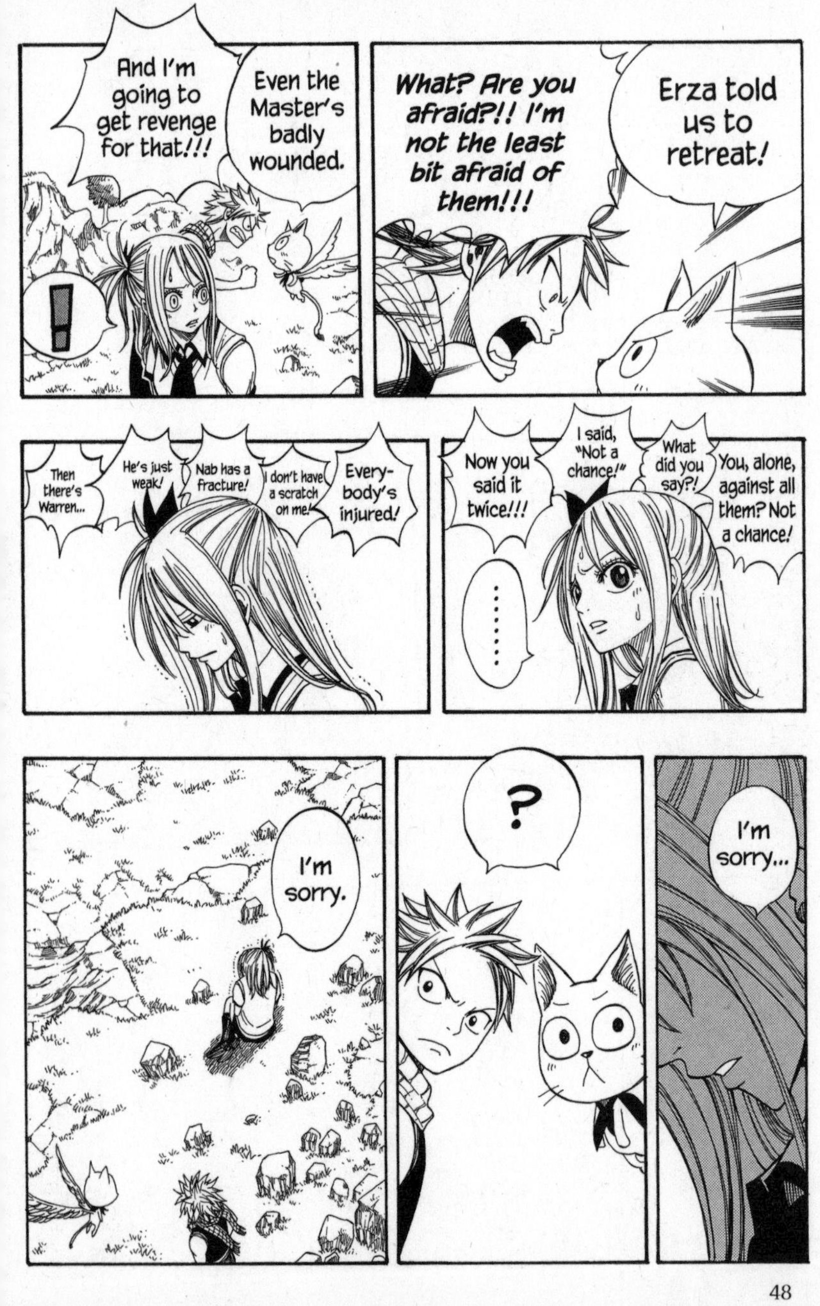
Erza told us to retreat!
What? Are you afraid?!! I'm not the least bit afraid of them!!!
Even the Master's badly wounded.
And I'm going to get revenge for that!!!
!
You, alone, against all them? Not a chance!
What did you say?!
I said, "Not a chance!"
Now you said it twice!!!
......
Every-body's injured!
I don't have a scratch on me!
Nab has a fracture!
He's just weak!
Then there's Warren...
I'm sorry...
?
I'm sorry.

GRIMP

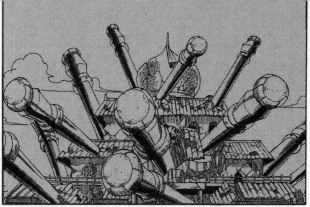

DOOM!!

SNIFF

It's all...my fault...

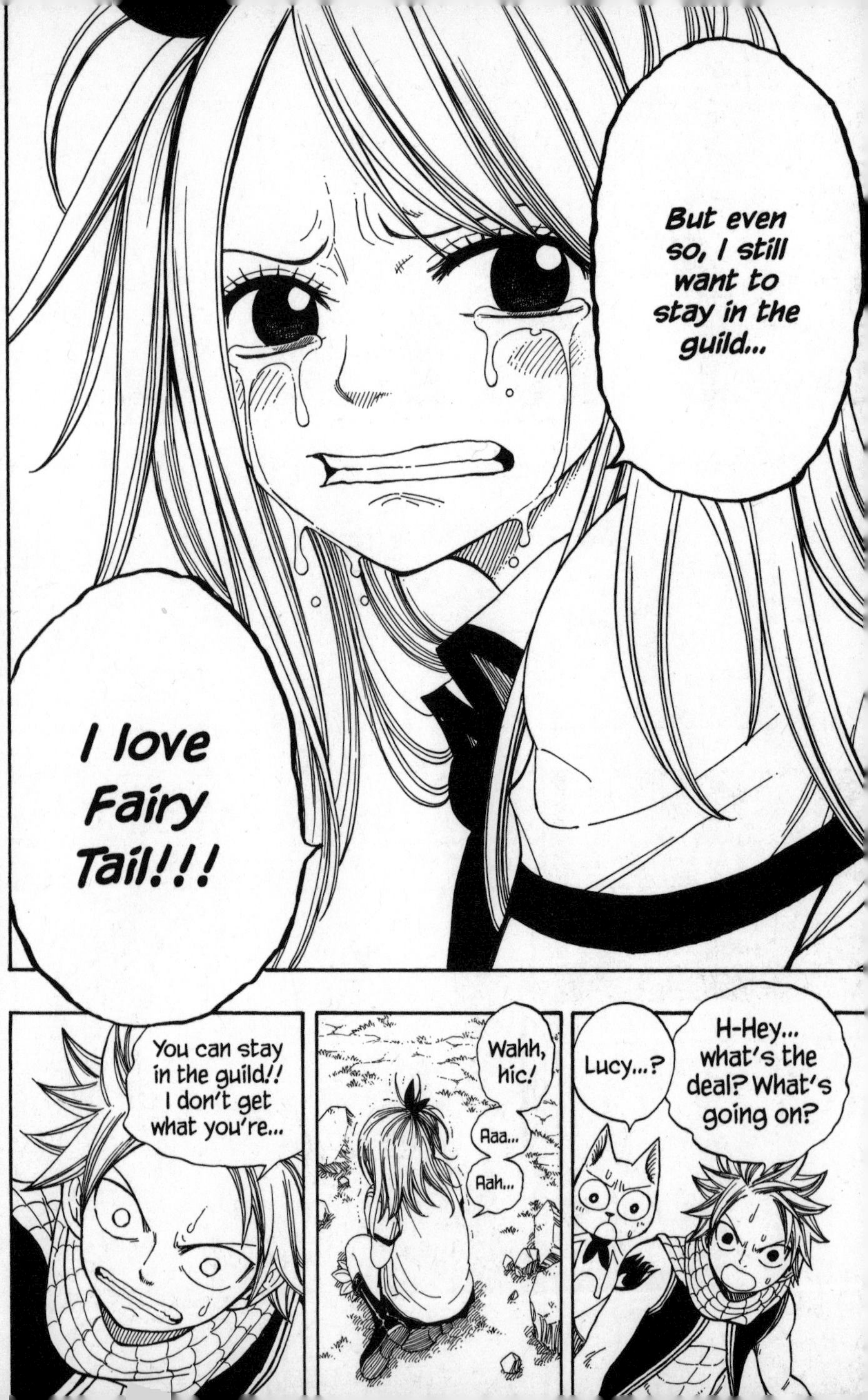
But even so, I still want to stay in the guild...
I love Fairy Tail!!!
H-Hey... what's the deal? What's going on?
Lucy...?
Wahh, hic!
Aaa...
Aah...
You can stay in the guild!! I don't get what you're...

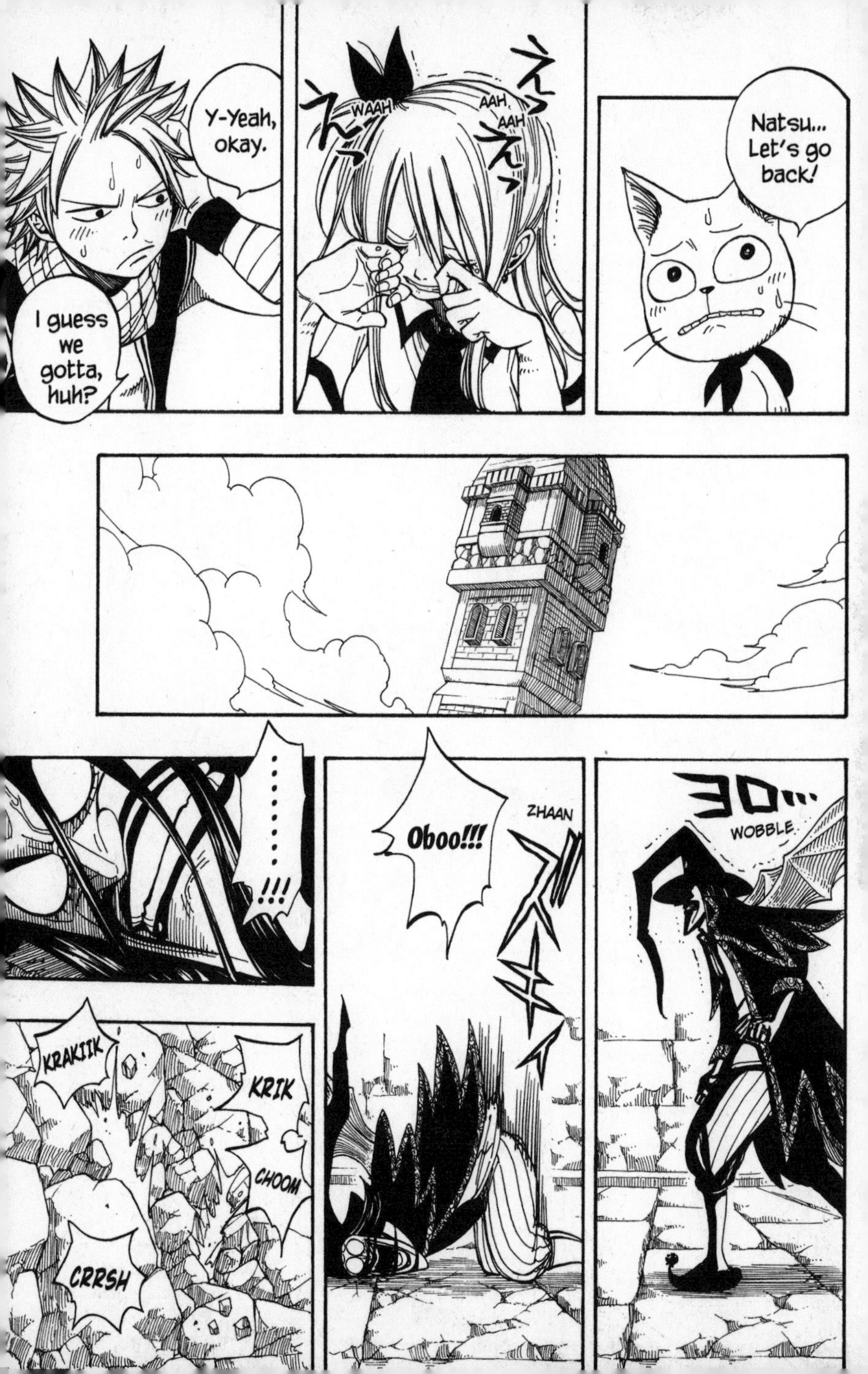
Natsu... Let's go back!
WAAH
AAH
AAH
Y-Yeah, okay.
I guess we gotta, huh?
WOBBLE
Oboo!!!
ZHAAN
......!!!
KRAKIIK
KRIK
CHOOM
CRRSH

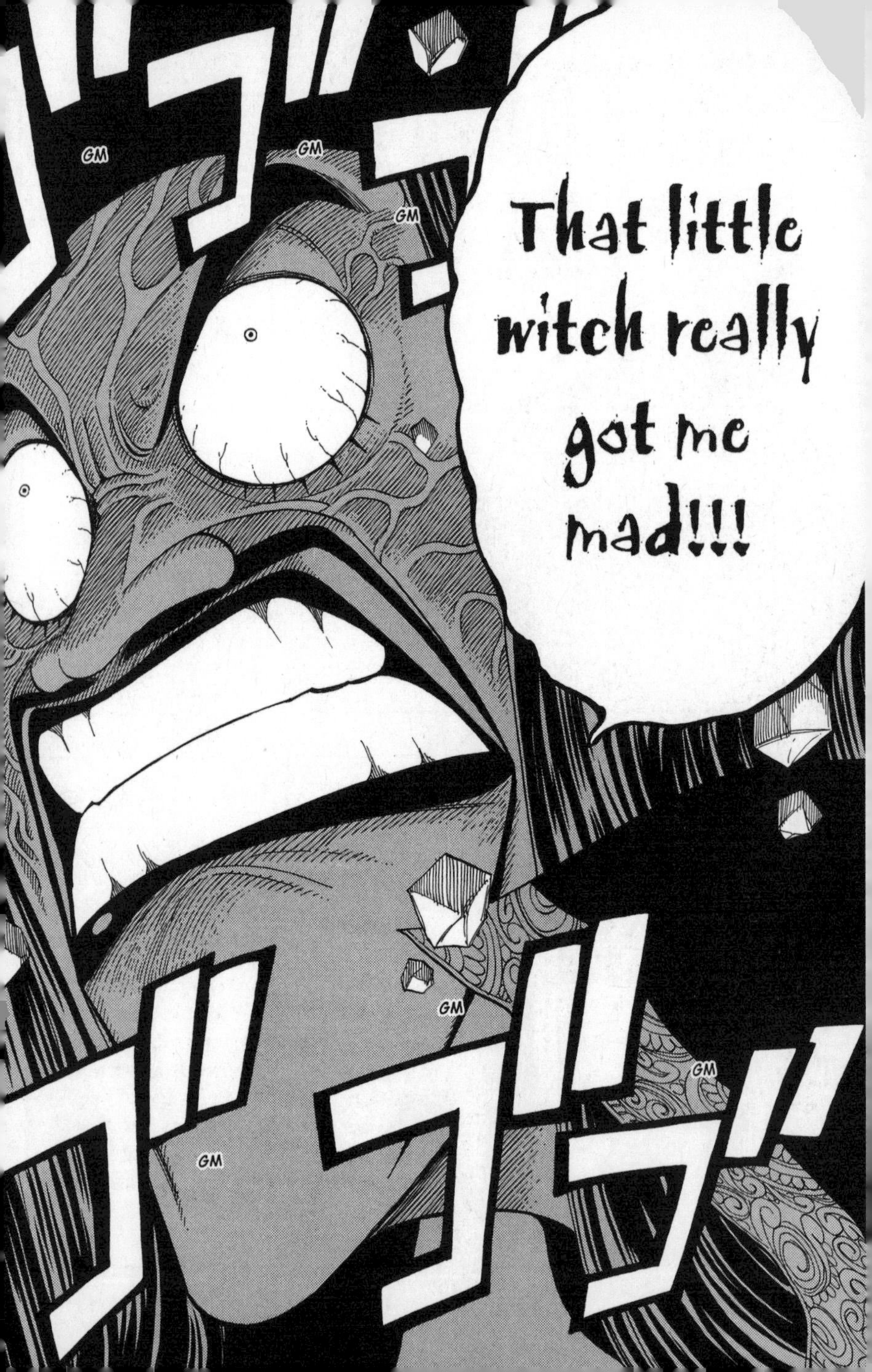
That little witch really got me mad!!!
GM
GM
GM
GM
GM
GM

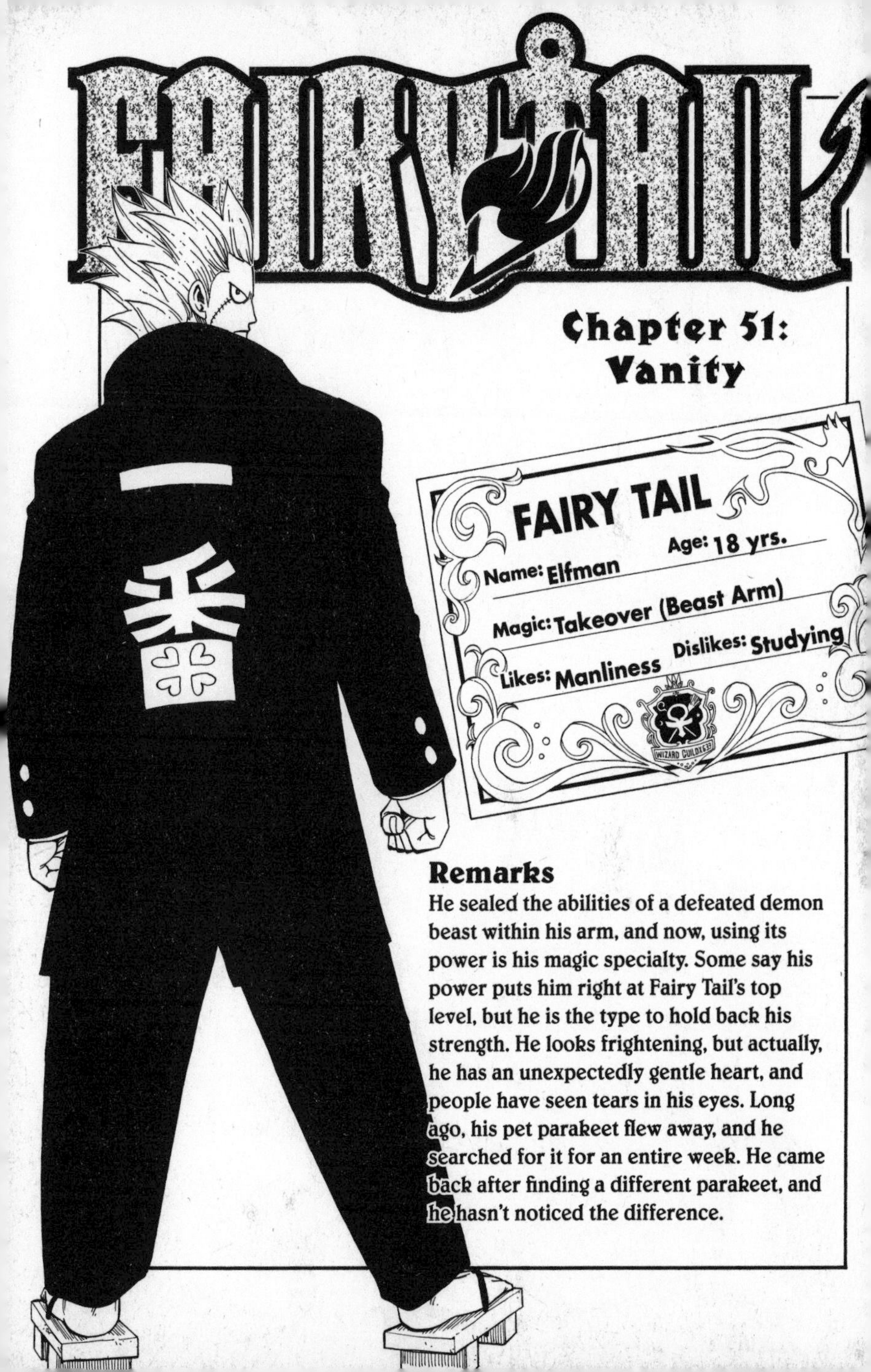

Chapter 51: Vanity

FAIRY TAIL

Name: Elfman **Age:** 18 yrs.

Magic: Takeover (Beast Arm)

Likes: Manliness **Dislikes:** Studying

WIZARD GUILD X633

Remarks

He sealed the abilities of a defeated demon beast within his arm, and now, using its power is his magic specialty. Some say his power puts him right at Fairy Tail's top level, but he is the type to hold back his strength. He looks frightening, but actually, he has an unexpectedly gentle heart, and people have seen tears in his eyes. Long ago, his pet parakeet flew away, and he searched for it for an entire week. He came back after finding a different parakeet, and he hasn't noticed the difference.

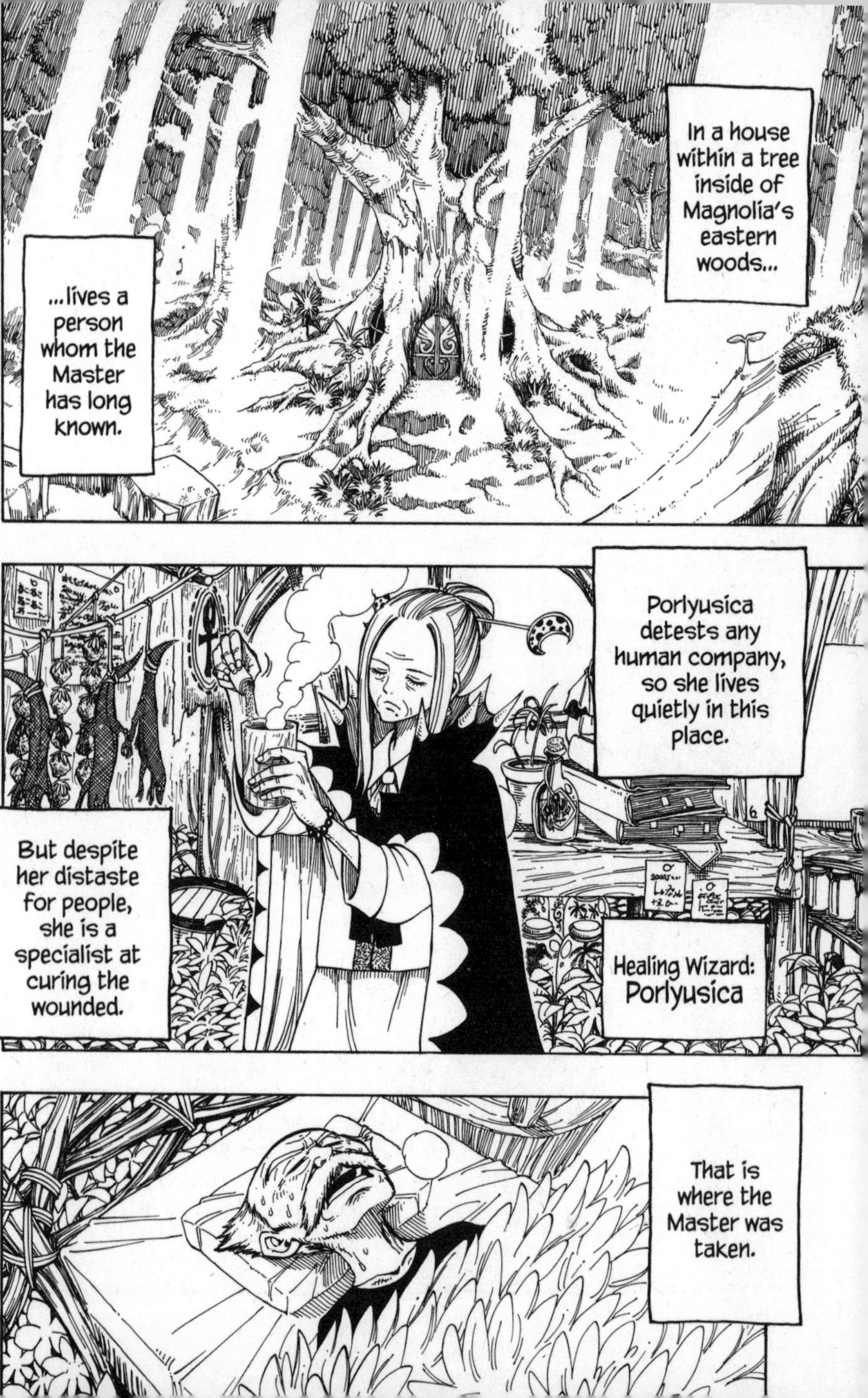
In a house within a tree inside of Magnolia's eastern woods...
...lives a person whom the Master has long known.
Porlyusica detests any human company, so she lives quietly in this place.
But despite her distaste for people, she is a specialist at curing the wounded.
Healing Wizard: Porlyusica
That is where the Master was taken.

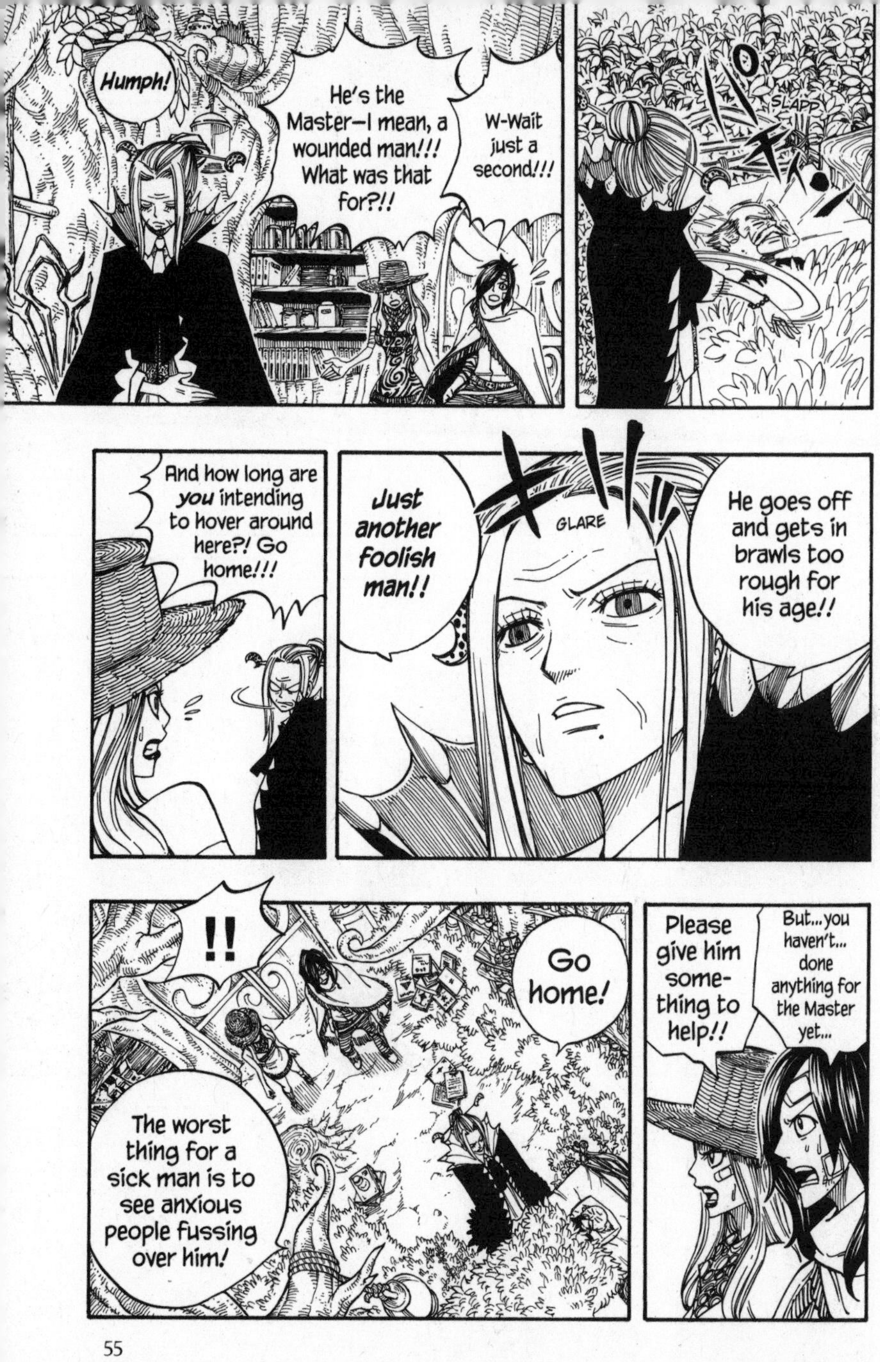
SLAPP
W-Wait just a second!!!
He's the Master—I mean, a wounded man!!! What was that for?!!
Humph!
He goes off and gets in brawls too rough for his age!!
GLARE
Just another foolish man!!
And how long are you intending to hover around here?! Go home!!!
But...you haven't... done anything for the Master yet...
Please give him some-thing to help!!
Go home!
!!
The worst thing for a sick man is to see anxious people fussing over him!

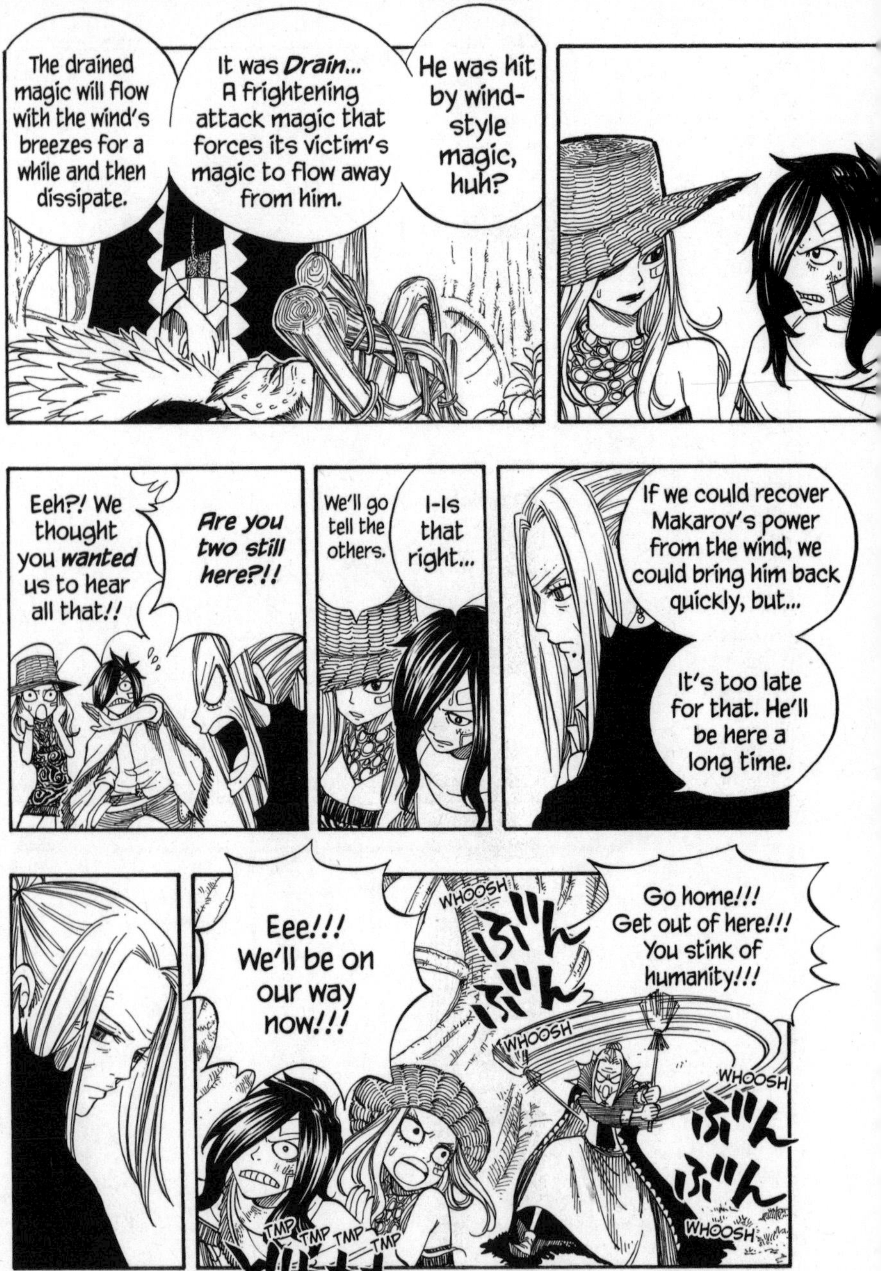
He was hit by wind-style magic, huh?
It was *Drain*... A frightening attack magic that forces its victim's magic to flow away from him.
The drained magic will flow with the wind's breezes for a while and then dissipate.
If we could recover Makarov's power from the wind, we could bring him back quickly, but...
It's too late for that. He'll be here a long time.
I-Is that right...
We'll go tell the others.
Are you two still here?!!
Eeh?! We thought you ***wanted*** us to hear all that!!
Go home!!! Get out of here!!! You stink of humanity!!!
WHOOSH
ぶん
ぶん
WHOOSH
WHOOSH
ぶん
ぶん
WHOOSH
Eee!!! We'll be on our way now!!!
TMP TMP TMP TMP
どたたたっ

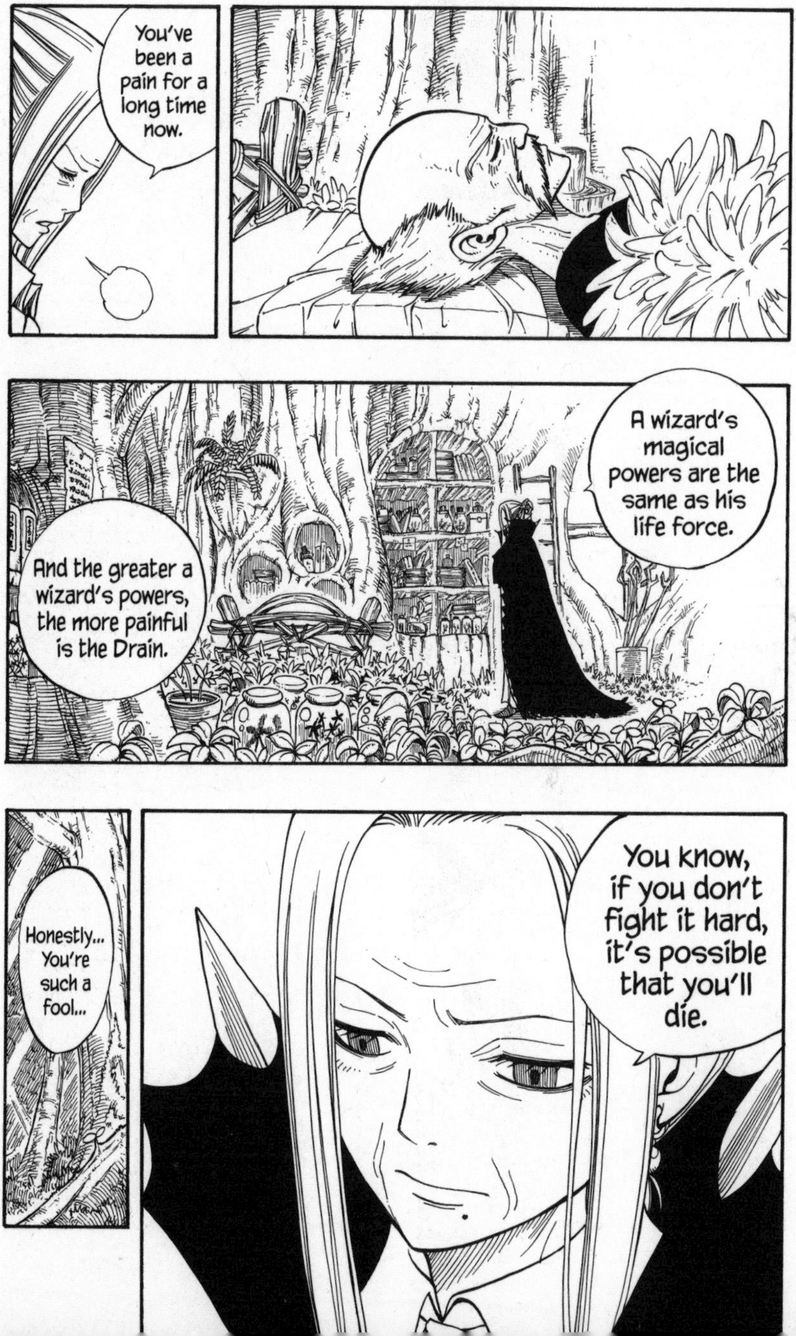
You've been a pain for a long time now.
A wizard's magical powers are the same as his life force.
And the greater a wizard's powers, the more painful is the Drain.
You know, if you don't fight it hard, it's possible that you'll die.
Honestly... You're such a fool...

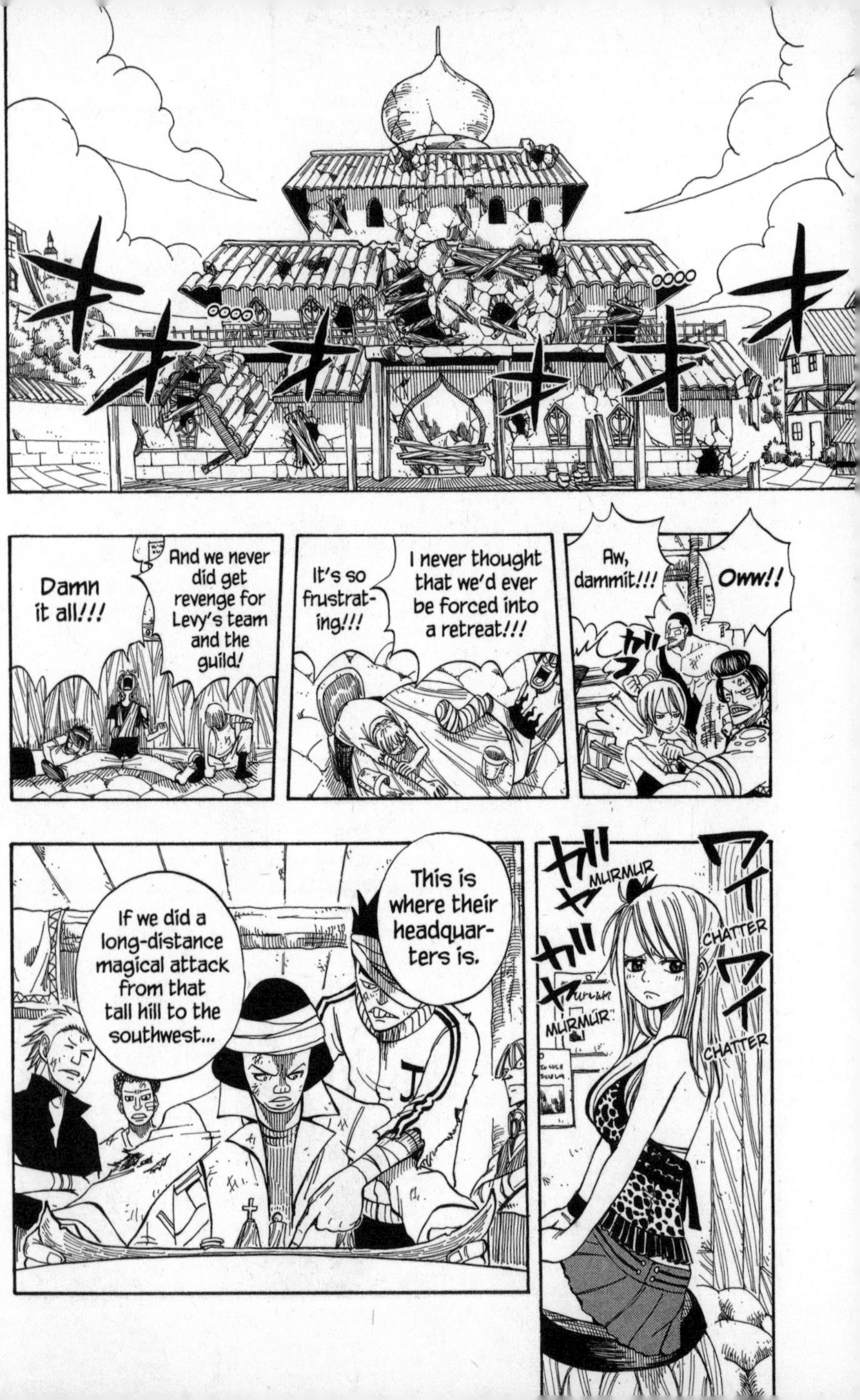
Oww!!
Aw, dammit!!!
I never thought that we'd ever be forced into a retreat!!!
It's so frustrat-ing!!!
And we never did get revenge for Levy's team and the guild!
Damn it all!!!
CHATTER
MURMUR
CHATTER
MURMUR
This is where their headquar-ters is.
If we did a long-distance magical attack from that tall hill to the southwest...

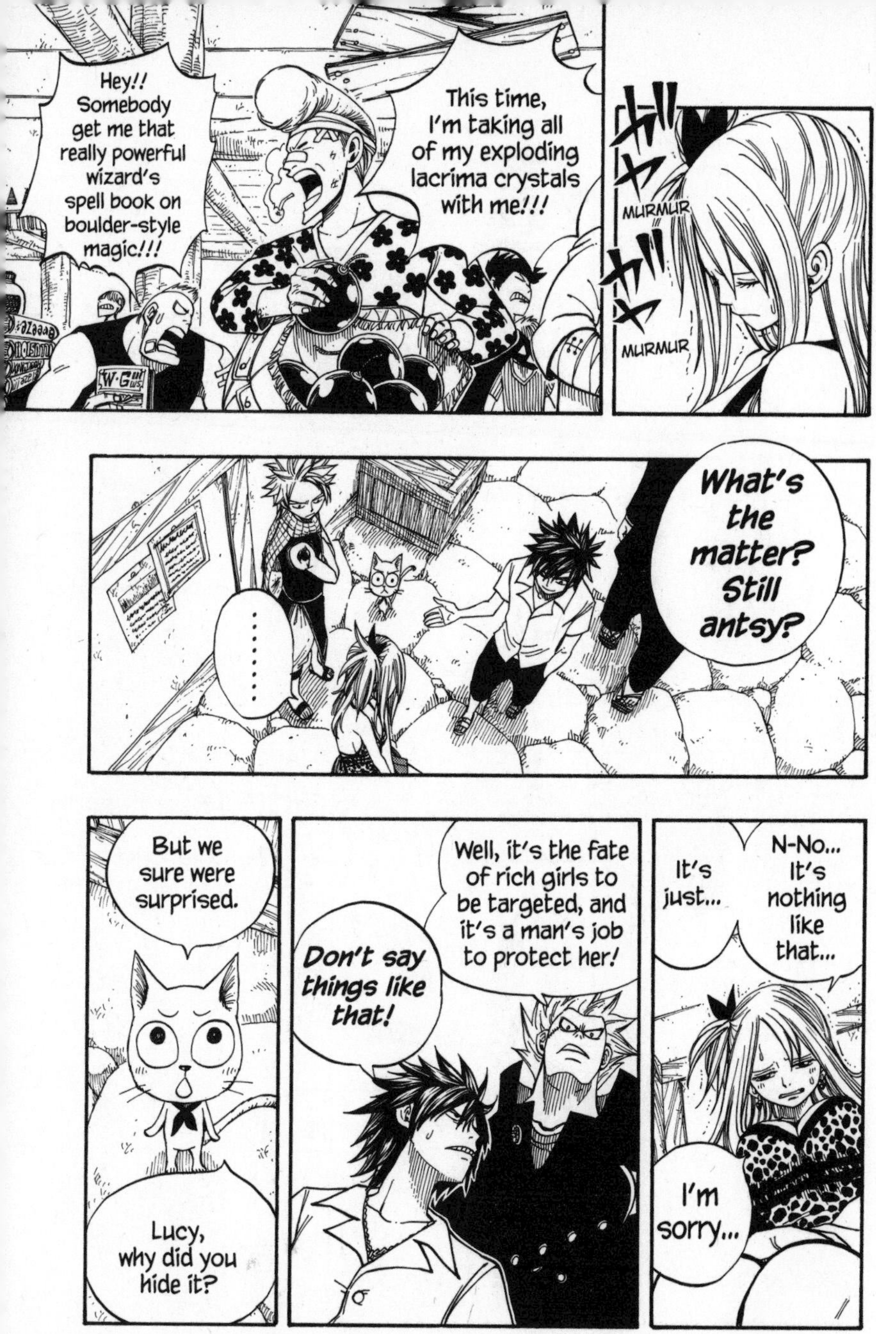
MURMUR
MURMUR
This time, I'm taking all of my exploding lacrima crystals with me!!!
Hey!! Somebody get me that really powerful wizard's spell book on boulder-style magic!!!
What's the matter? Still antsy?
......
N-No... It's nothing like that...
It's just...
I'm sorry...
Well, it's the fate of rich girls to be targeted, and it's a man's job to protect her!
Don't say things like that!
But we sure were surprised.
Lucy, why did you hide it?

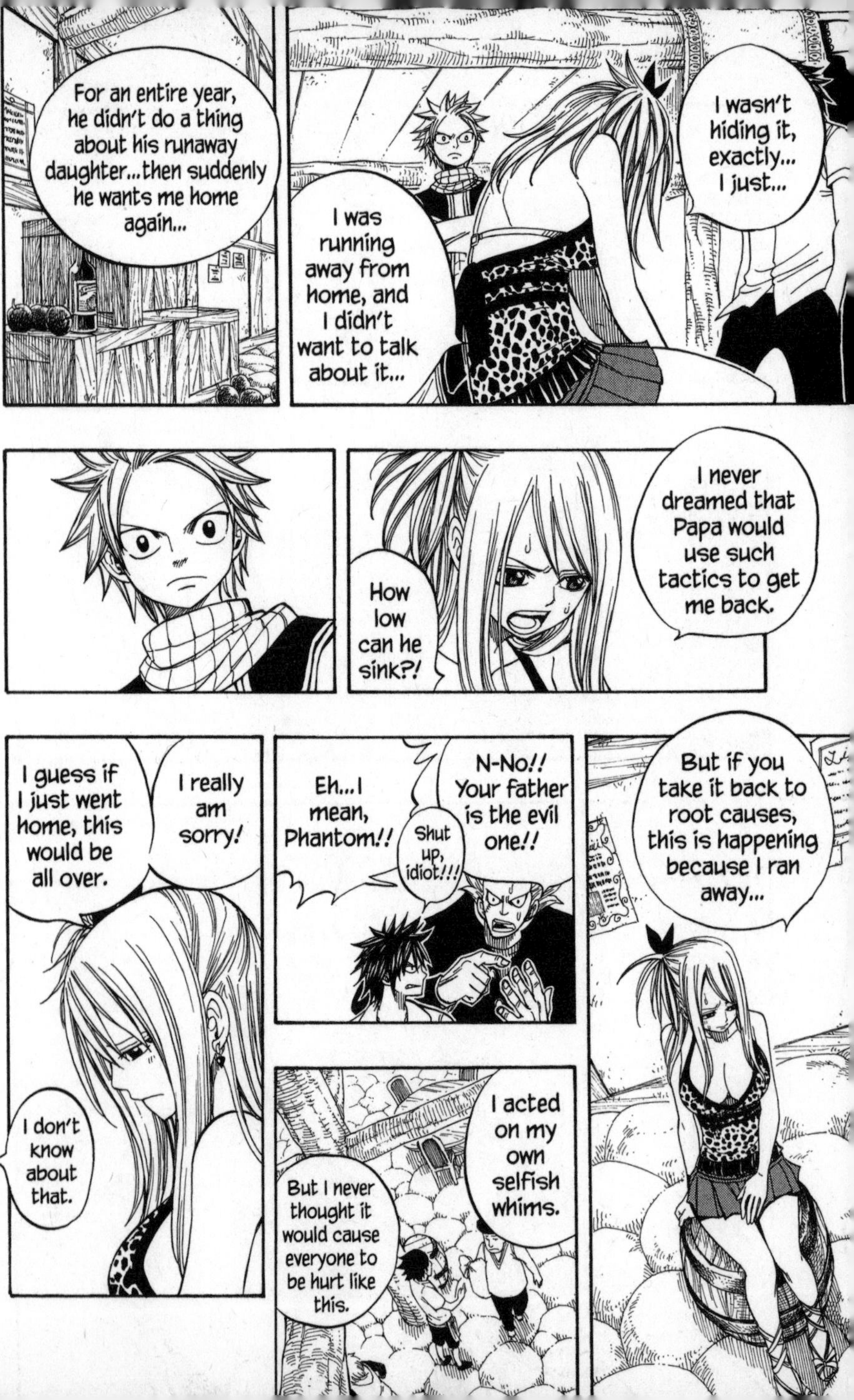
I wasn't hiding it, exactly... I just...
I was running away from home, and I didn't want to talk about it...
For an entire year, he didn't do a thing about his runaway daughter...then suddenly he wants me home again...
I never dreamed that Papa would use such tactics to get me back.
How low can he sink?!
But if you take it back to root causes, this is happening because I ran away...
N-No!! Your father is the evil one!!
Shut up, idiot!!!
Eh...I mean, Phantom!!
I acted on my own selfish whims.
But I never thought it would cause everyone to be hurt like this.
I really am sorry!
I guess if I just went home, this would be all over.
I don't know about that.

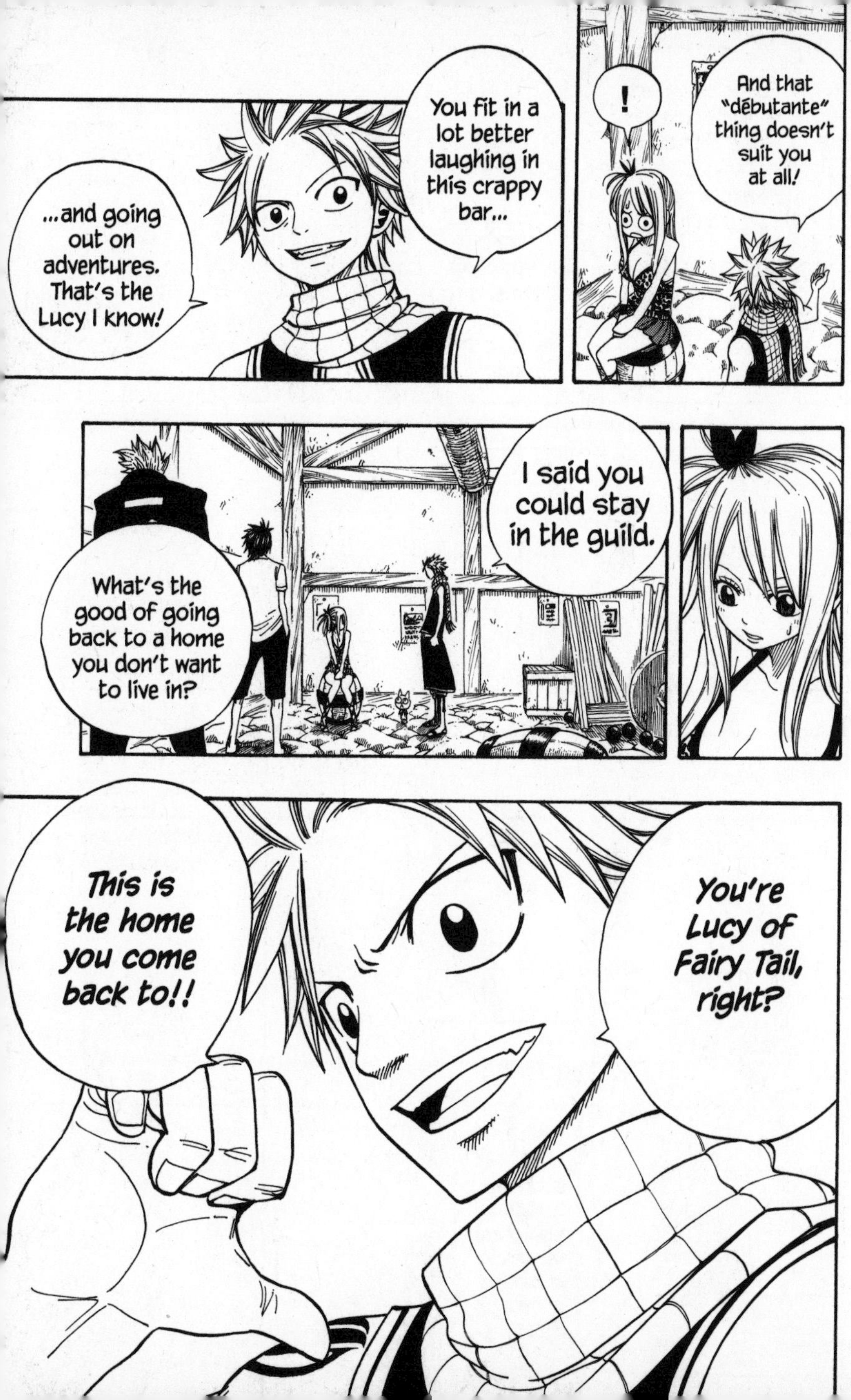
!
And that "débutante" thing doesn't suit you at all!
You fit in a lot better laughing in this crappy bar...
...and going out on adventures. That's the Lucy I know!
I said you could stay in the guild.
What's the good of going back to a home you don't want to live in?
You're Lucy of Fairy Tail, right?
This is the home you come back to!!

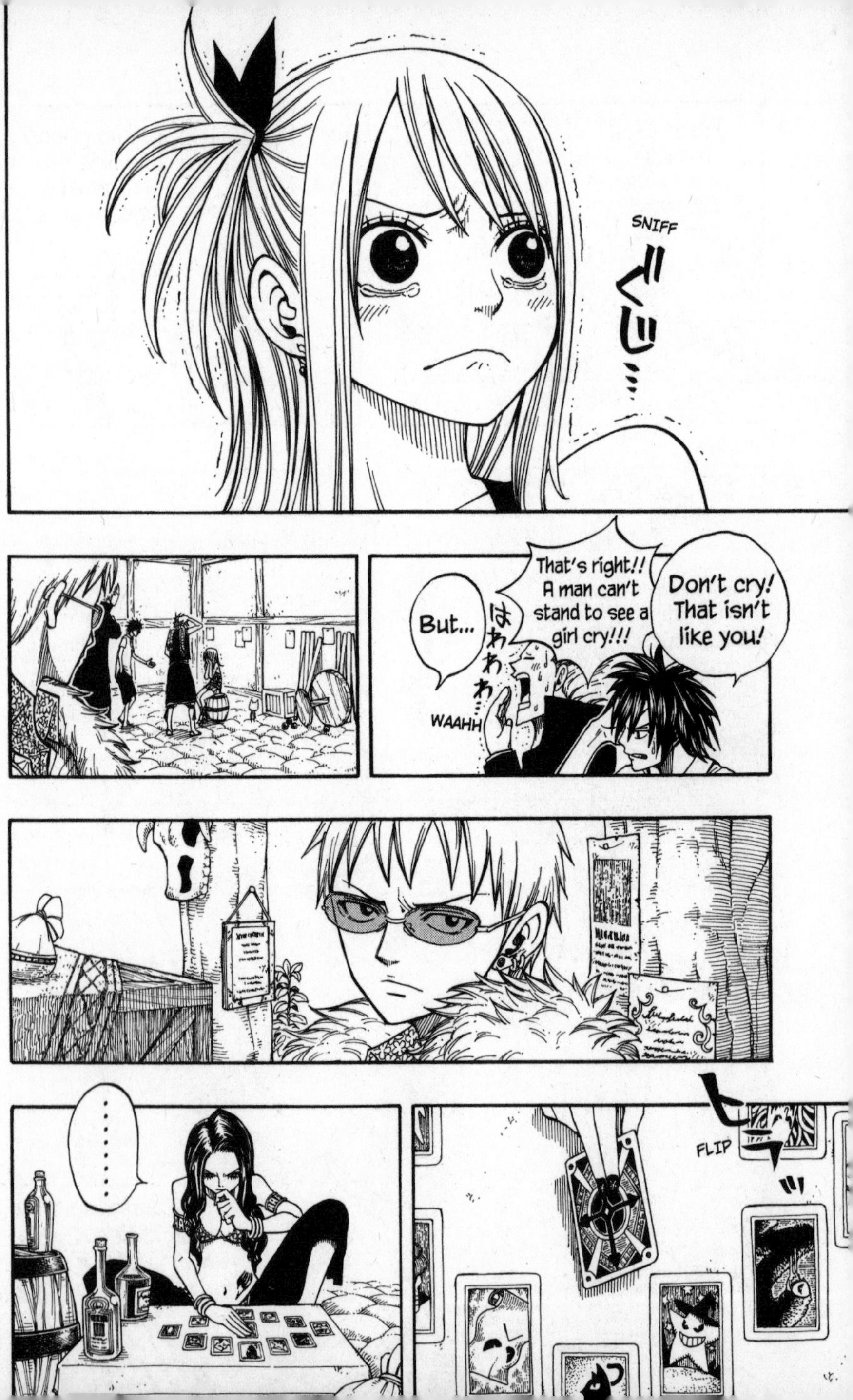
SNIFF
ぐじ…
Don't cry! That isn't like you!
That's right!! A man can't stand to see a girl cry!!!
But...
はわわわ…
WAAHH
FLIP
……

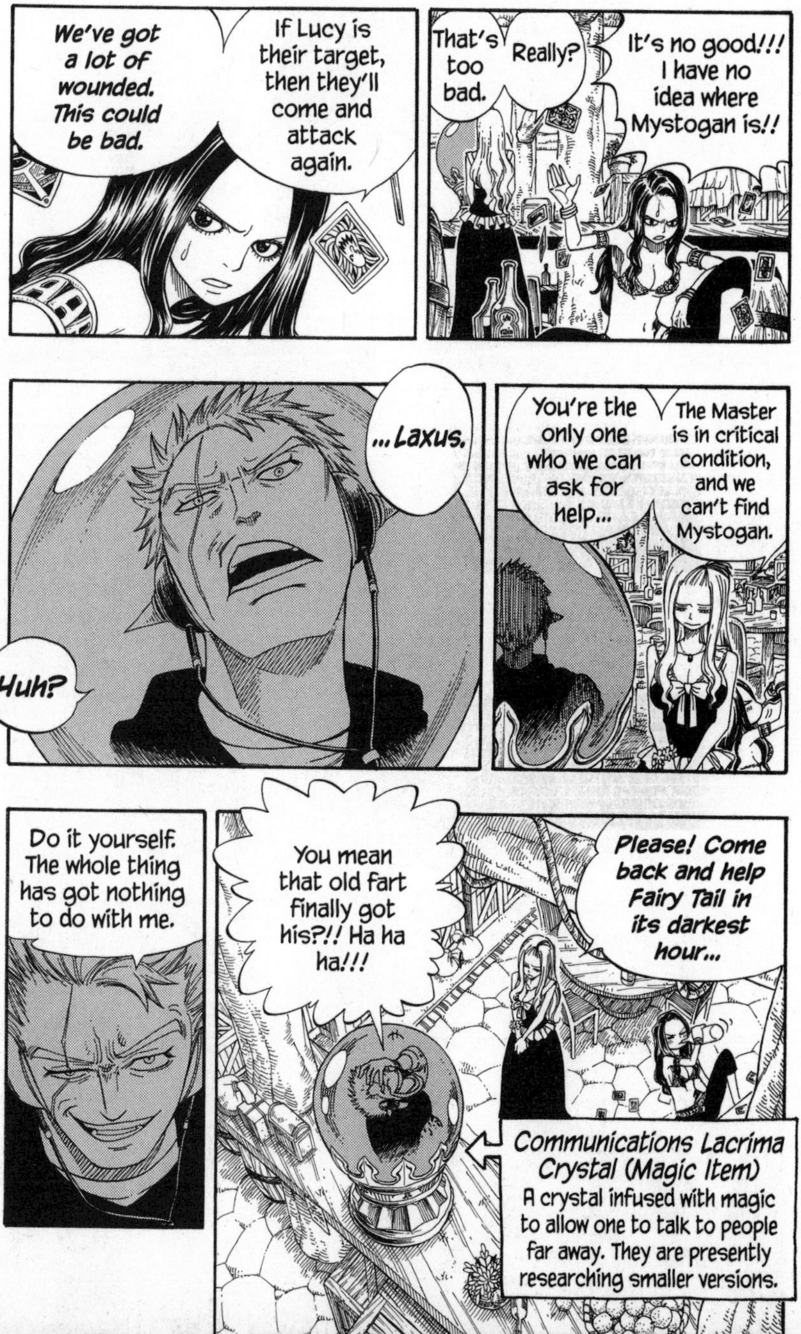
It's no good!!! I have no idea where Mystogan is!!
Really?
That's too bad.
If Lucy is their target, then they'll come and attack again.
We've got a lot of wounded. This could be bad.
The Master is in critical condition, and we can't find Mystogan.
You're the only one who we can ask for help...
...Laxus.
Huh?
Please! Come back and help Fairy Tail in its darkest hour...
You mean that old fart finally got his?!! Ha ha ha!!!
Communications Lacrima Crystal (Magic Item)
A crystal infused with magic to allow one to talk to people far away. They are presently researching smaller versions.
Do it yourself. The whole thing has got nothing to do with me.

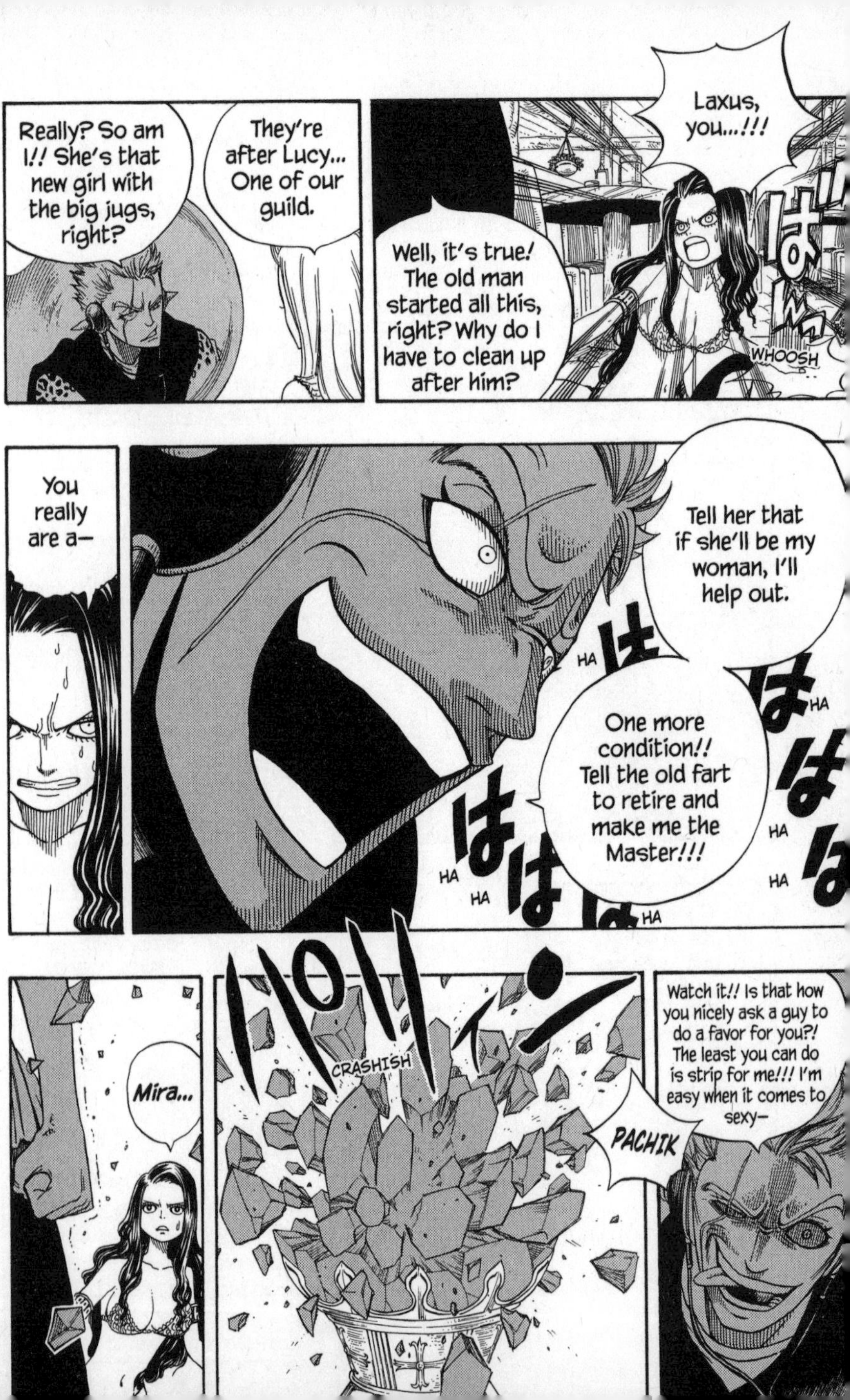
Laxus, you...!!!
WHOOSH
They're after Lucy... One of our guild.
Really? So am I!! She's that new girl with the big jugs, right?
Well, it's true! The old man started all this, right? Why do I have to clean up after him?
Tell her that if she'll be my woman, I'll help out.
HA HA HA HA HA HA HA HA
One more condition!! Tell the old fart to retire and make me the Master!!!
You really are a—
Watch it!! Is that how you nicely ask a guy to do a favor for you?! The least you can do is strip for me!!! I'm easy when it comes to sexy—
PACHIK
CRASHISH
Mira...

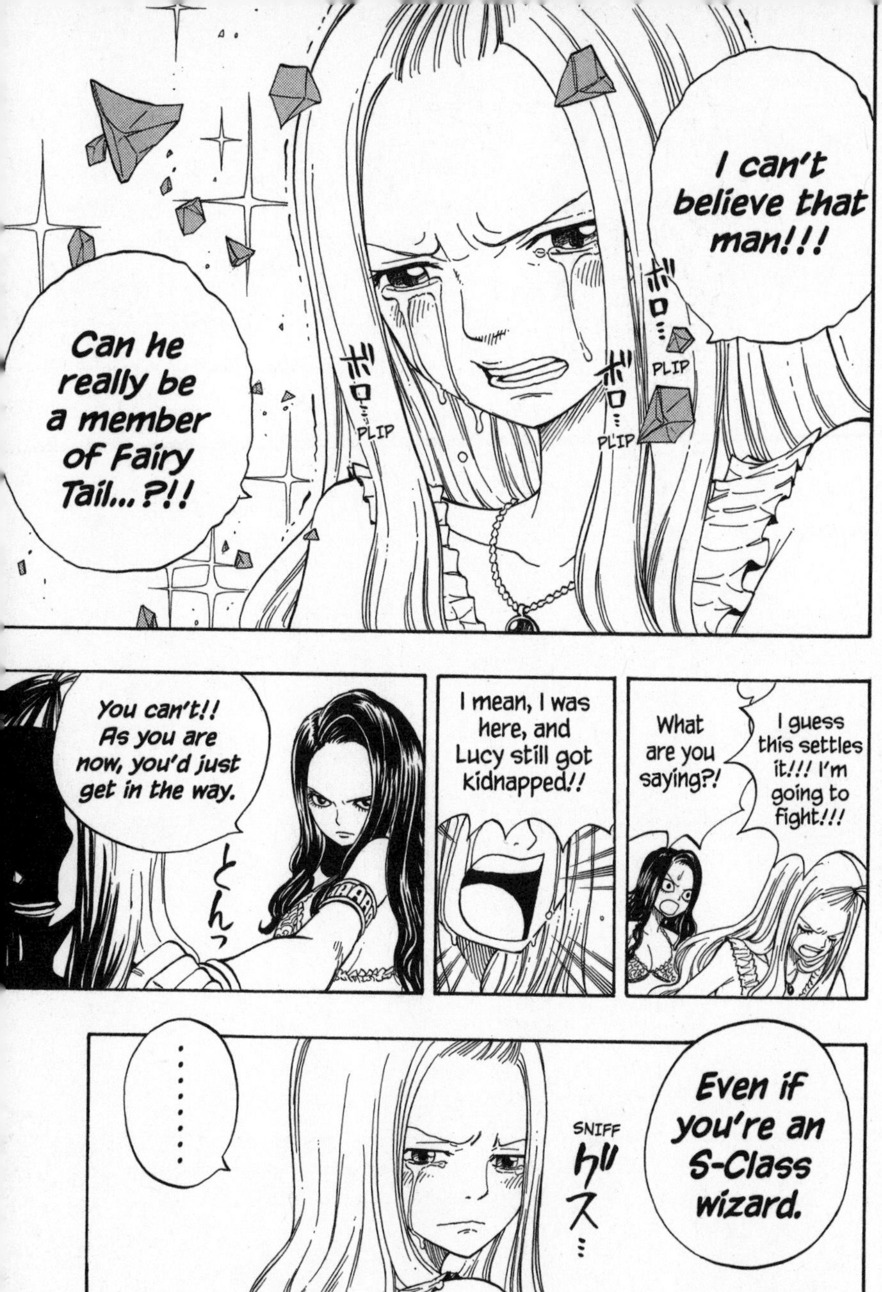
I can't believe that man!!!
Can he really be a member of Fairy Tail...?!!
ボロ…
PLIP
ボロ…
PLIP
ボロ…
PLIP
You can't!! As you are now, you'd just get in the way.
I mean, I was here, and Lucy still got kidnapped!!
I guess this settles it!!! I'm going to fight!!!
What are you saying?!
Even if you're an S-Class wizard.
……
SNIFF
グズ…

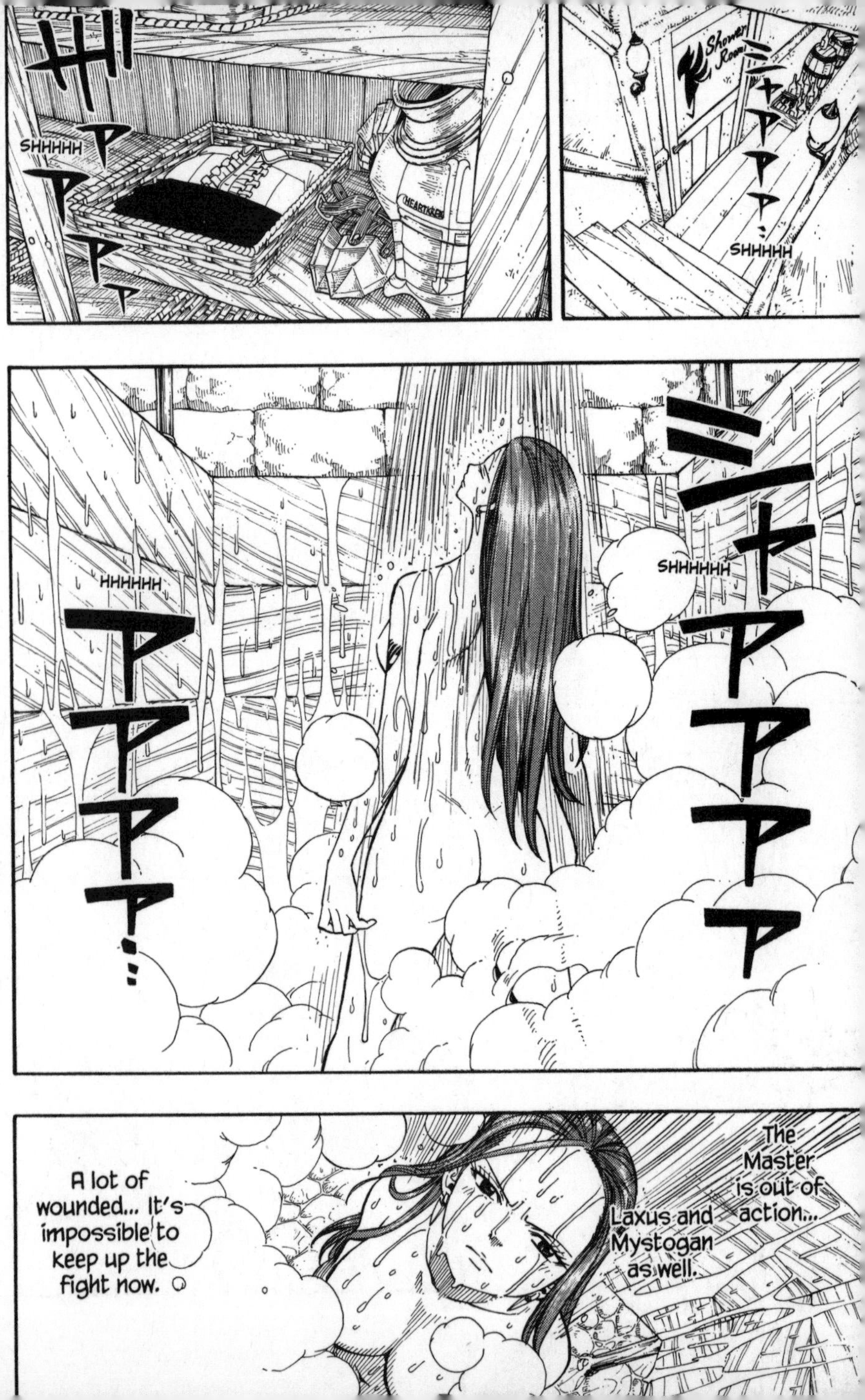
Shower Room
SHHHHH
SHHHHH
SHHHHHH
HHHHHH
The Master is out of action...
Laxus and Mystogan as well.
A lot of wounded... It's impossible to keep up the fight now.

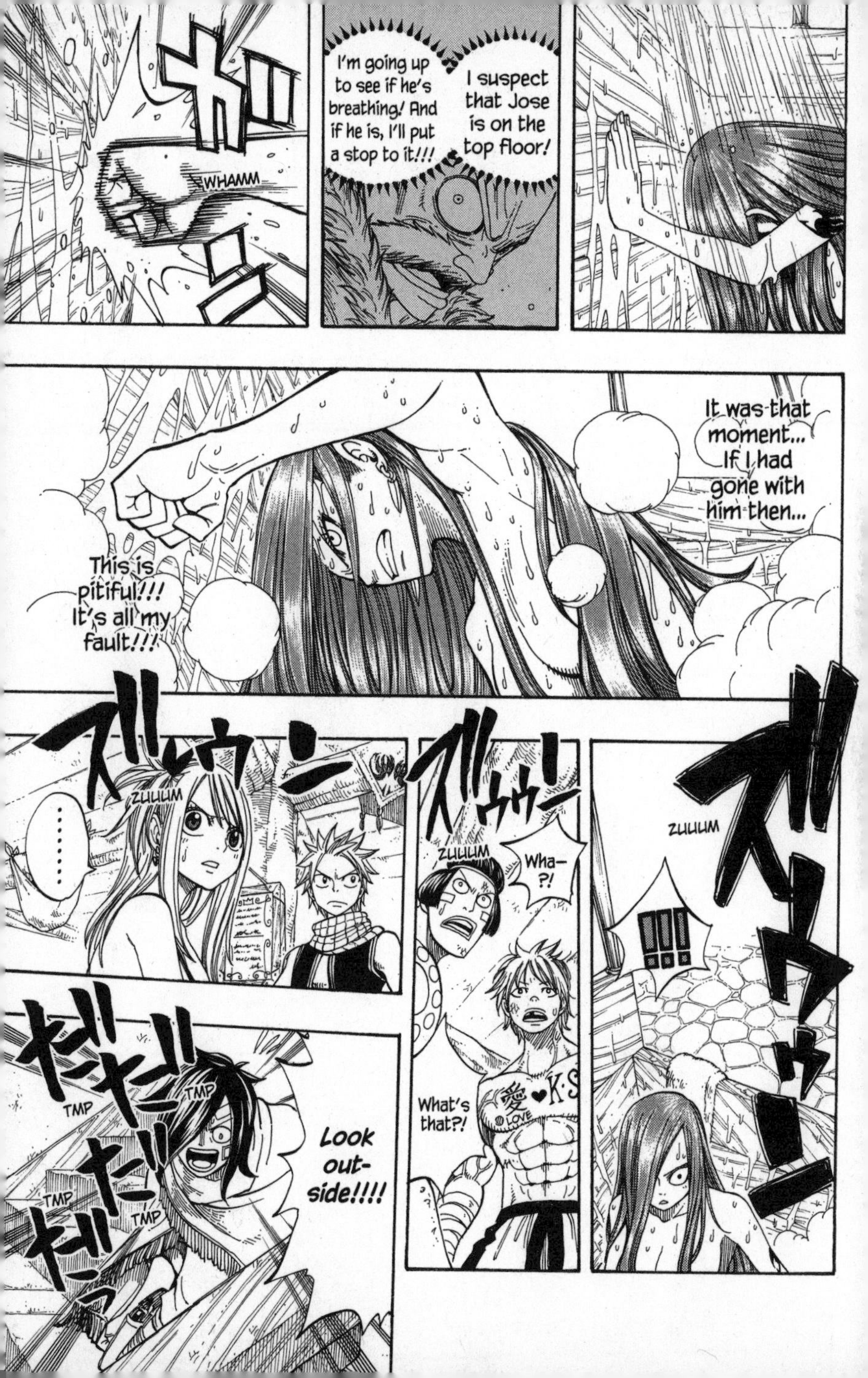
I suspect that Jose is on the top floor!
I'm going up to see if he's breathing! And if he is, I'll put a stop to it!!!
WHAMM
It was that moment... If I had gone with him then...
This is pitiful!!! It's all my fault!!!
ZUUUM
!!!
ZUUUM
Wha-?!
What's that?!
ZUUUM
......
TMP
TMP
TMP
TMP
Look out-side!!!!

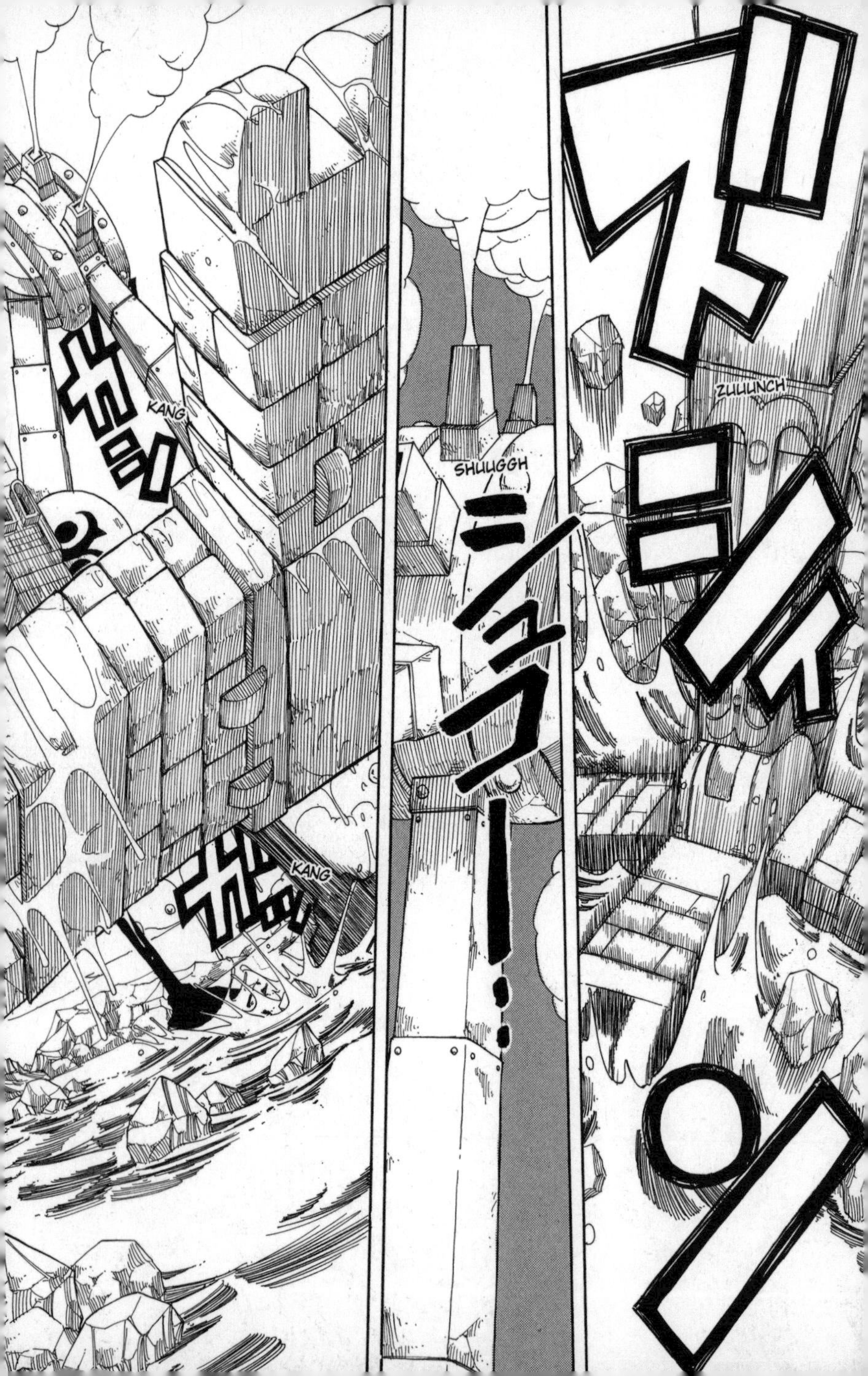
ZUUUNCH
SHUUGGH
KANG
KANG

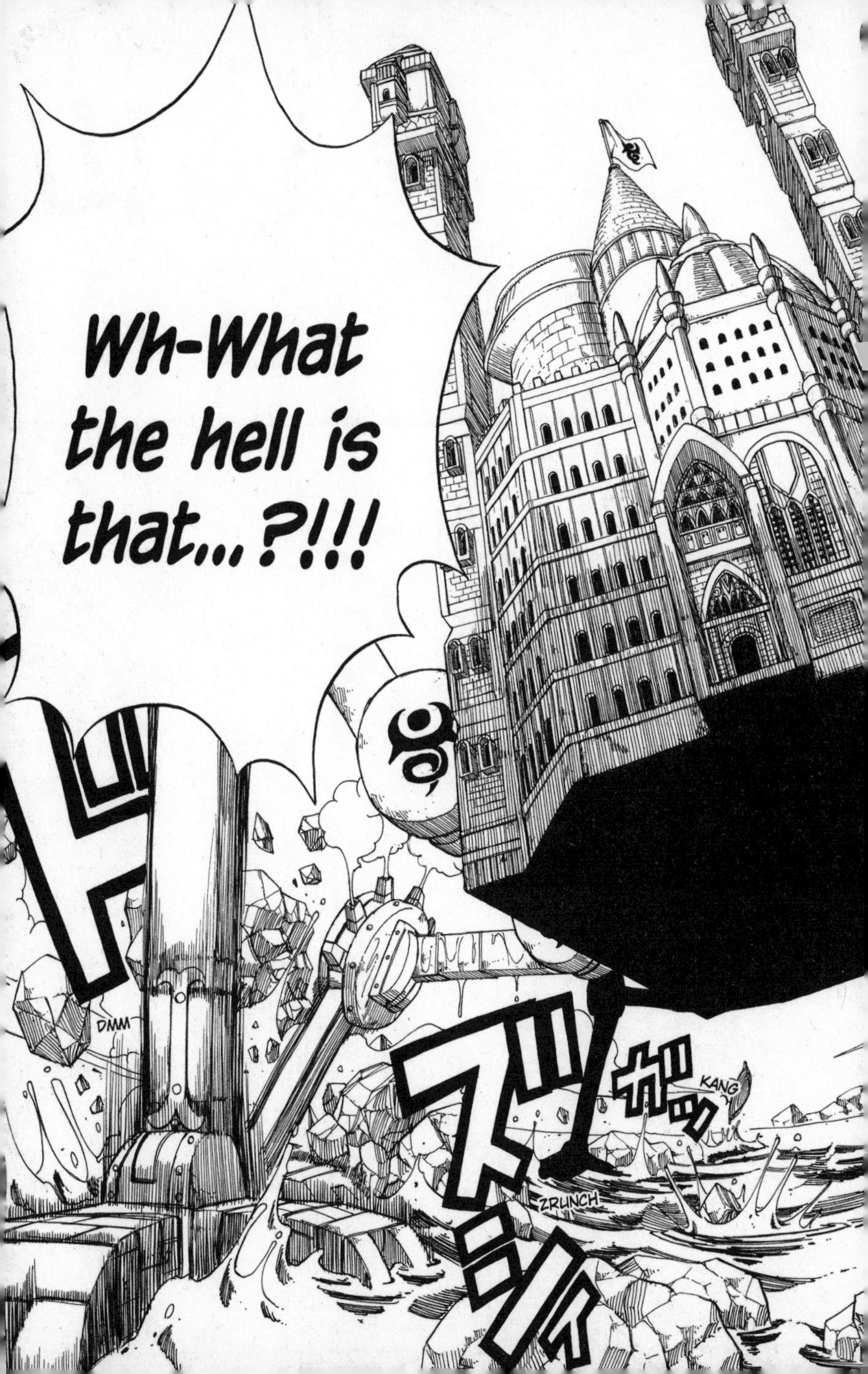

Wh-What the hell is that...?!!!
DMM
KANG
ZRUNCH

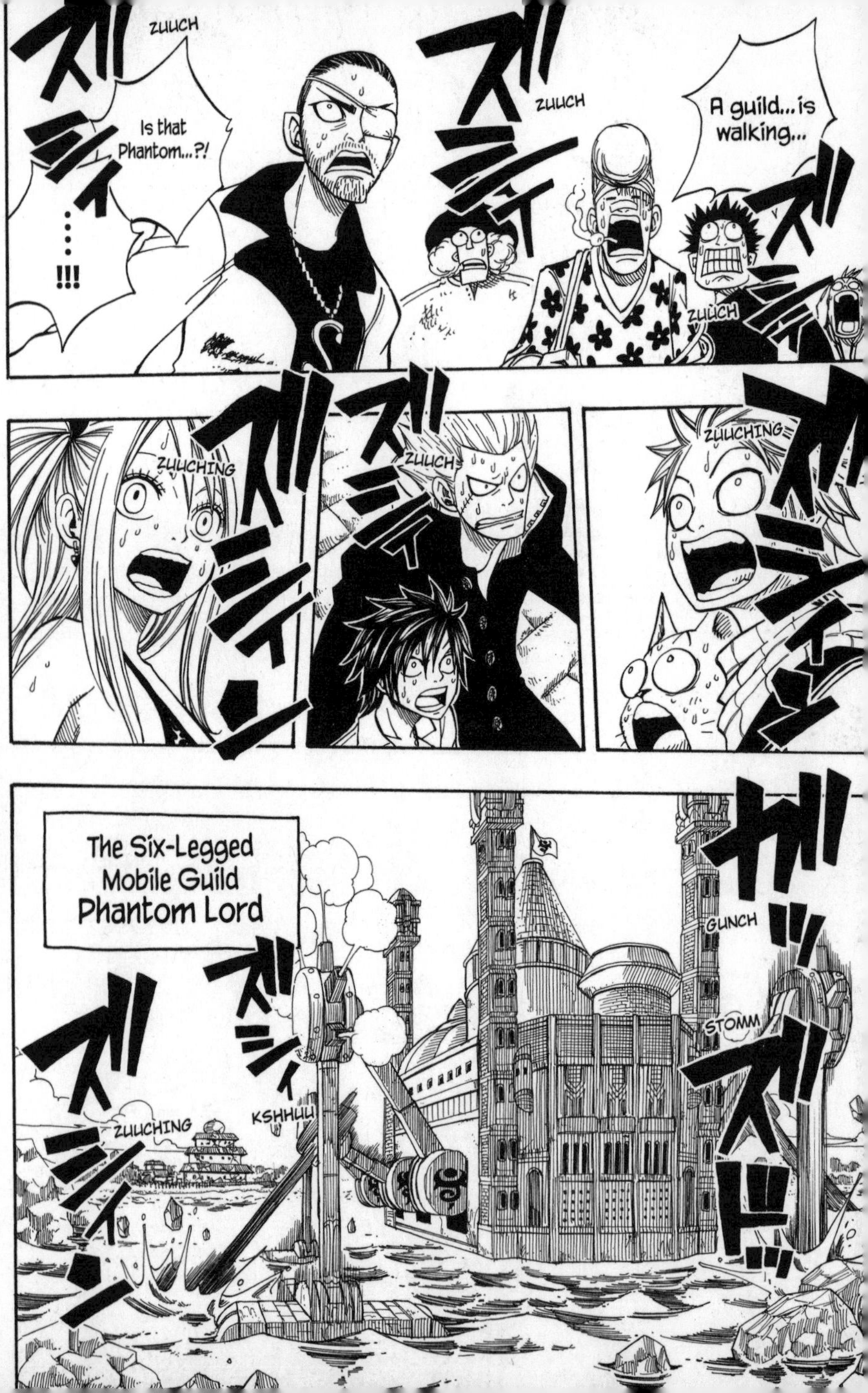
A guild...is walking...
ZUUCH
ZUUCH
Is that Phantom...?!
ZUUCH
ZUUCHING
ZUUCH
ZUUCHING
GUNCH
STOMM
The Six-Legged Mobile Guild Phantom Lord
KSHHUU
ZUUCHING

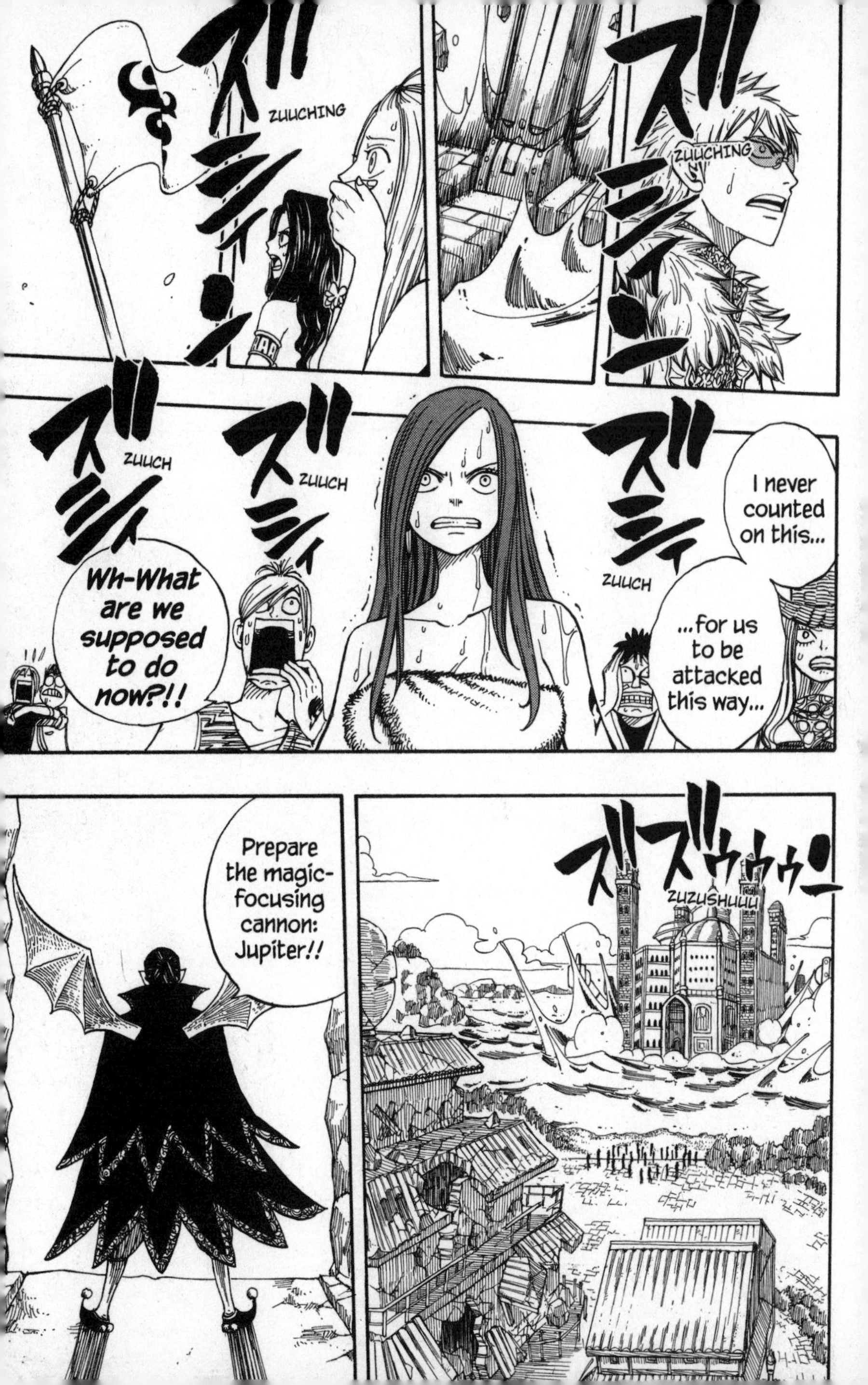
ZUUCHING
ZUUCHING
ZUUCH
I never counted on this...
...for us to be attacked this way...
ZUUCH
ZUUCH
Wh-What are we supposed to do now?!!
ZUZUSHUUU
Prepare the magic-focusing cannon: Jupiter!!

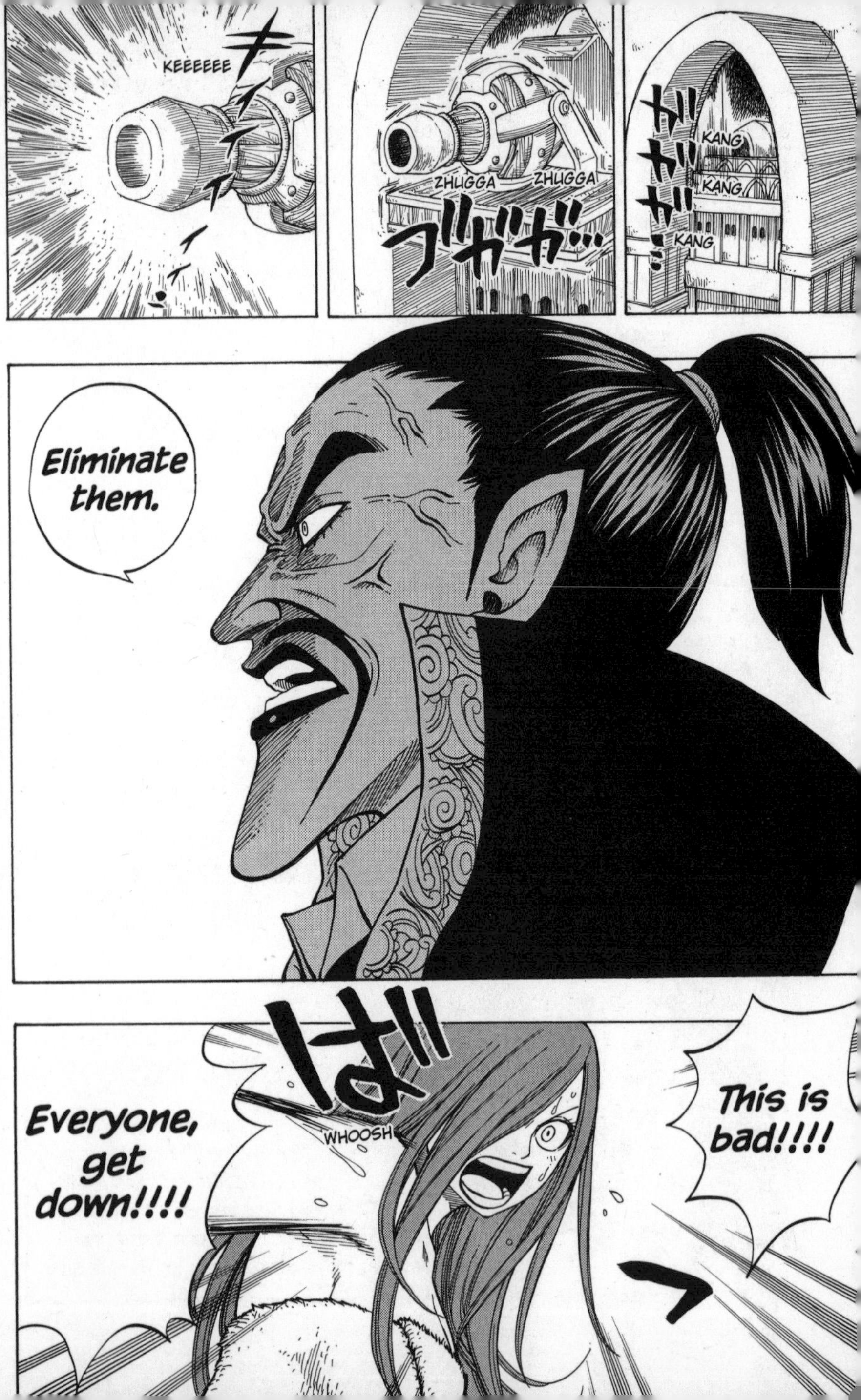
KANG
KANG
KANG
ZHUGGA
ZHUGGA
KEEEEEE
Eliminate them.
This is bad!!!!
WHOOSH
Everyone, get down!!!!

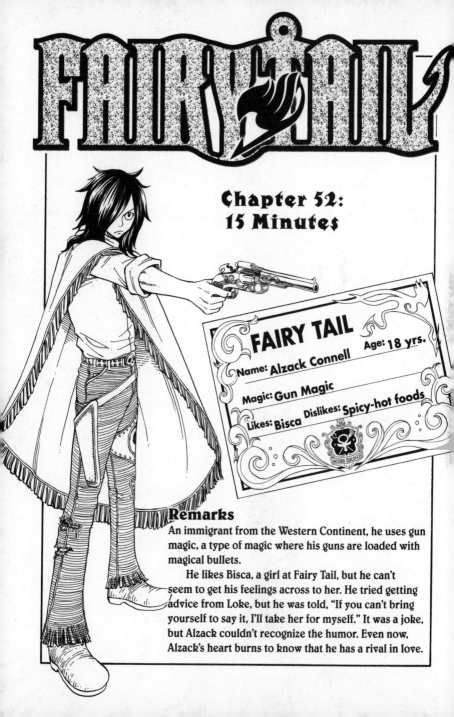

FAIRY TAIL

Chapter 52: 15 Minutes

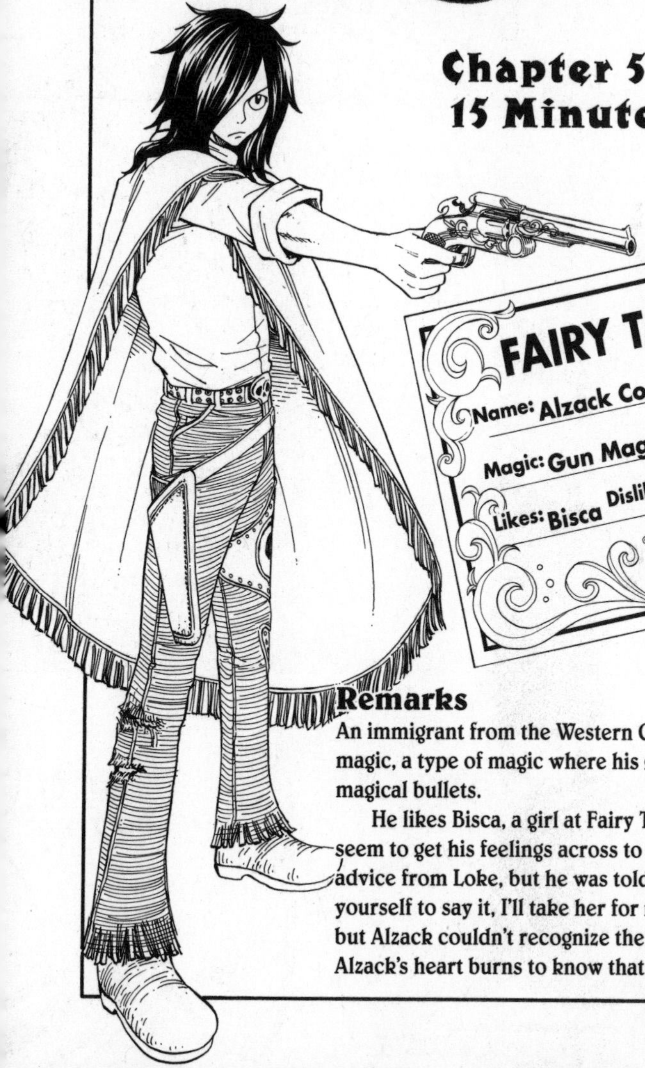

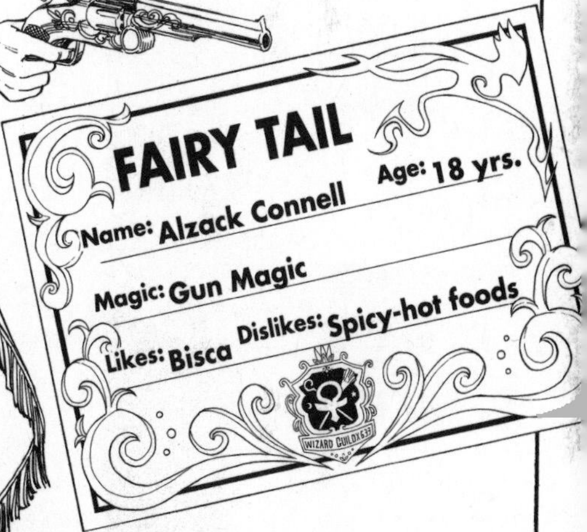
FAIRY TAIL
Age: 18 yrs.
Name: Alzack Connell
Magic: Gun Magic
Likes: Bisca
Dislikes: Spicy-hot foods
WIZARD GUILD

Remarks

An immigrant from the Western Continent, he uses gun magic, a type of magic where his guns are loaded with magical bullets.

He likes Bisca, a girl at Fairy Tail, but he can't seem to get his feelings across to her. He tried getting advice from Loke, but he was told, "If you can't bring yourself to say it, I'll take her for myself." It was a joke, but Alzack couldn't recognize the humor. Even now, Alzack's heart burns to know that he has a rival in love.

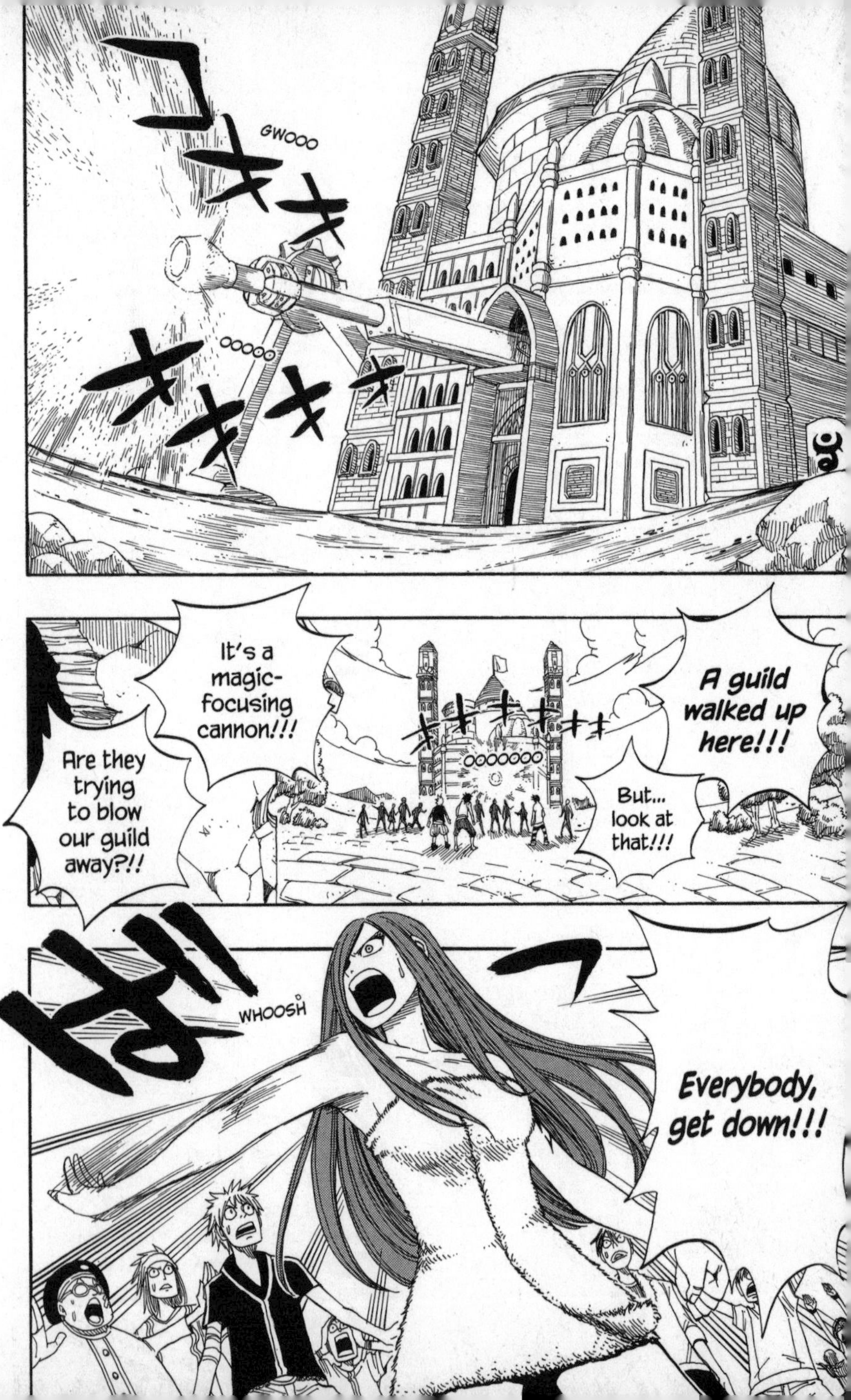
GWOOO
OOOOO
A guild walked up here!!!
But... look at that!!!
OOOOOOO
It's a magic-focusing cannon!!!
Are they trying to blow our guild away?!!
Everybody, get down!!!
WHOOSH

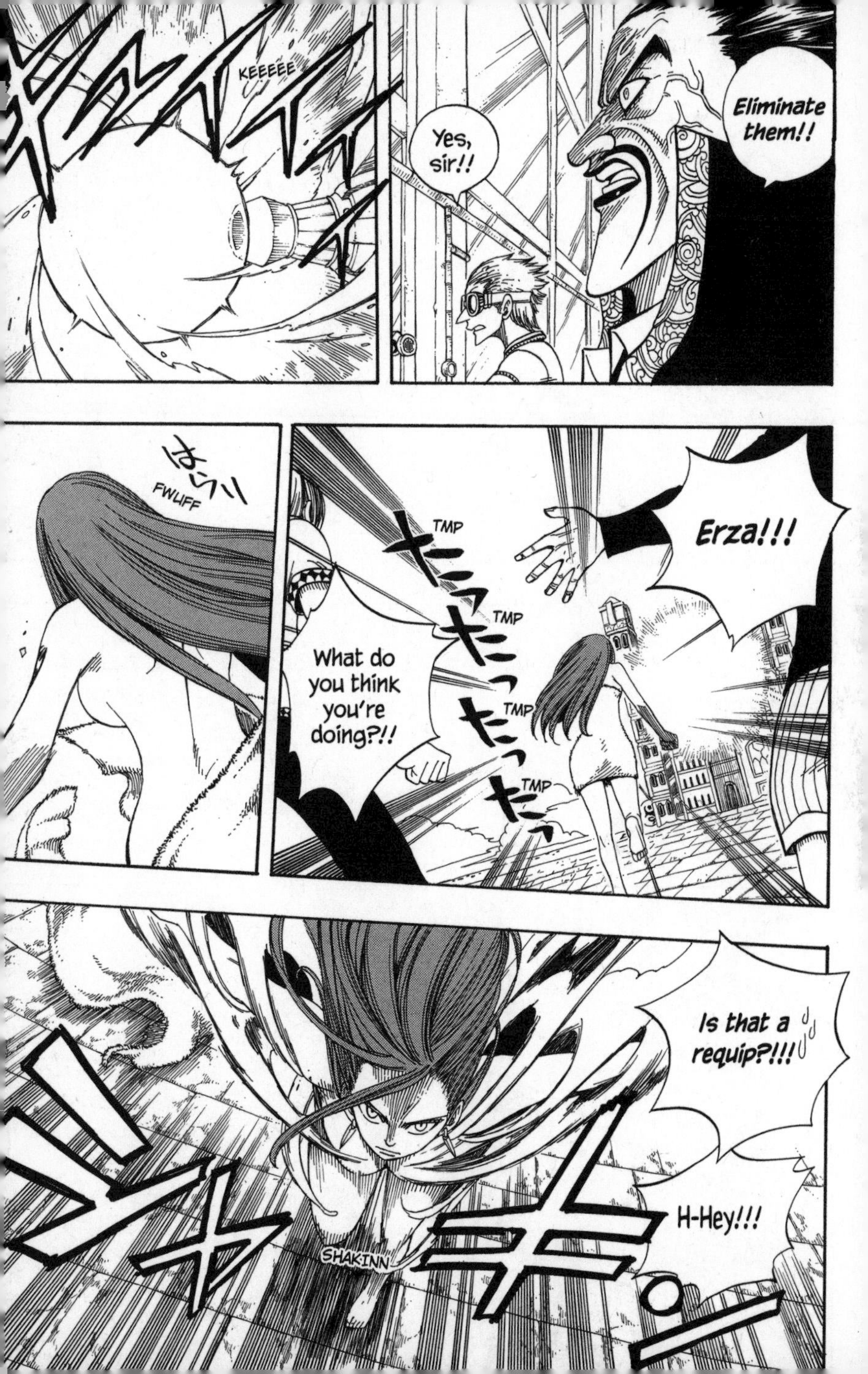
Eliminate them!!
Yes, sir!!
KEEEEE
Erza!!!
TMP
TMP
TMP
TMP
What do you think you're doing?!!
FWUFF
Is that a requip?!!!
H-Hey!!!
SHAKINN

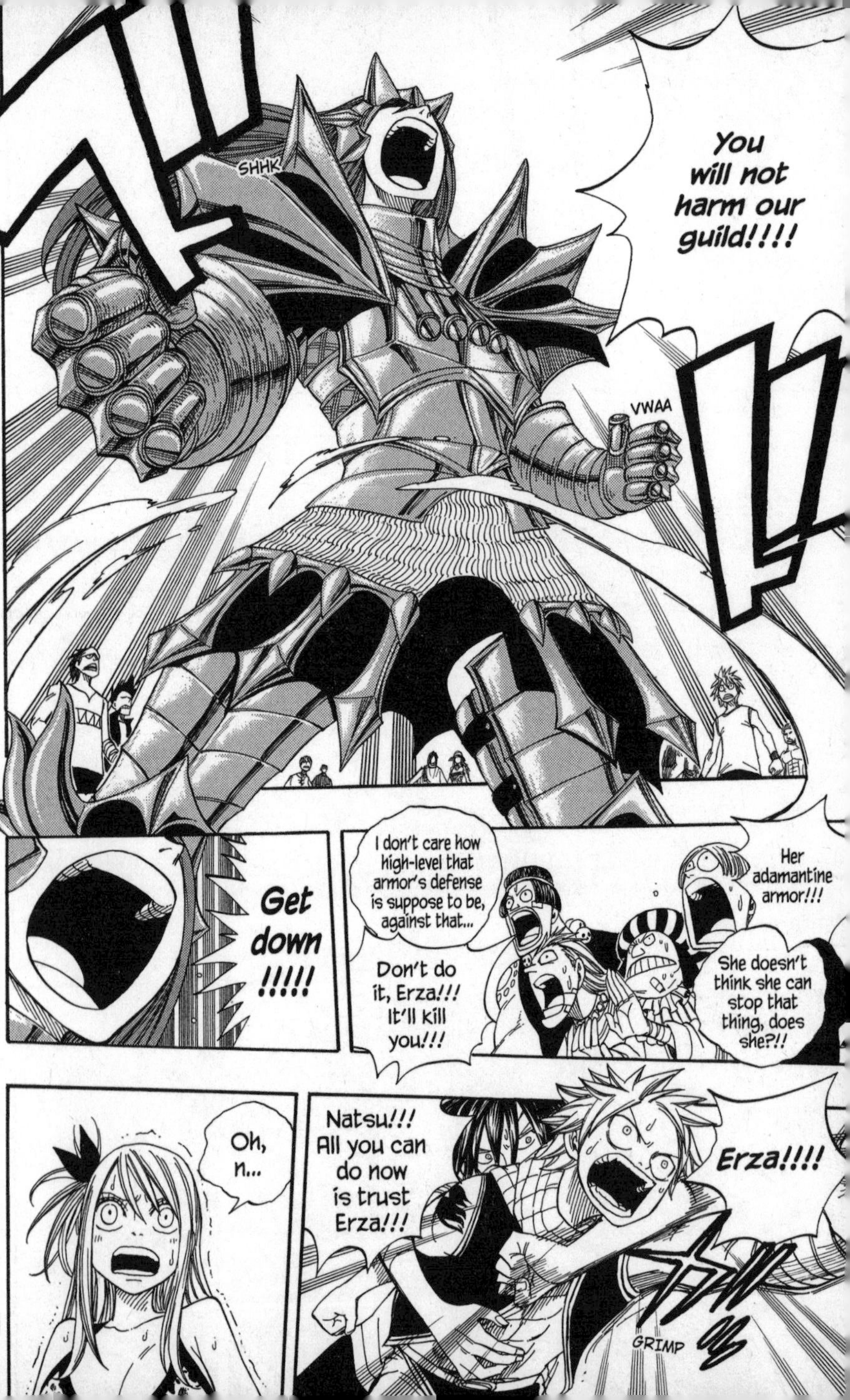
You will not harm our guild!!!!
VWAA
SHHK
Her adamantine armor!!!
She doesn't think she can stop that thing, does she?!!
I don't care how high-level that armor's defense is suppose to be, against that...
Don't do it, Erza!!! It'll kill you!!!
Get down!!!!!
Erza!!!!
Natsu!!! All you can do now is trust Erza!!!
GRIMP
Oh, n...

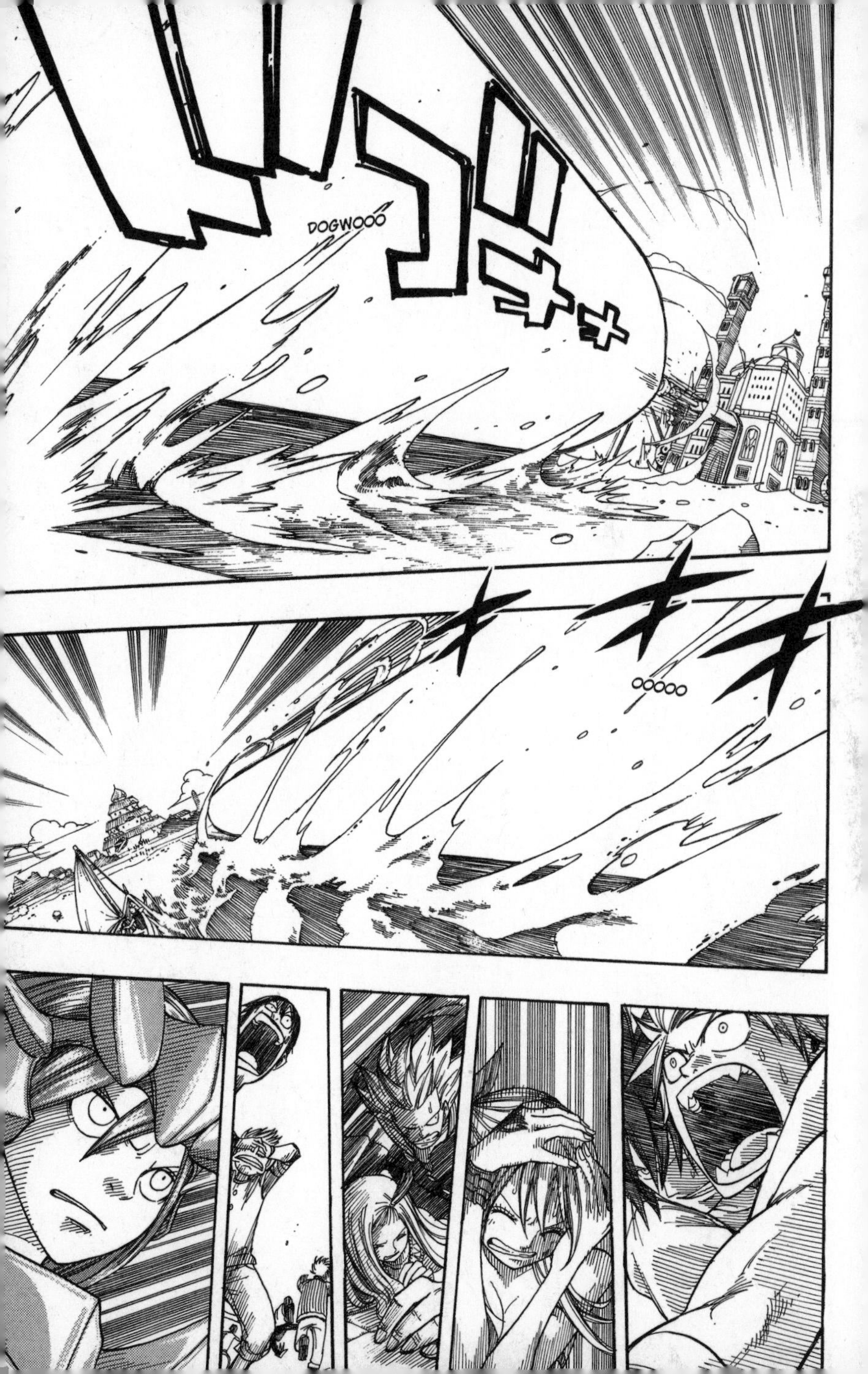
DOGWOOO
OOOOO

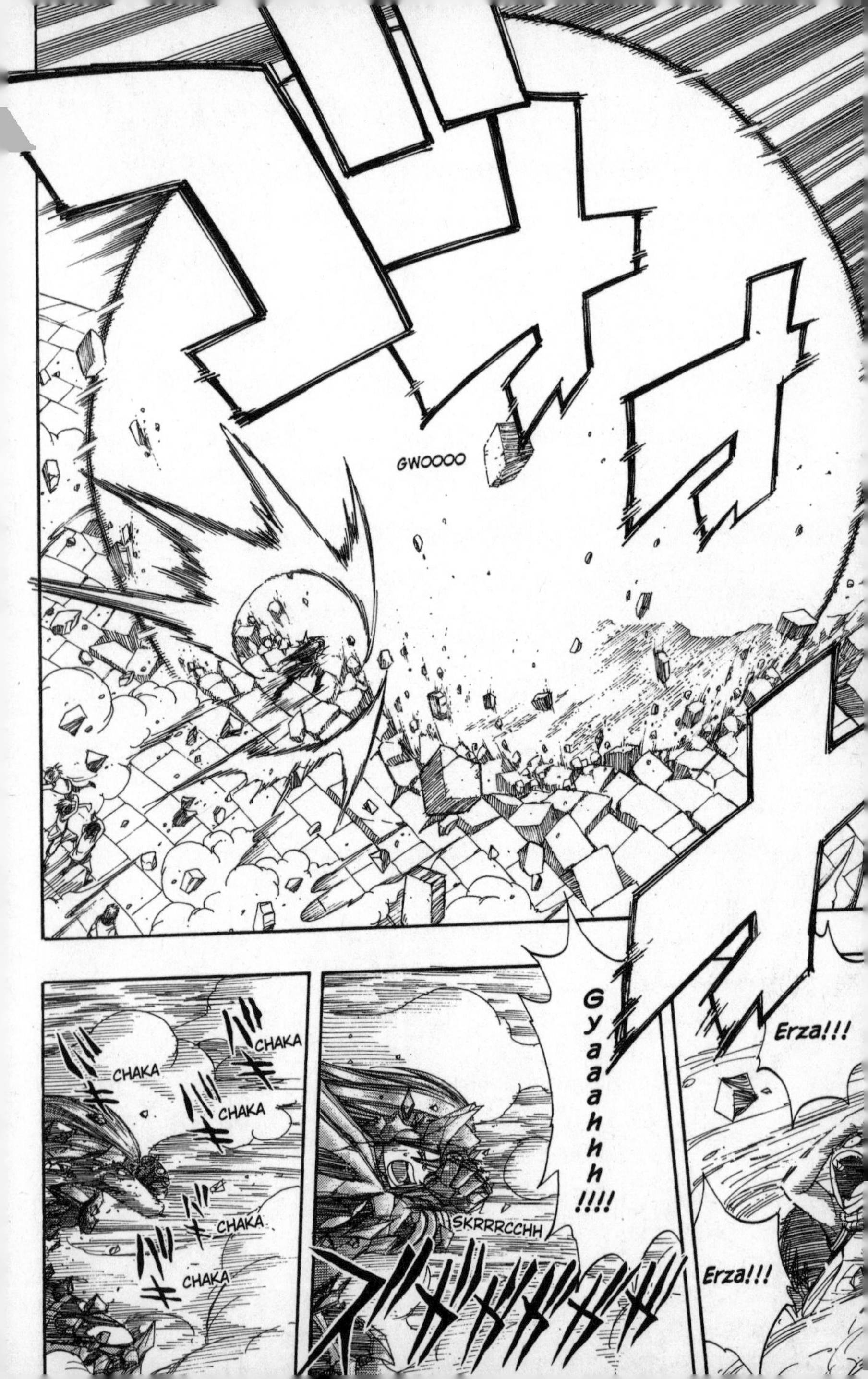
GWOOOO
Erza!!!
Erza!!!
Gyaaahhh!!!!
SKRRRCCHH
CHAKA
CHAKA
CHAKA
CHAKA
CHAKA

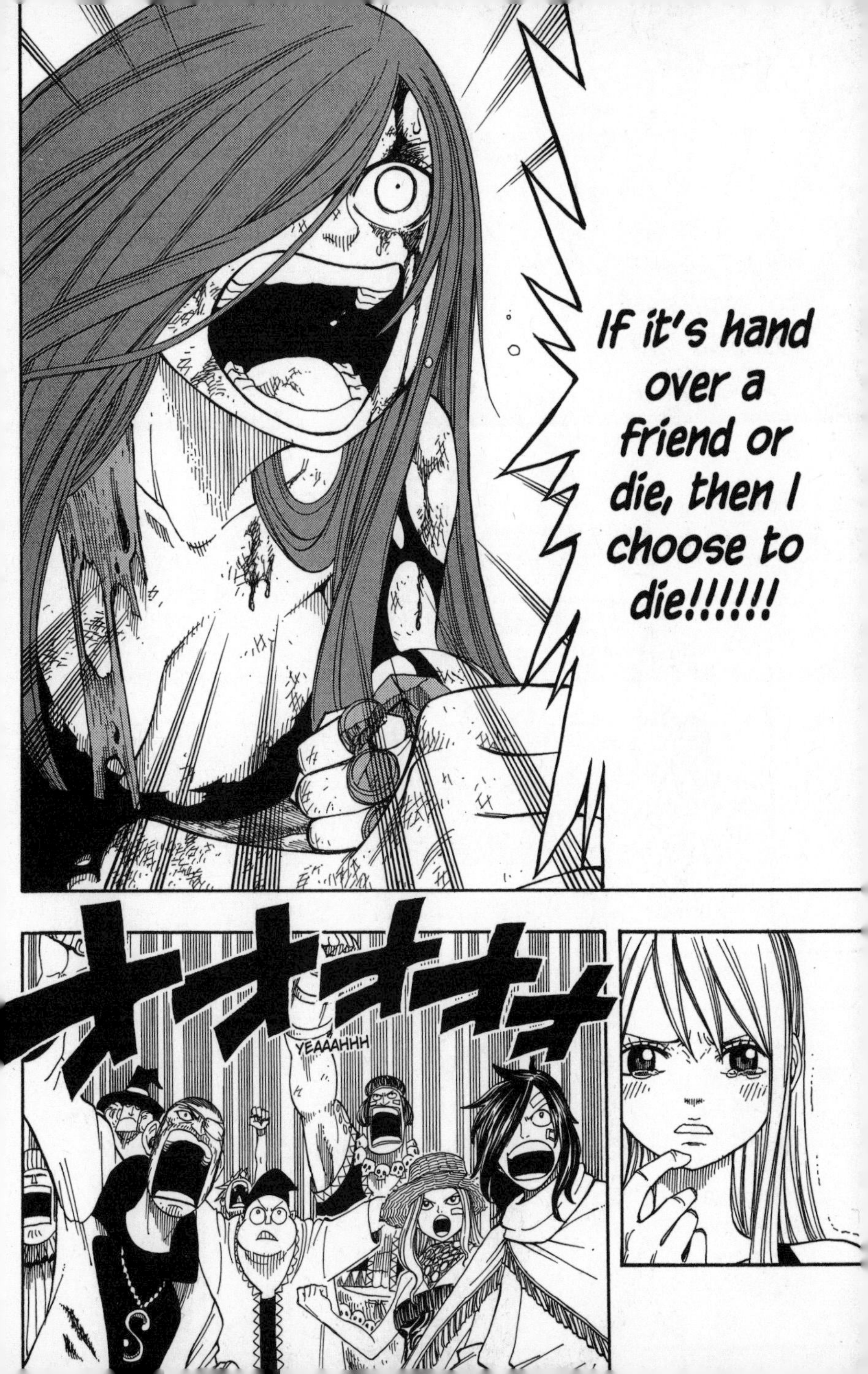
If it's hand over a friend or die, then I choose to die!!!!!!
オオオオオ
YEAAAHHH

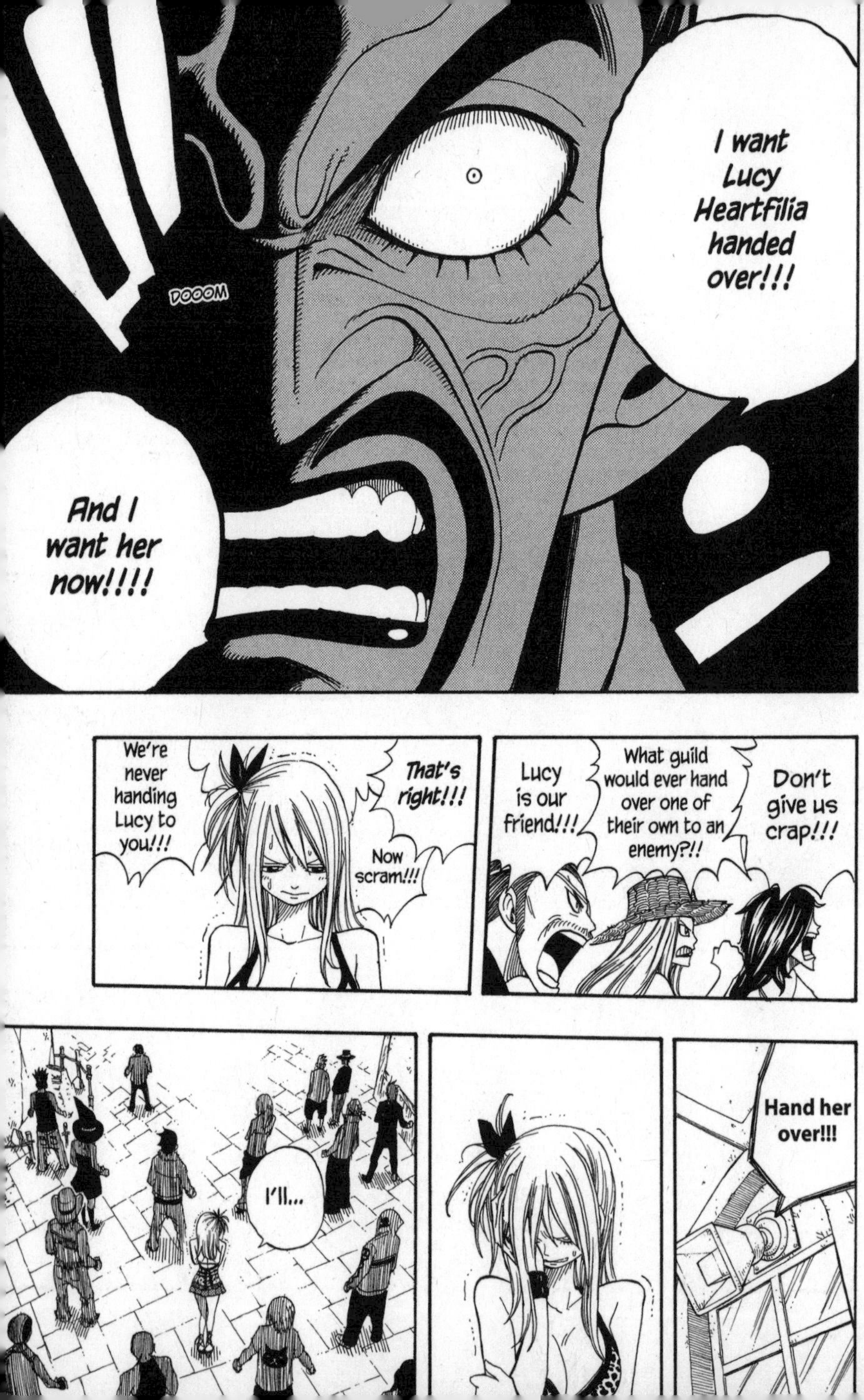
I want Lucy Heartfilia handed over!!!
DOOOM
And I want her now!!!!
Don't give us crap!!!
What guild would ever hand over one of their own to an enemy?!!
Lucy is our friend!!!
That's right!!!
Now scram!!!
We're never handing Lucy to you!!!
Hand her over!!!
I'll...

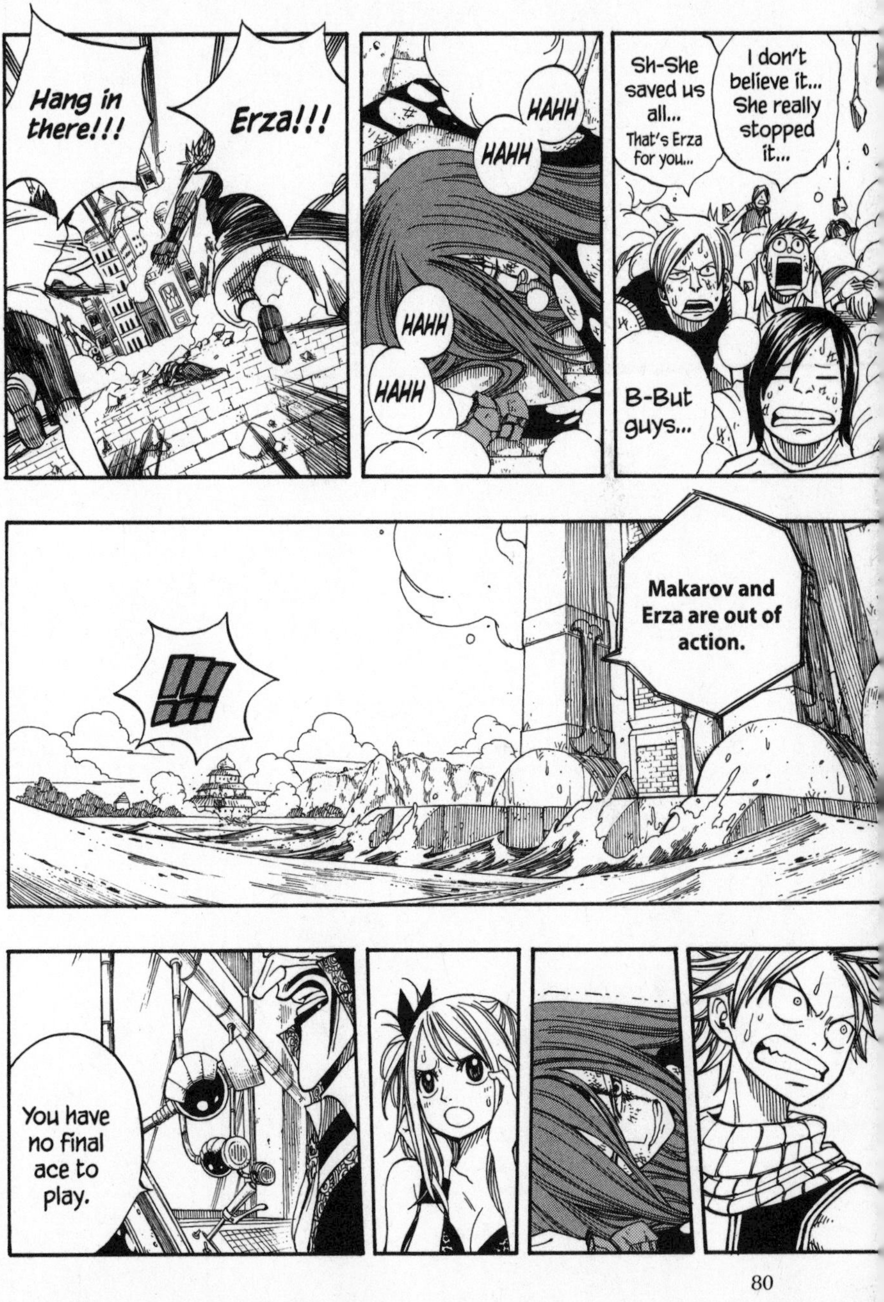
I don't believe it... She really stopped it...
Sh-She saved us all...
That's Erza for you...
B-But guys...
HAHH
HAHH
HAHH
HAHH
Erza!!!
Hang in there!!!
Makarov and Erza are out of action.
!!
You have no final ace to play.

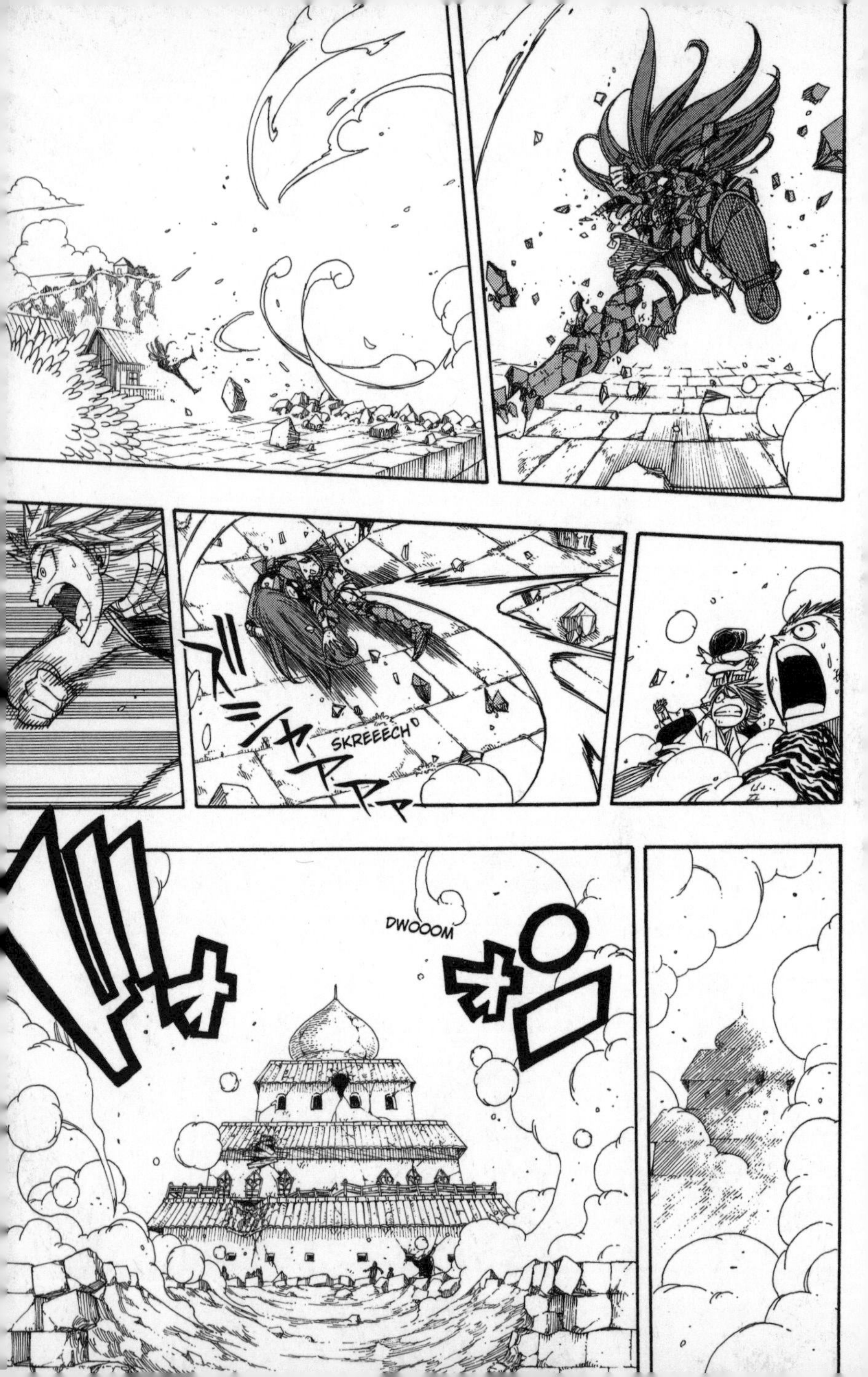
ズシャアアァ
SKREEECH
DWOOOM

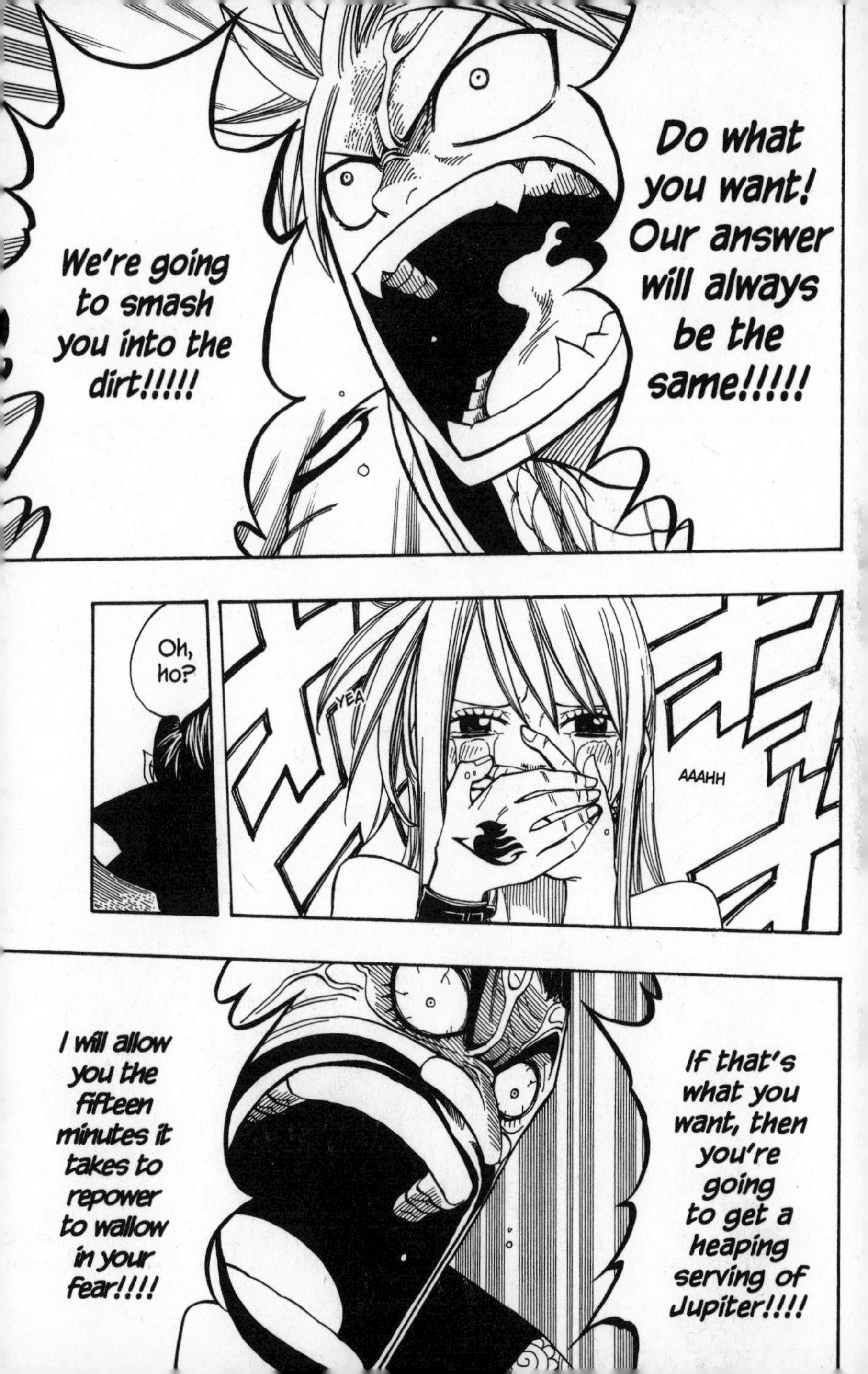
Do what you want! Our answer will always be the same!!!!!
We're going to smash you into the dirt!!!!!
YEA
AAAHH
Oh, ho?
If that's what you want, then you're going to get a heaping serving of Jupiter!!!!
I will allow you the fifteen minutes it takes to repower to wallow in your fear!!!!

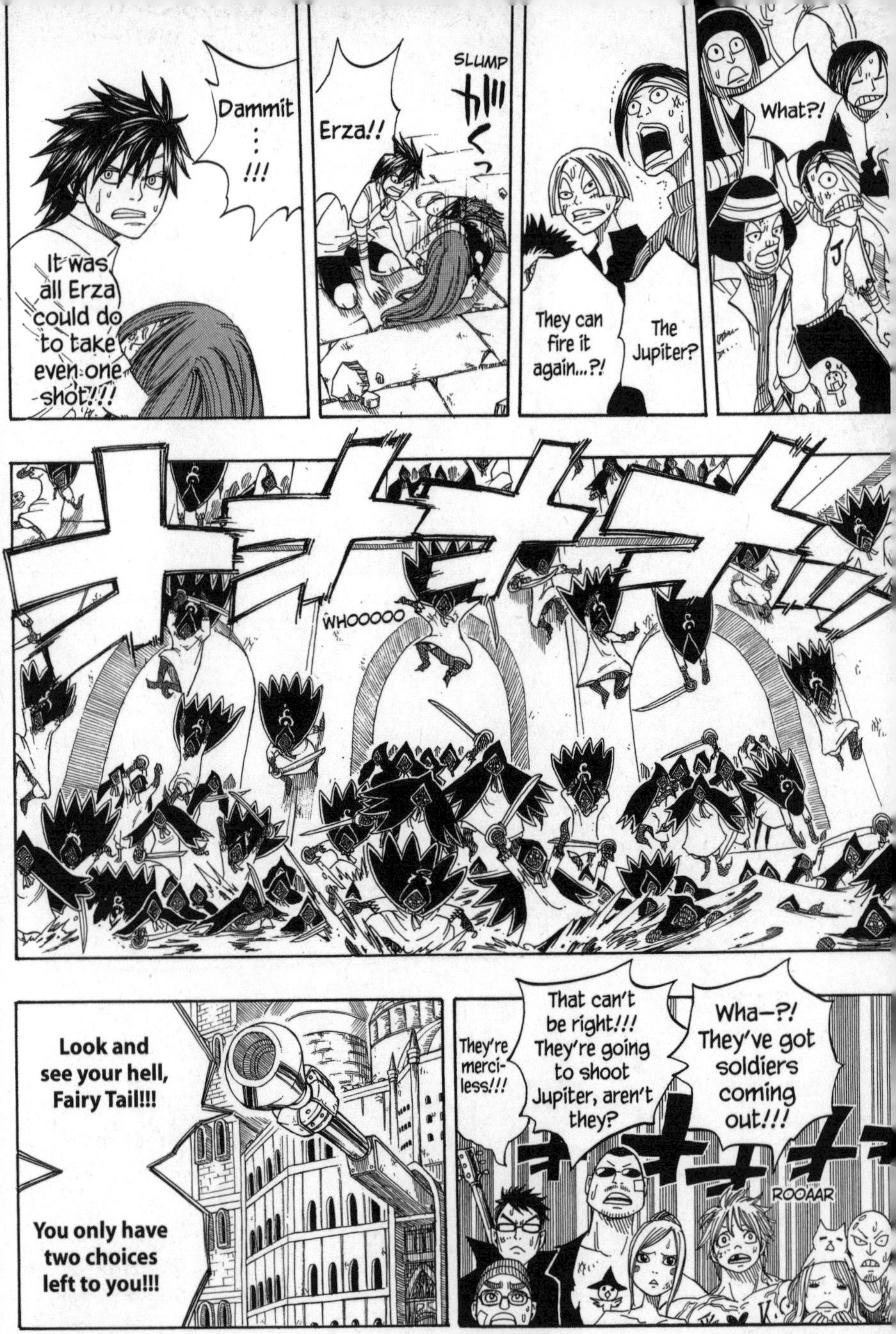

What?!
The Jupiter?
They can fire it again...?!
SLUMP
Erza!!
Dammit...!!!
It was all Erza could do to take even one shot!!!
WHOOOOO
Wha—?! They've got soldiers coming out!!!
That can't be right!!! They're going to shoot Jupiter, aren't they?
They're merciless!!!
ROOAAR
Look and see your hell, Fairy Tail!!!
You only have two choices left to you!!!

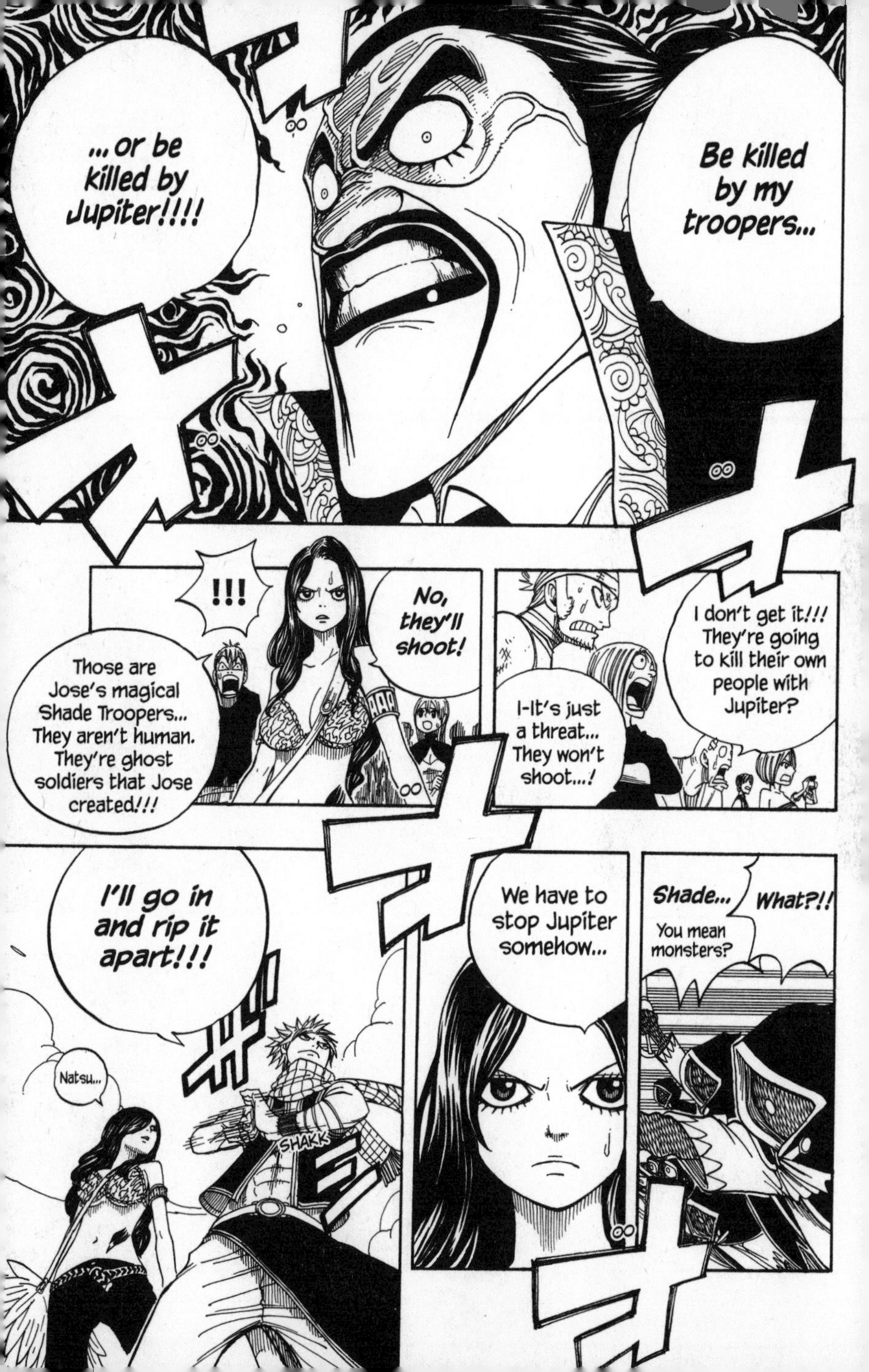
Be killed by my troopers...
...or be killed by Jupiter!!!!
I don't get it!!! They're going to kill their own people with Jupiter?
I-It's just a threat... They won't shoot...!
No, they'll shoot!
!!!
Those are Jose's magical Shade Troopers... They aren't human. They're ghost soldiers that Jose created!!!
What?!!
Shade...
You mean monsters?
We have to stop Jupiter somehow...
I'll go in and rip it apart!!!
SHAKK
Natsu...

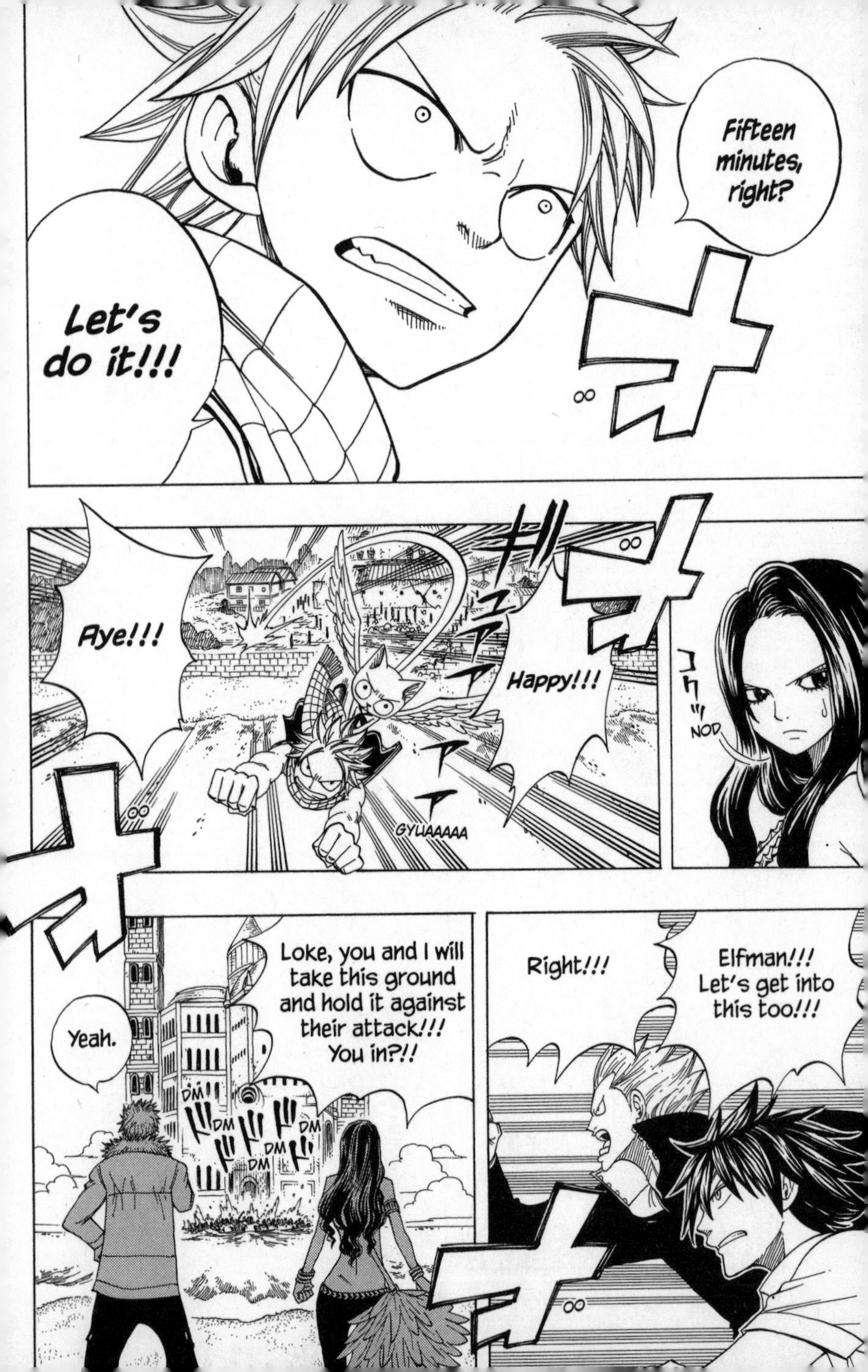
Fifteen minutes, right?
Let's do it!!!
コクッ
NOD
Happy!!!
Aye!!!
GYUAAAAA
Elfman!!! Let's get into this too!!!
Right!!!
Loke, you and I will take this ground and hold it against their attack!!! You in?!!
Yeah.
DM DM DM DM DM

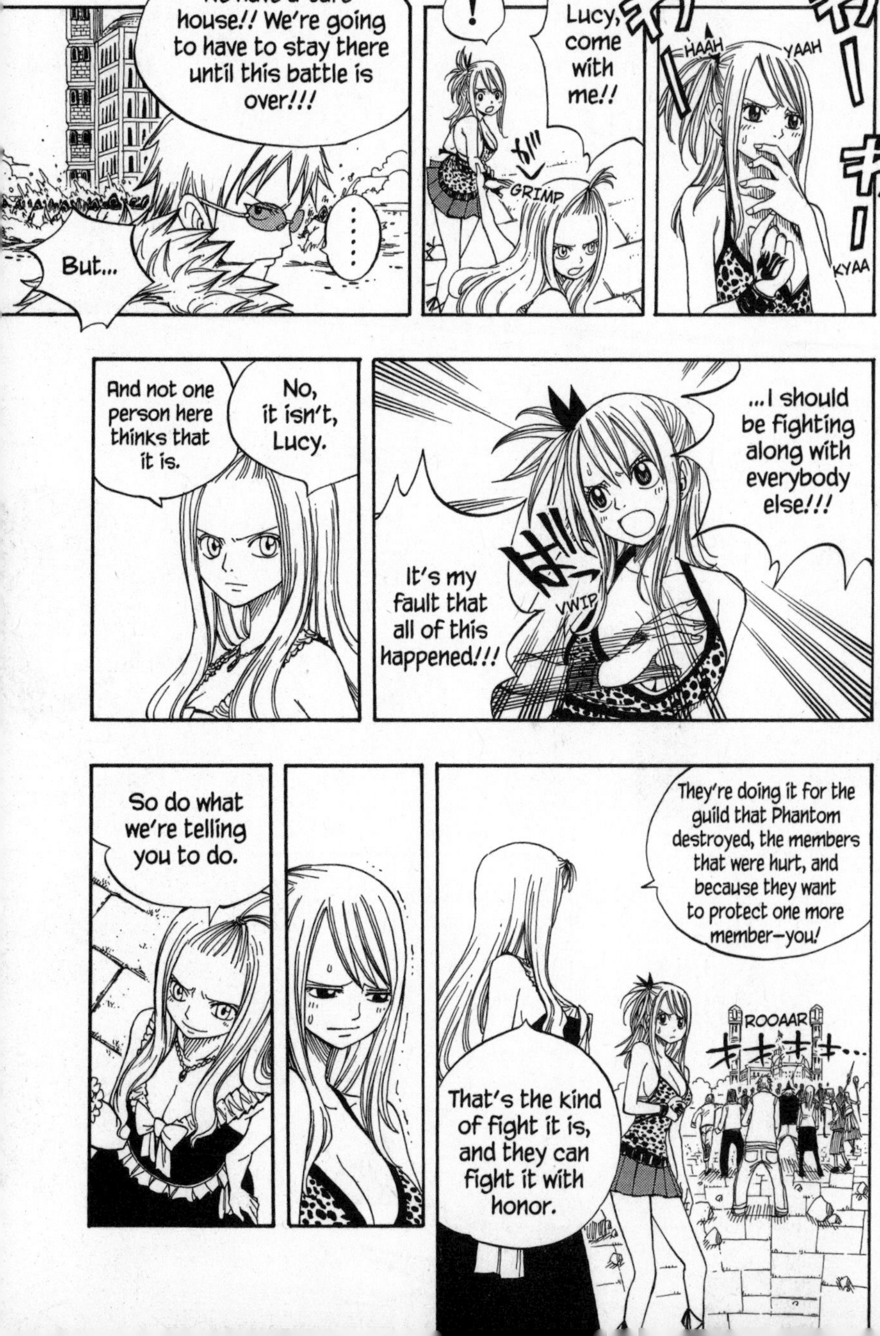
HAAH
YAAH
KYAA
!
Lucy, come with me!!
GRIMP
We have a safe-house!! We're going to have to stay there until this battle is over!!!
......
But...
...I should be fighting along with everybody else!!!
VWIP
It's my fault that all of this happened!!!
No, it isn't, Lucy.
And not one person here thinks that it is.
They're doing it for the guild that Phantom destroyed, the members that were hurt, and because they want to protect one more member—you!
ROOAAR
That's the kind of fight it is, and they can fight it with honor.
So do what we're telling you to do.

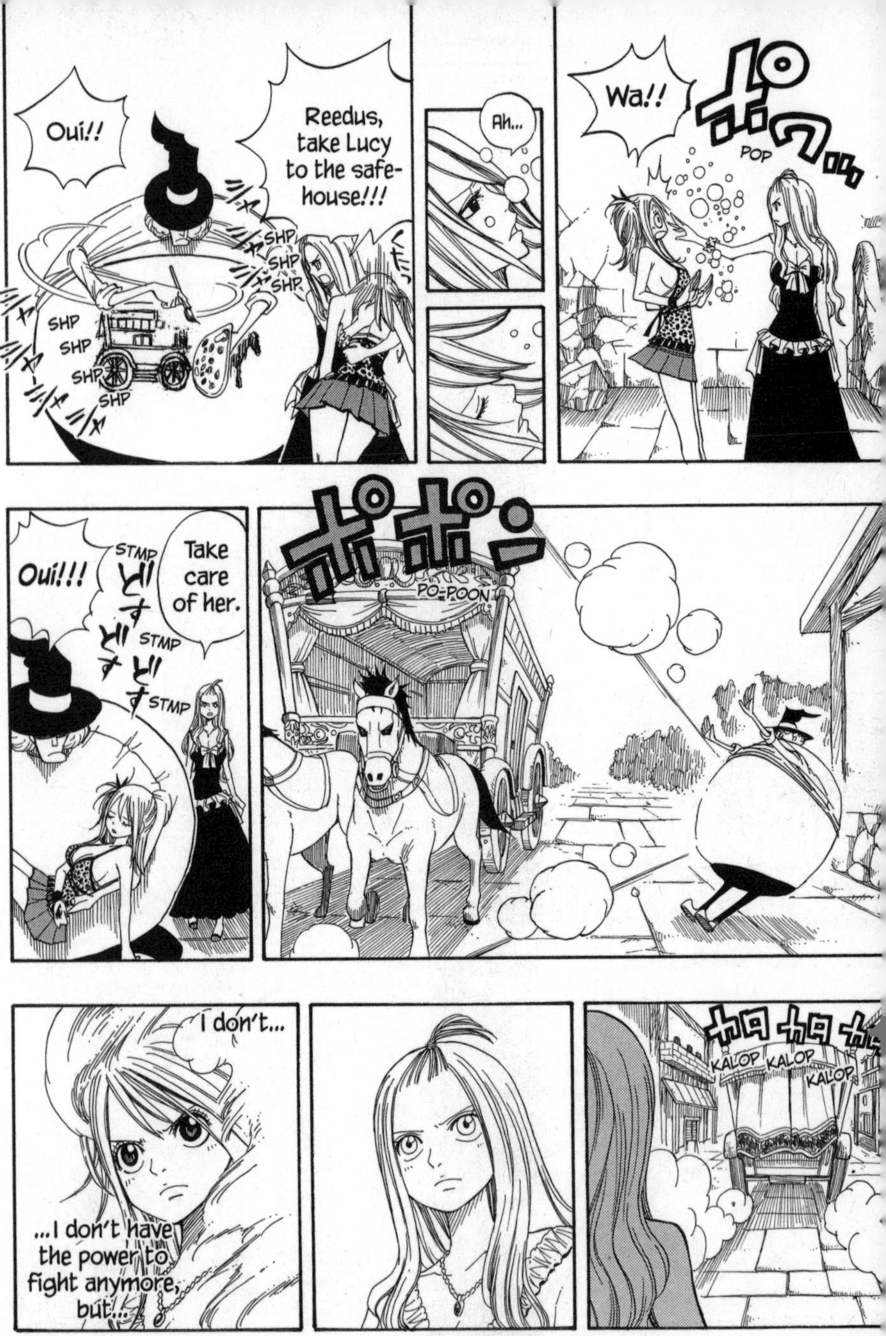
Wa!!
POP
Ah...
Reedus, take Lucy to the safe-house!!!
Oui!!
SHP
SHP
SHP
SHP
SHP
SHP
SHP
ポポン
PO-POON
Take care of her.
Oui!!!
STMP
STMP
STMP
KALOP KALOP KALOP
I don't...
...I don't have the power to fight anymore, but...

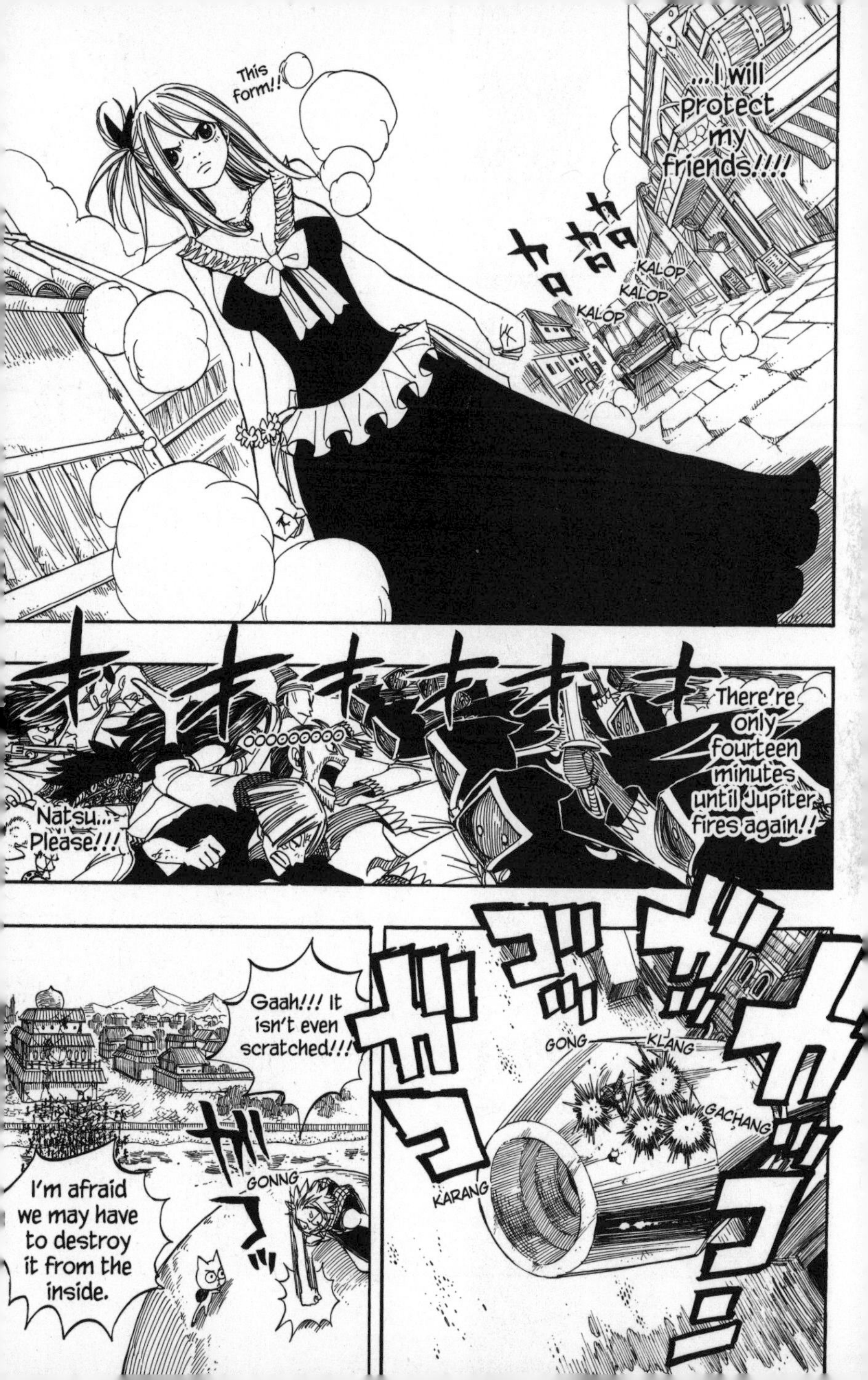
...I will protect my friends!!!!
KALOP
KALOP
KALOP
This form!!
There're only fourteen minutes until Jupiter fires again!!
OOOOOOOOOO
Natsu... Please!!!
GONG
KLANG
GACHANG
KARANG
Gaah!!! It isn't even scratched!!!
GONNG
I'm afraid we may have to destroy it from the inside.

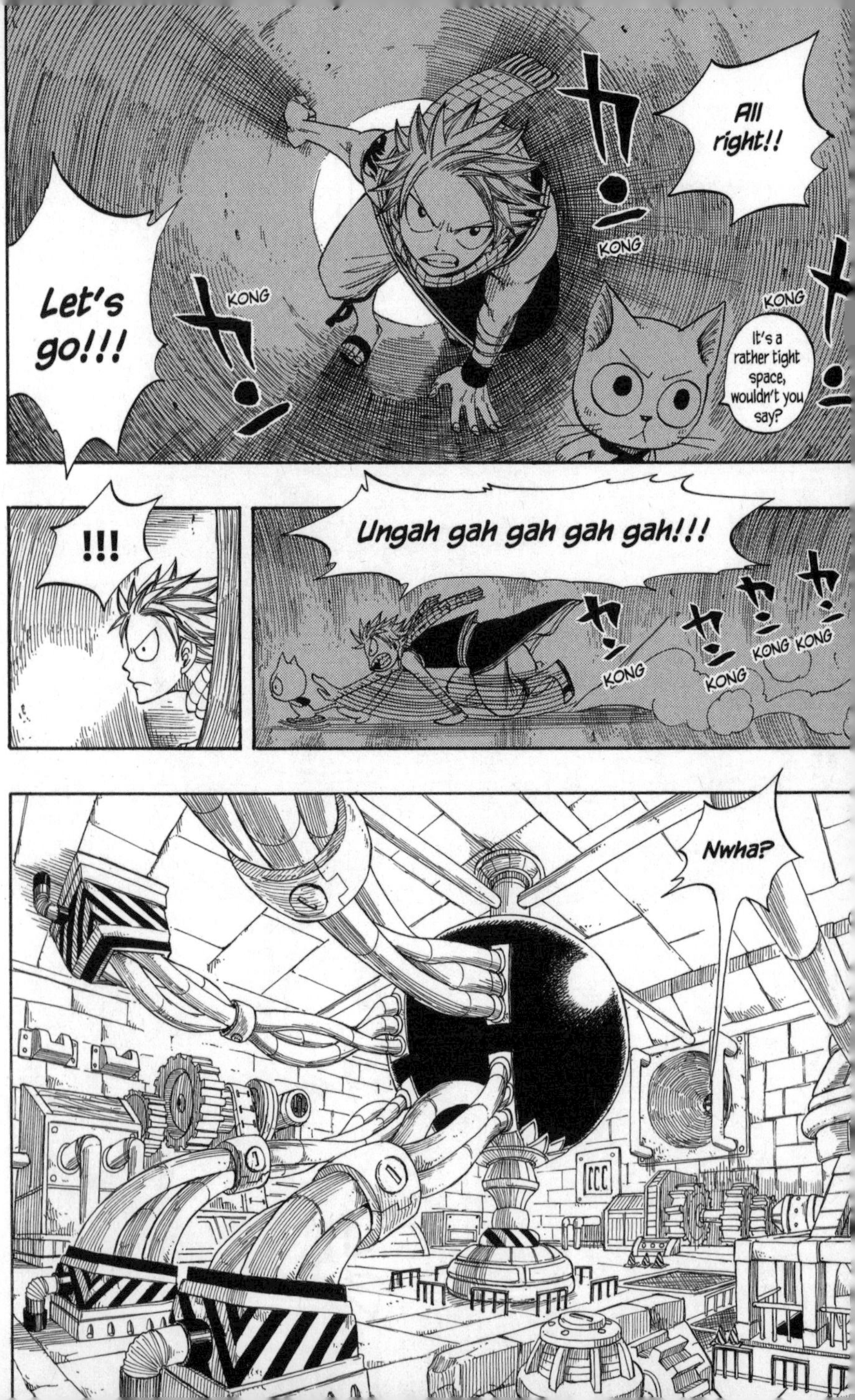
All right!!
KONG
KONG
It's a rather tight space, wouldn't you say?
KONG
Let's go!!!
Ungah gah gah gah gah!!!
KONG KONG
KONG
KONG
!!!
Nwha?

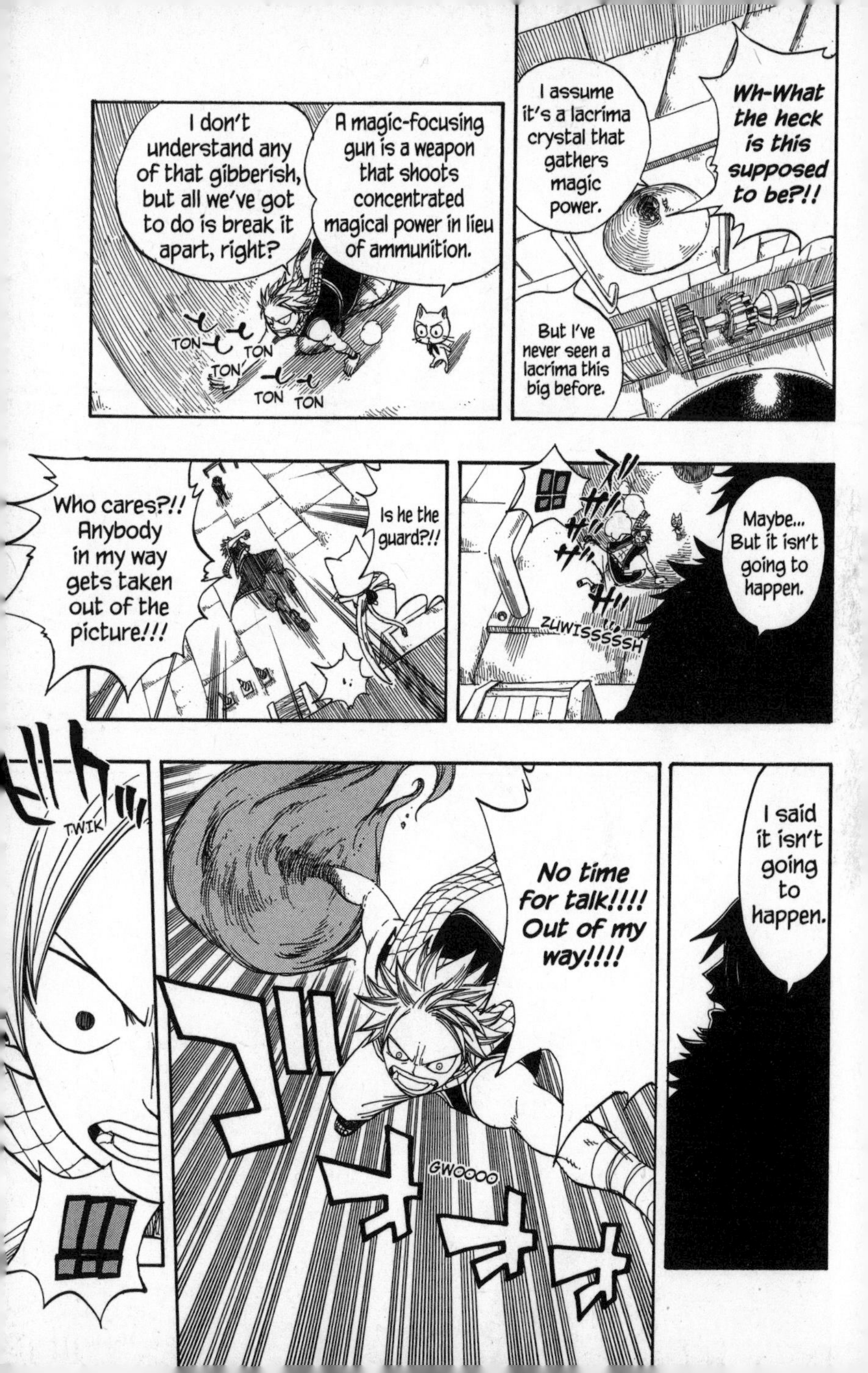
Wh-What the heck is this supposed to be?!!
I assume it's a lacrima crystal that gathers magic power.
But I've never seen a lacrima this big before.
A magic-focusing gun is a weapon that shoots concentrated magical power in lieu of ammunition.
I don't understand any of that gibberish, but all we've got to do is break it apart, right?
TON TON TON TON TON
Maybe... But it isn't going to happen.
ZUWISSSSSH
Is he the guard?!!
Who cares?!! Anybody in my way gets taken out of the picture!!!
I said it isn't going to happen.
No time for talk!!!! Out of my way!!!!
GWOOOO
TWIK

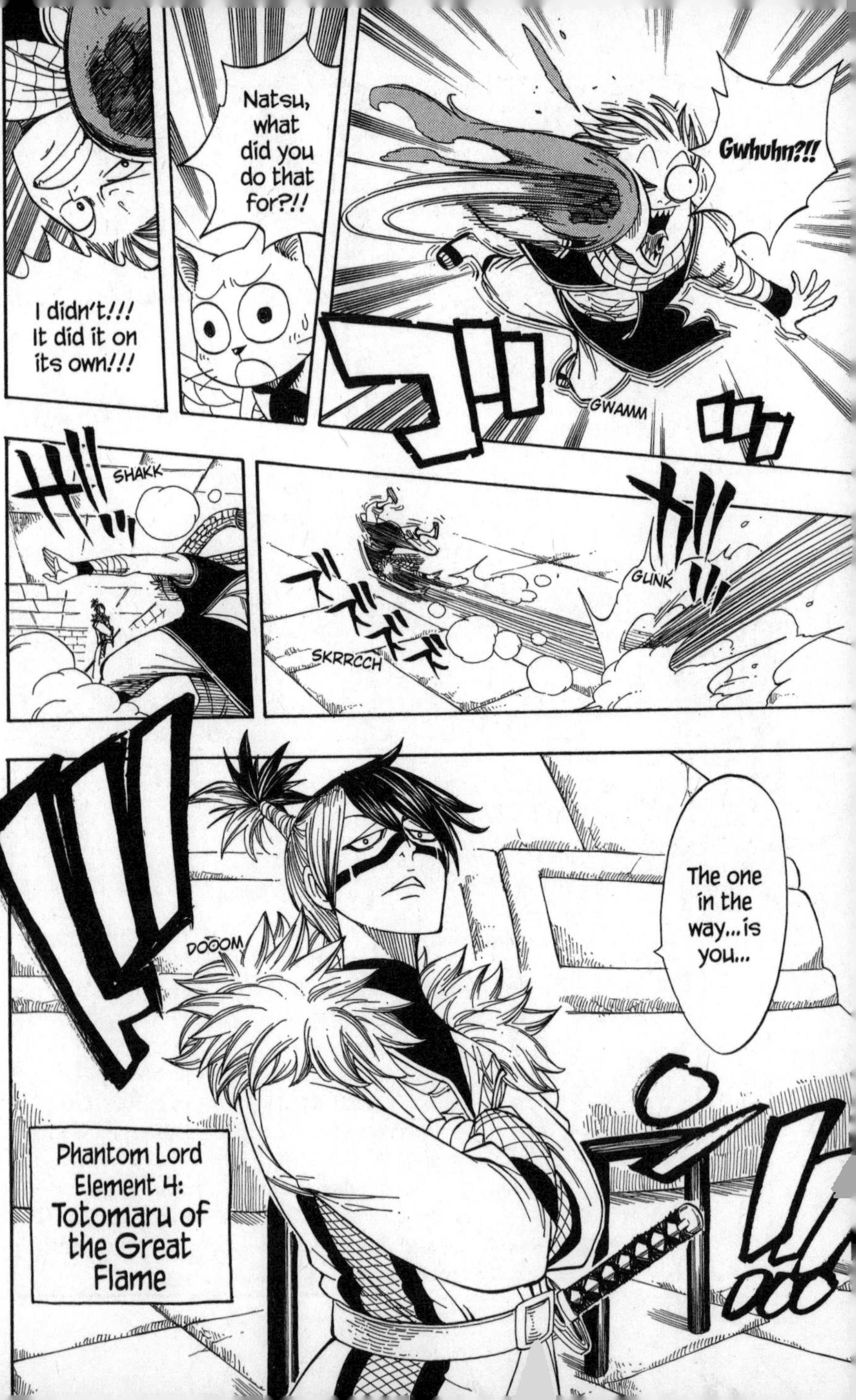
Gwhuhn?!!
GWAMM
Natsu, what did you do that for?!!
I didn't!!! It did it on its own!!!
GUNK
SKRRCH
SHAKK
The one in the way...is you...
DOOOM
Phantom Lord Element 4: Totomaru of the Great Flame

FAIRY TAIL

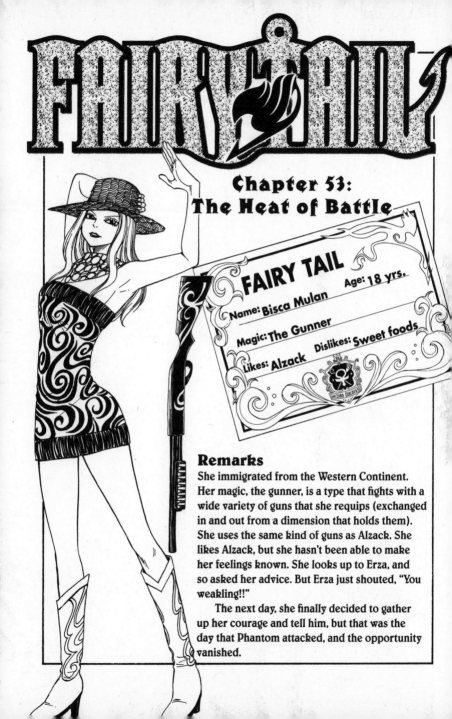

Chapter 53: The Heat of Battle

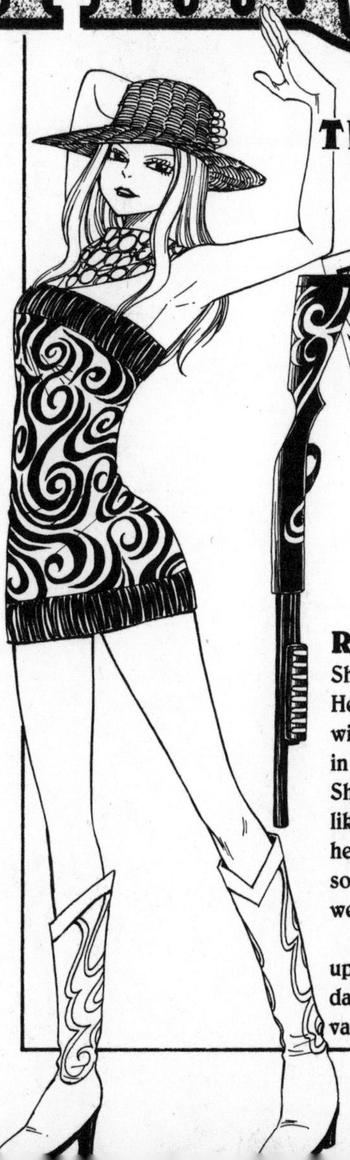

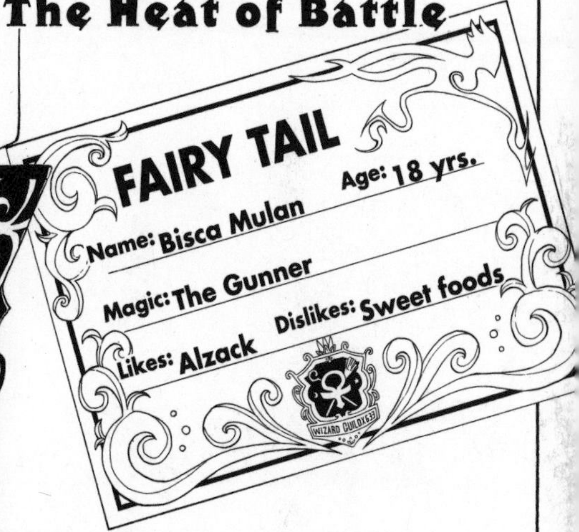
FAIRY TAIL
Age: 18 yrs.
Name: Bisca Mulan
Magic: The Gunner
Likes: Alzack
Dislikes: Sweet foods

Remarks

She immigrated from the Western Continent. Her magic, the gunner, is a type that fights with a wide variety of guns that she requips (exchanged in and out from a dimension that holds them). She uses the same kind of guns as Alzack. She likes Alzack, but she hasn't been able to make her feelings known. She looks up to Erza, and so asked her advice. But Erza just shouted, "You weakling!!"

The next day, she finally decided to gather up her courage and tell him, but that was the day that Phantom attacked, and the opportunity vanished.

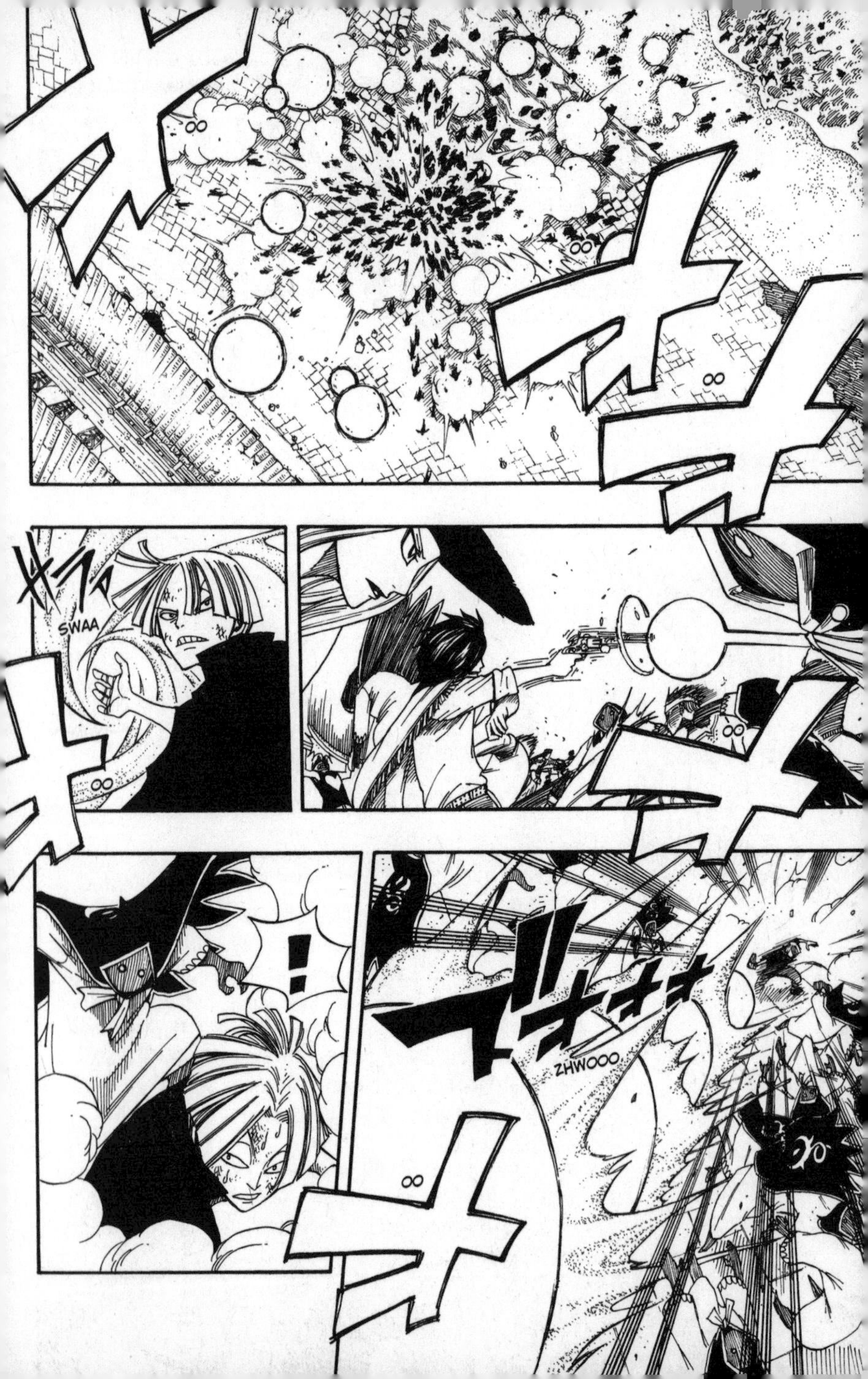
SWAA
ZHWOOO
!

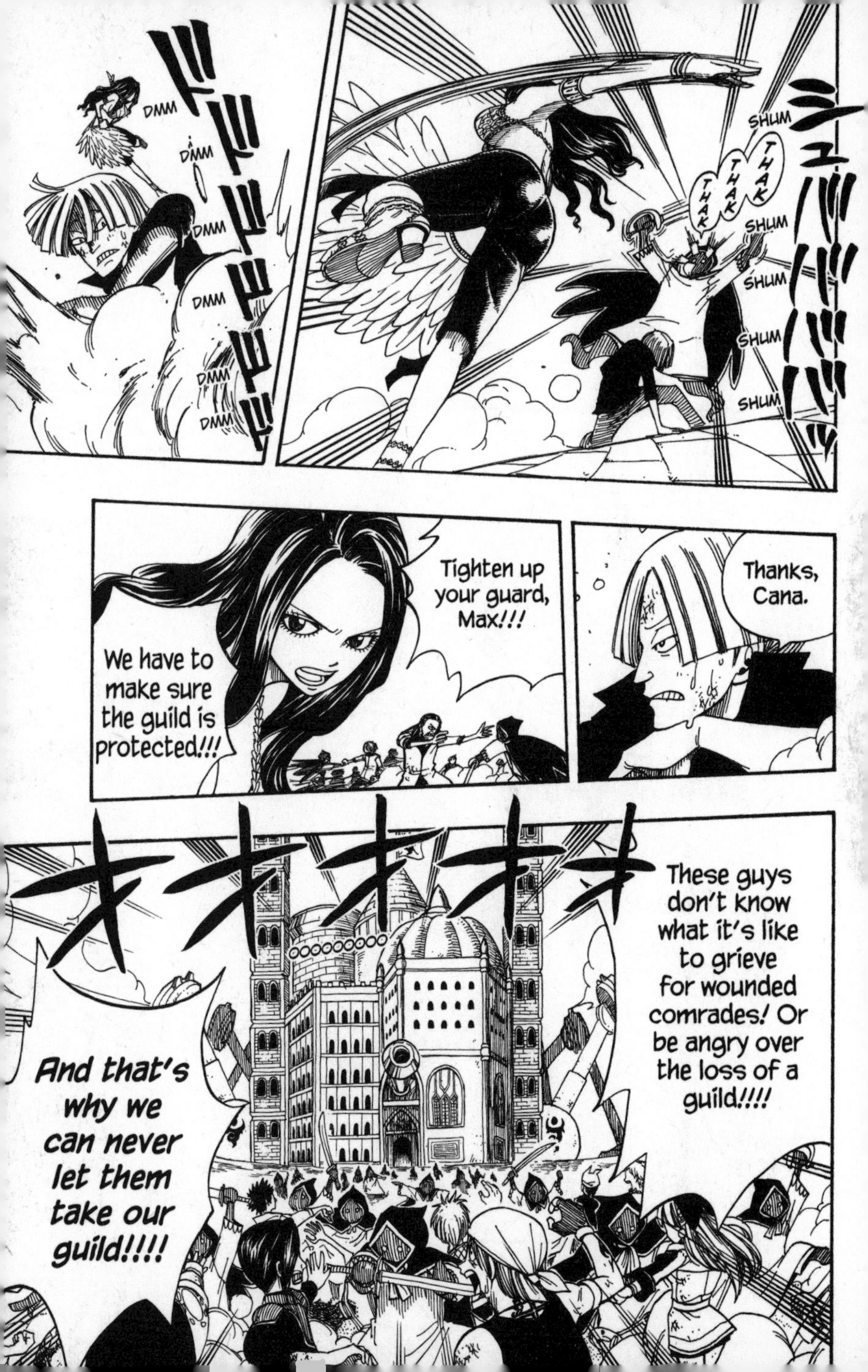
SHUM
THAK THAK THAK
SHUM
SHUM
SHUM
SHUM
DMM
DMM
DMM
DMM
DMM
DMM
Thanks, Cana.
Tighten up your guard, Max!!!
We have to make sure the guild is protected!!!
オオオオオ
These guys don't know what it's like to grieve for wounded comrades! Or be angry over the loss of a guild!!!!
And that's why we can never let them take our guild!!!!

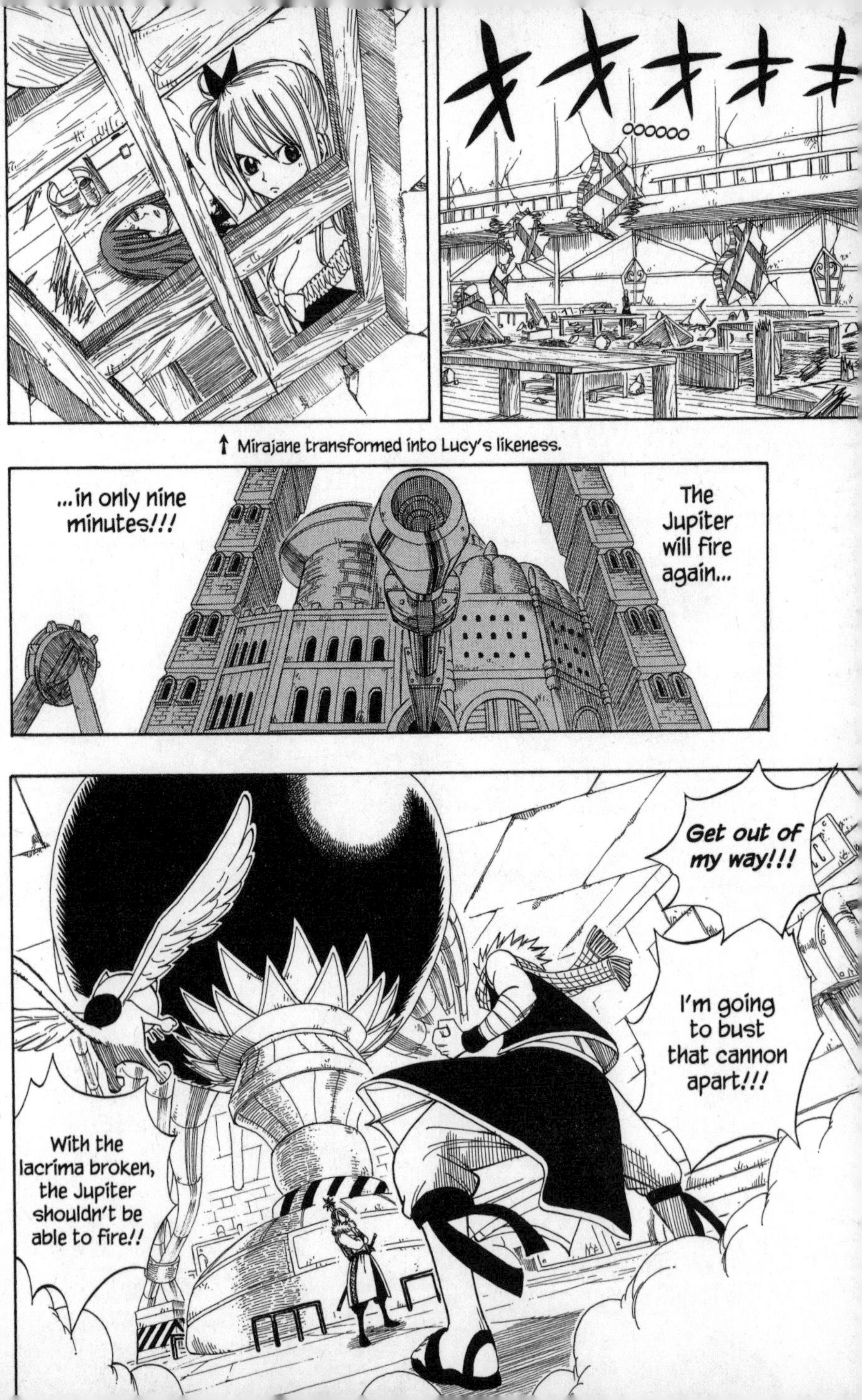
OOOOOO
↑ Mirajane transformed into Lucy's likeness.
The Jupiter will fire again...
...in only nine minutes!!!
Get out of my way!!!
I'm going to bust that cannon apart!!!
With the lacrima broken, the Jupiter shouldn't be able to fire!!

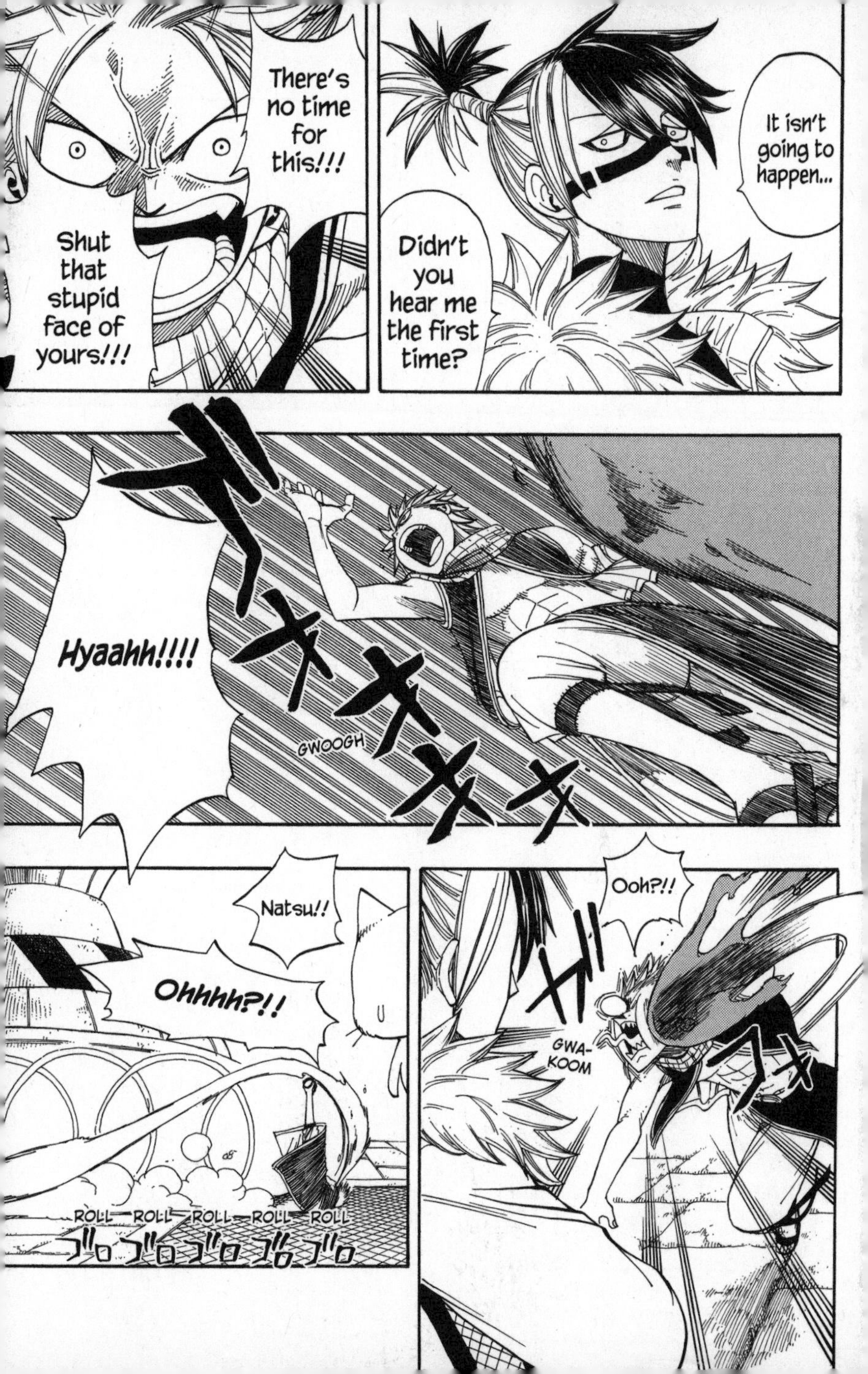
It isn't going to happen...
Didn't you hear me the first time?
There's no time for this!!!
Shut that stupid face of yours!!!
Hyaahh!!!!
GWOOGH
Ooh?!!
GWA-KOOM
Natsu!!
Ohhhh?!!
ROLL ROLL ROLL ROLL ROLL
ゴロゴロゴロゴロゴロ

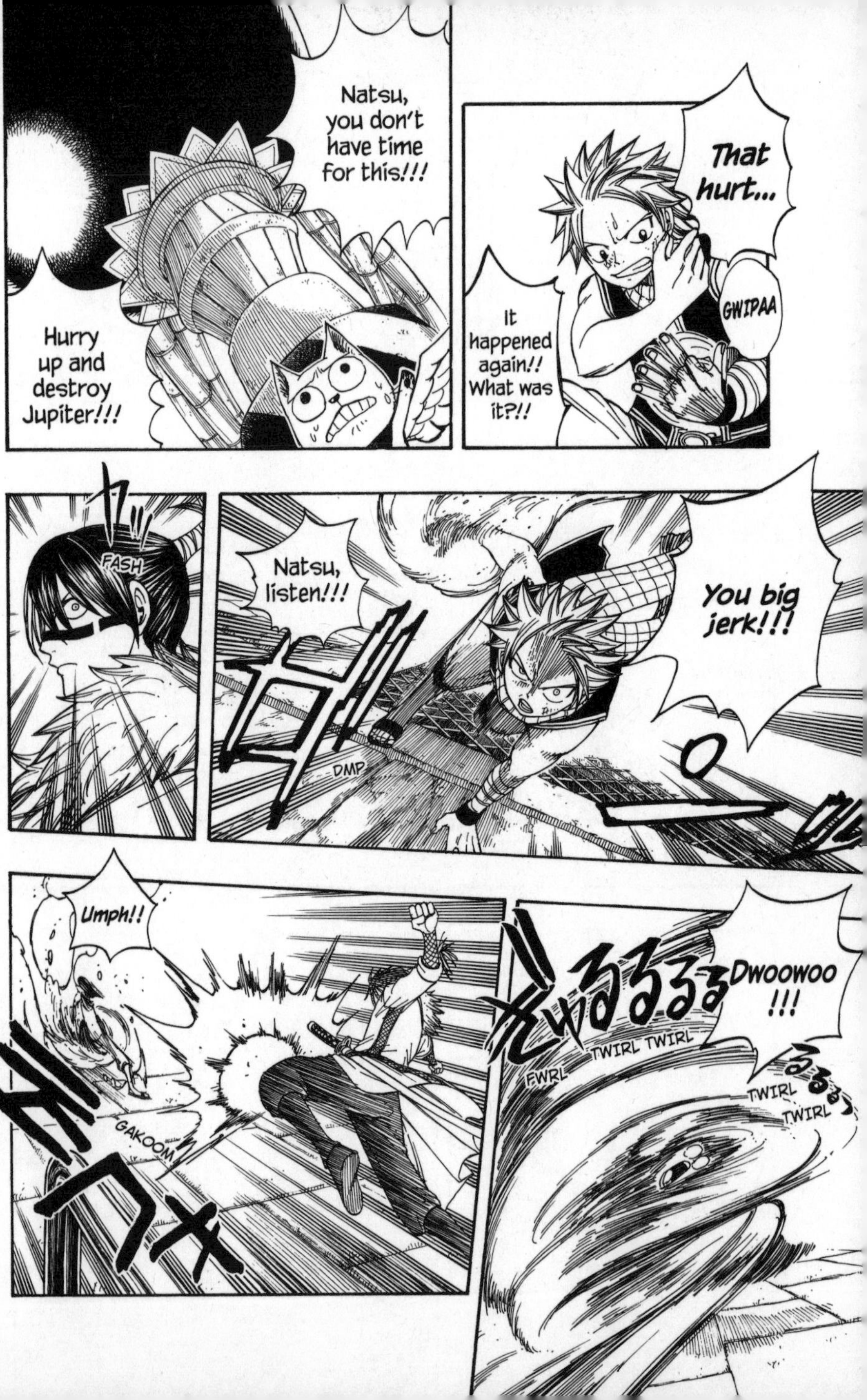
That hurt...
GWIPAA
It happened again!! What was it?!!
Natsu, you don't have time for this!!!
Hurry up and destroy Jupiter!!!
You big jerk!!!
Natsu, listen!!!
DMP
FASH
Dwoowoo !!!
TWIRL TWIRL
FWRL
TWIRL TWIRL
Umph!!
GAKOOM

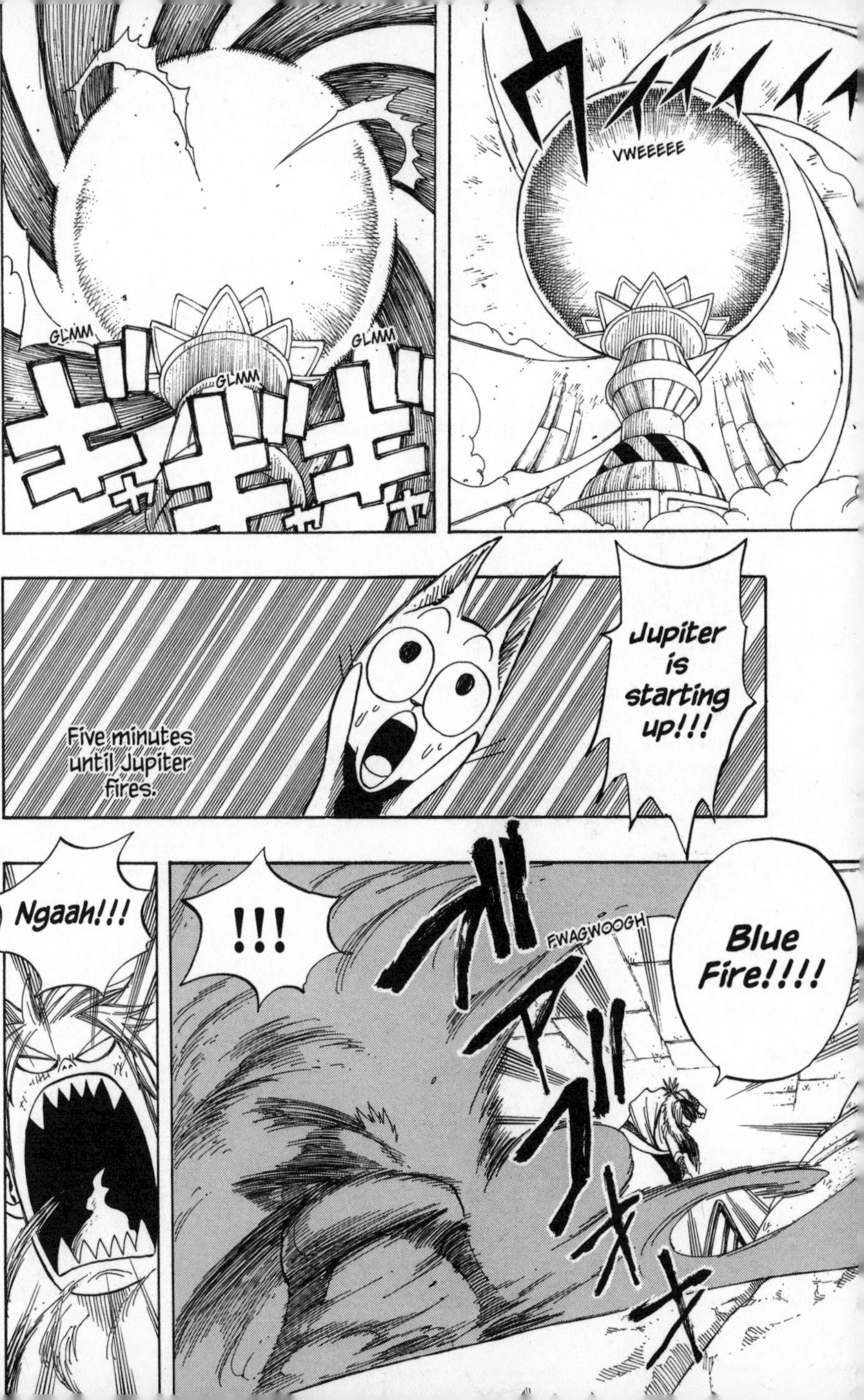
VWEEEEE
GLMM
GLMM
GLMM
Jupiter is starting up!!!
Five minutes until Jupiter fires.
Blue Fire!!!!
FWAGWOOGH
!!!
Ngaah!!!

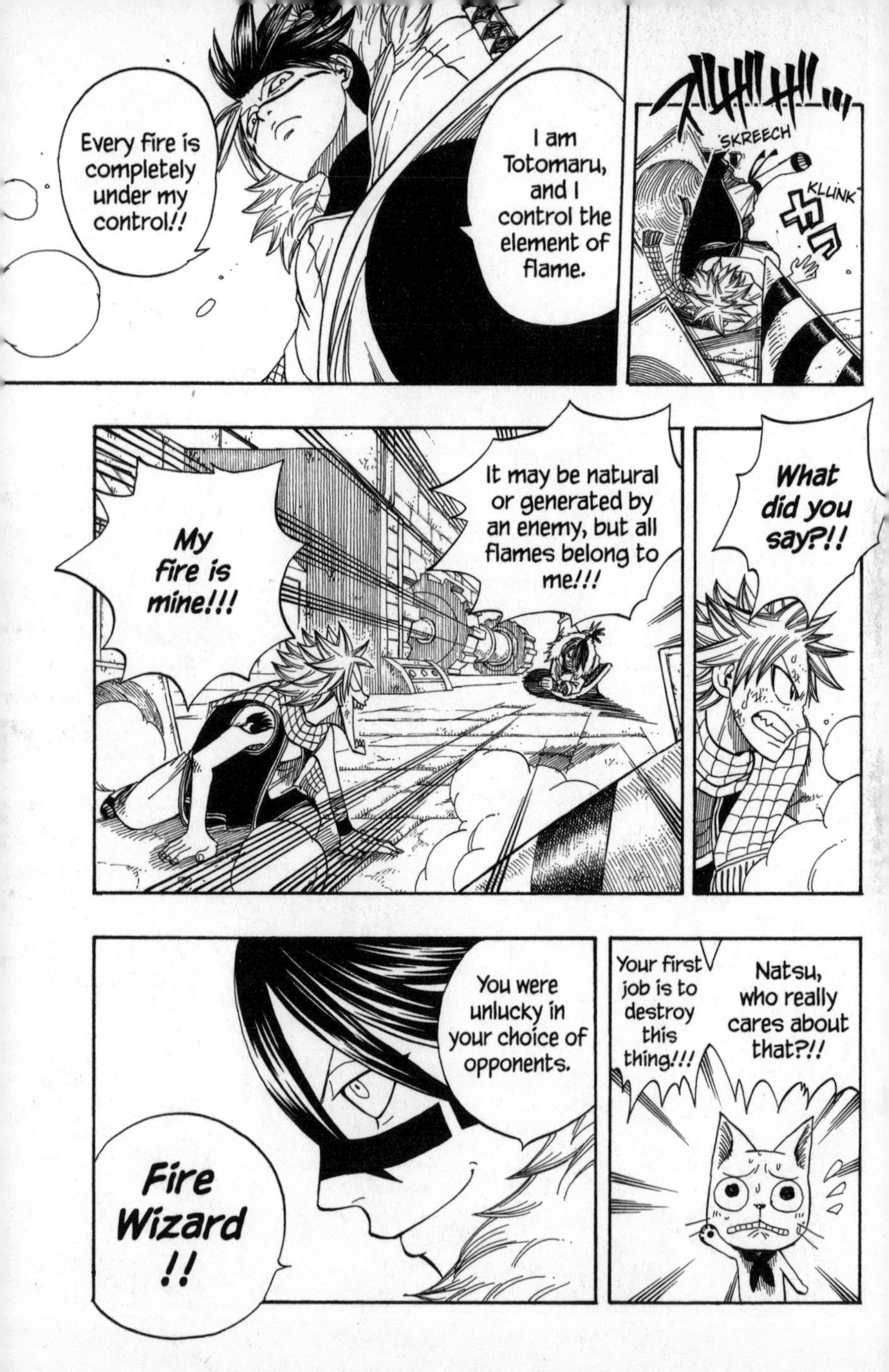
SKREECH
KLUNK
I am Totomaru, and I control the element of flame.
Every fire is completely under my control!!
What did you say?!!
It may be natural or generated by an enemy, but all flames belong to me!!!
My fire is mine!!!
Natsu, who really cares about that?!!
Your first job is to destroy this thing!!!
You were unlucky in your choice of opponents.
Fire Wizard!!

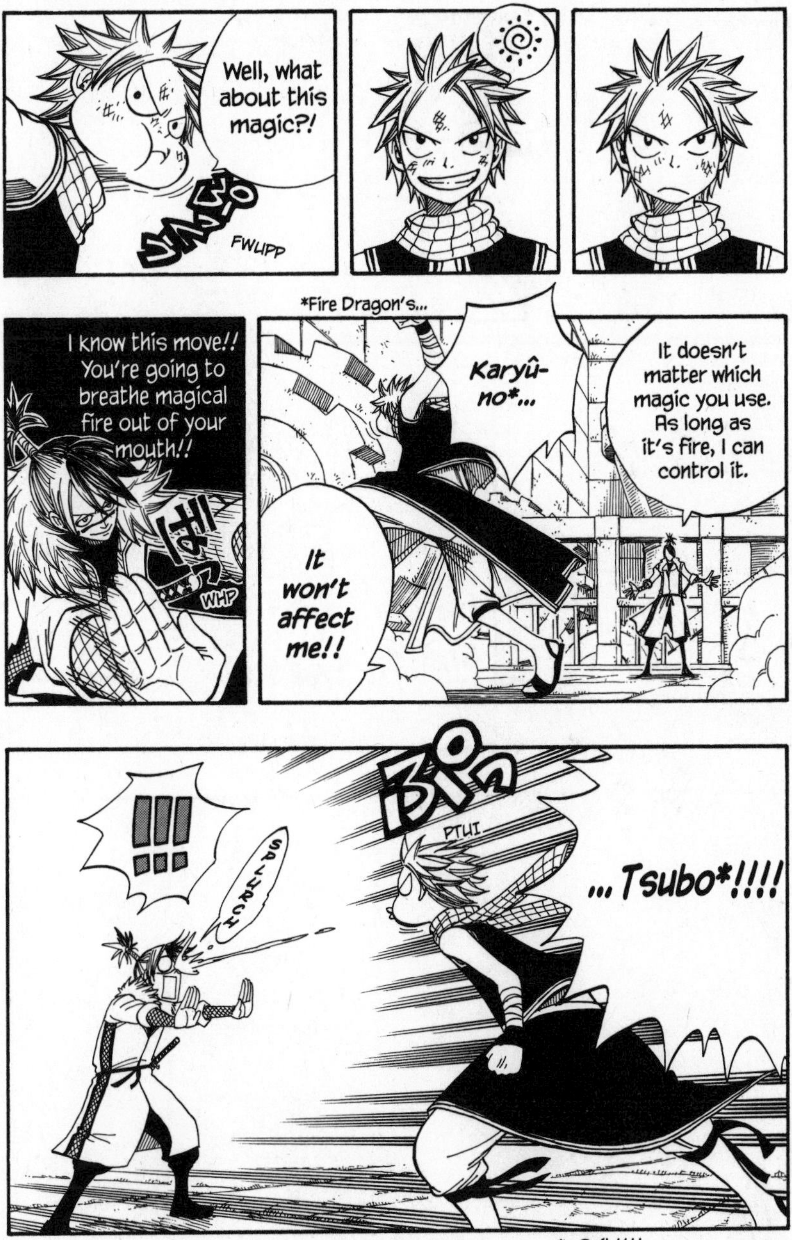
Well, what about this magic?!
FWUPP
It doesn't matter which magic you use. As long as it's fire, I can control it.
Karyû-no*...
It won't affect me!!
I know this move!! You're going to breathe magical fire out of your mouth!!
WHP
...Tsubo*!!!!
PTUI
!!!!
SPLURCH

*Fire Dragon's...

*...Spit!!!!

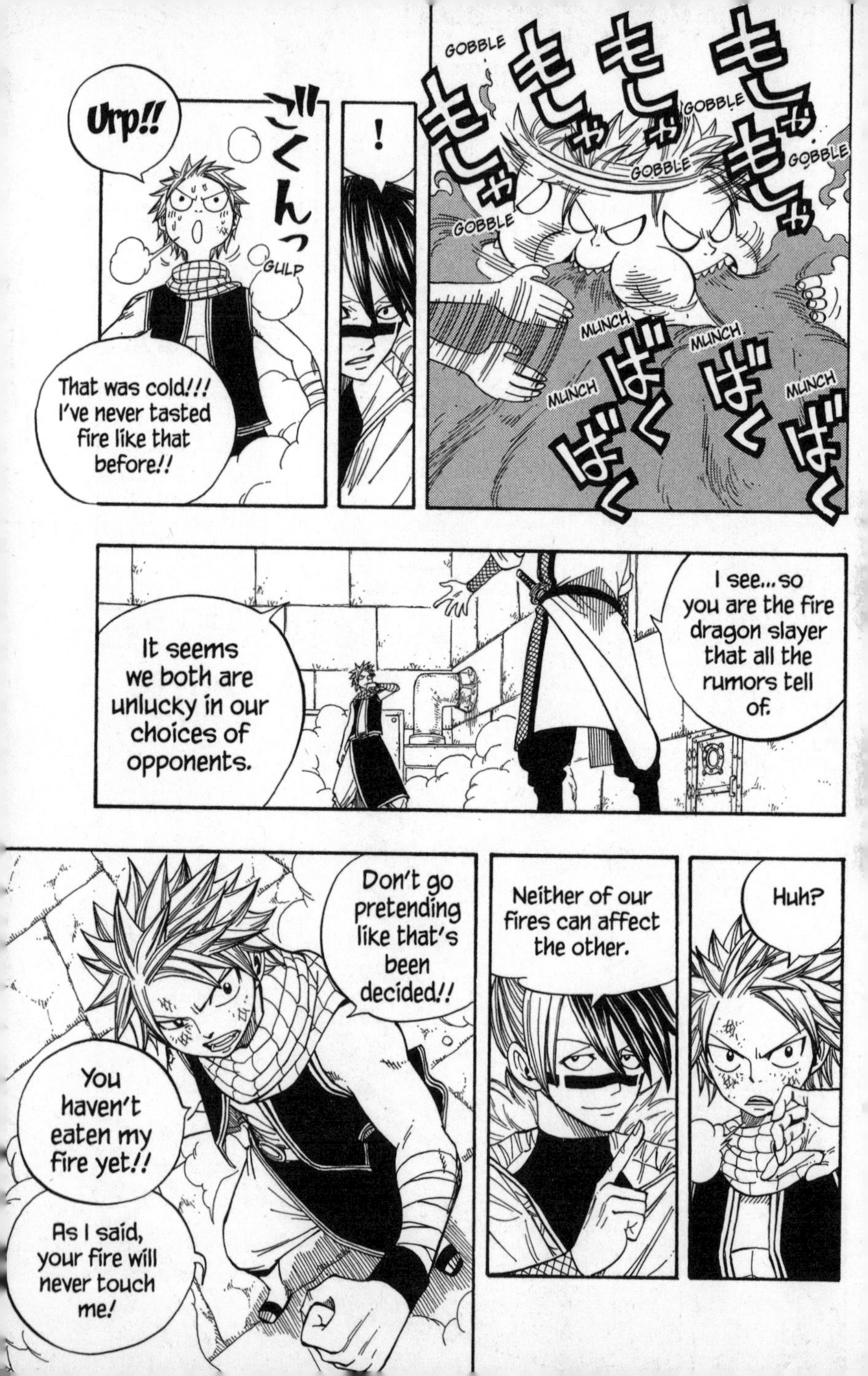
もしゃもしゃもしゃもしゃもしゃもしゃ
GOBBLE
GOBBLE
GOBBLE
GOBBLE
GOBBLE
ばくばくばくばくばくばく
MUNCH
MUNCH
MUNCH
MUNCH
!
Urp!!
ごくんっ
GULP
That was cold!!! I've never tasted fire like that before!!
I see...so you are the fire dragon slayer that all the rumors tell of.
It seems we both are unlucky in our choices of opponents.
Huh?
Neither of our fires can affect the other.
Don't go pretending like that's been decided!!
You haven't eaten my fire yet!!
As I said, your fire will never touch me!

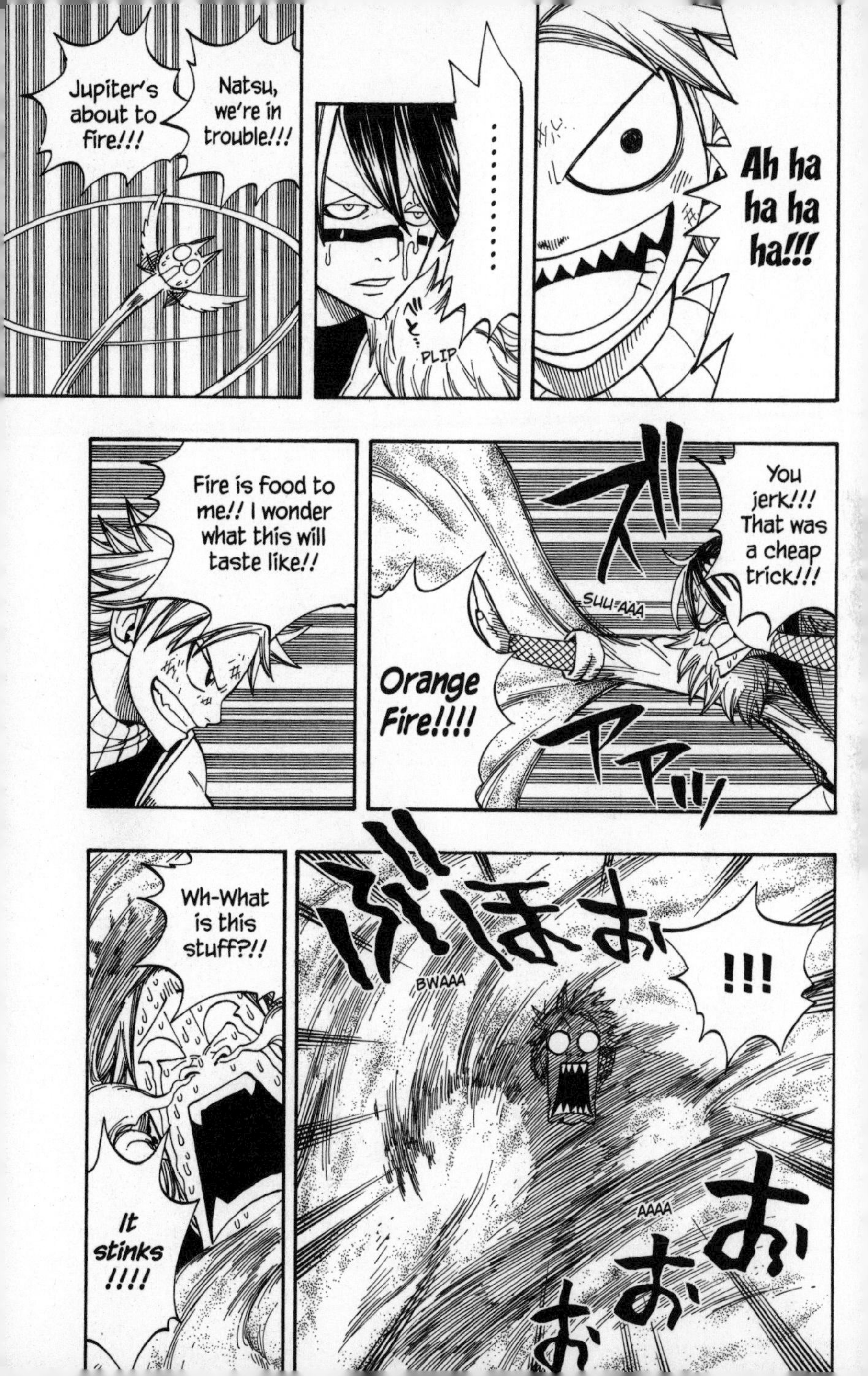
Ah ha ha ha ha!!!
......
PLIP
Natsu, we're in trouble!!!
Jupiter's about to fire!!!
You jerk!!! That was a cheap trick!!!
SUU-AAA
Orange Fire!!!!
Fire is food to me!! I wonder what this will taste like!!
BWAAA
!!!
AAAA
Wh-What is this stuff?!!
It stinks!!!!

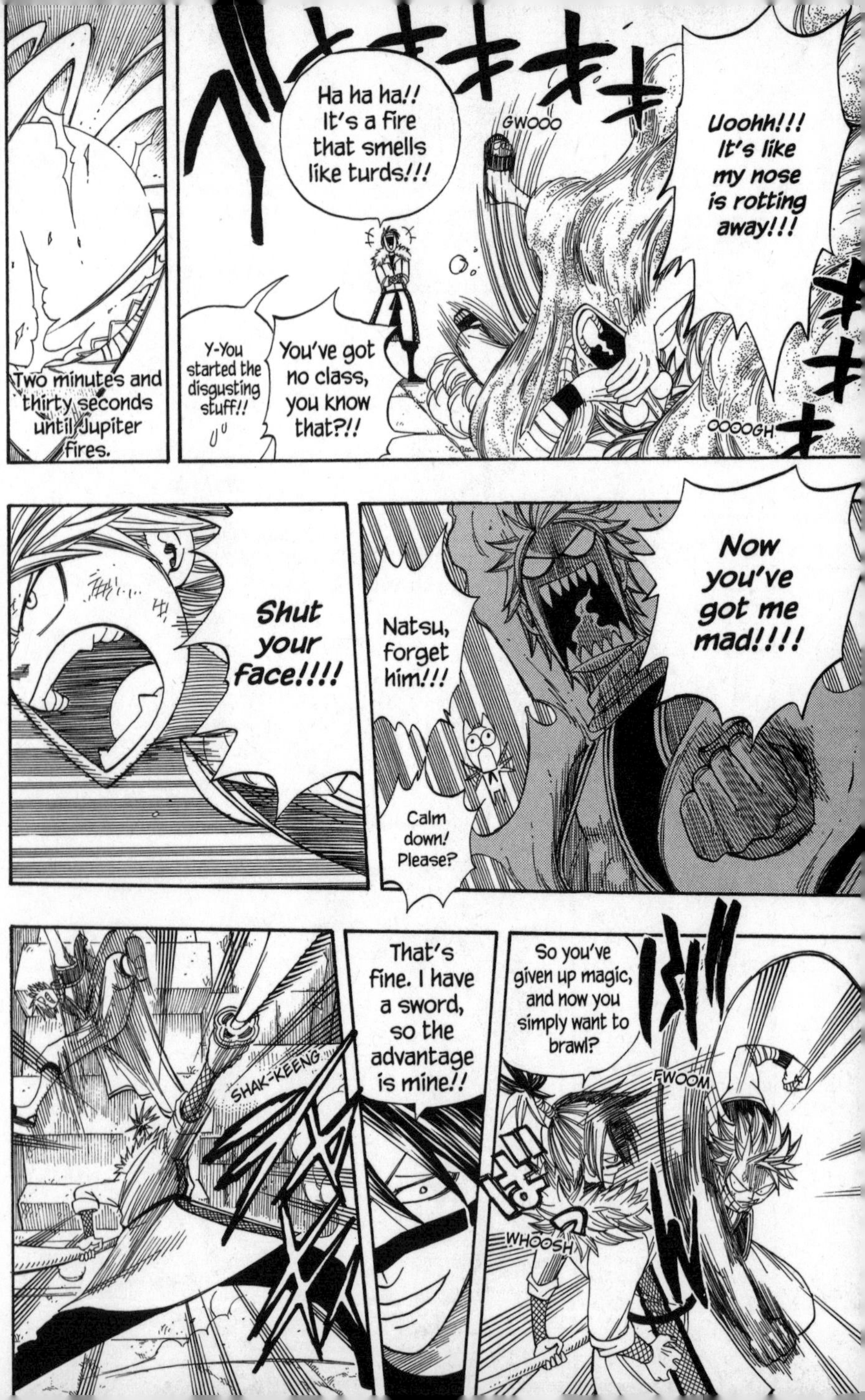
Uoohh!!! It's like my nose is rotting away!!!
GWOOO
OOOOGH
Ha ha ha!! It's a fire that smells like turds!!!
You've got no class, you know that?!!
Y-You started the disgusting stuff!!
Two minutes and thirty seconds until Jupiter fires.
Now you've got me mad!!!!
Natsu, forget him!!!
Calm down! Please?
Shut your face!!!!
So you've given up magic, and now you simply want to brawl?
FWOOM
WHOOSH
That's fine. I have a sword, so the advantage is mine!!
SHAK-KEENG

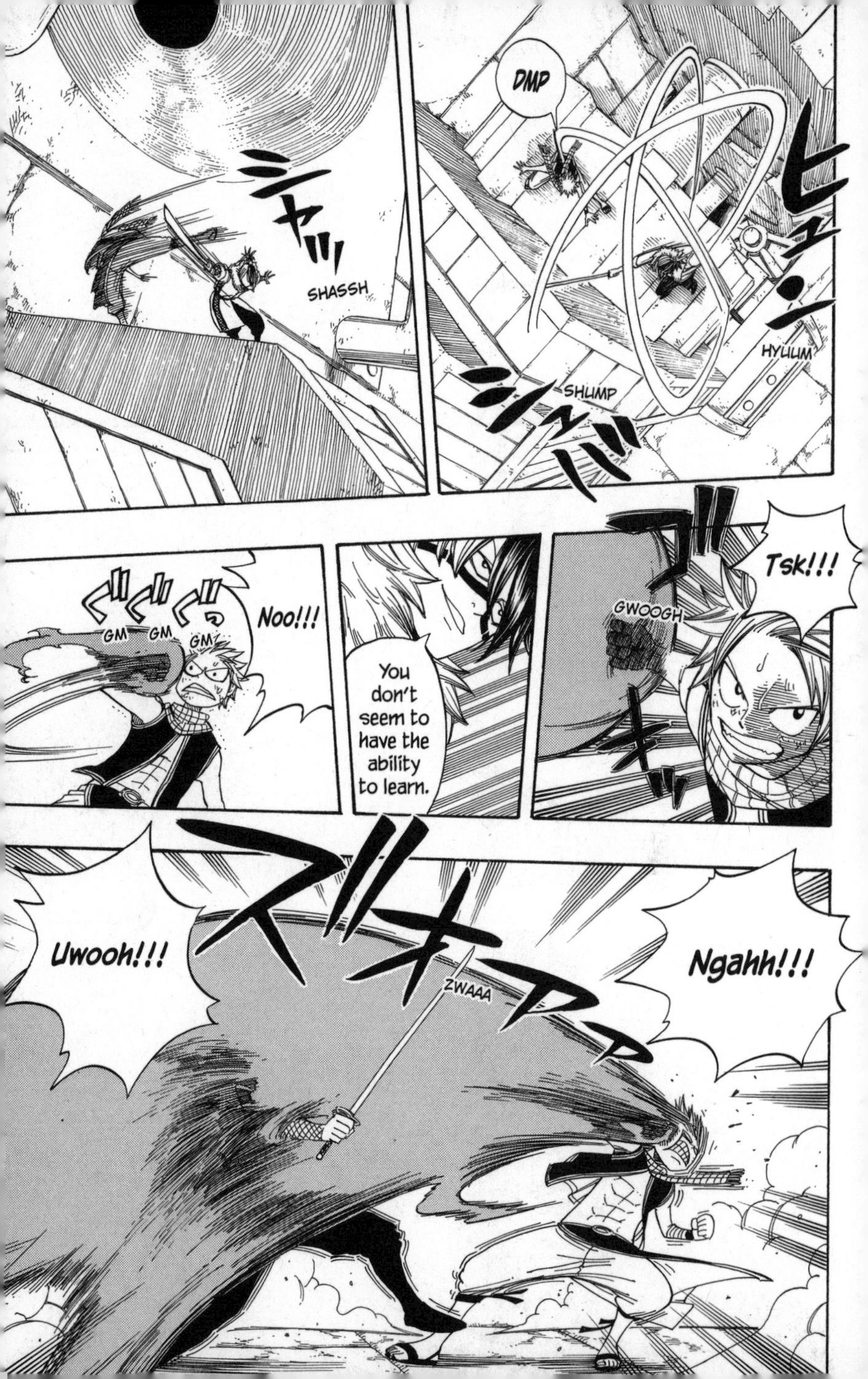
DMP
HYUUM
SHUMP
SHASSH
Tsk!!!
GWOOGH
You don't seem to have the ability to learn.
GM GM GM
Noo!!!
Ngahh!!!
ZWAAA
Uwooh!!!

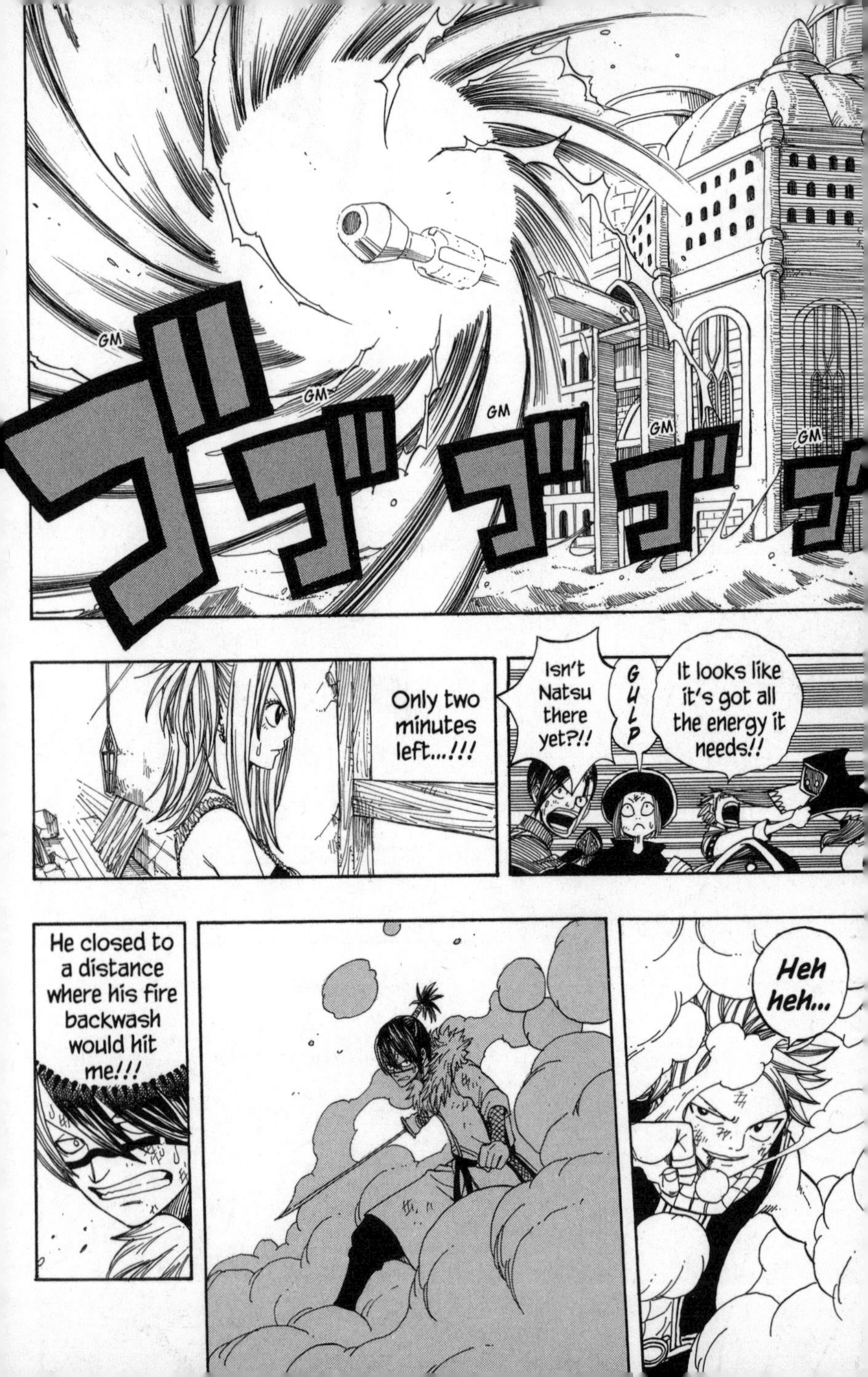
GM
GM
GM
GM
GM
It looks like it's got all the energy it needs!!
GULP
Isn't Natsu there yet?!!
Only two minutes left...!!!
Heh heh...
He closed to a distance where his fire backwash would hit me!!!

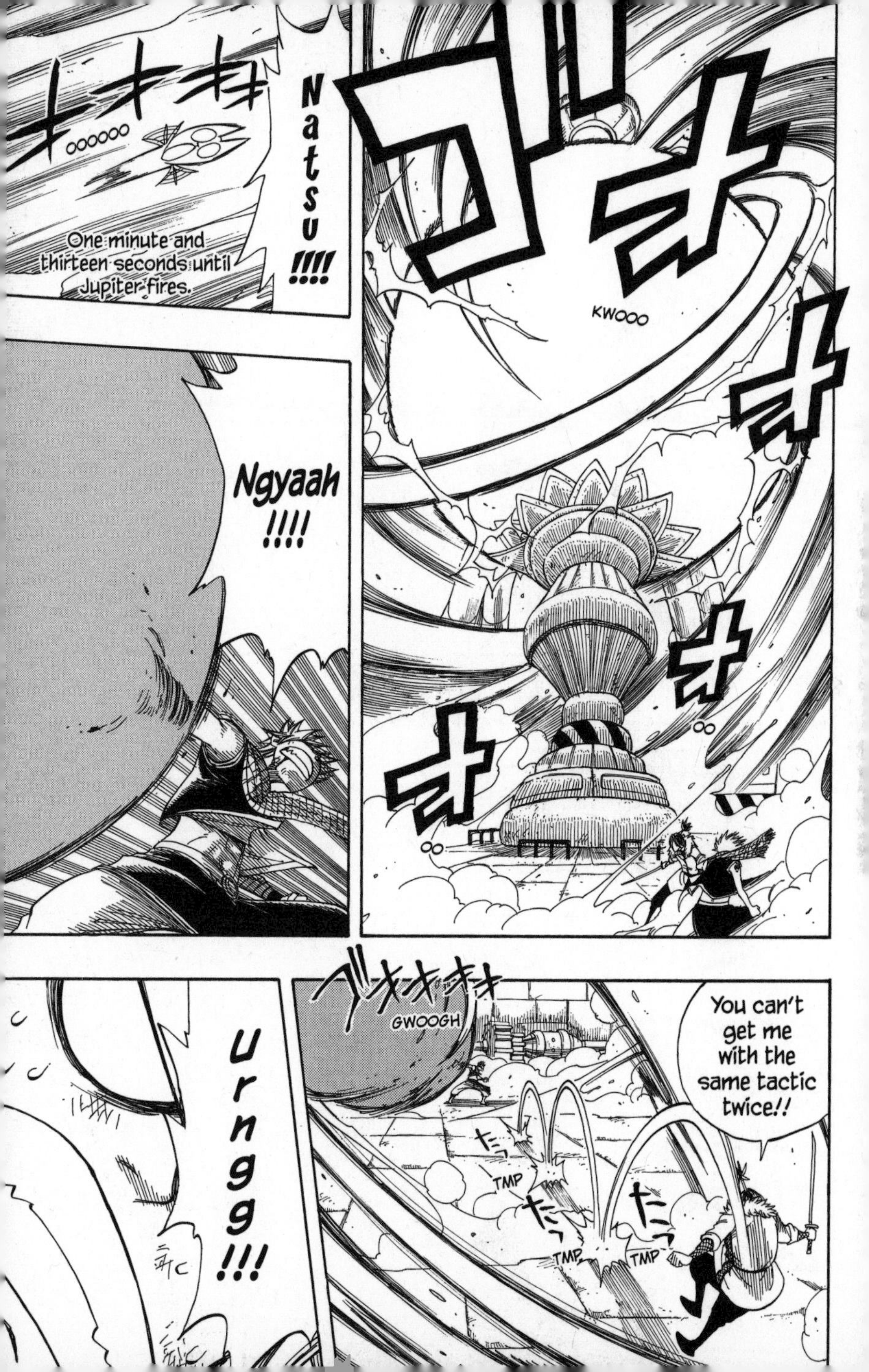
KWOOO
Natsu!!!!
oooooo
One minute and thirteen seconds until Jupiter fires.
Ngyaah!!!!
GWOOGH
You can't get me with the same tactic twice!!
TMP
TMP
TMP
Urngg!!!

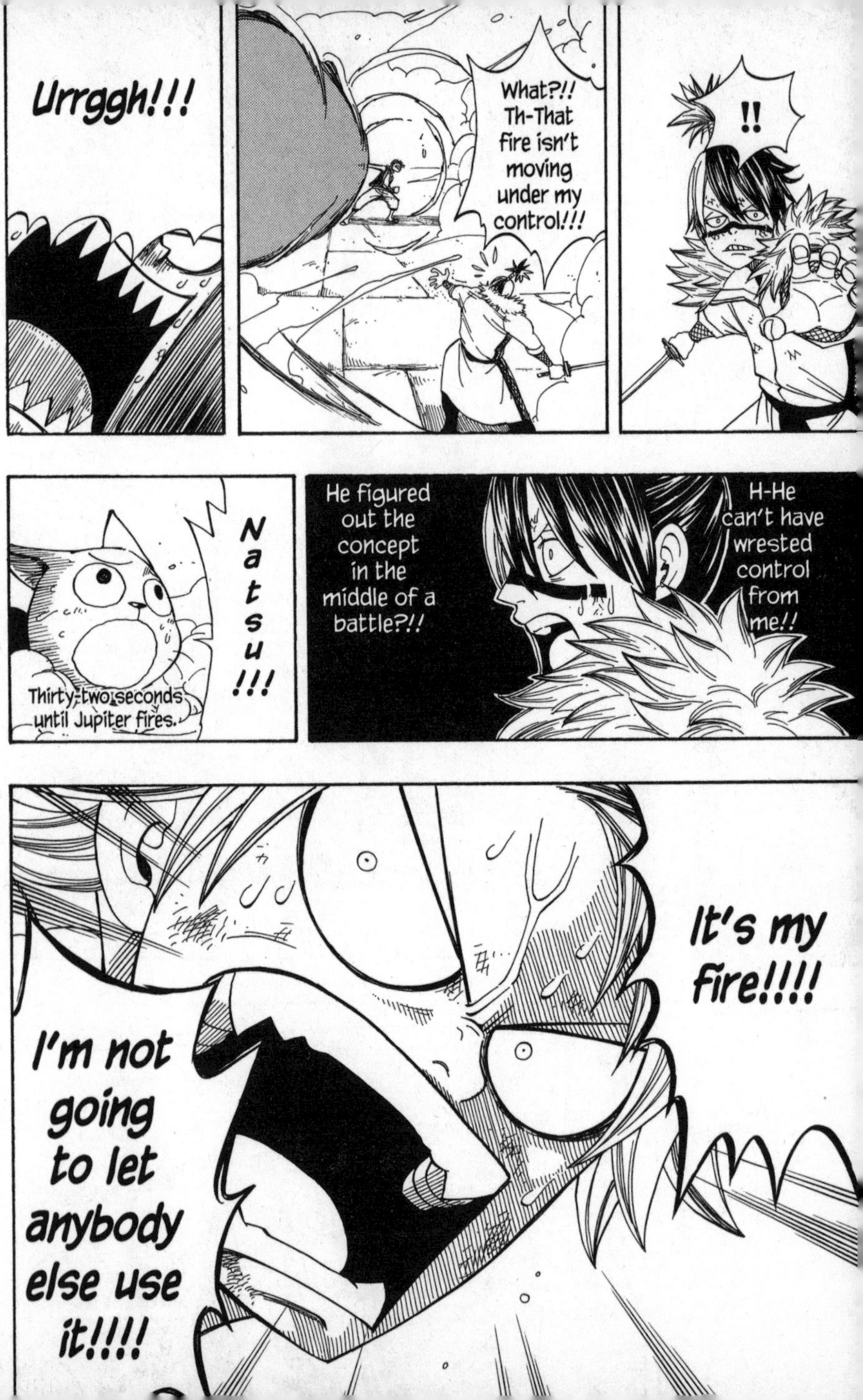
!!
What?!! Th-That fire isn't moving under my control!!!
Urrggh!!!
H-He can't have wrested control from me!!
He figured out the concept in the middle of a battle?!!
Natsu!!!
Thirty-two seconds until Jupiter fires.
It's my fire!!!!
I'm not going to let anybody else use it!!!!

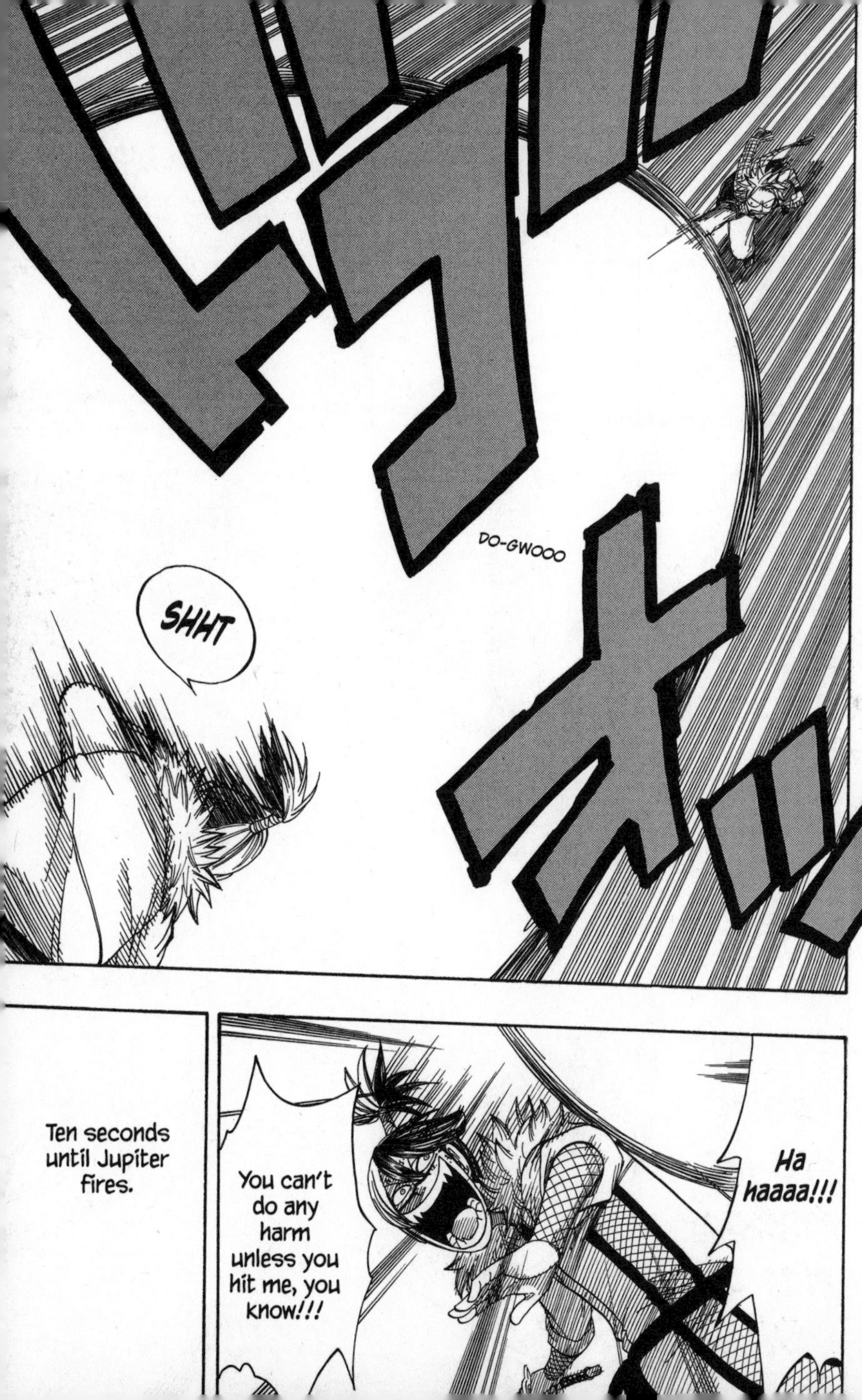
DO-GWOOO
SHHT
Ha haaaa!!!
You can't do any harm unless you hit me, you know!!!
Ten seconds until Jupiter fires.

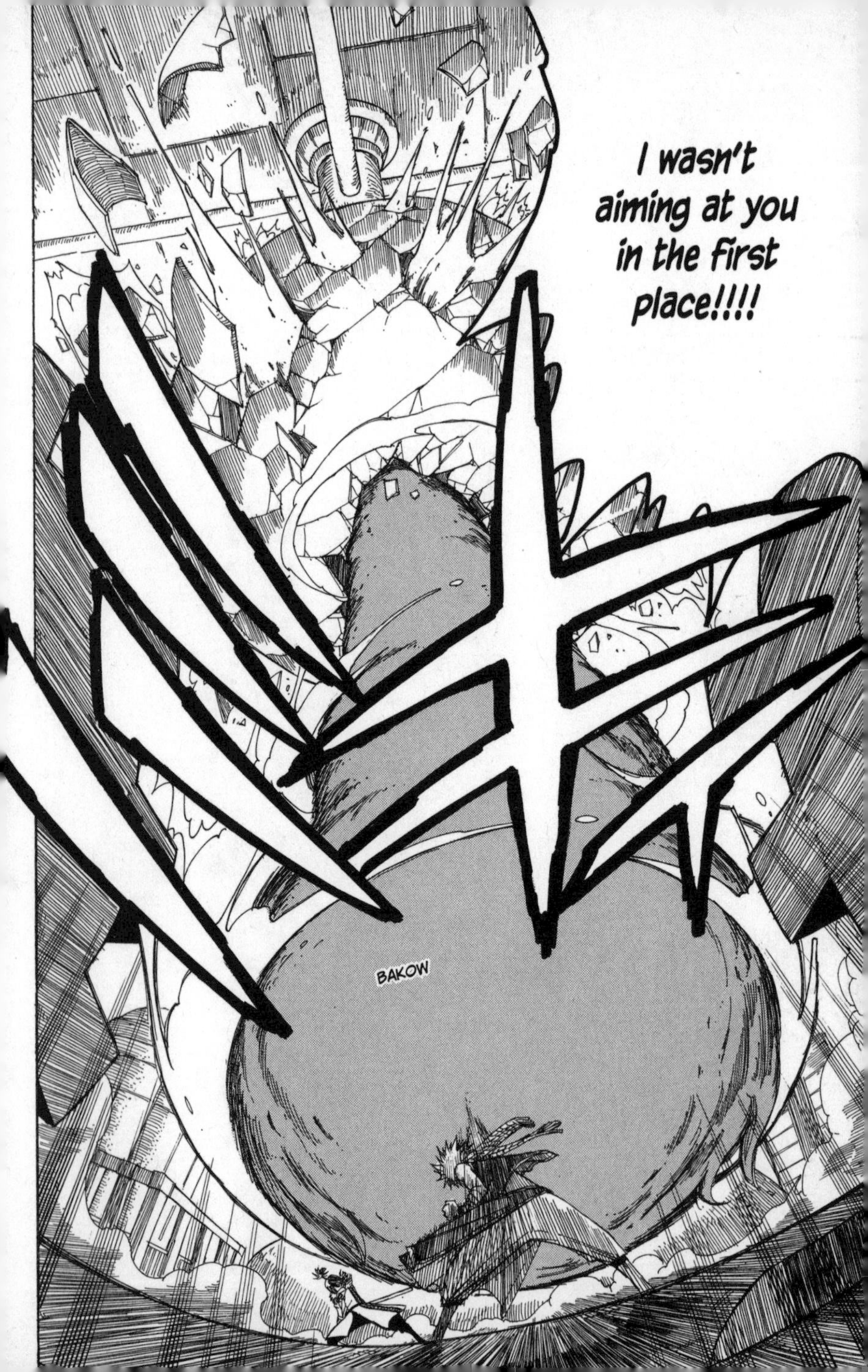
I wasn't aiming at you in the first place!!!!
BAKOW

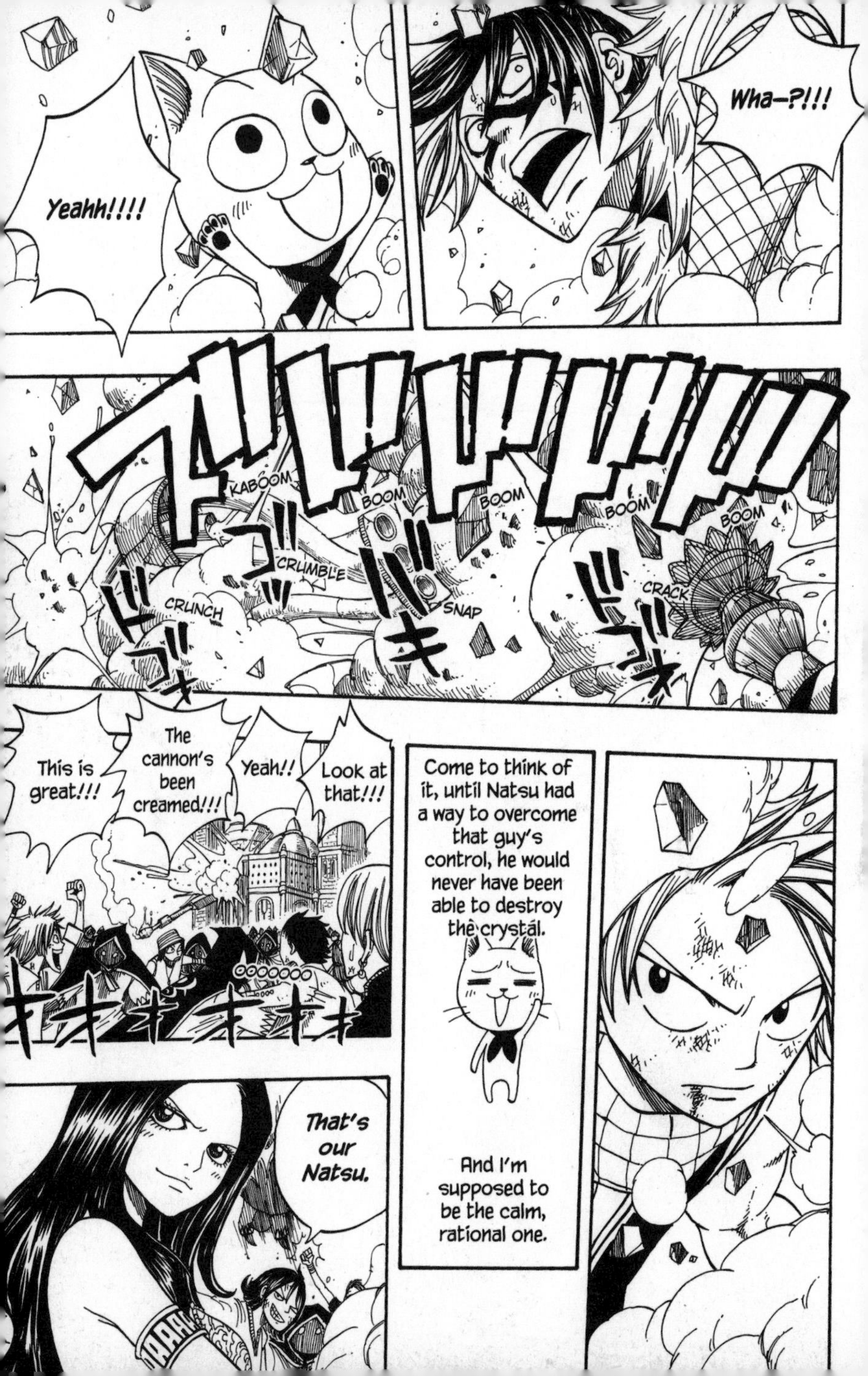
Wha–?!!!
Yeahh!!!!
BOOM
BOOM
CRACK
BOOM
SNAP
BOOM
CRUMBLE
KABOOM
CRUNCH
Come to think of it, until Natsu had a way to overcome that guy's control, he would never have been able to destroy the crystal.
And I'm supposed to be the calm, rational one.
Look at that!!!
Yeah!!
The cannon's been creamed!!!
This is great!!!
OOOOOOO
That's our Natsu.

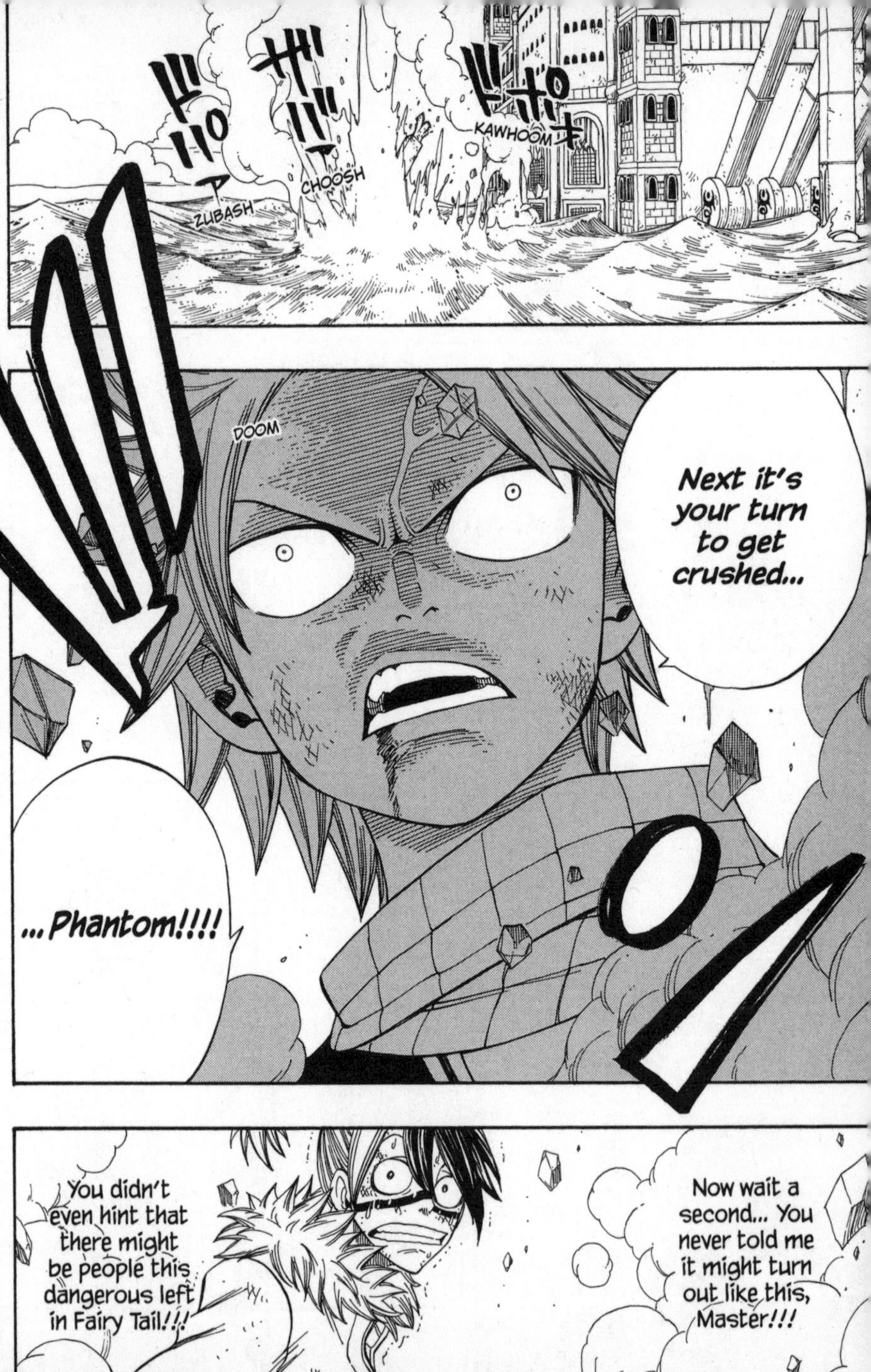
KAWHOOM
CHOOSH
ZUBASH
DOOM
Next it's your turn to get crushed...
...Phantom!!!!
Now wait a second... You never told me it might turn out like this, Master!!!
You didn't even hint that there might be people this dangerous left in Fairy Tail!!!

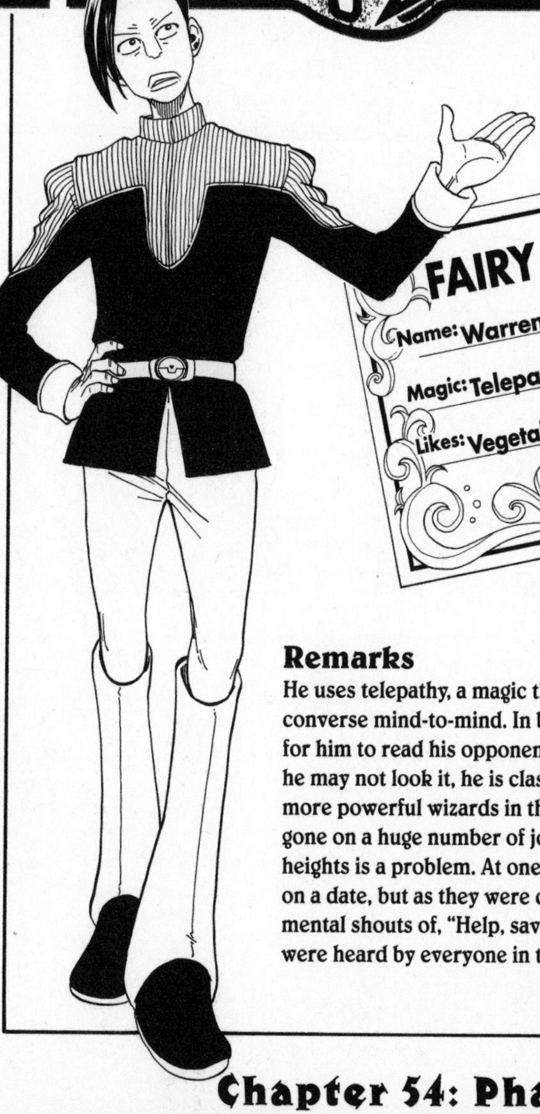

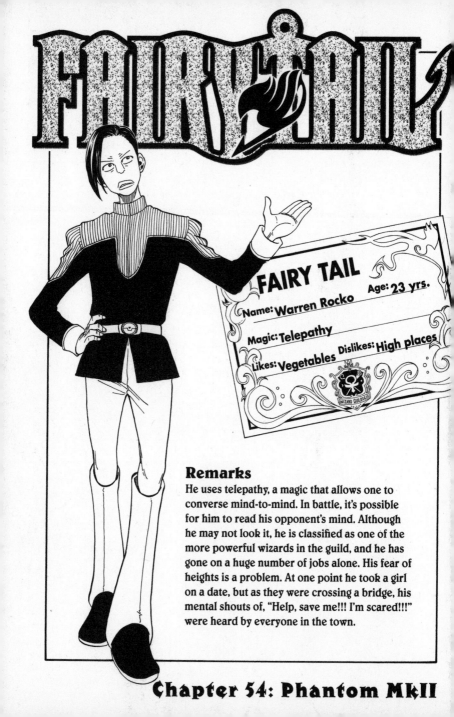

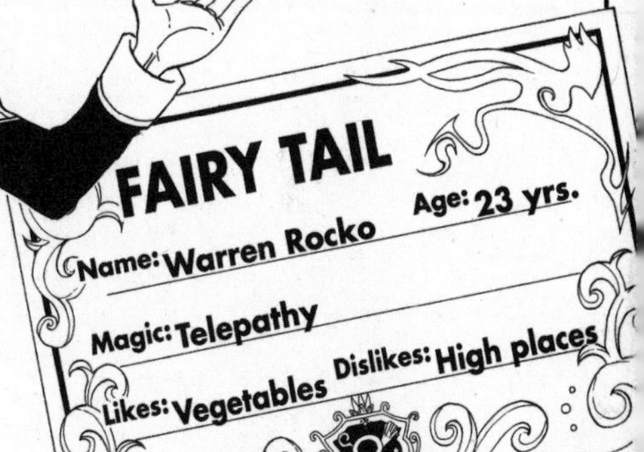
FAIRY TAIL
Age: 23 yrs.
Name: Warren Rocko
Magic: Telepathy
Likes: Vegetables
Dislikes: High places
WIZARD GUILD

Remarks

He uses telepathy, a magic that allows one to converse mind-to-mind. In battle, it's possible for him to read his opponent's mind. Although he may not look it, he is classified as one of the more powerful wizards in the guild, and he has gone on a huge number of jobs alone. His fear of heights is a problem. At one point he took a girl on a date, but as they were crossing a bridge, his mental shouts of, "Help, save me!!! I'm scared!!!" were heard by everyone in the town.

Chapter 54: Phantom MkII

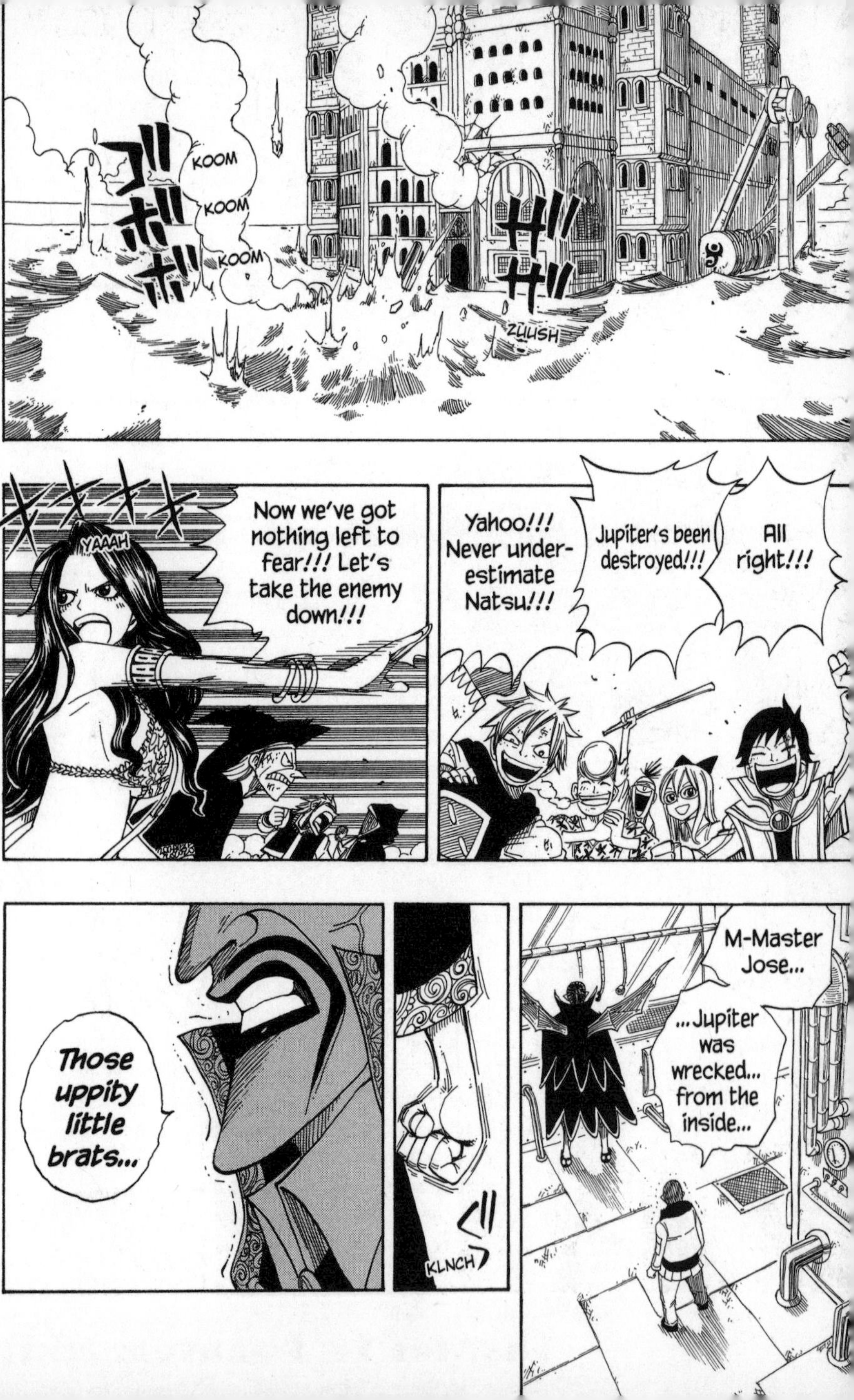
ザザ
ZUUSH
ゴボボ
KOOM
KOOM
KOOM
All right!!!
Jupiter's been destroyed!!!
Yahoo!!! Never under-estimate Natsu!!!
Now we've got nothing left to fear!!! Let's take the enemy down!!!
YAAAH
M-Master Jose...
...Jupiter was wrecked... from the inside...
KLNCH
Those uppity little brats...

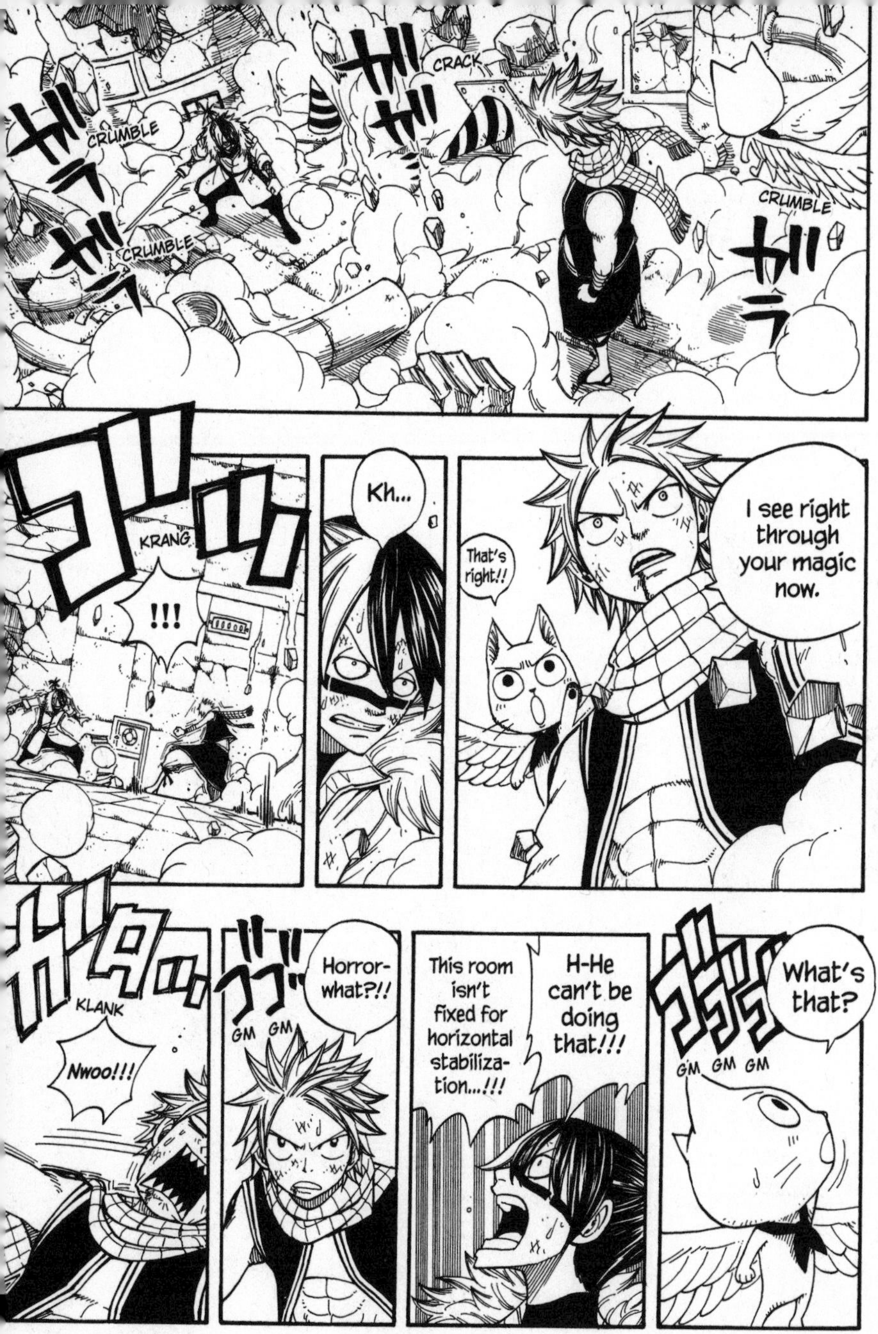
CRACK
CRUMBLE
CRUMBLE
CRUMBLE
I see right through your magic now.
That's right!!
Kh...
KRANG
!!!
What's that?
GM GM GM
H-He can't be doing that!!!
This room isn't fixed for horizontal stabiliza-tion...!!!
Horror-what?!!
GM GM
KLANK
Nwoo!!!

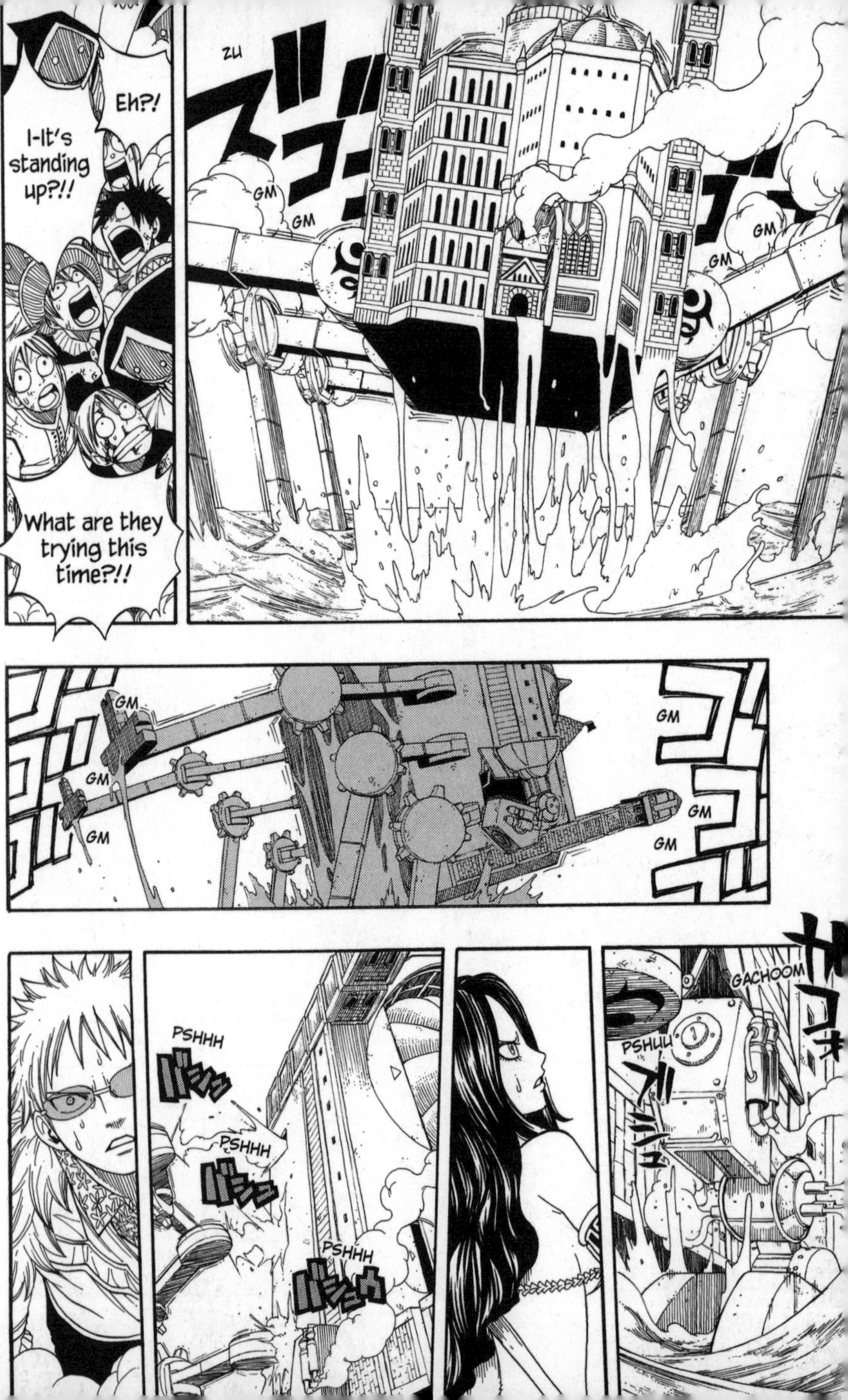
ZU
GM
GM
GM
GM
Eh?!
I-It's standing up?!!
What are they trying this time?!!
GM
GM
GM
GM
GM
GM
GACHOOM
PSHUU
PSHHH
PSHHH
PSHHH

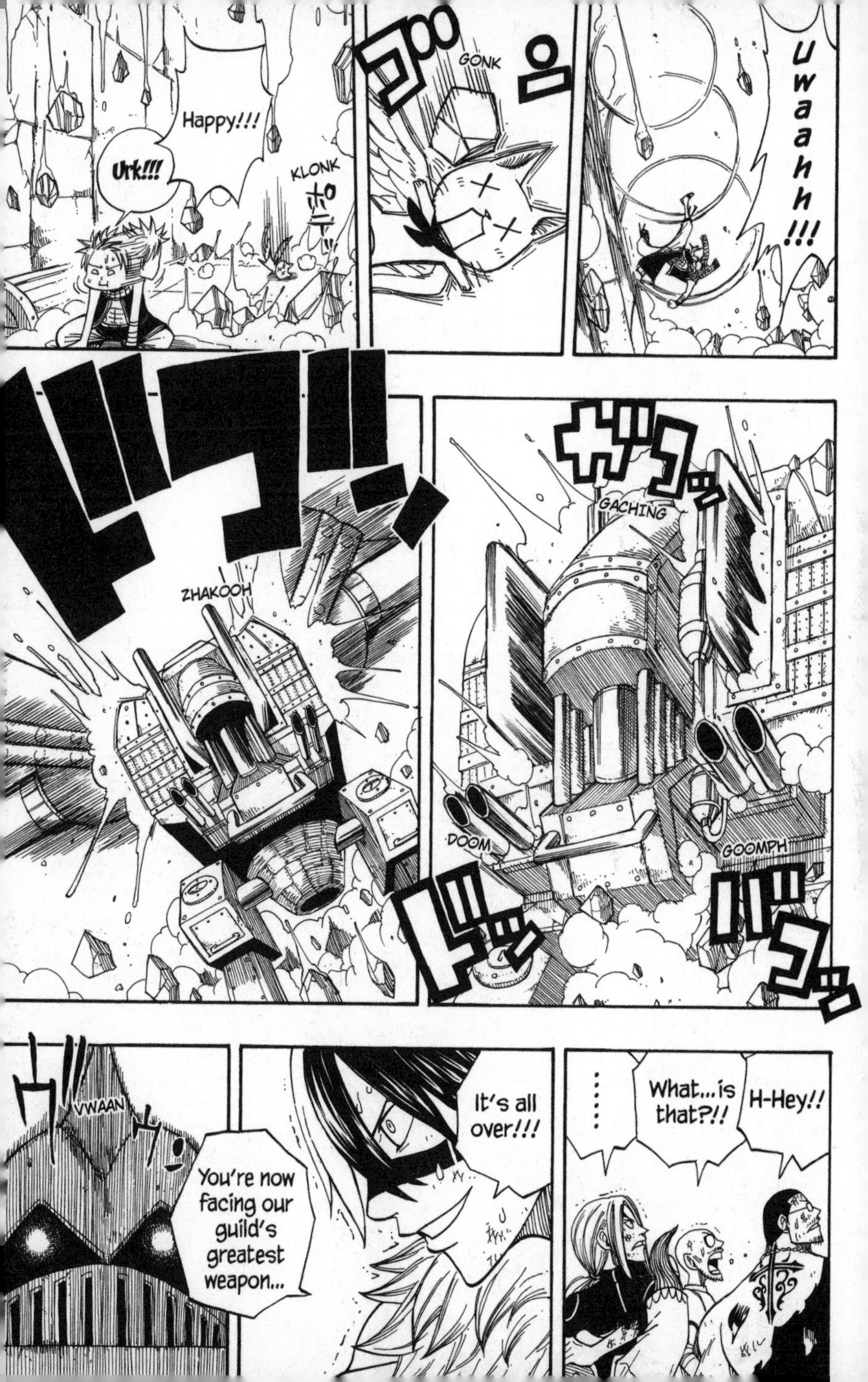
Uwaahh!!!
GONK
Happy!!!
Urk!!!
KLONK
GACHING
DOOM
GOOMPH
ZHAKOOH
H-Hey!!
What...is that?!!
......
It's all over!!!
VWAAN
You're now facing our guild's greatest weapon...

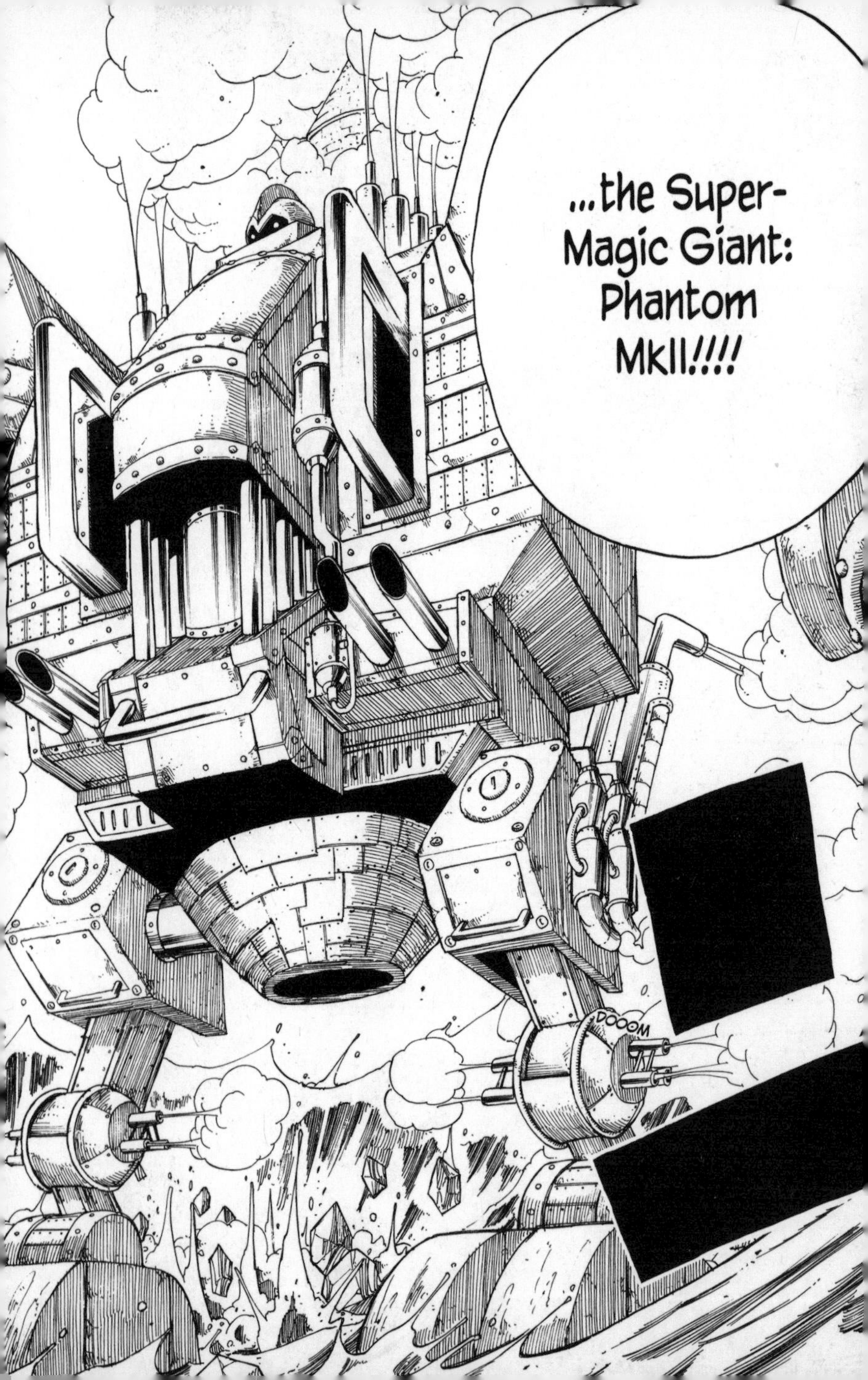
...the Super-Magic Giant: Phantom MkII!!!!
[redacted]
DOOOM
[redacted]

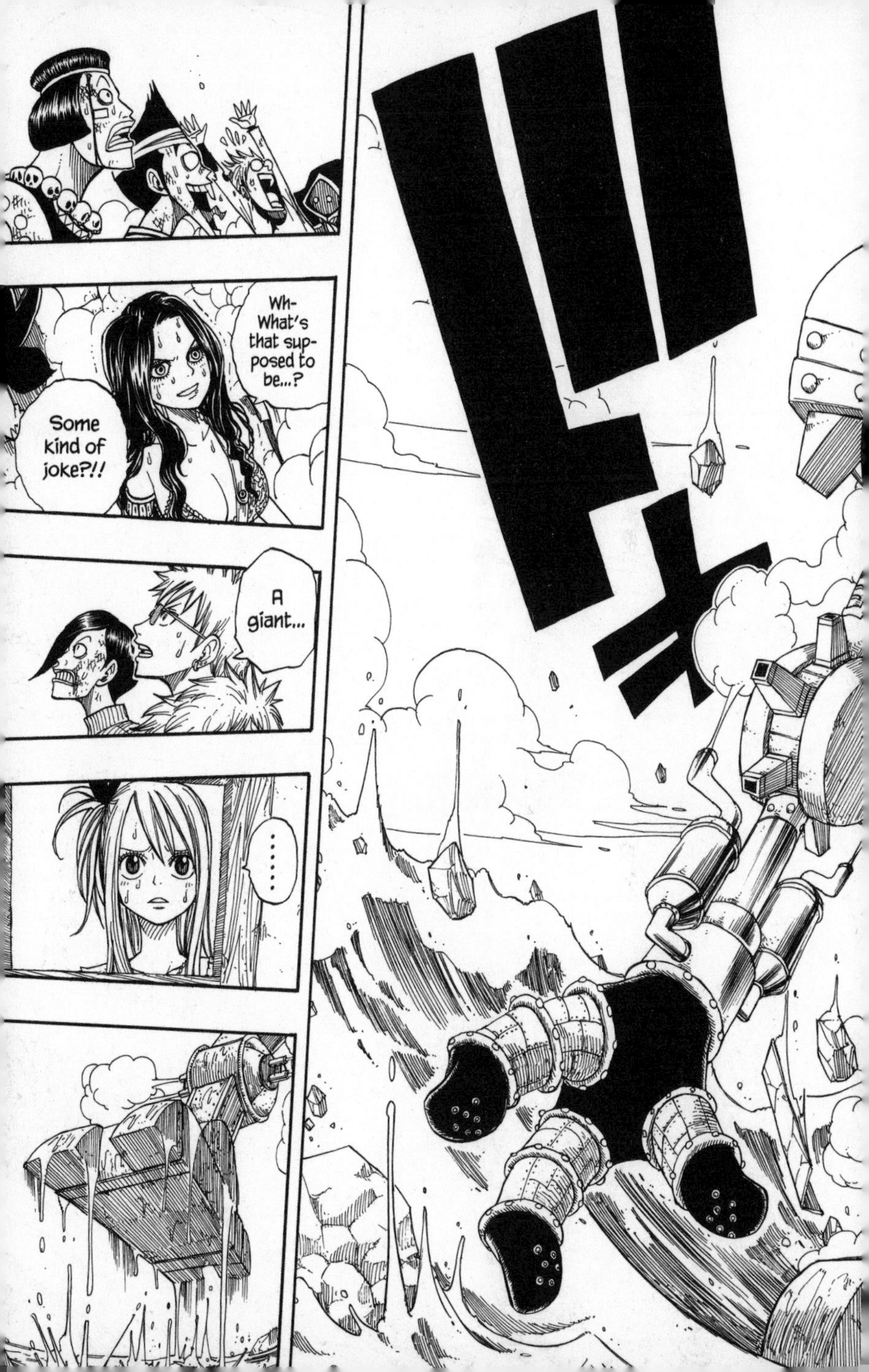
Wh- What's that sup-posed to be...?
Some kind of joke?!!
A giant...
......

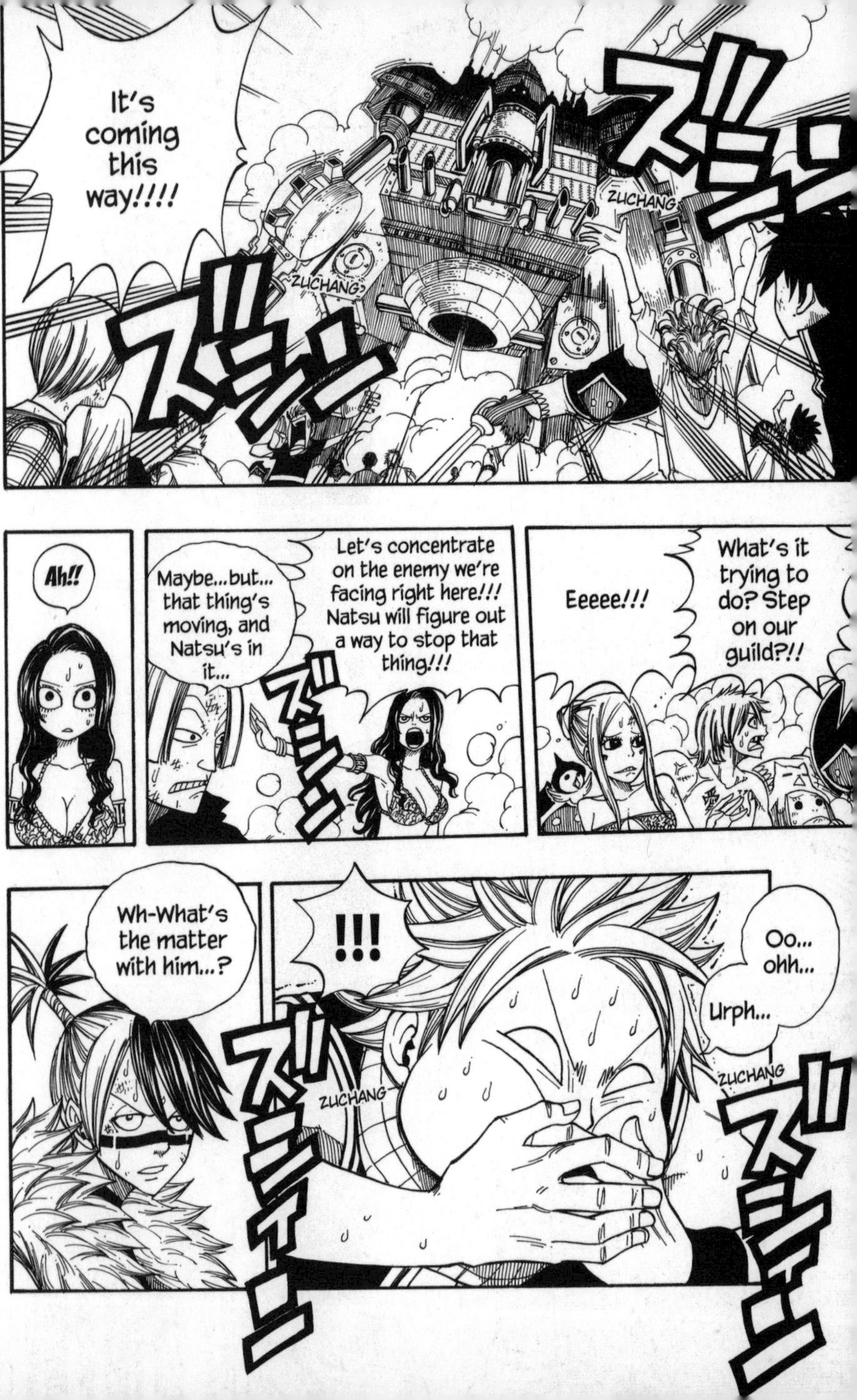
ZUCHANG
It's coming this way!!!!
ZUCHANG
What's it trying to do? Step on our guild?!!
Eeeee!!!
Let's concentrate on the enemy we're facing right here!!! Natsu will figure out a way to stop that thing!!!
Maybe...but... that thing's moving, and Natsu's in it...
Ah!!
Oo... ohh...
Urph...
ZUCHANG
!!!
ZUCHANG
Wh-What's the matter with him...?

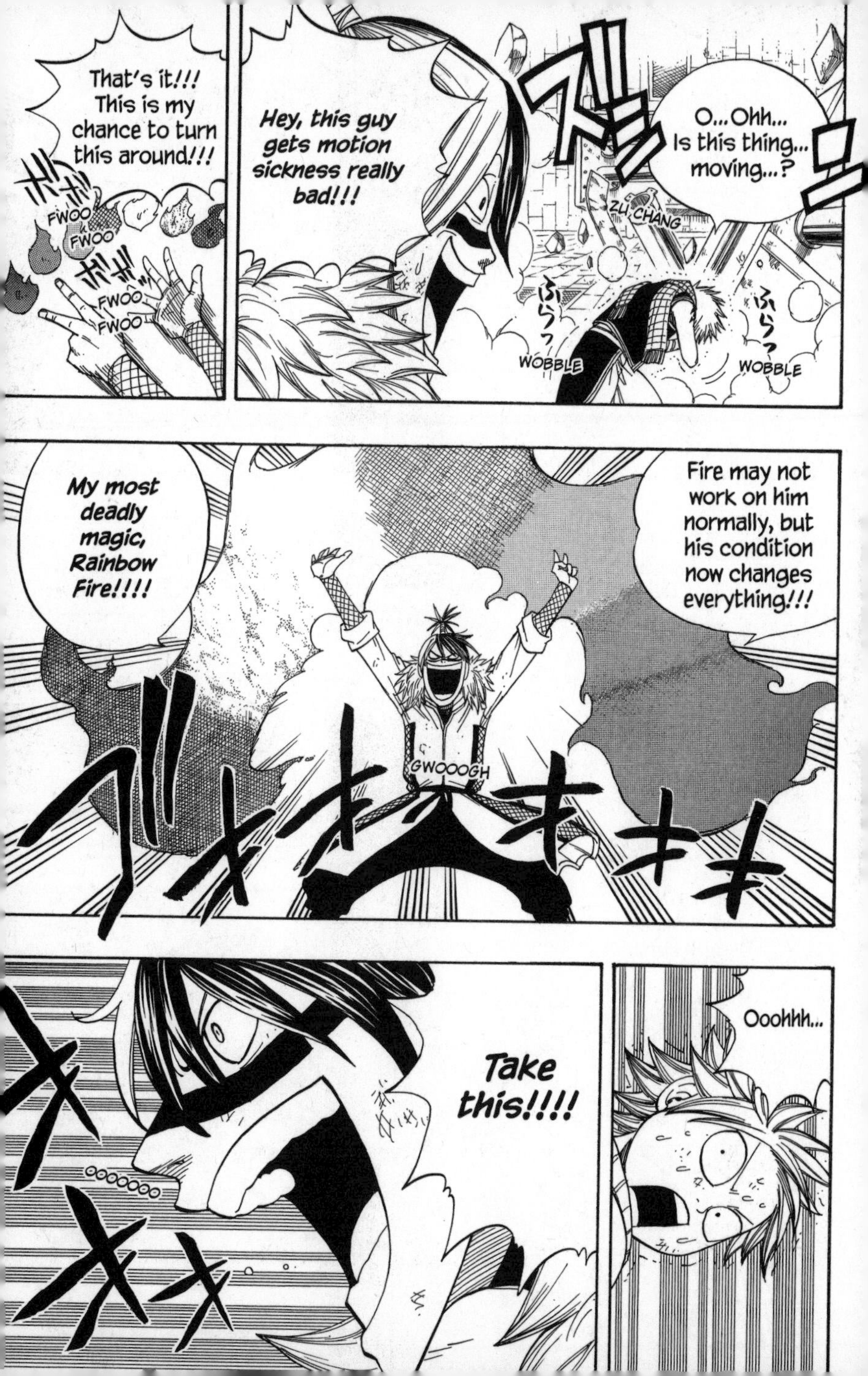

O...Ohh...
Is this thing...
moving...?
ZU CHANG
ふらっ
WOBBLE
ふらっ
WOBBLE
Hey, this guy
gets motion
sickness really
bad!!!
That's it!!!
This is my
chance to turn
this around!!!
FWOO
FWOO
FWOO
FWOO
Fire may not
work on him
normally, but
his condition
now changes
everything!!!
My most
deadly
magic,
Rainbow
Fire!!!!
GWOOOGH
Ooohhh...
Take
this!!!!
OOOOOOO

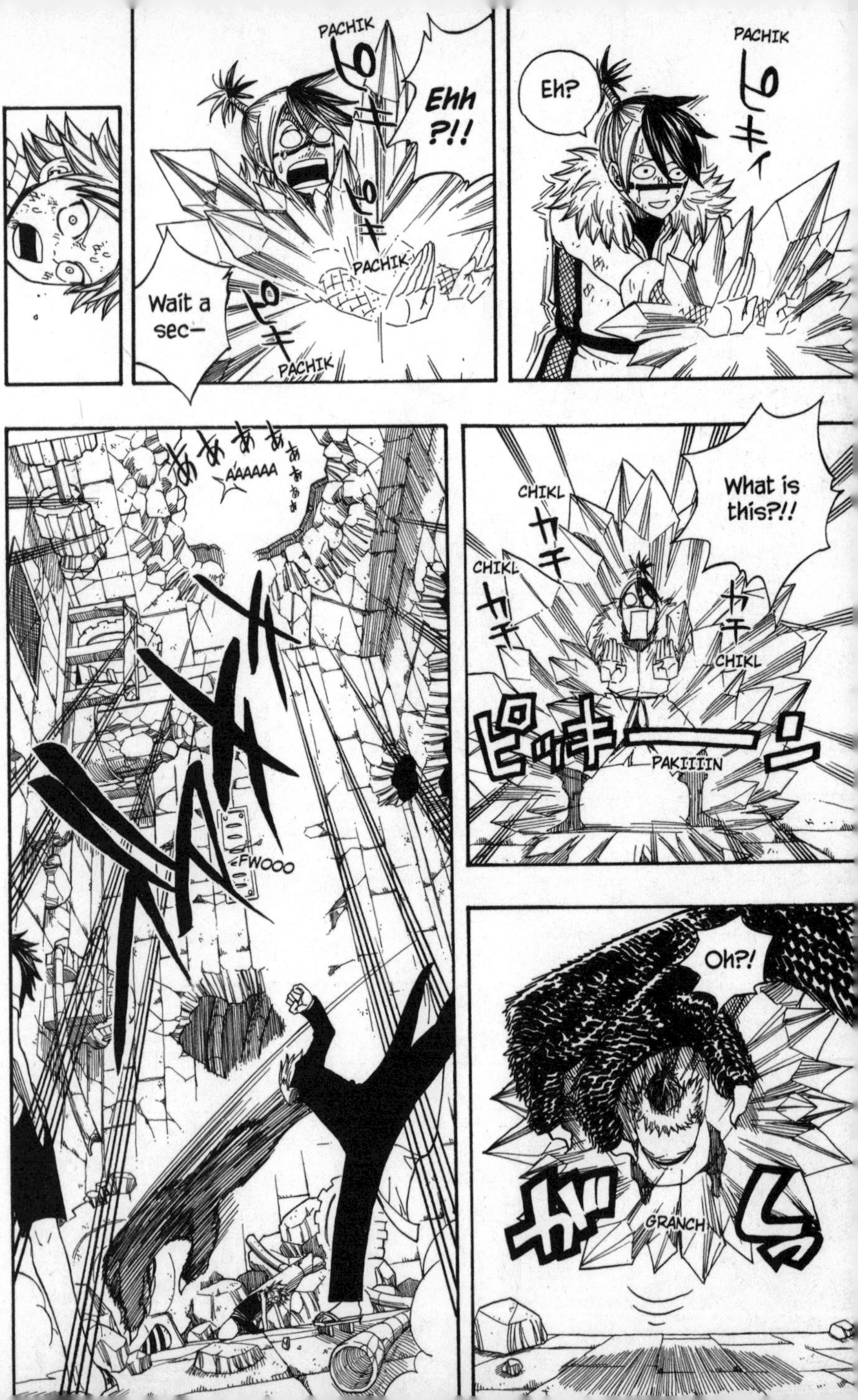
PACHIK
Eh?
PACHIK
Ehh ?!!
PACHIK
PACHIK
Wait a sec—
What is this?!!
CHIKL
CHIKL
CHIKL
PAKIIIIN
Oh?!
GRANCH
AAAAAA
FWOOO

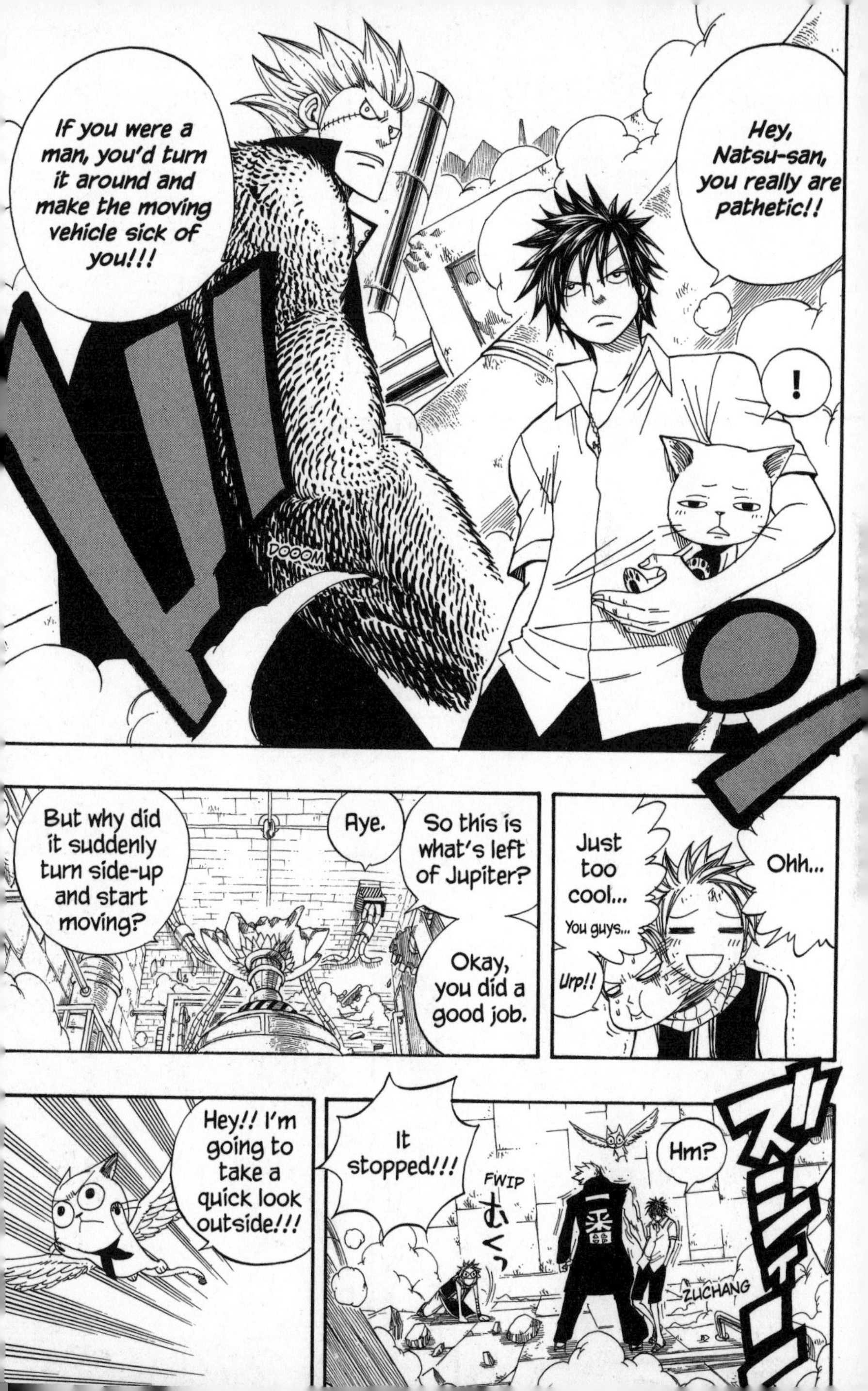

Hey, Natsu-san, you really are pathetic!!
If you were a man, you'd turn it around and make the moving vehicle sick of you!!!
!
DOOOM
Ohh...
Just too cool...
You guys...
Urp!!
So this is what's left of Jupiter?
Aye.
But why did it suddenly turn side-up and start moving?
Okay, you did a good job.
Hm?
It stopped!!!
FWIP
むくっ
ZUCHANG
Hey!! I'm going to take a quick look outside!!!

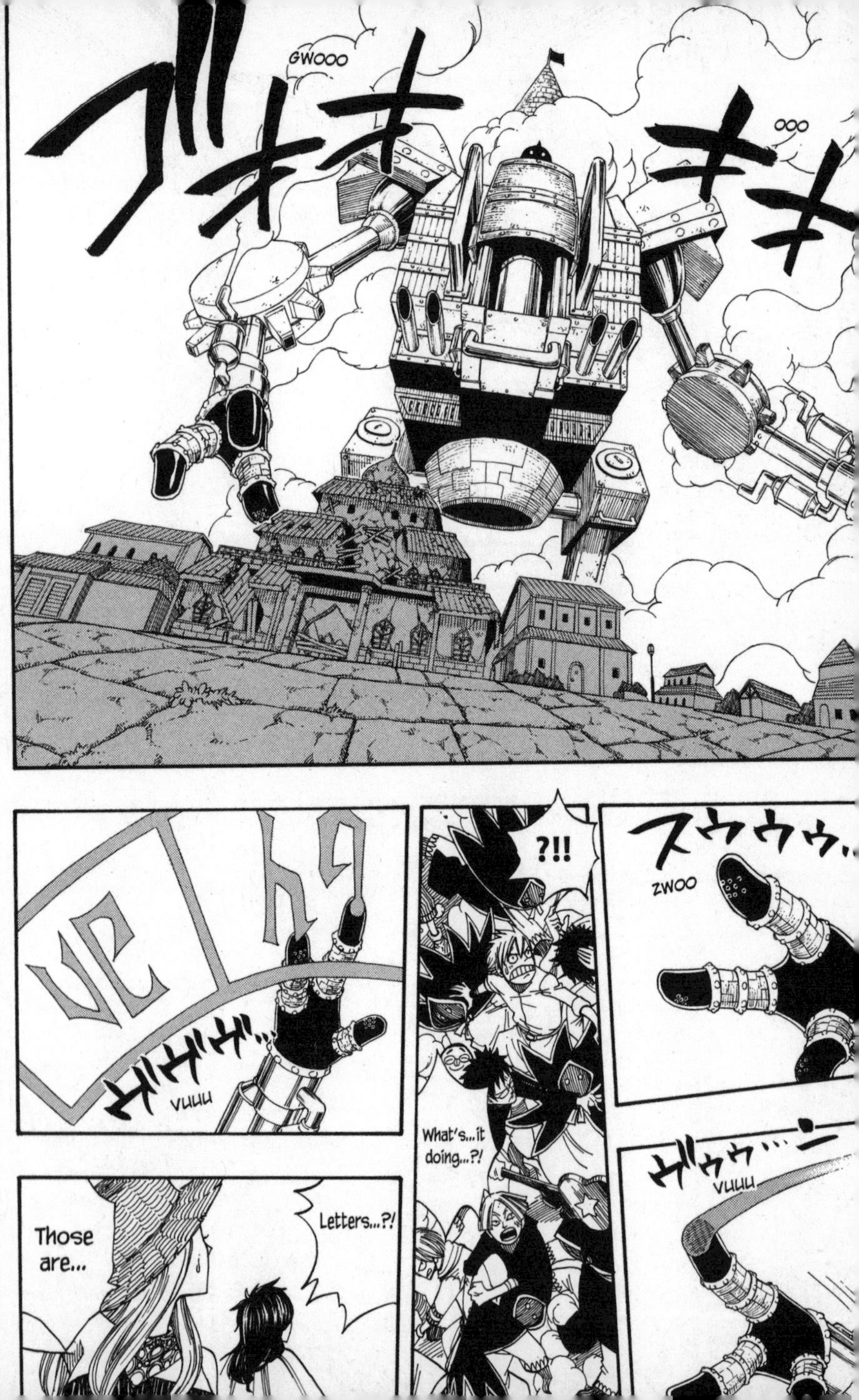
GWOOO
OOO
ZWOO
VUUU
?!!
What's...it doing...?!
VUUU
Letters...?!
Those are...

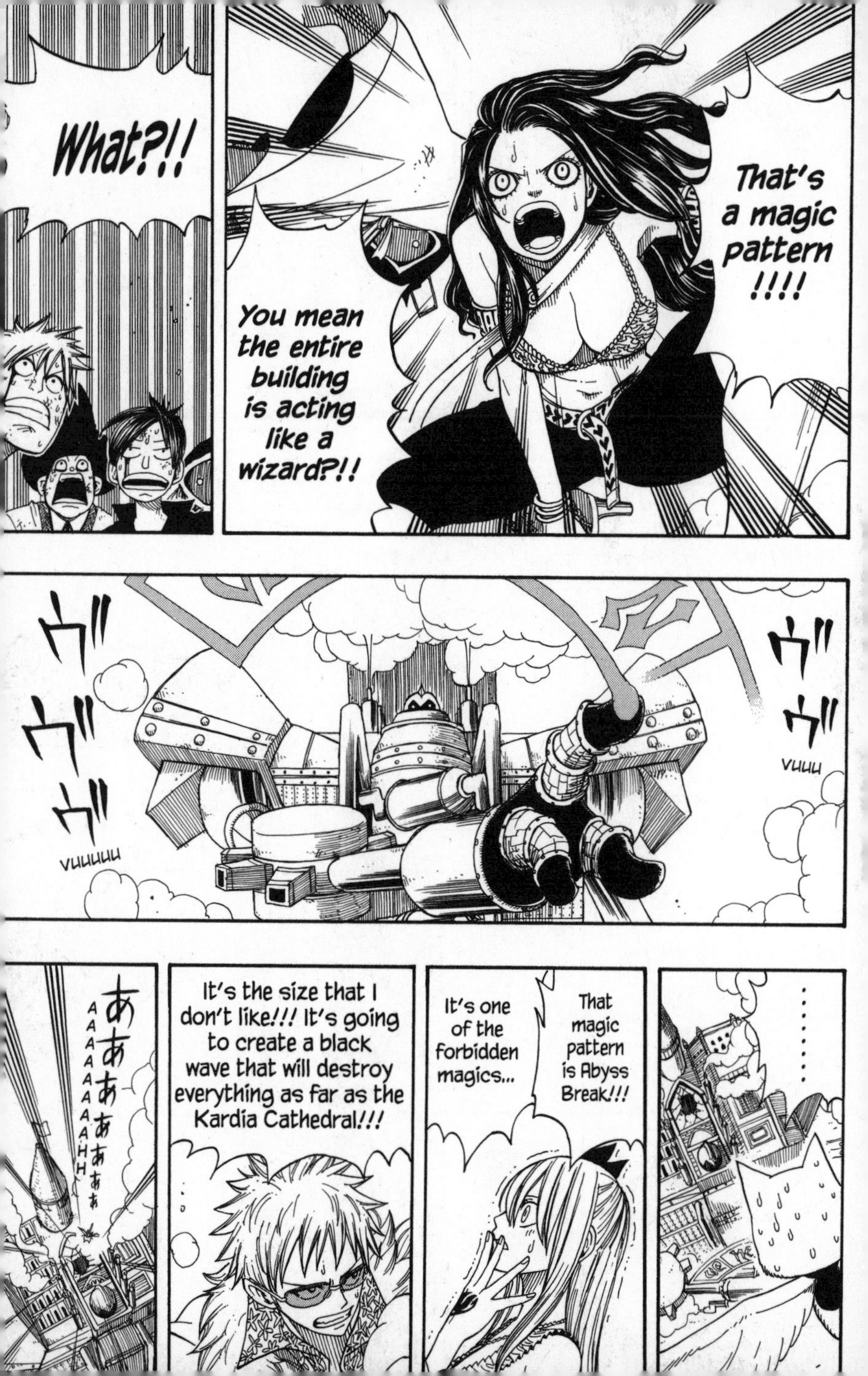
That's a magic pattern !!!!
You mean the entire building is acting like a wizard?!!
What?!!
ヴヴ
VUUU
ヴヴヴ
VUUUUU
......
That magic pattern is Abyss Break!!!
It's one of the forbidden magics...
It's the size that I don't like!!! It's going to create a black wave that will destroy everything as far as the Kardia Cathedral!!!
ああああああ
AAAAAAAAHH

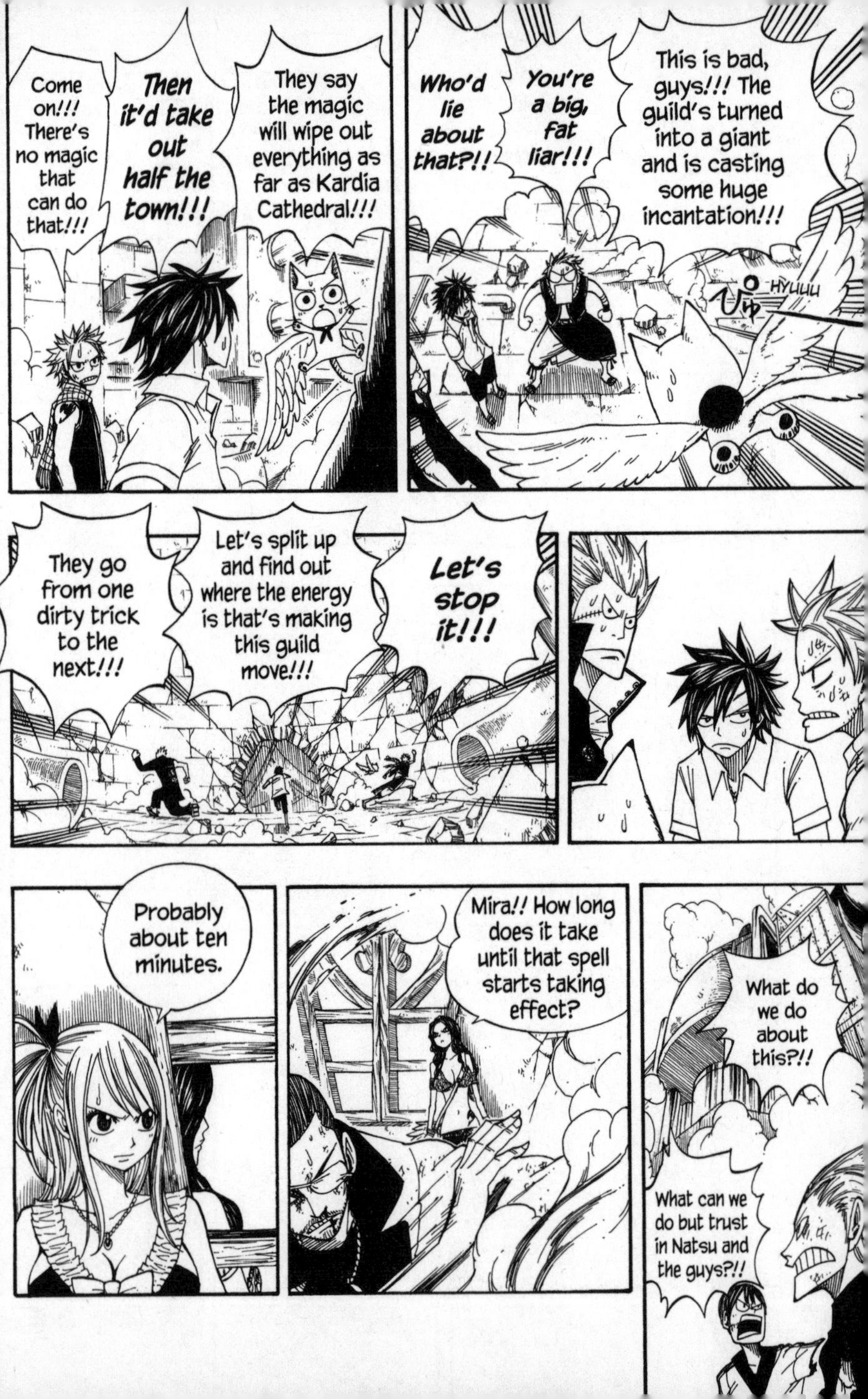
This is bad, guys!!! The guild's turned into a giant and is casting some huge incantation!!!
HYUUU
You're a big, fat liar!!!
Who'd lie about that?!!
They say the magic will wipe out everything as far as Kardia Cathedral!!!
Then it'd take out half the town!!!
Come on!!! There's no magic that can do that!!!
Let's stop it!!!
Let's split up and find out where the energy is that's making this guild move!!!
They go from one dirty trick to the next!!!
What do we do about this?!!
What can we do but trust in Natsu and the guys?!!
Mira!! How long does it take until that spell starts taking effect?
Probably about ten minutes.

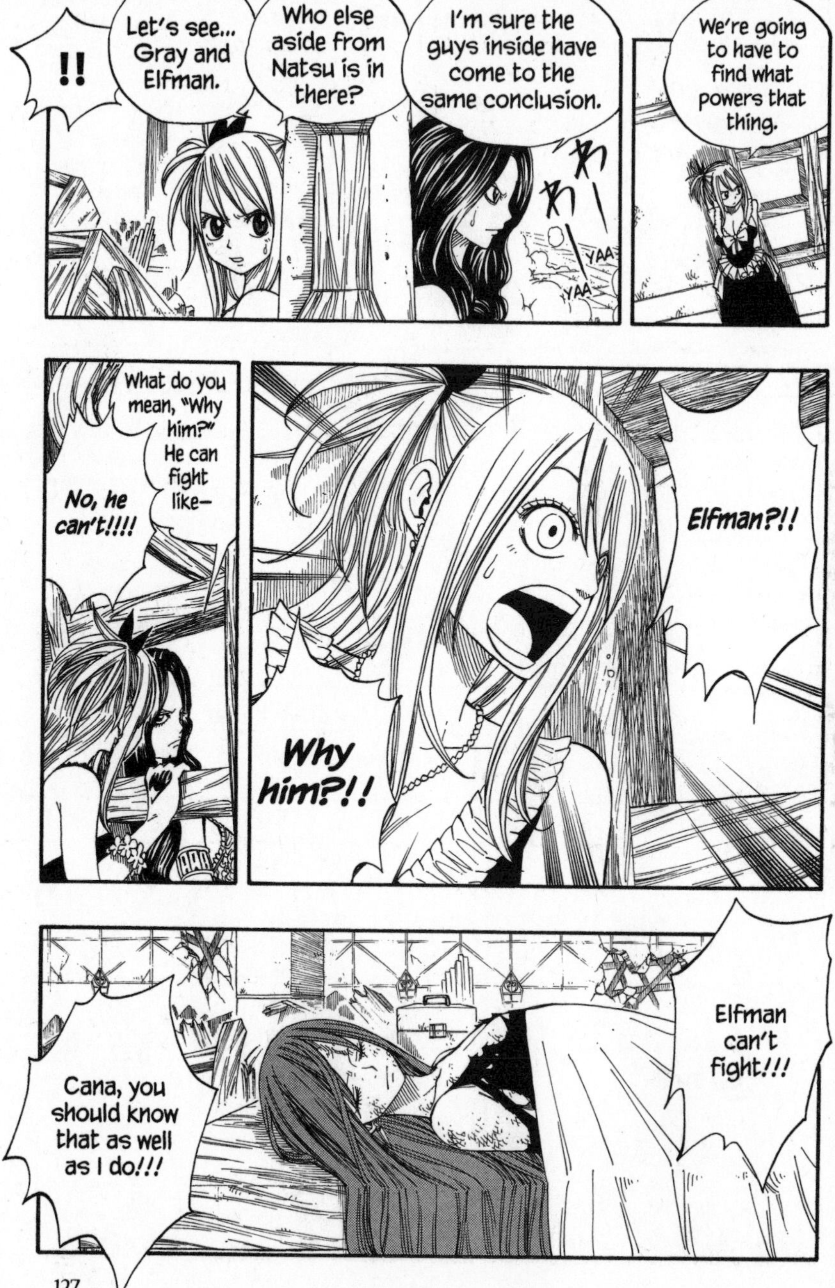
We're going to have to find what powers that thing.
I'm sure the guys inside have come to the same conclusion.
YAA
YAA
Who else aside from Natsu is in there?
Let's see... Gray and Elfman.
!!
Elfman?!!
Why him?!!
What do you mean, "Why him?" He can fight like—
No, he can't!!!!
Elfman can't fight!!!
Cana, you should know that as well as I do!!!

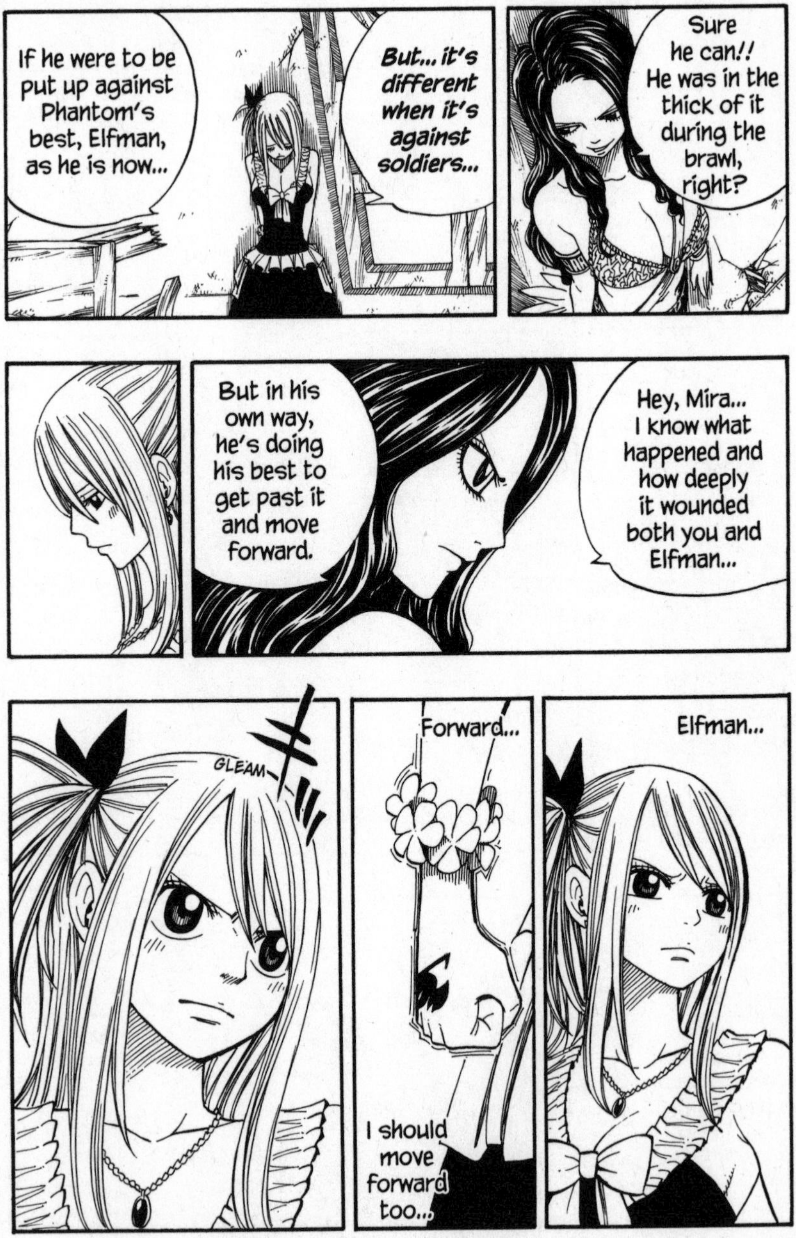

Sure he can!! He was in the thick of it during the brawl, right?
But... it's different when it's against soldiers...
If he were to be put up against Phantom's best, Elfman, as he is now...
Hey, Mira... I know what happened and how deeply it wounded both you and Elfman...
But in his own way, he's doing his best to get past it and move forward.
Elfman...
Forward...
I should move forward too...
GLEAM

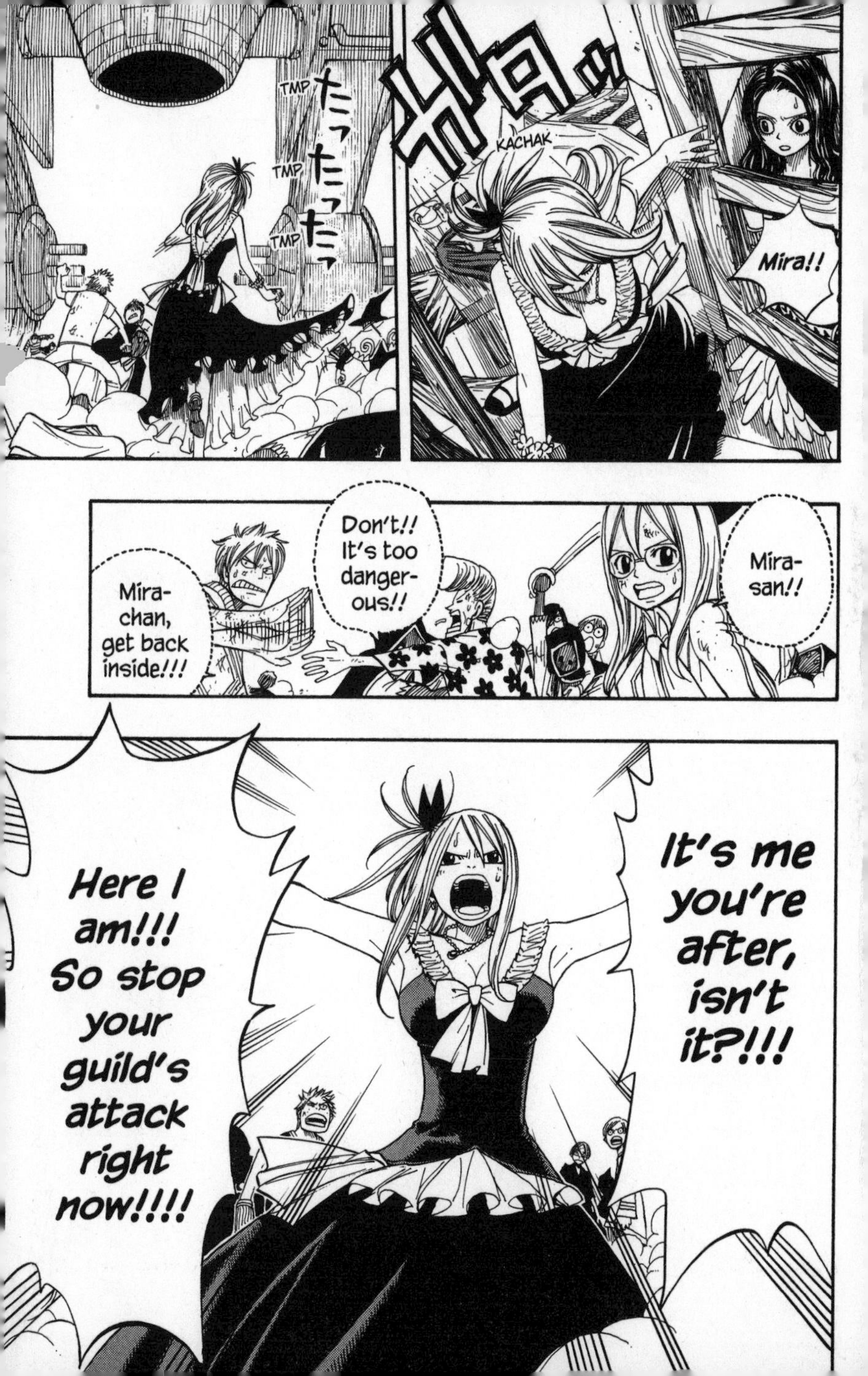
KACHAK
Mira!!
TMP
たっ
TMP
たっ
TMP
たっ
Mira-san!!
Don't!! It's too danger-ous!!
Mira-chan, get back inside!!!
It's me you're after, isn't it?!!!
Here I am!!! So stop your guild's attack right now!!!!

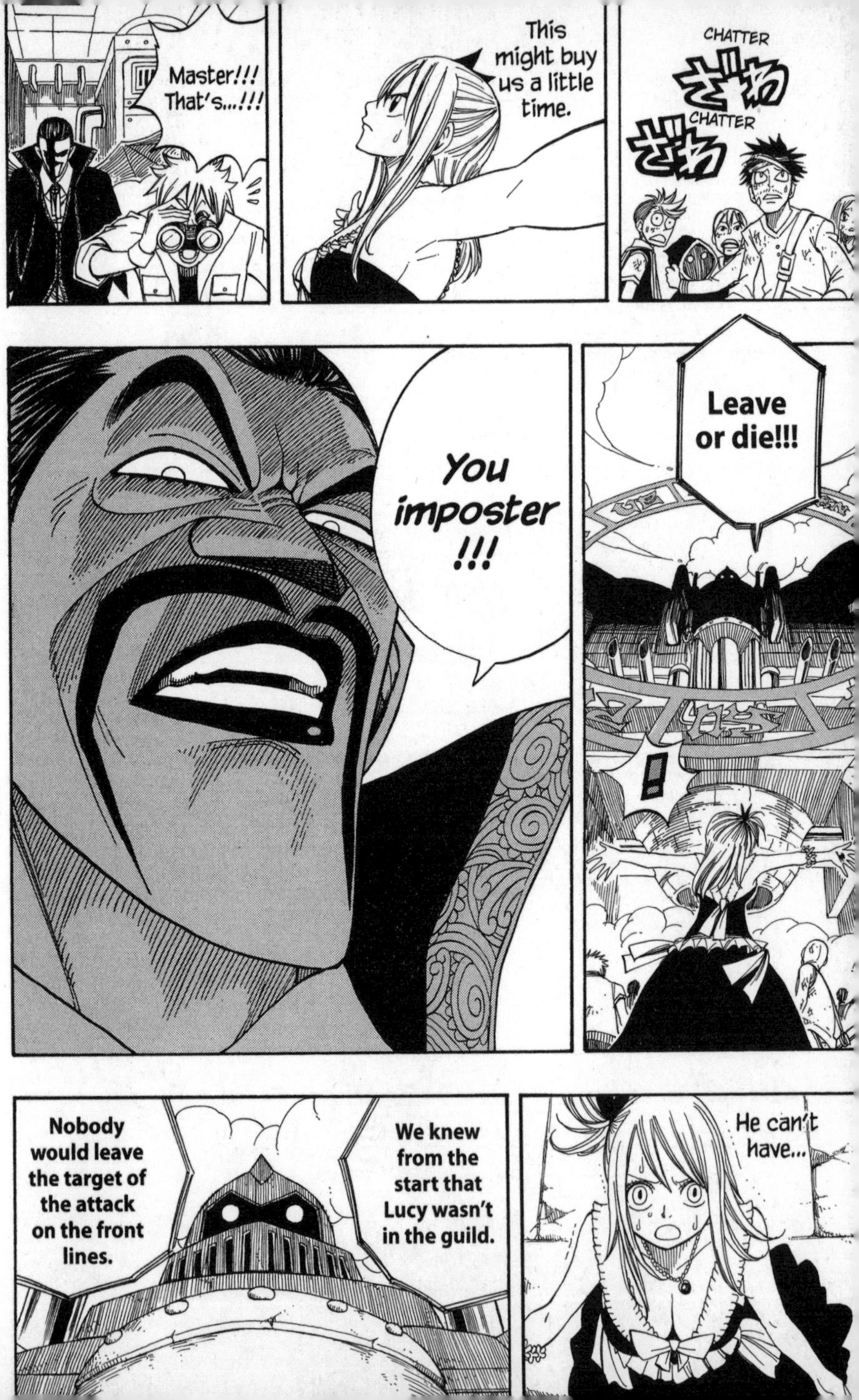
CHATTER
CHATTER
This might buy us a little time.
Master!!! That's...!!!
Leave or die!!!
!
You imposter!!!
He can't have...
We knew from the start that Lucy wasn't in the guild.
Nobody would leave the target of the attack on the front lines.

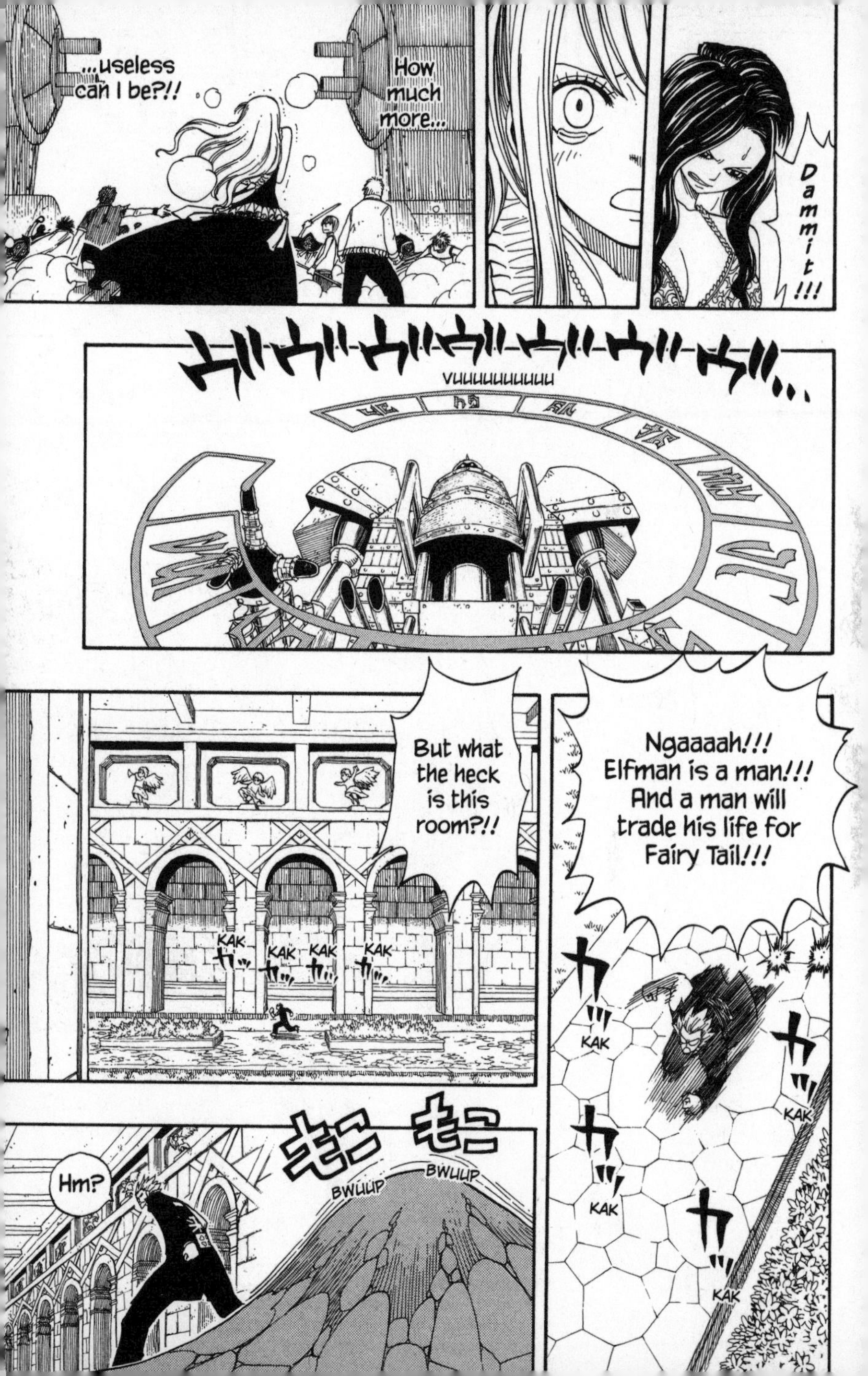
Dammit!!!
How much more...
...useless can I be?!!
VUUUUUUUUUU
Ngaaaah!!! Elfman is a man!!! And a man will trade his life for Fairy Tail!!!
KAK
KAK
KAK
KAK
But what the heck is this room?!!
KAK
KAK
KAK
KAK
BWUUP
BWUUP
Hm?

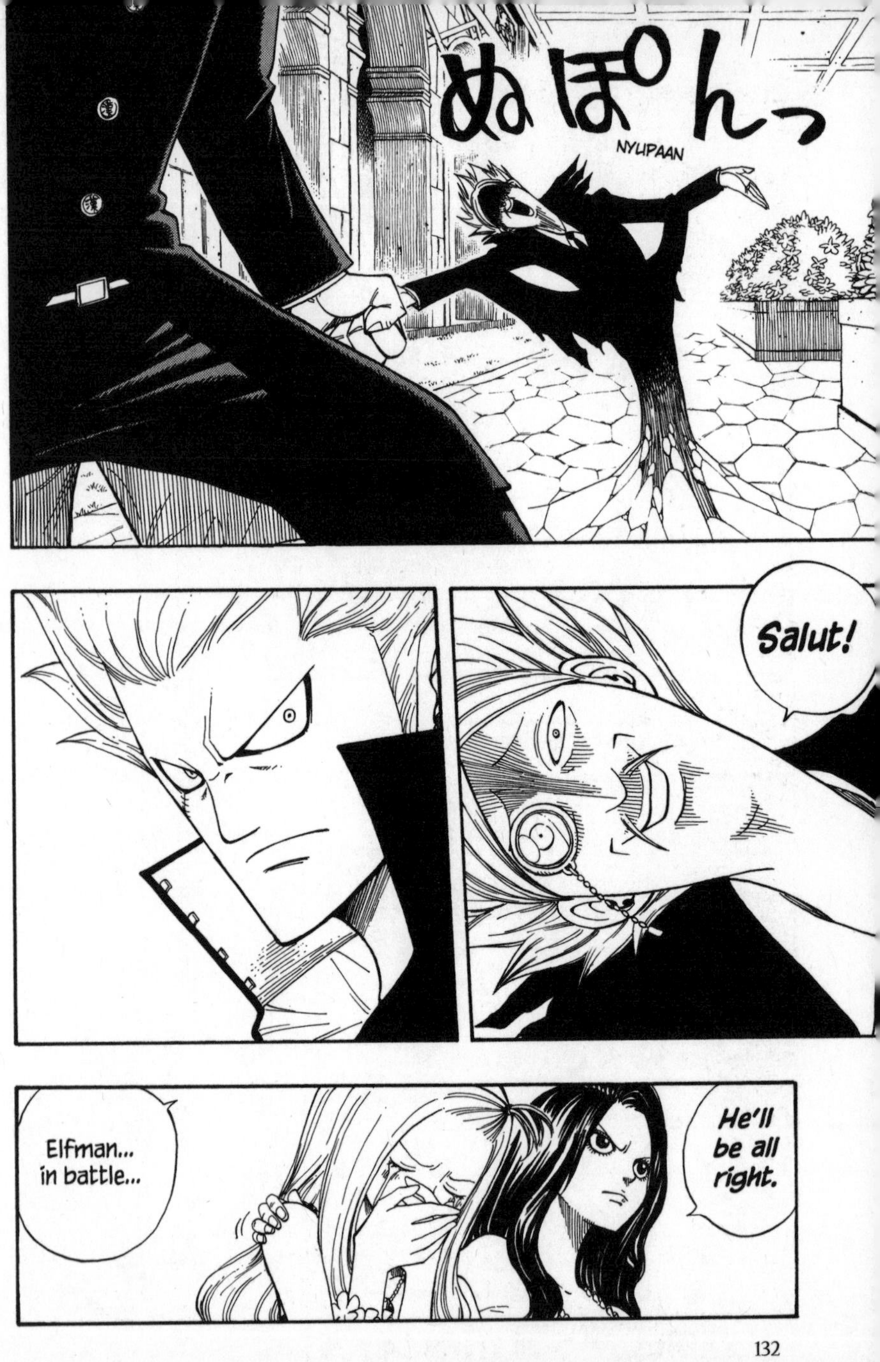
ぬぽんっ
NYUPAAN
Salut!
He'll be all right.
Elfman... in battle...

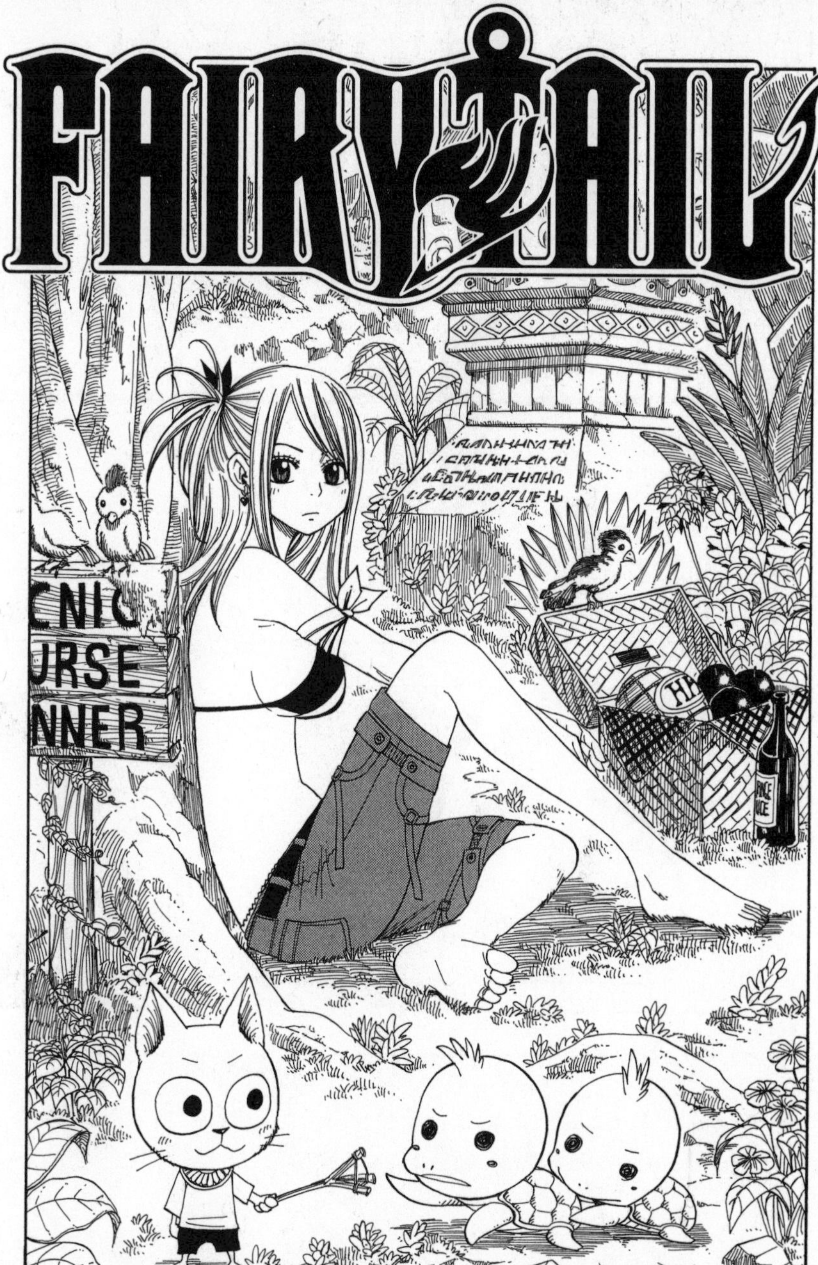
FAIRY TAIL
CNIC
URSE
NNER

Chapter 55:
So No One Sees the Tears

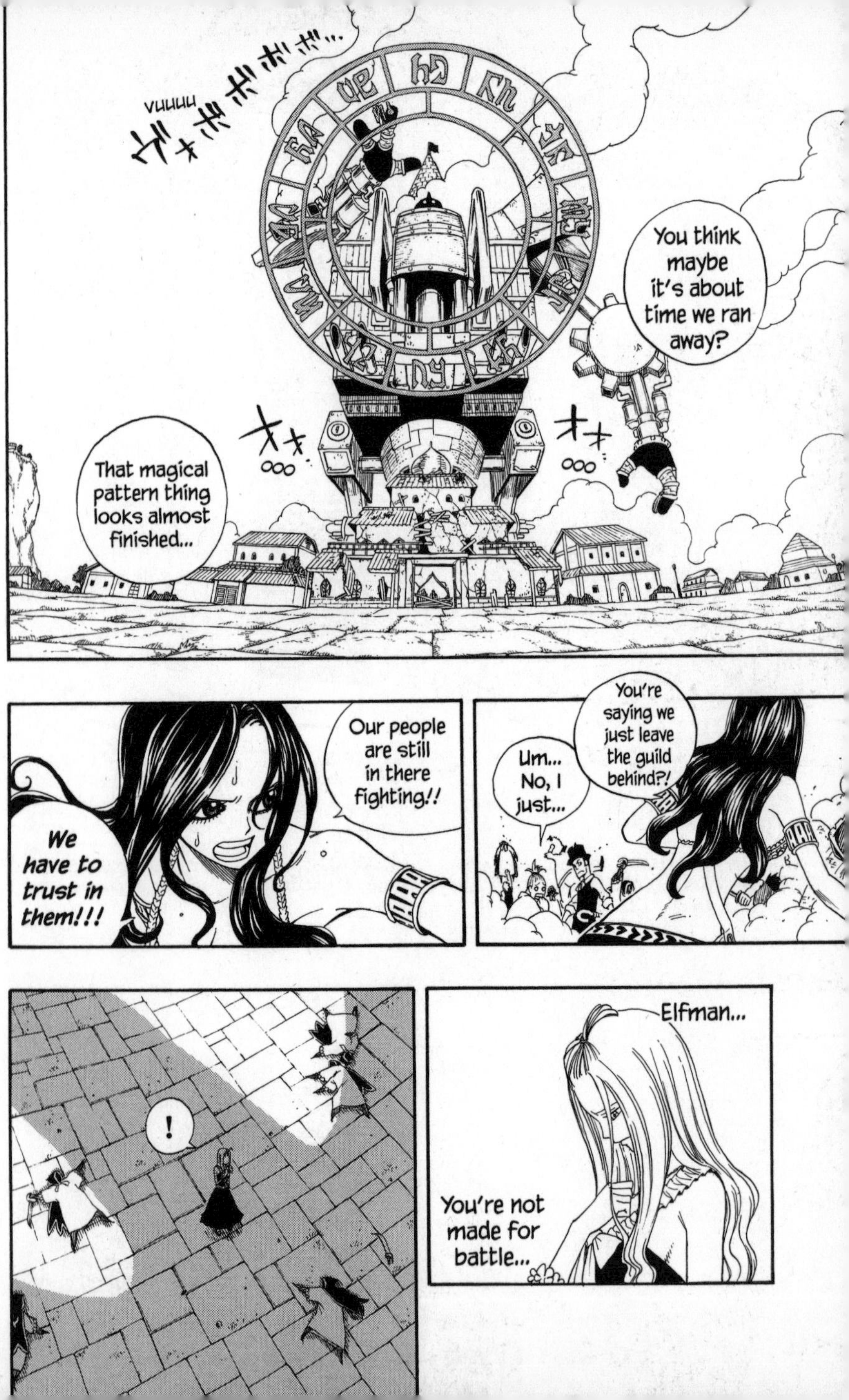
VUUUU
You think maybe it's about time we ran away?
That magical pattern thing looks almost finished...
You're saying we just leave the guild behind?!
Um... No, I just...
Our people are still in there fighting!!
We have to trust in them!!!
Elfman...
You're not made for battle...
!

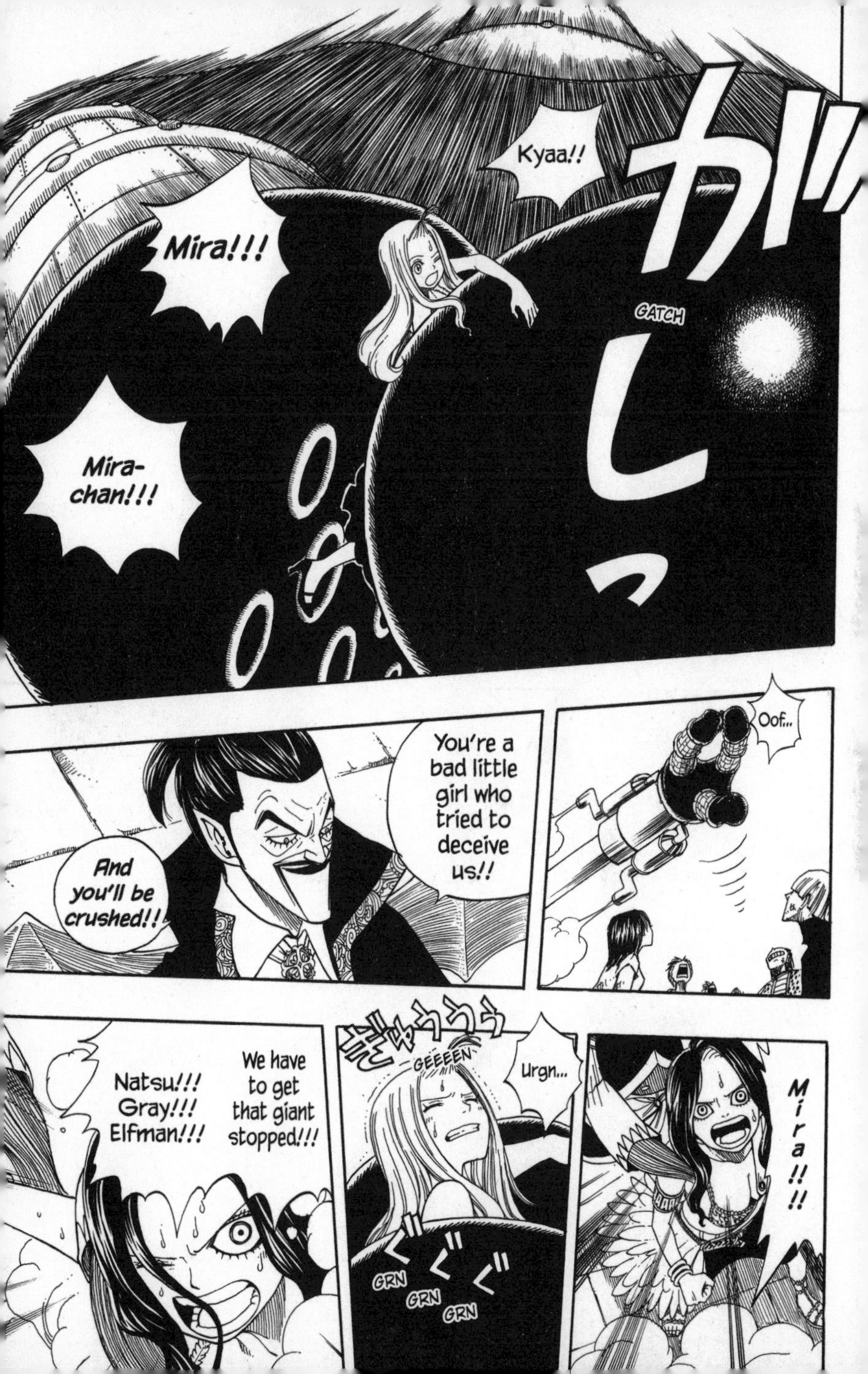

GATCH
Kyaa!!
Mira!!!
Mira-chan!!!
Oof...
You're a bad little girl who tried to deceive us!!
And you'll be crushed!!
Mira!!!!
GEEEEN
Urgn...
GRN GRN GRN
We have to get that giant stopped!!!
Natsu!!! Gray!!! Elfman!!!

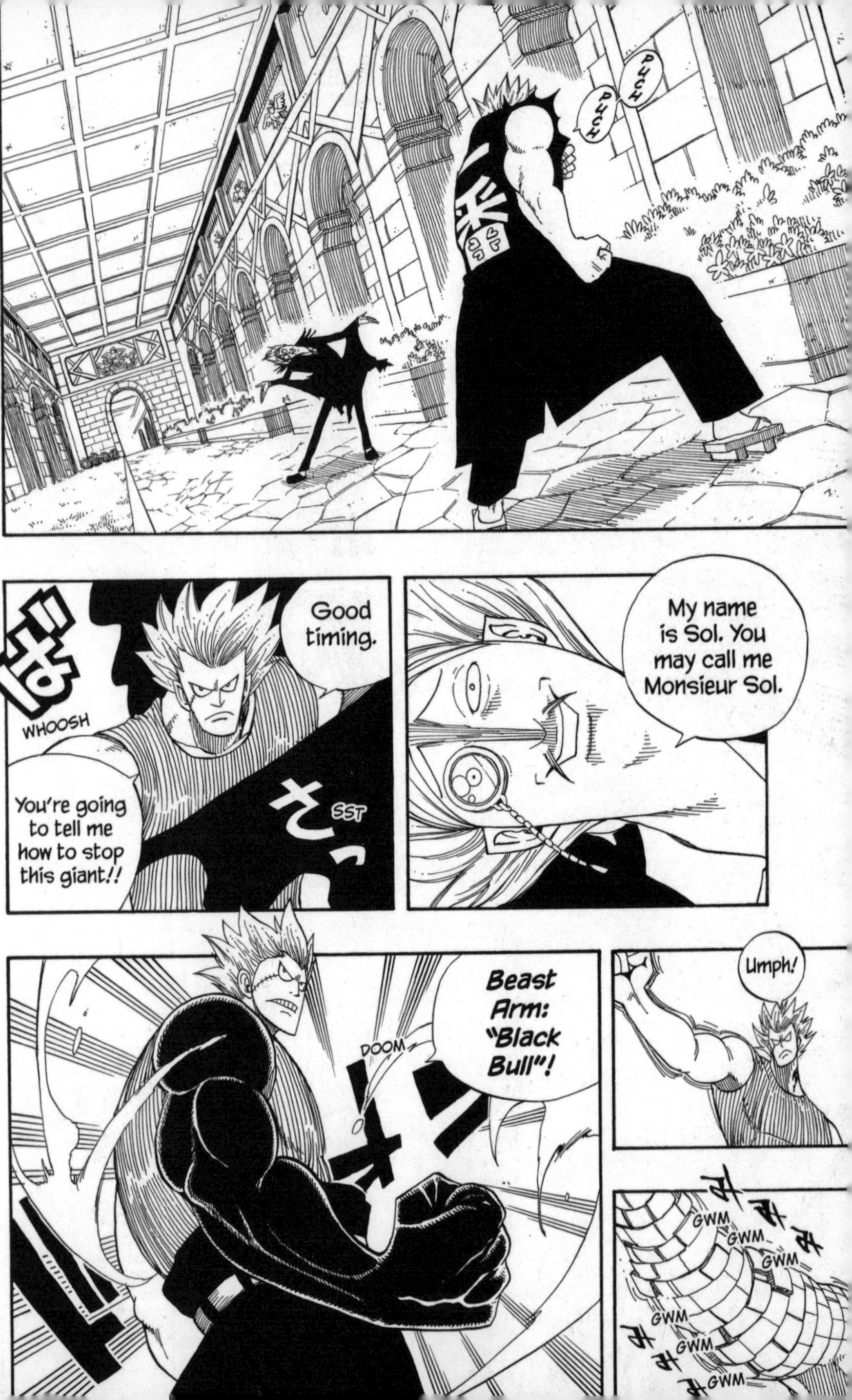
PUCH
PUCH
My name is Sol. You may call me Monsieur Sol.
Good timing.
WHOOSH
You're going to tell me how to stop this giant!!
SST
Umph!
GWM GWM GWM GWM GWM GWM GWM
Beast Arm: "Black Bull"!
DOOM

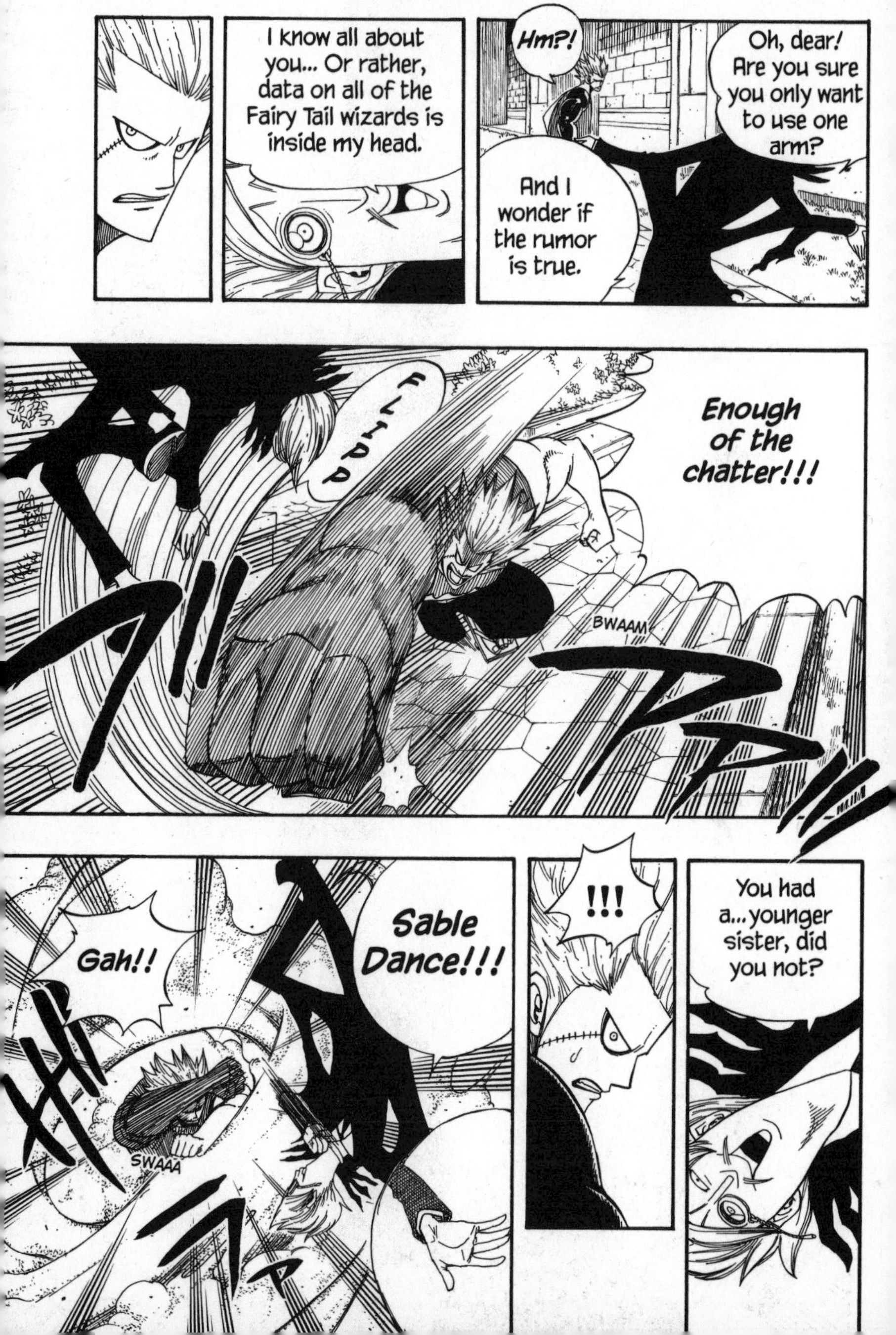
Oh, dear! Are you sure you only want to use one arm?
Hm?!
And I wonder if the rumor is true.
I know all about you... Or rather, data on all of the Fairy Tail wizards is inside my head.
Enough of the chatter!!!
FLIPP
BWAAM
You had a...younger sister, did you not?
!!!
Sable Dance!!!
Gah!!
SWAAA

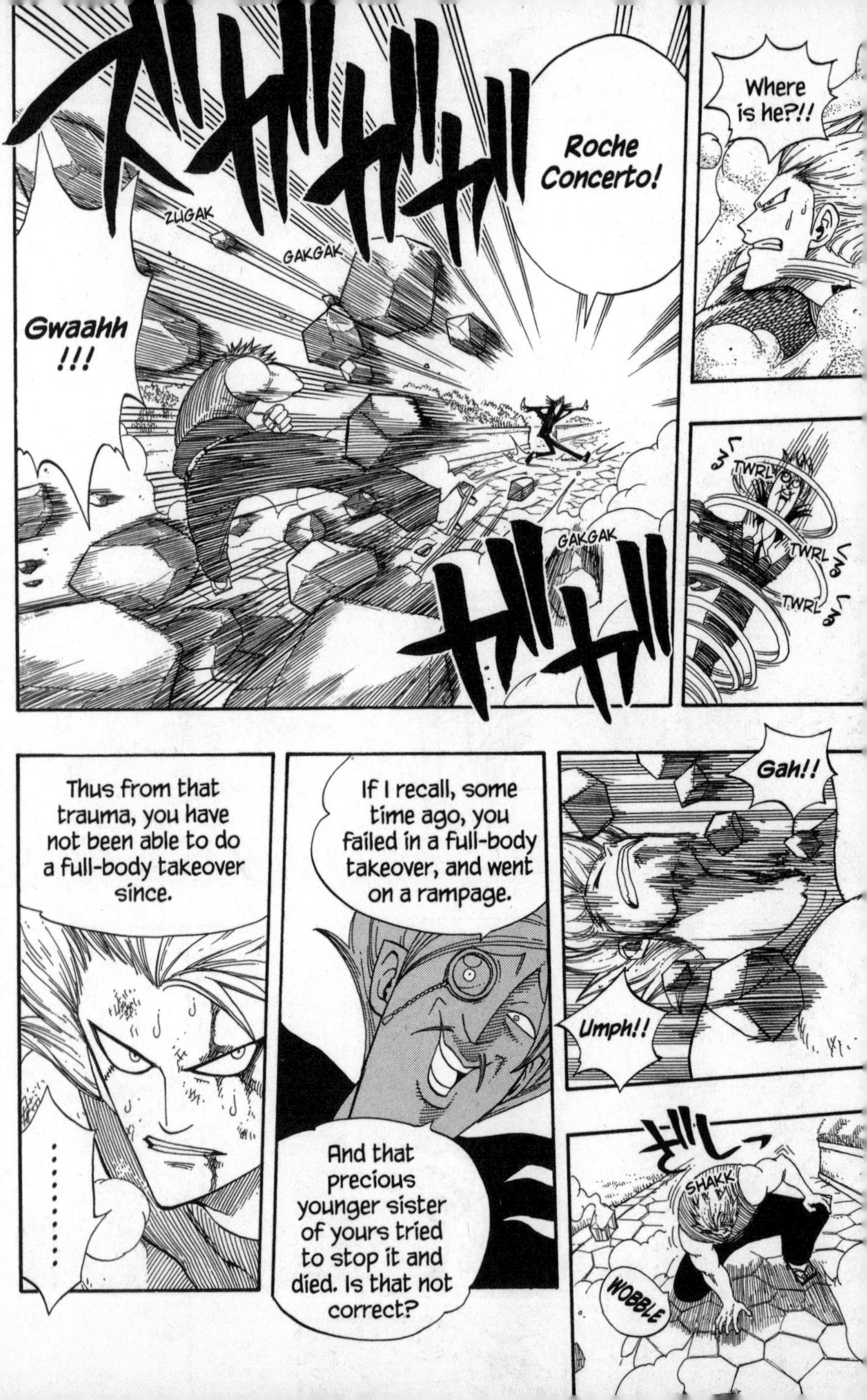
Where is he?!!
TWRL
TWRL
TWRL
Roche Concerto!
ZUGAK
GAKGAK
Gwaahh!!!
GAKGAK
Gah!!
Umph!!
SHAKK
WOBBLE
If I recall, some time ago, you failed in a full-body takeover, and went on a rampage.
And that precious younger sister of yours tried to stop it and died. Is that not correct?
Thus from that trauma, you have not been able to do a full-body takeover since.
....

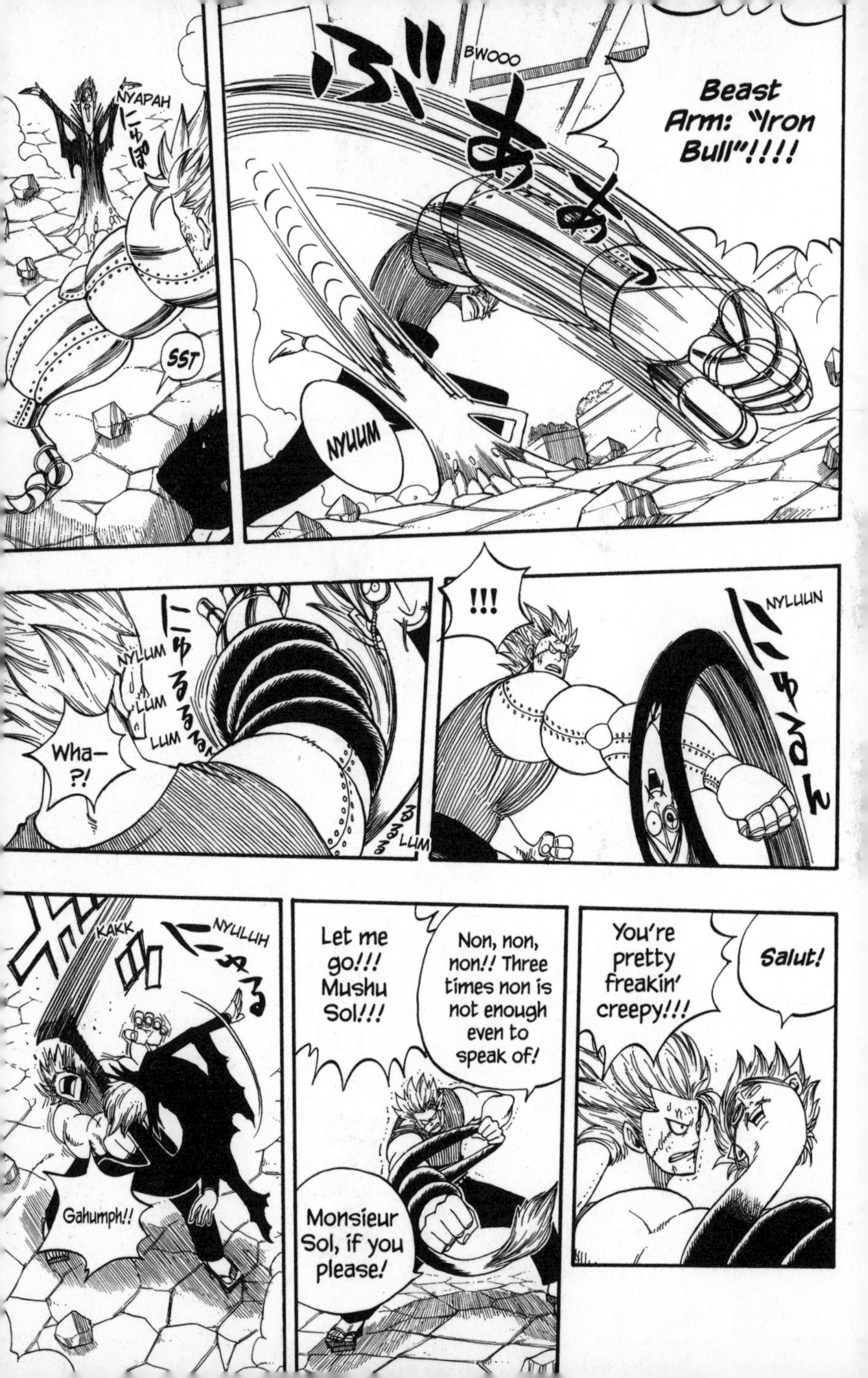

BWOOO
Beast Arm: "Iron Bull"!!!!
NYUUM
NYAPAH
SST
!!!
NYLUUN
NYLUM
LUM
LUM
Wha-?!
LUM
Salut!
You're pretty freakin' creepy!!!
Non, non, non!! Three times non is not enough even to speak of!
Let me go!!! Mushu Sol!!!
Monsieur Sol, if you please!
KAKK
NYULUH
Gahumph!!

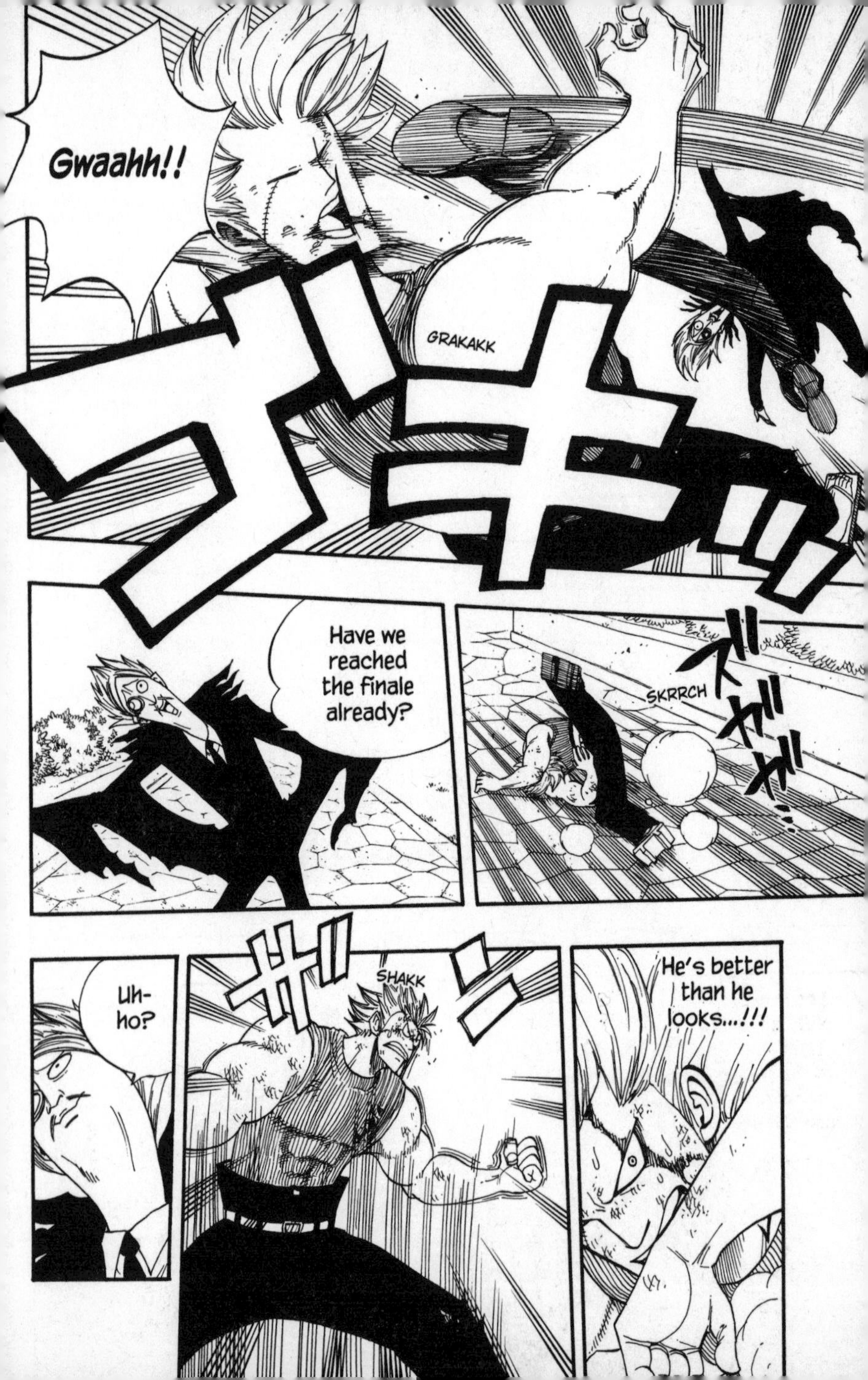
Gwaahh!!
GRAKAKK
SKRRCH
Have we reached the finale already?
He's better than he looks...!!!
SHAKK
Uh-ho?

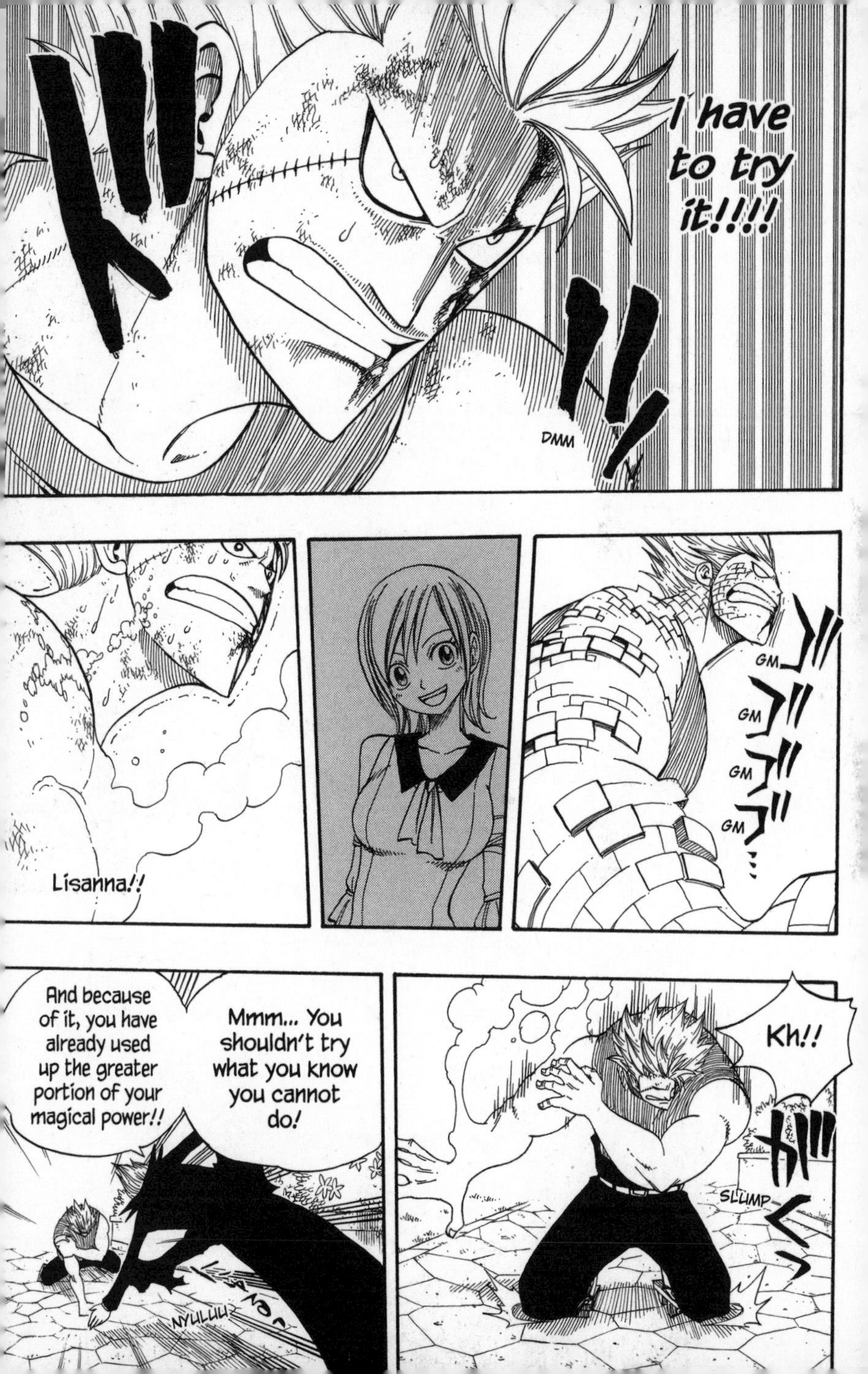
I have to try it!!!!
DMM
GM
GM
GM
GM
Lisanna!!
Kh!!
SLUMP
Mmm... You shouldn't try what you know you cannot do!
And because of it, you have already used up the greater portion of your magical power!!
NYULUU

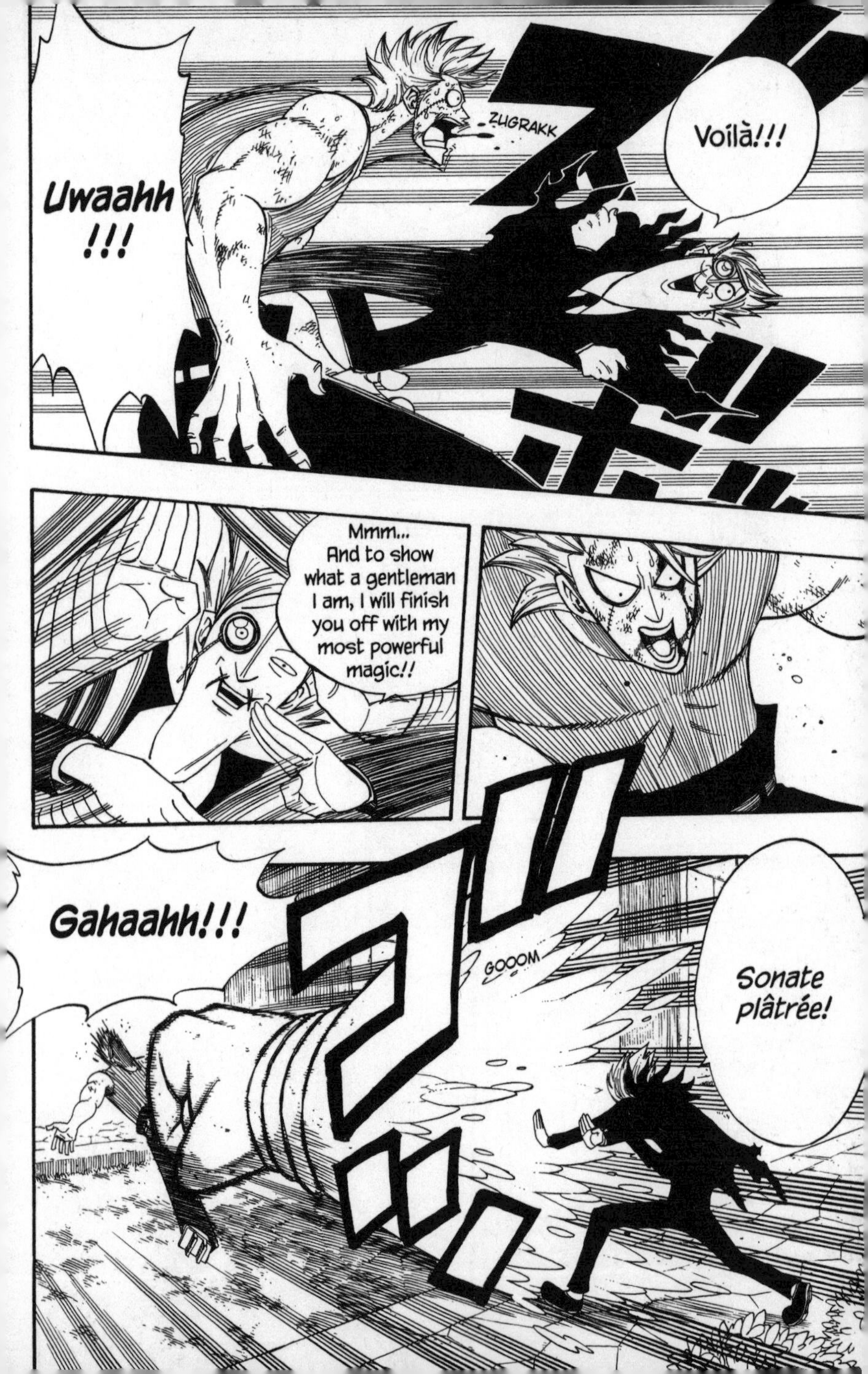
Voilà!!!
ZUGRAKK
Uwaahh !!!
Mmm... And to show what a gentleman I am, I will finish you off with my most powerful magic!!
Sonate plâtrée!
GOOOM
Gahaahh!!!

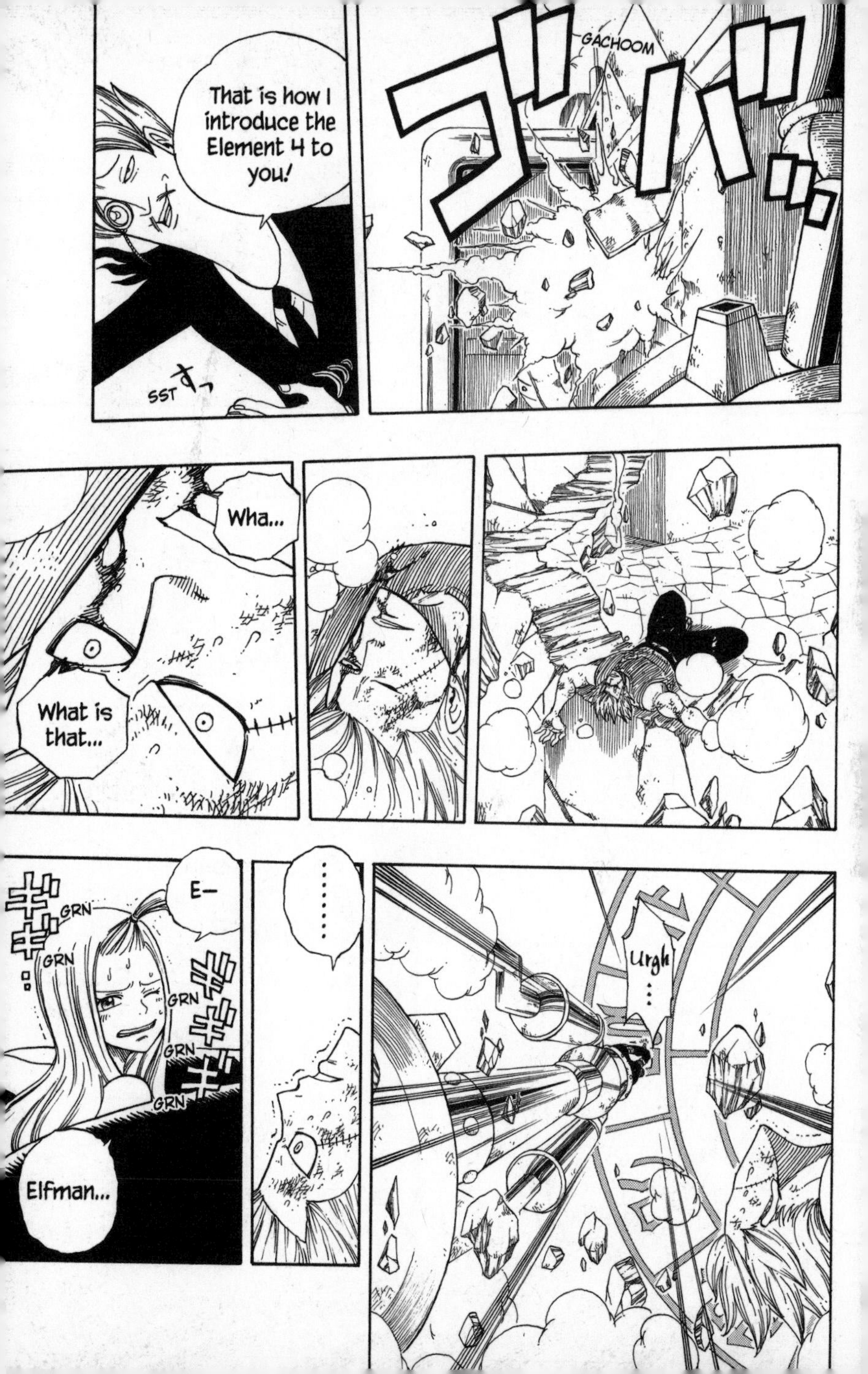
GACHOOM
That is how I introduce the Element 4 to you!
SST
Wha...
What is that...
Urgh...
....
E–
GRN
GRN
GRN
GRN
GRN
Elfman...

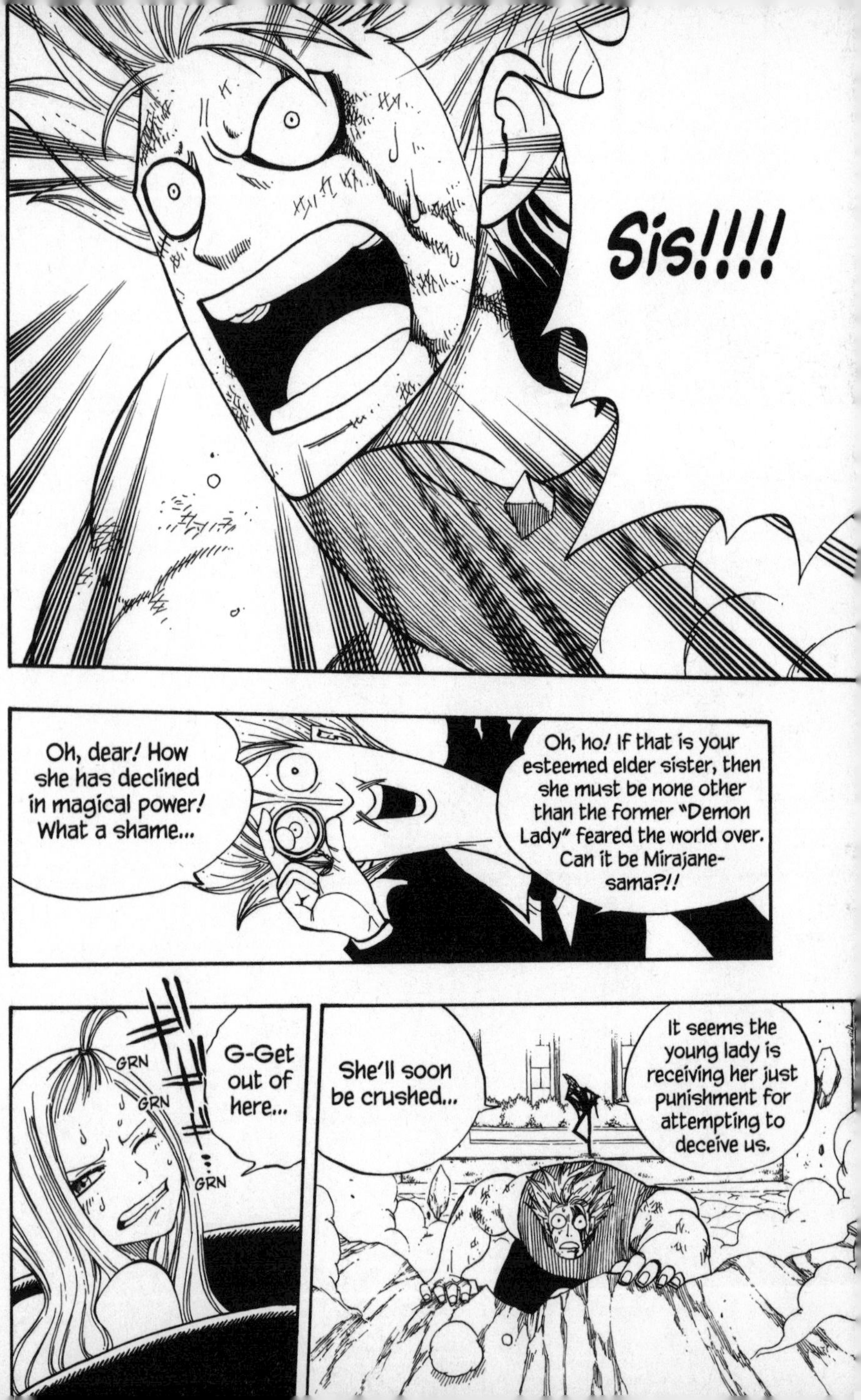
Sis!!!!
Oh, ho! If that is your esteemed elder sister, then she must be none other than the former "Demon Lady" feared the world over. Can it be Mirajane-sama?!!
Oh, dear! How she has declined in magical power! What a shame...
It seems the young lady is receiving her just punishment for attempting to deceive us.
She'll soon be crushed...
GRN
GRN
GRN
G-Get out of here...

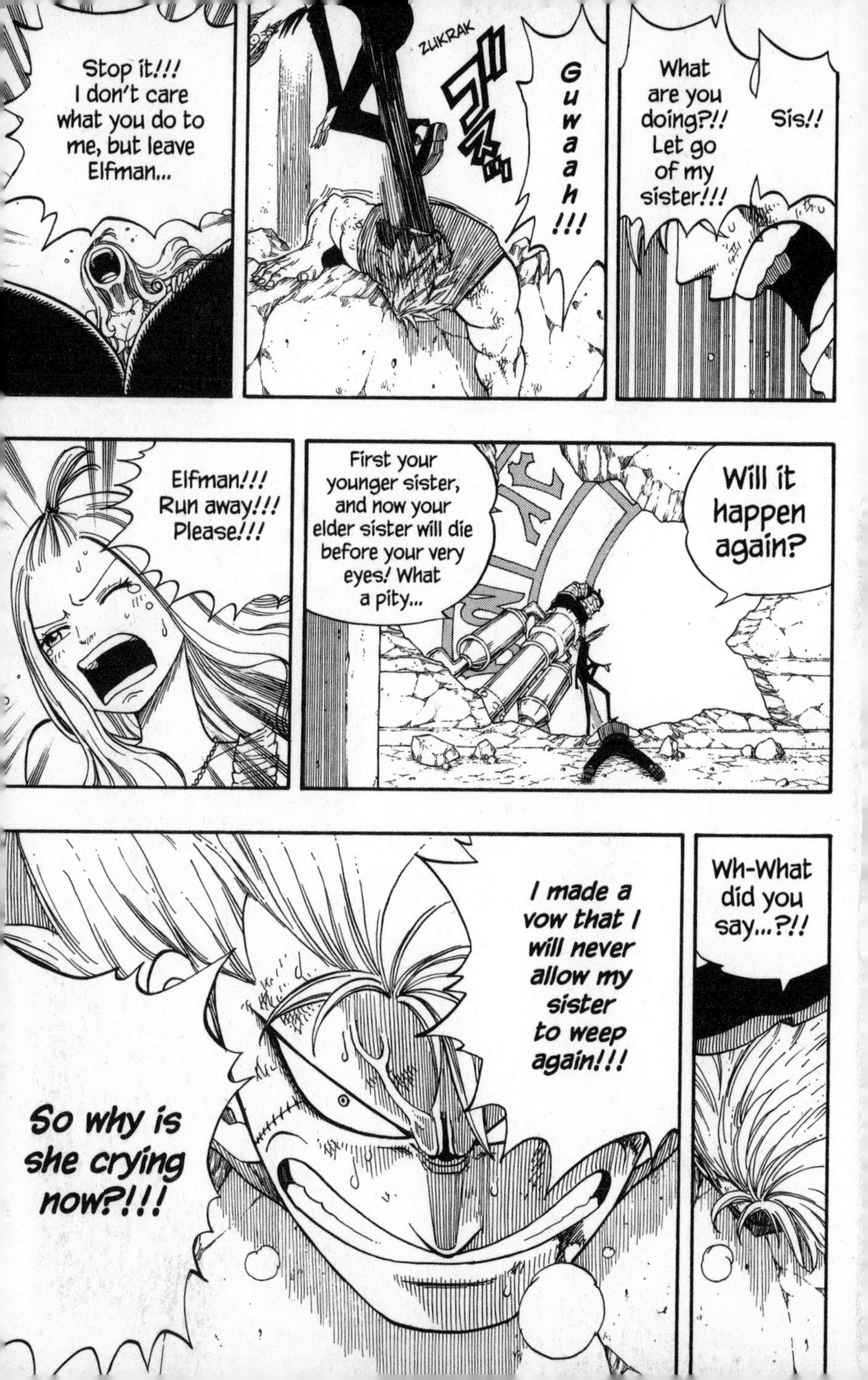
Sis!!
What are you doing?!! Let go of my sister!!!
ZUKRAK
Guwaah!!!
Stop it!!! I don't care what you do to me, but leave Elfman...
Will it happen again?
First your younger sister, and now your elder sister will die before your very eyes! What a pity...
Elfman!!! Run away!!! Please!!!
Wh-What did you say...?!!
I made a vow that I will never allow my sister to weep again!!!
So why is she crying now?!!!

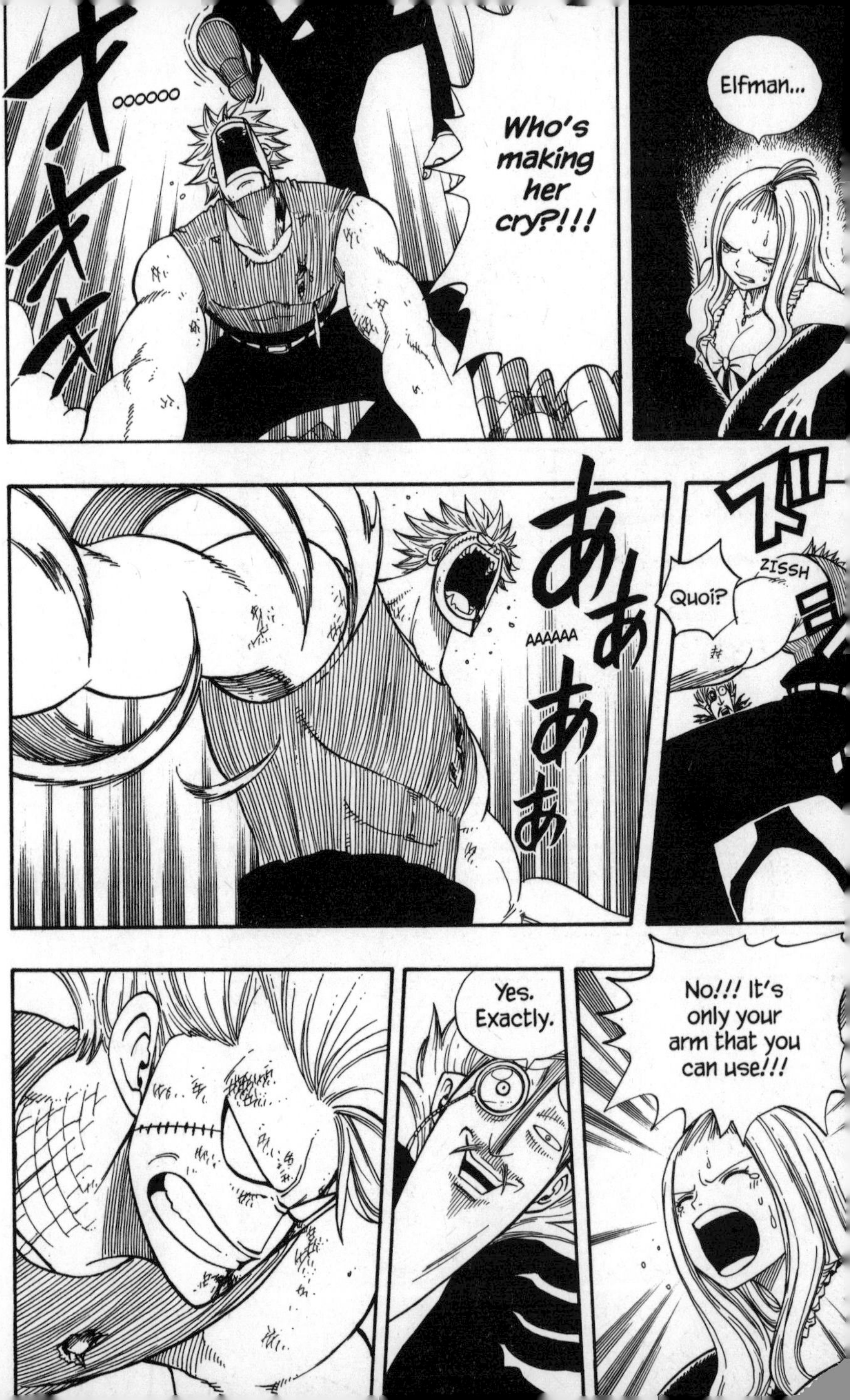

Elfman...
オォォォ
OOOOOO
Who's making her cry?!!!
ズ
ZISSH
Quoi?
ああああ
AAAAAA
No!!! It's only your arm that you can use!!!
Yes. Exactly.

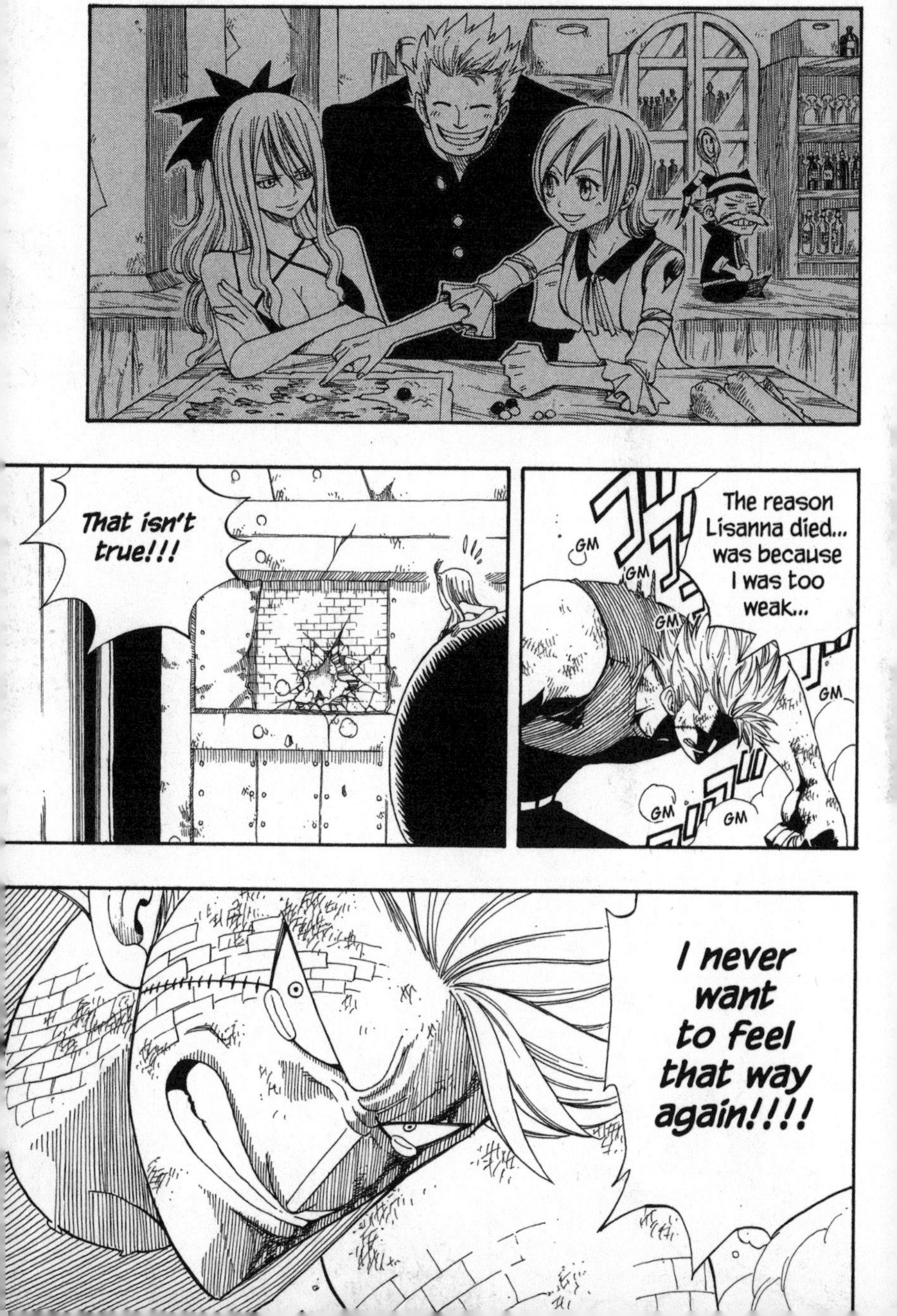
The reason Lisanna died... was because I was too weak...
GM
GM
GM
GM
GM
GM
That isn't true!!!
I never want to feel that way again!!!!

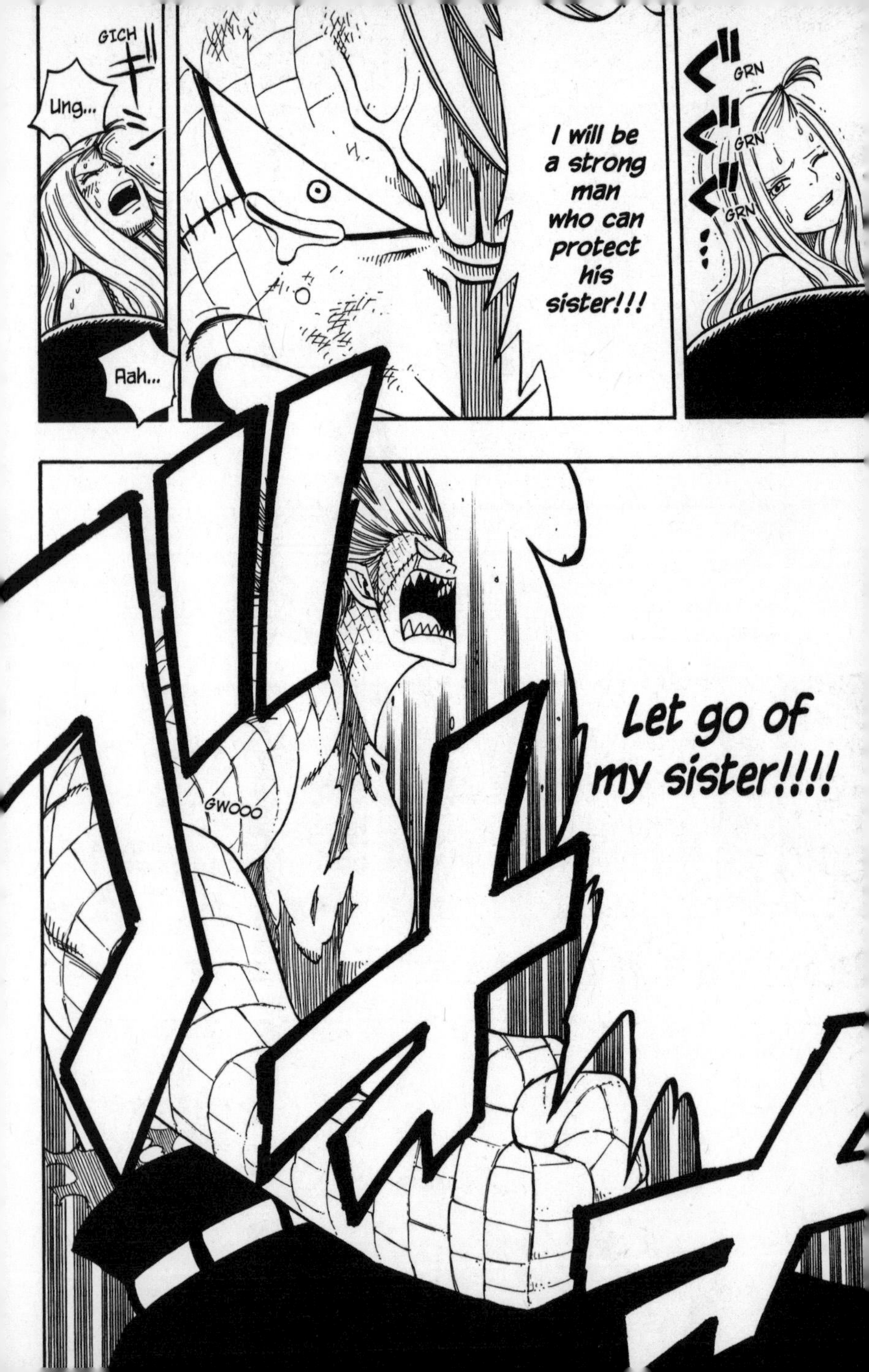
GRN
GRN
GRN
I will be a strong man who can protect his sister!!!
GICH
Ung...
Aah...
Let go of my sister!!!!
GWOOO

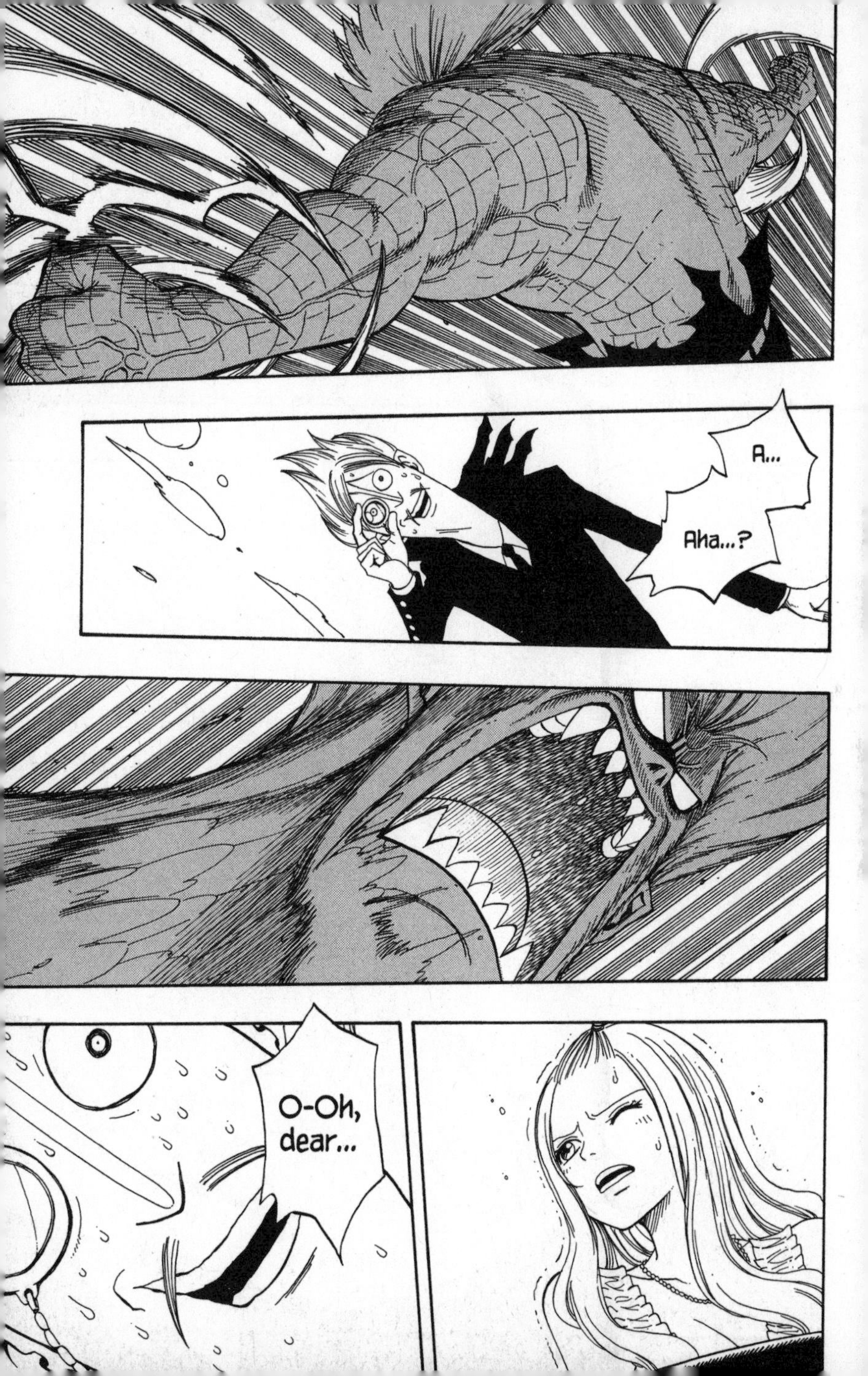
A...
Aha...?
O-Oh, dear...

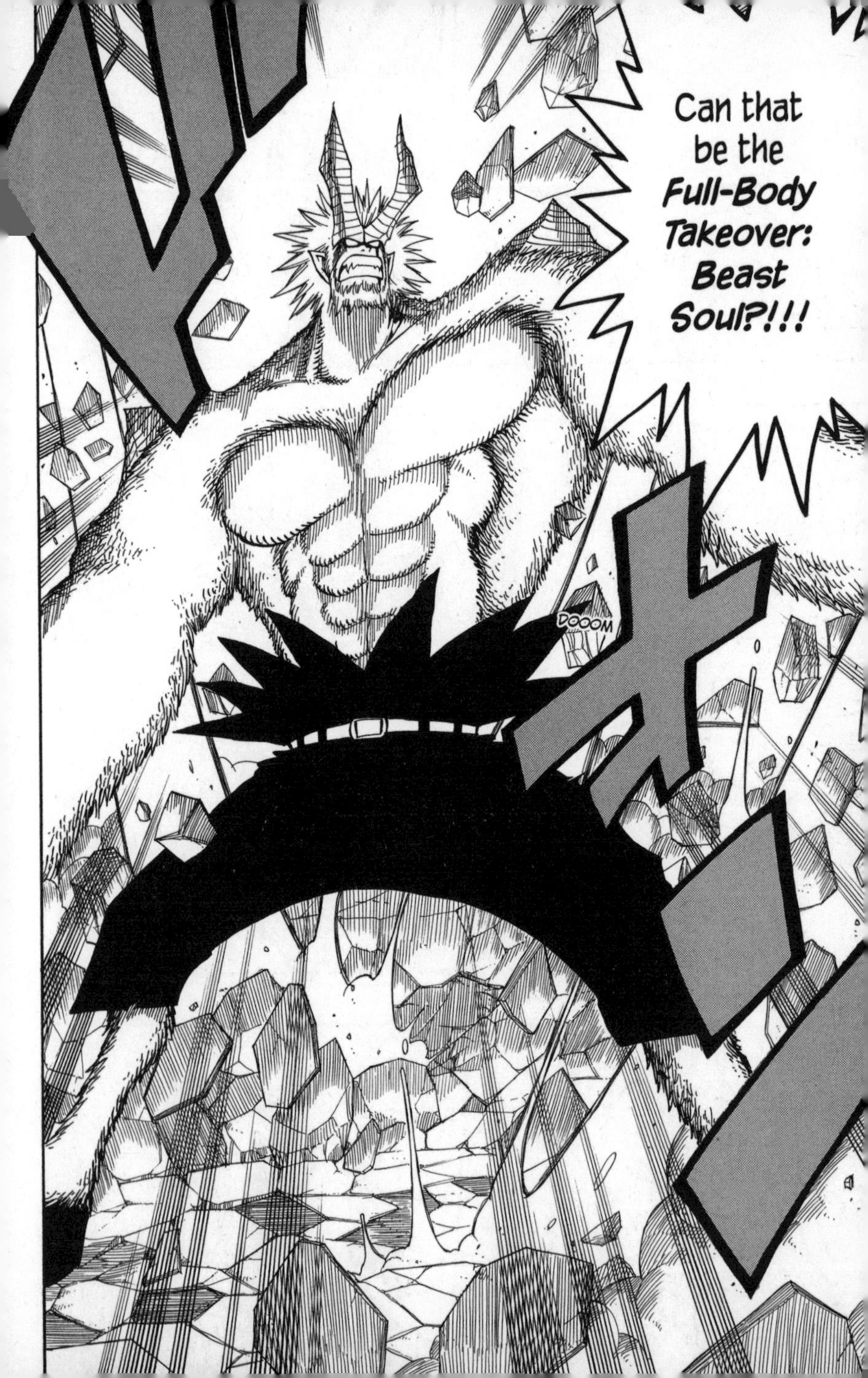
Can that be the *Full-Body Takeover: Beast Soul?!!!*
DOOOM

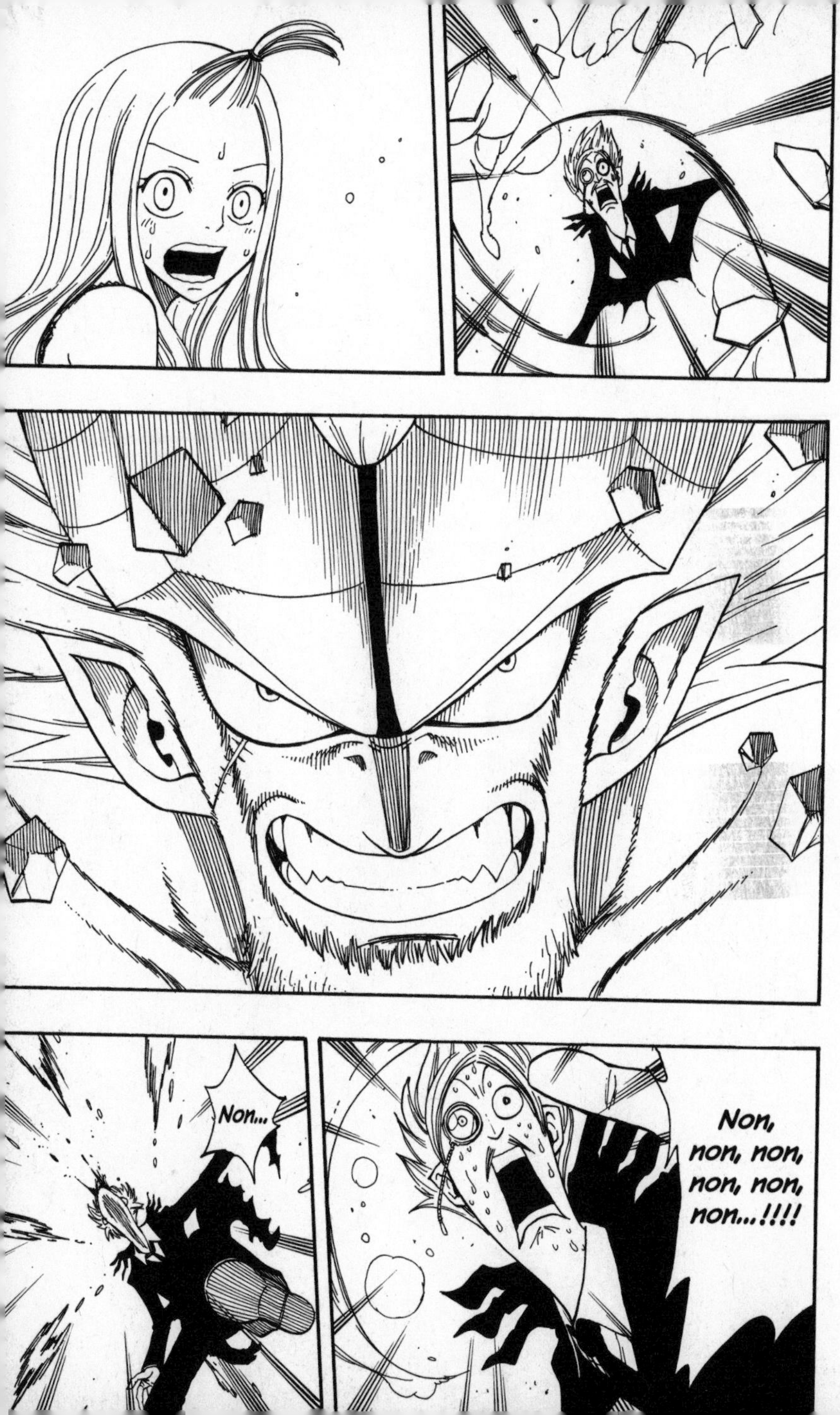
Non, non, non, non, non, non...!!!!
Non...

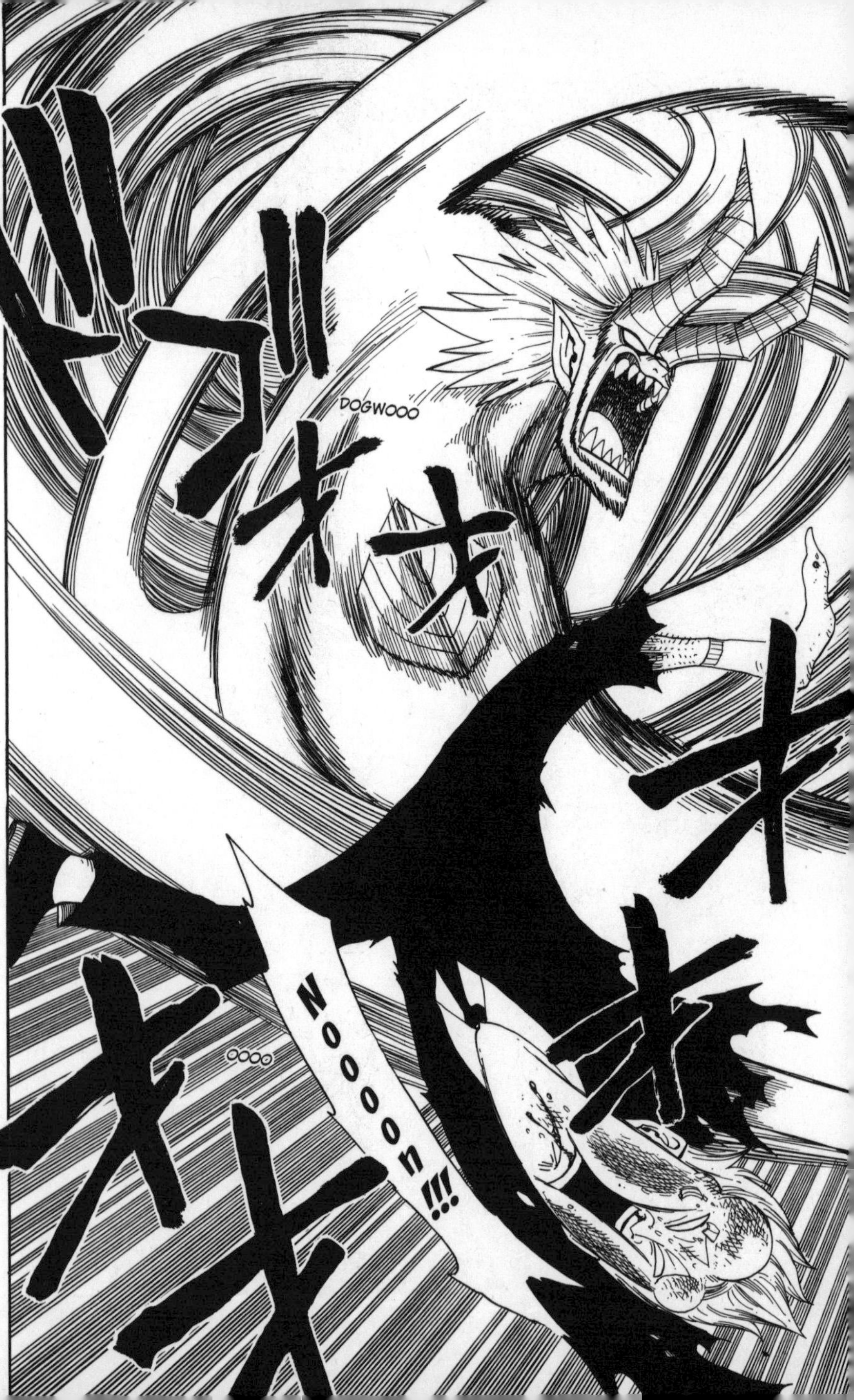
DOGWOOO
Nooooon!!!
oooo

FAIRY TAIL

Chapter 56: A Flower Blooms in the Rain

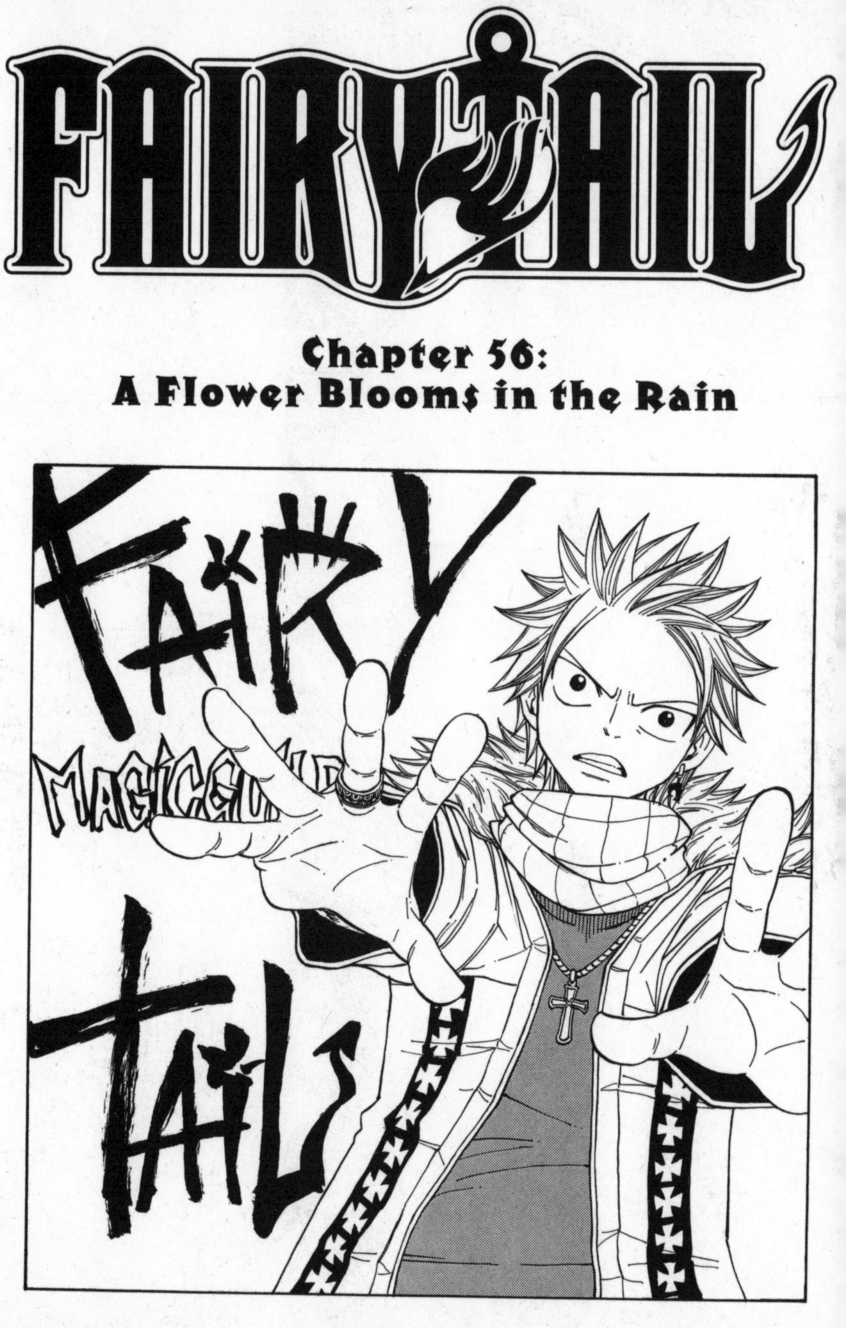
FAIRY
TAIL

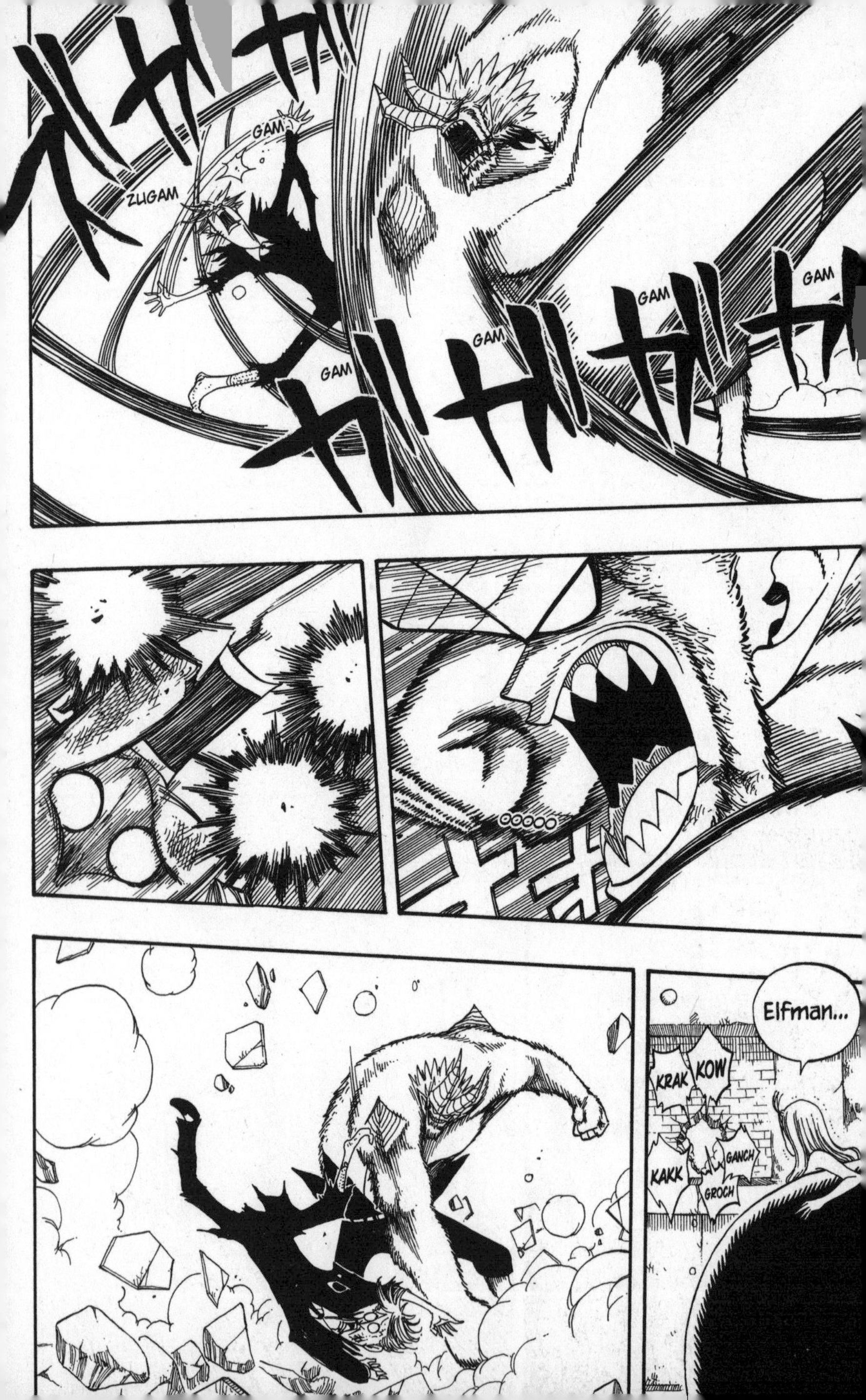
GAM
GAM
GAM
GAM
GAM
ZUGAM
Elfman...
KOW
KRAK
GANCH
KAKK
GROCH

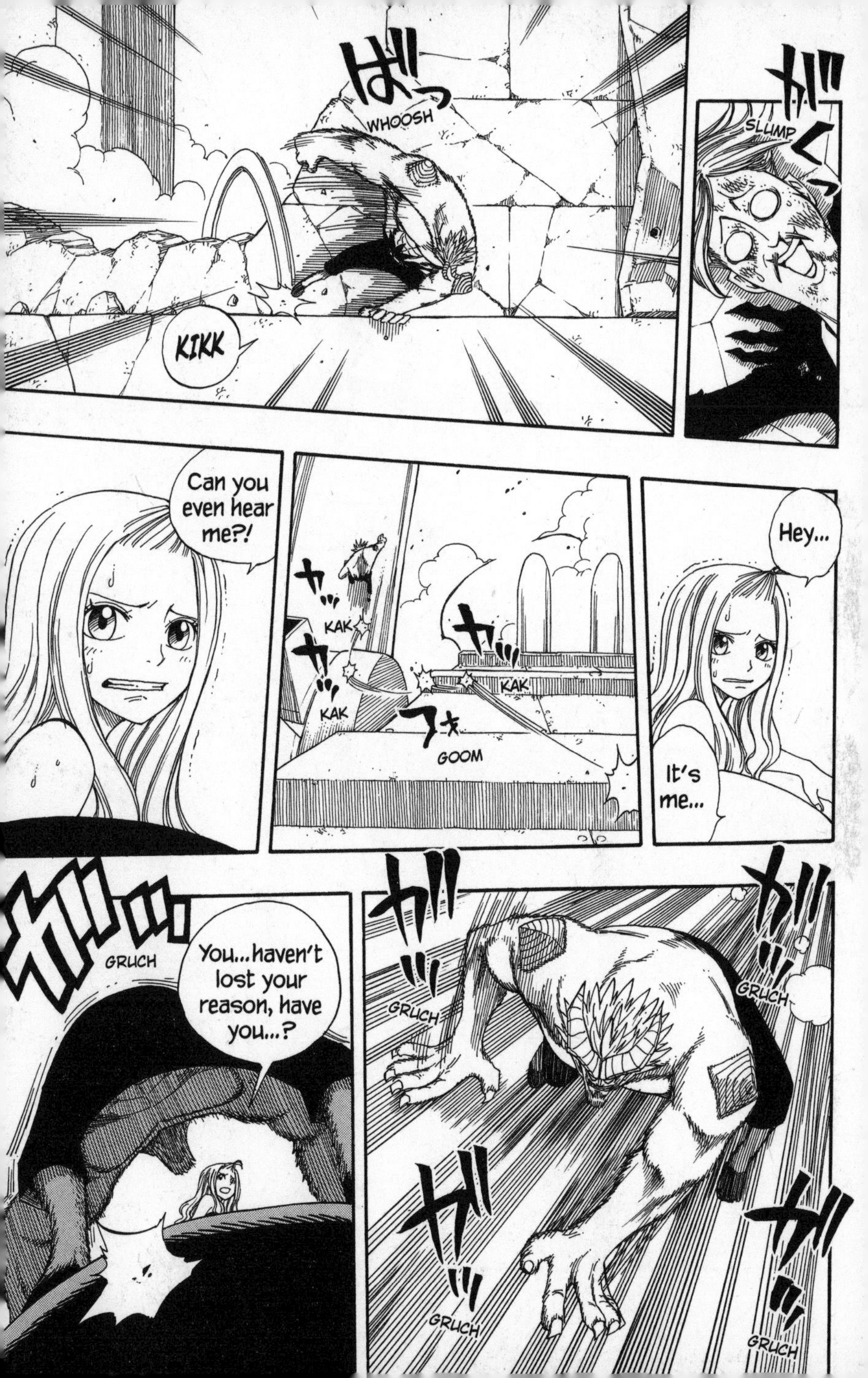
SLUMP
WHOOSH
KIKK
Hey...
It's me...
KAK
KAK
KAK
GOOM
Can you even hear me?!
GRUCH
GRUCH
GRUCH
GRUCH
GRUCH
You...haven't lost your reason, have you...?

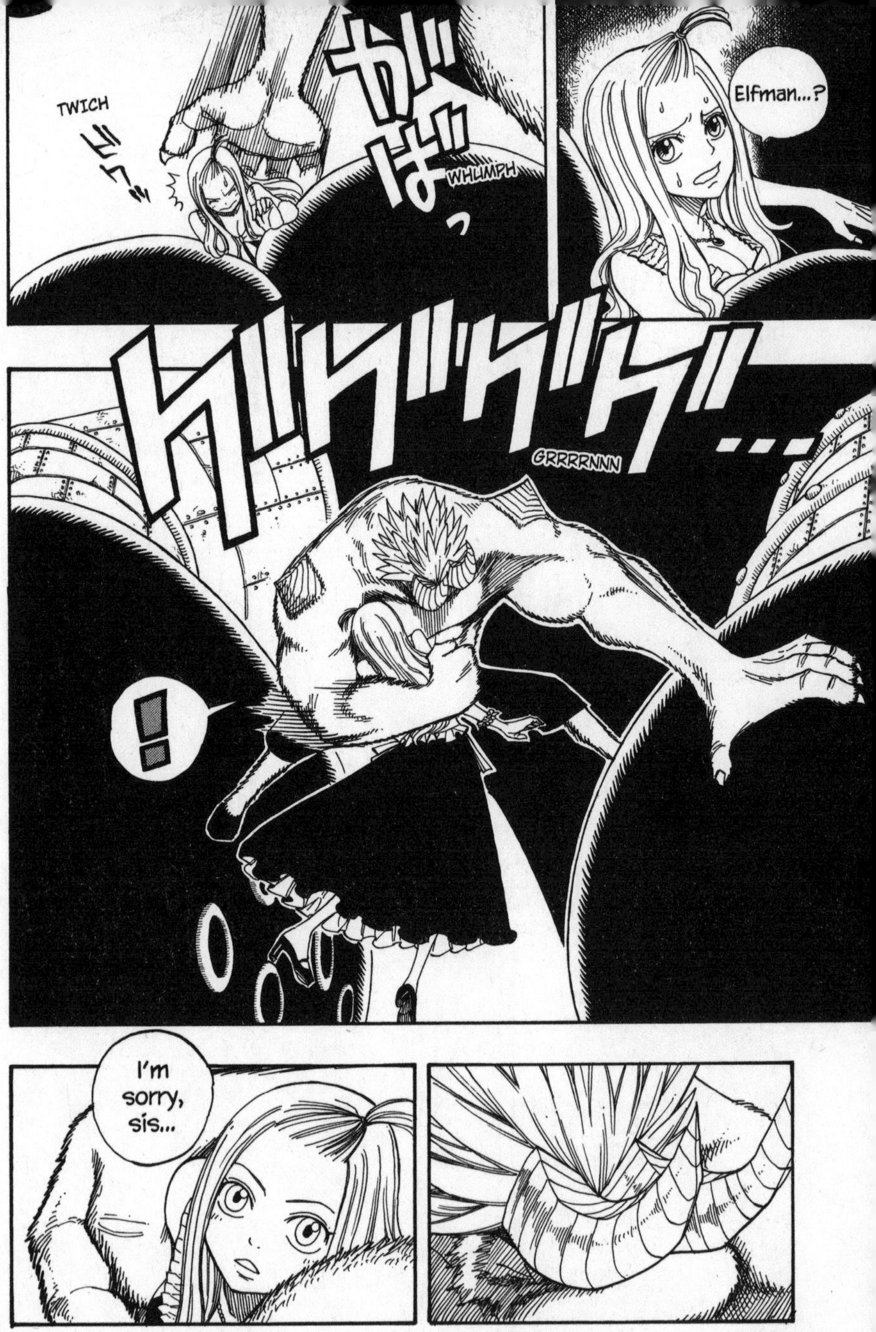

Elfman...?
TWICH
WHUMPH
GRRRRNNN
!
I'm sorry, sis...

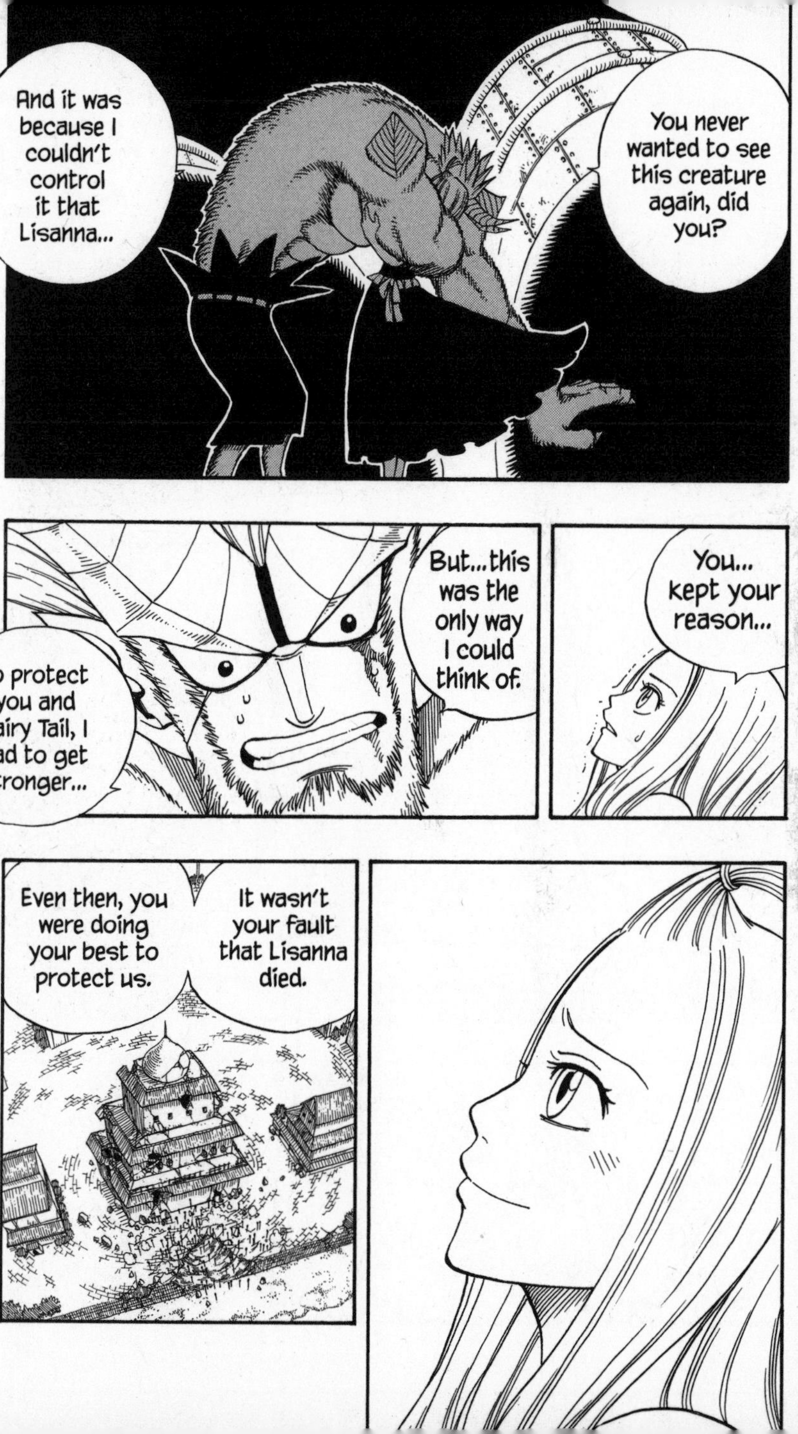
You never wanted to see this creature again, did you?
And it was because I couldn't control it that Lisanna...
You... kept your reason...
But...this was the only way I could think of.
To protect you and Fairy Tail, I had to get stronger...
It wasn't your fault that Lisanna died.
Even then, you were doing your best to protect us.

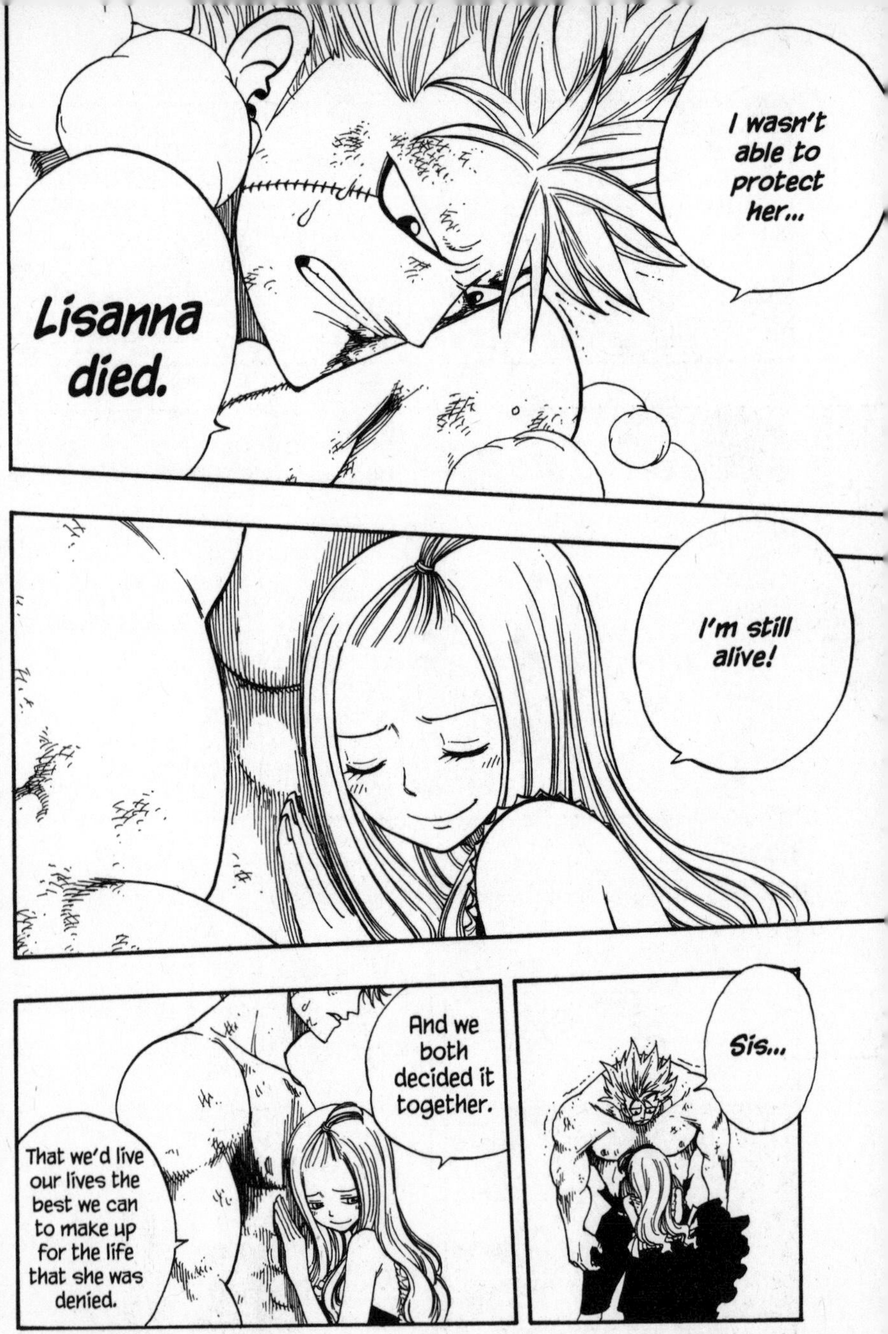
I wasn't able to protect her...
Lisanna died.
I'm still alive!
Sis...
And we both decided it together.
That we'd live our lives the best we can to make up for the life that she was denied.

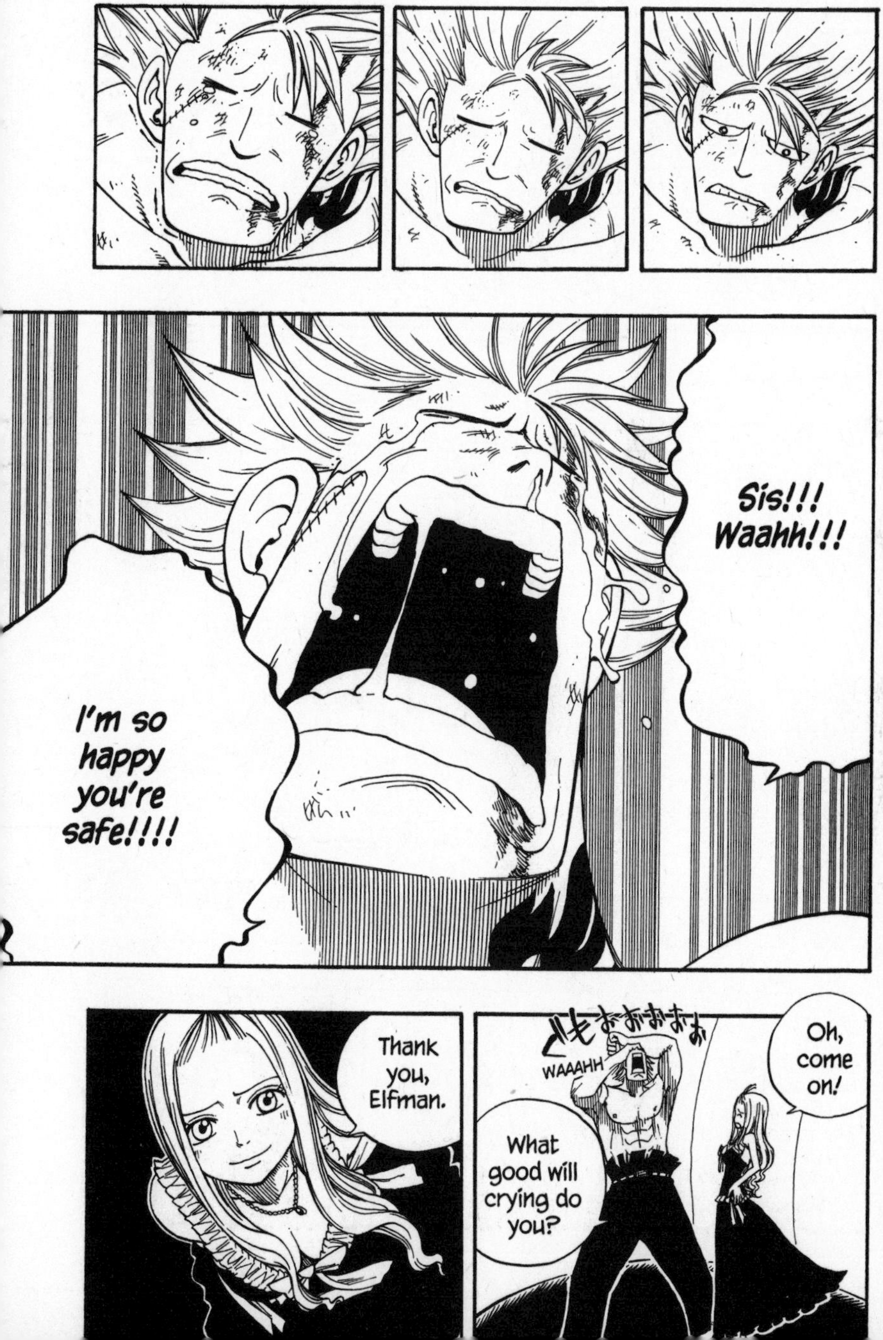
Sis!!! Waahh!!!
I'm so happy you're safe!!!!
Oh, come on!
WAAAHH
What good will crying do you?
Thank you, Elfman.

Wh-What is it, sis?!!

!

VUU
VUU
VUU VUU
VUU

The speed it's writing the pattern by...

It's slower than it used to be.

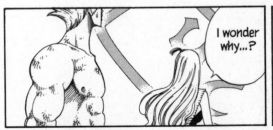

I wonder why...?

Eh?!

160

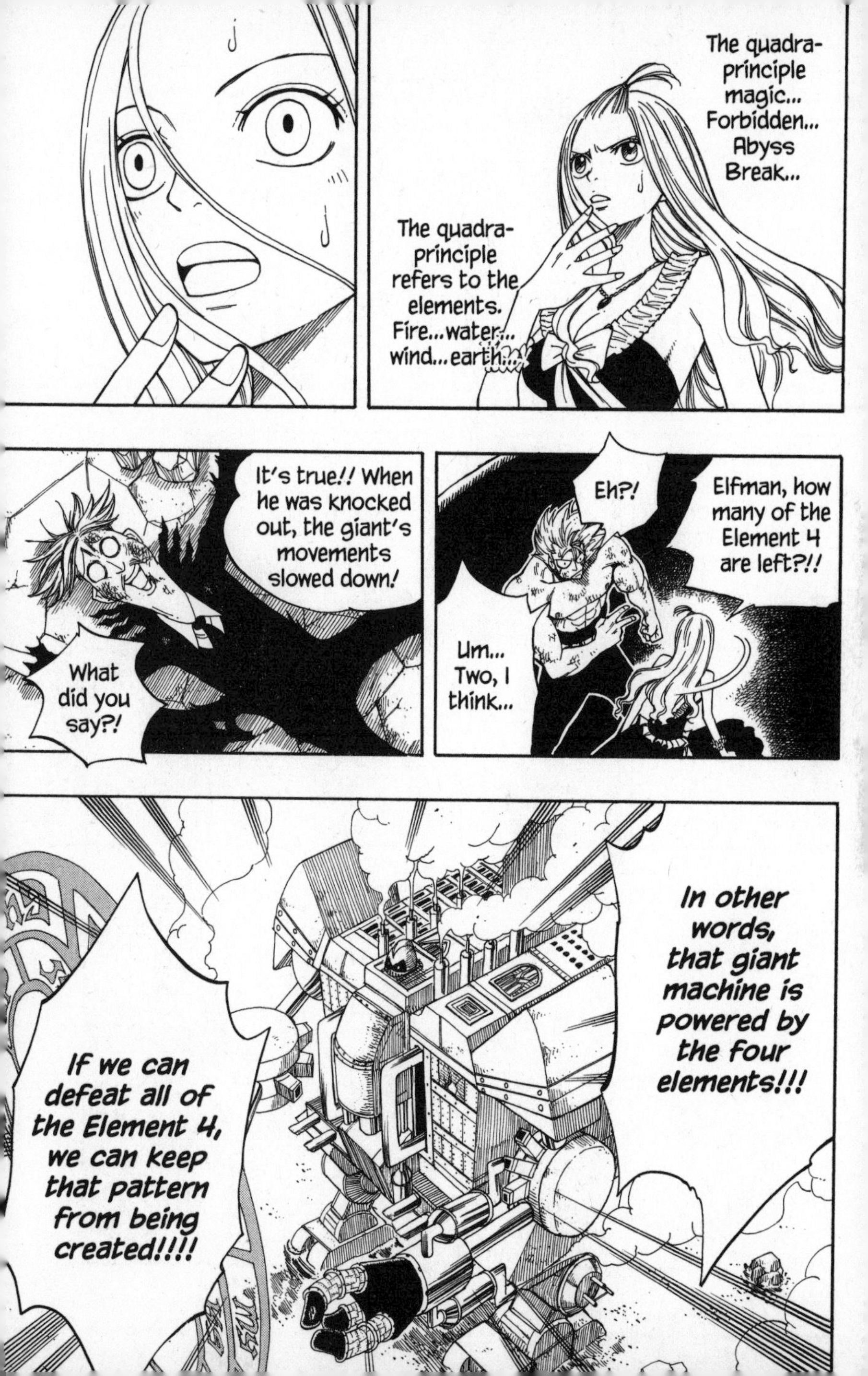
The quadra-principle magic... Forbidden... Abyss Break...
The quadra-principle refers to the elements. Fire...water... wind...earth...
Elfman, how many of the Element 4 are left?!!
Eh?!
Um... Two, I think...
It's true!! When he was knocked out, the giant's movements slowed down!
What did you say?!
In other words, that giant machine is powered by the four elements!!!
If we can defeat all of the Element 4, we can keep that pattern from being created!!!!

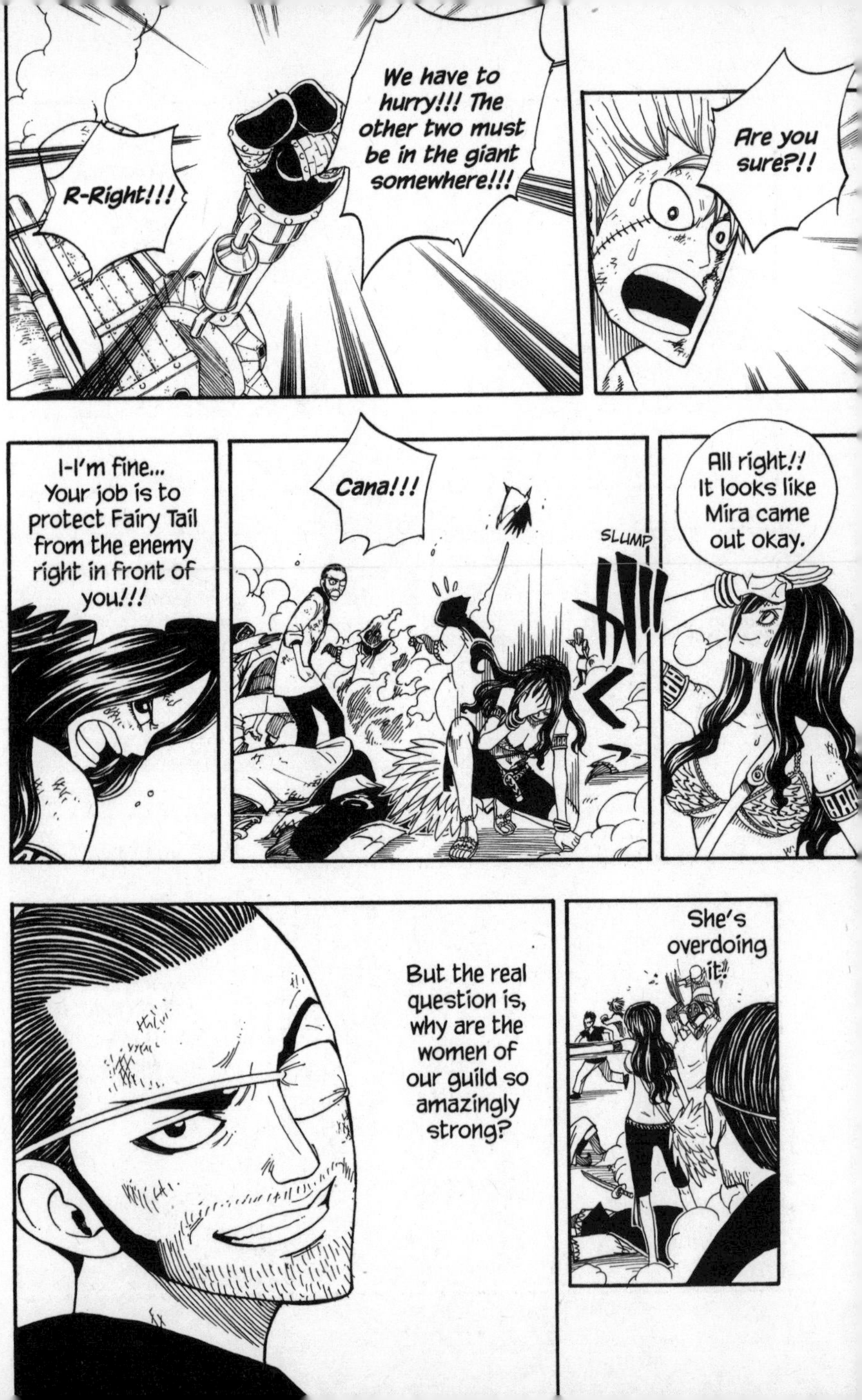
Are you sure?!!
We have to hurry!!! The other two must be in the giant somewhere!!!
R-Right!!!
All right!! It looks like Mira came out okay.
Cana!!!
SLUMP
I-I'm fine... Your job is to protect Fairy Tail from the enemy right in front of you!!!
She's overdoing it!!
But the real question is, why are the women of our guild so amazingly strong?

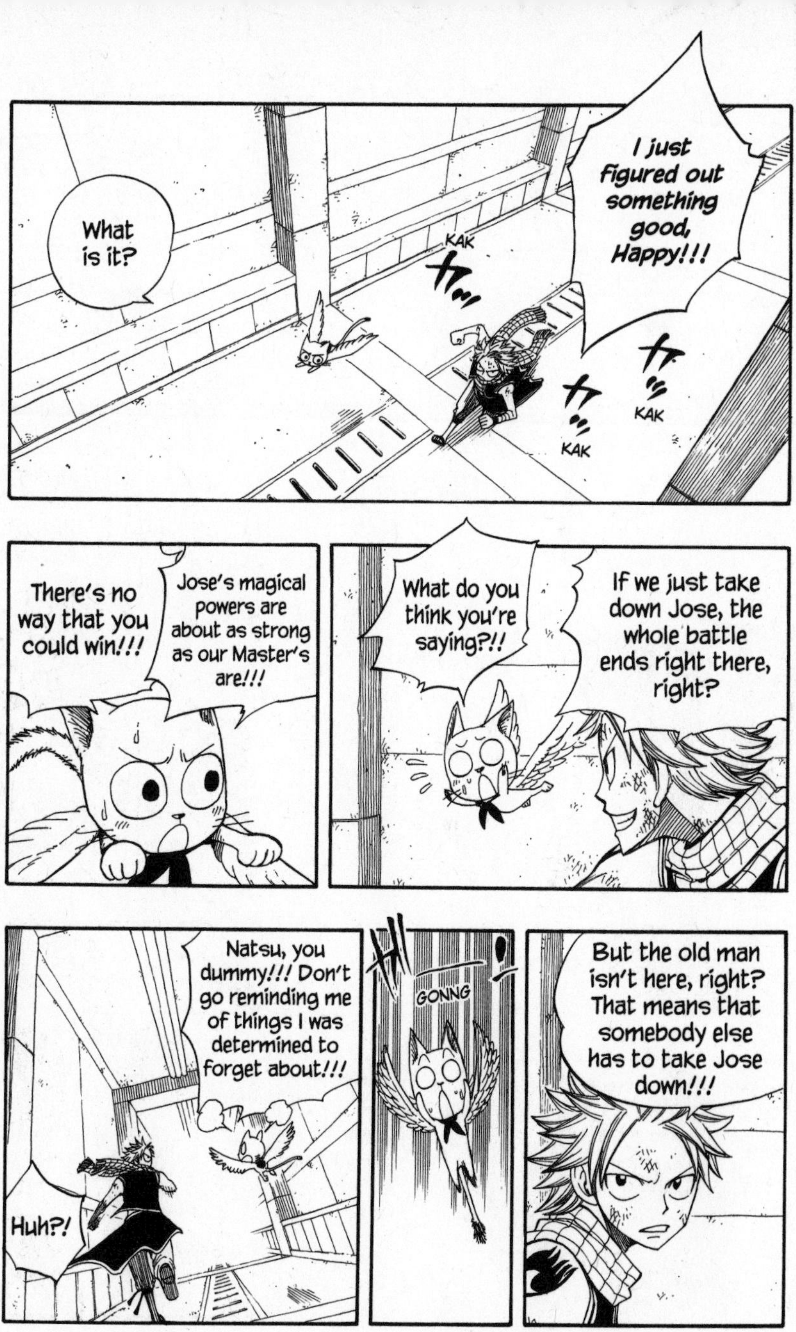
I just figured out something good, Happy!!!
KAK
KAK
KAK
What is it?
If we just take down Jose, the whole battle ends right there, right?
What do you think you're saying?!!
Jose's magical powers are about as strong as our Master's are!!!
There's no way that you could win!!!
But the old man isn't here, right? That means that somebody else has to take Jose down!!!
GONNG
Natsu, you dummy!!! Don't go reminding me of things I was determined to forget about!!!
Huh?!

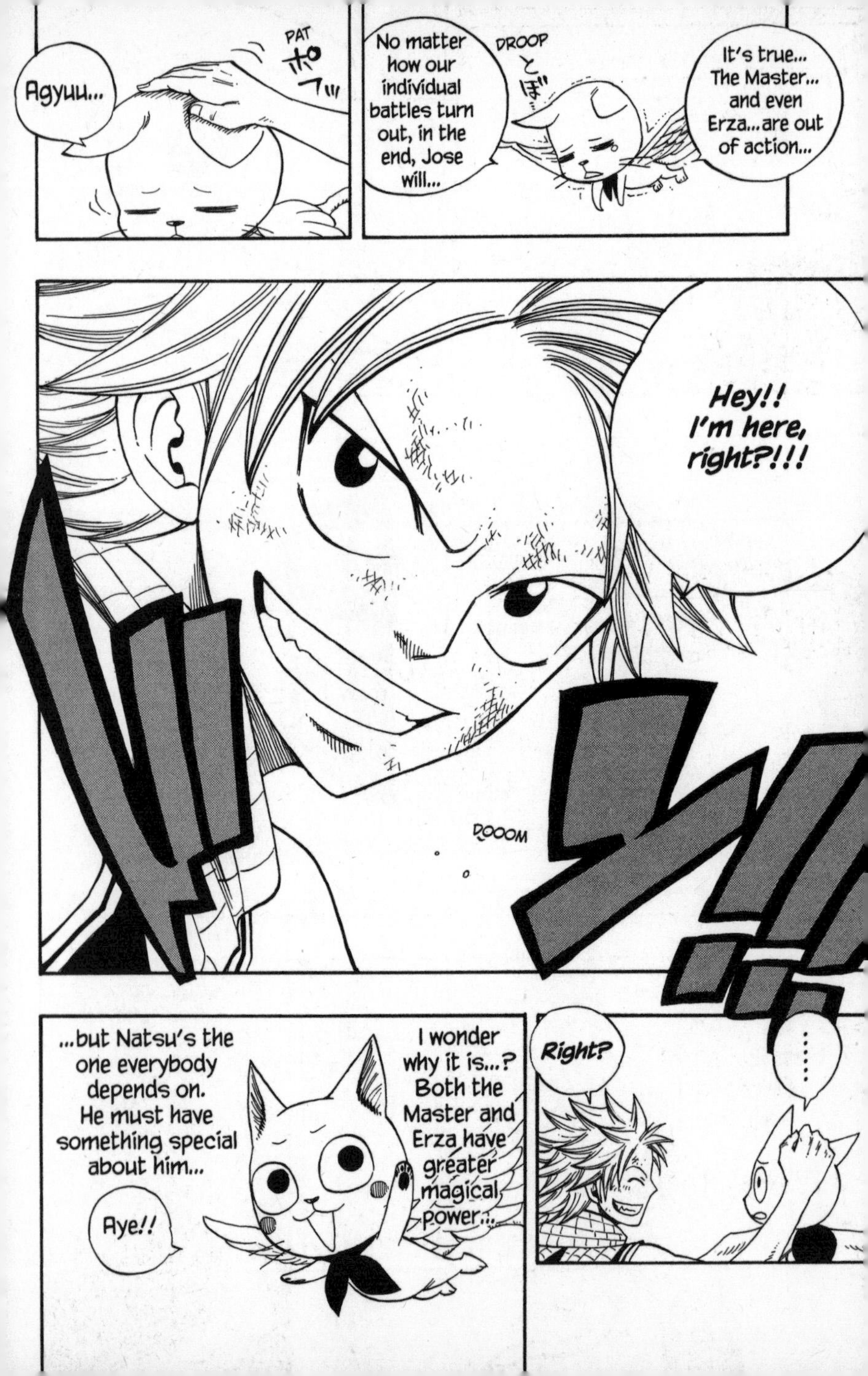
It's true... The Master... and even Erza...are out of action...
No matter how our individual battles turn out, in the end, Jose will...
DROOP
とぼ
PAT
ポフッ
Agyuu...
Hey!! I'm here, right?!!!
DOOOM
......
Right?
I wonder why it is...? Both the Master and Erza have greater magical power...
...but Natsu's the one everybody depends on. He must have something special about him...
Aye!!

!!
HYUOOO
It's so sad...
Wha-?!!
Wings of fire will deaden and fall...
Ahh... All that will remain is the corpse of a dragon...
Huh?
Natsu... That guy's one of the Element 4!!!

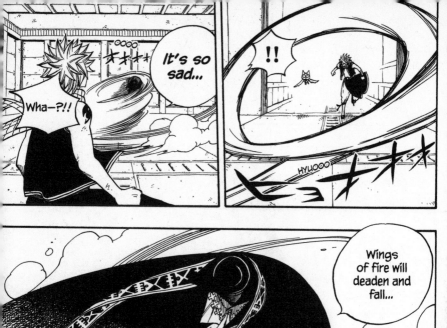

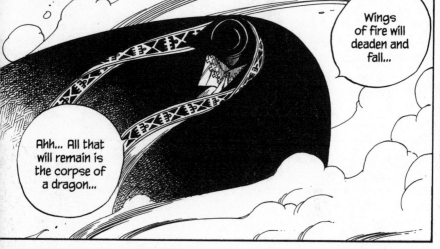

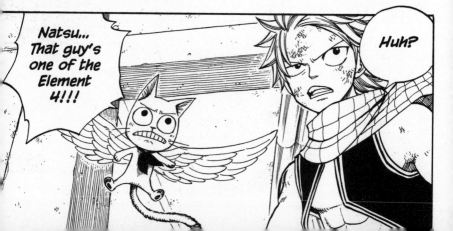

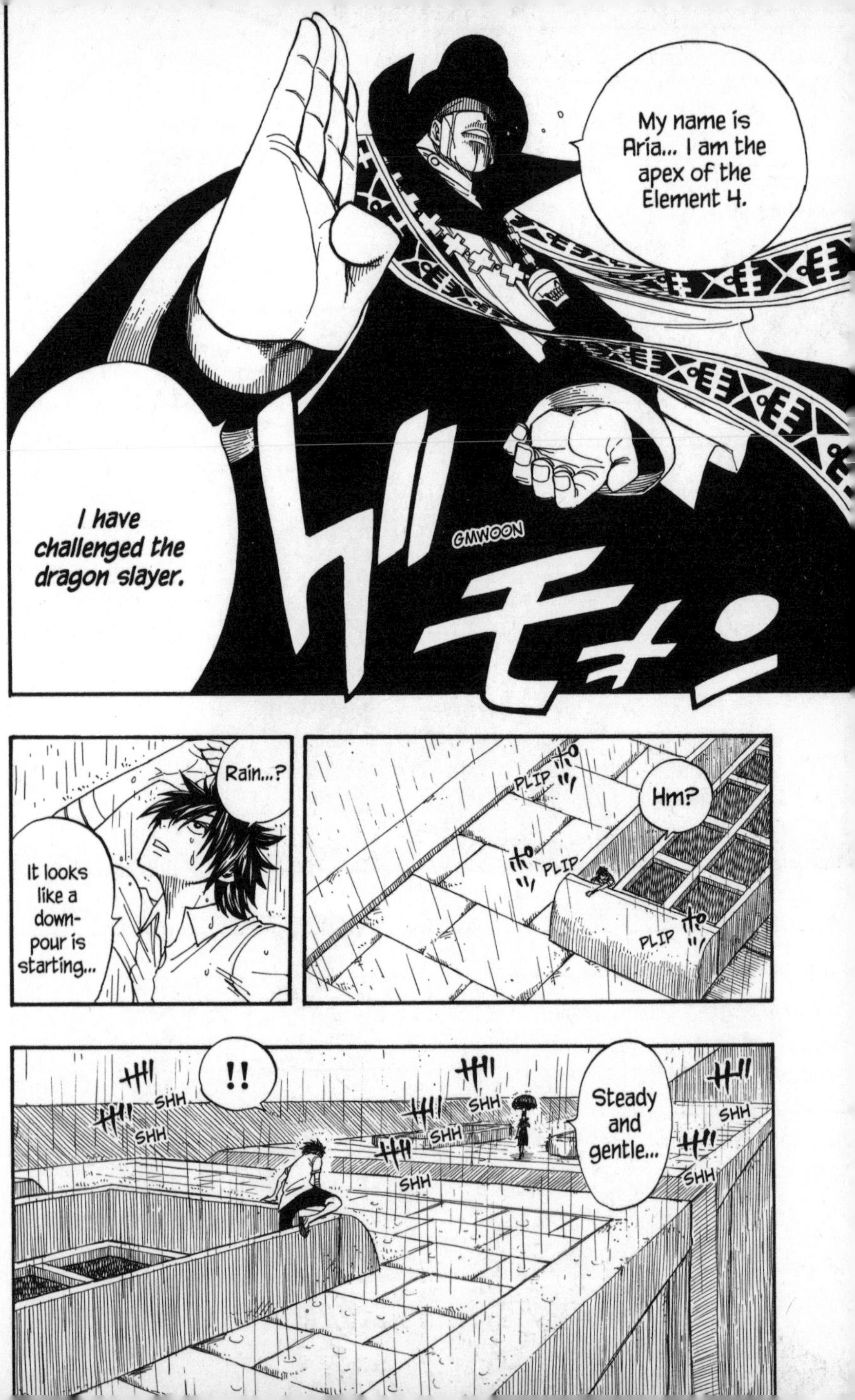
My name is Aria... I am the apex of the Element 4.
GMWOON
I have challenged the dragon slayer.
PLIP
Hm?
PLIP
PLIP
Rain...?
It looks like a down-pour is starting...
SHH
Steady and gentle...
SHH
SHH
SHH
SHH
!!
SHH
SHH

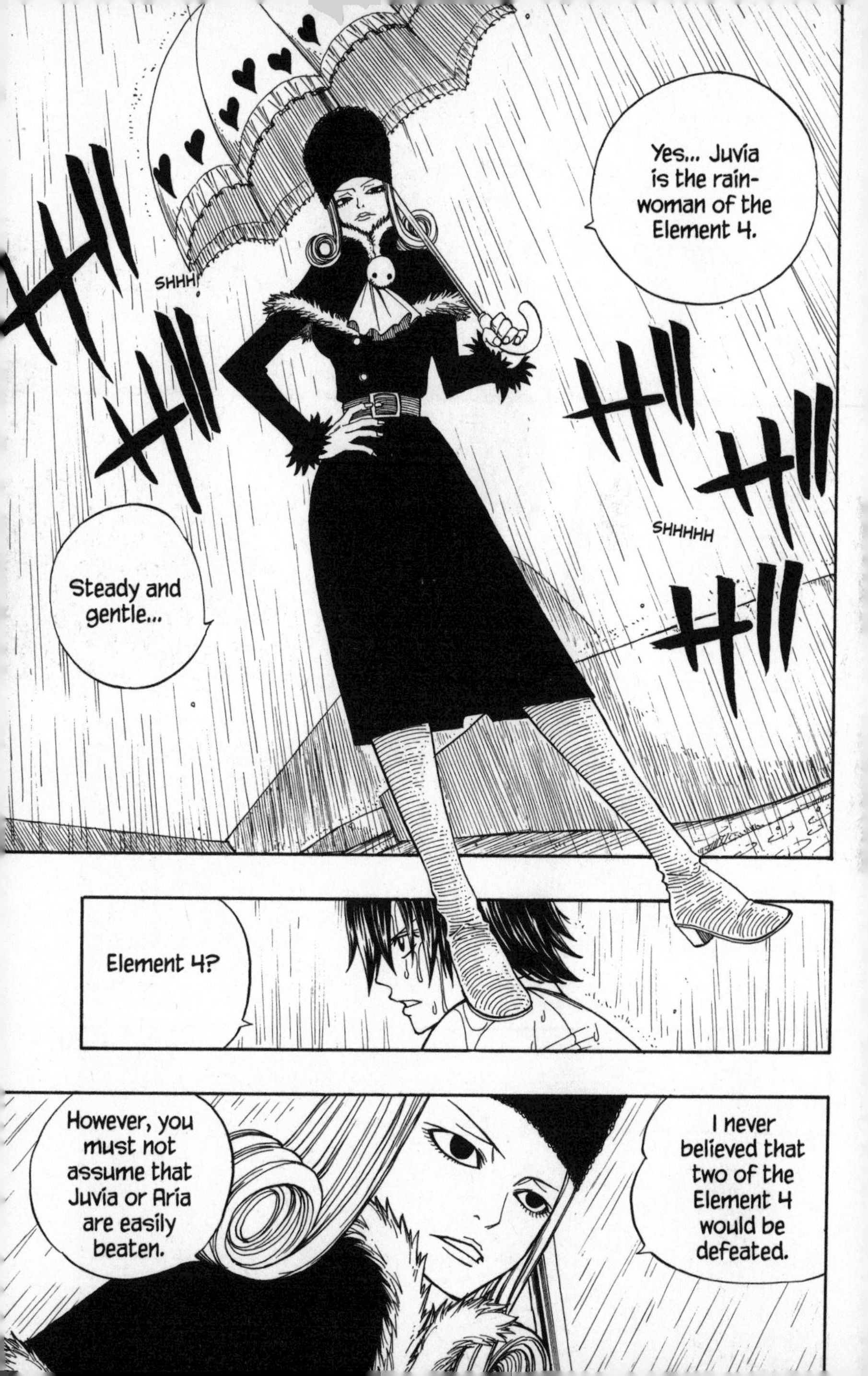
Yes... Juvia is the rain-woman of the Element 4.
SHHH!
SHHHHH
Steady and gentle...
Element 4?
I never believed that two of the Element 4 would be defeated.
However, you must not assume that Juvia or Aria are easily beaten.

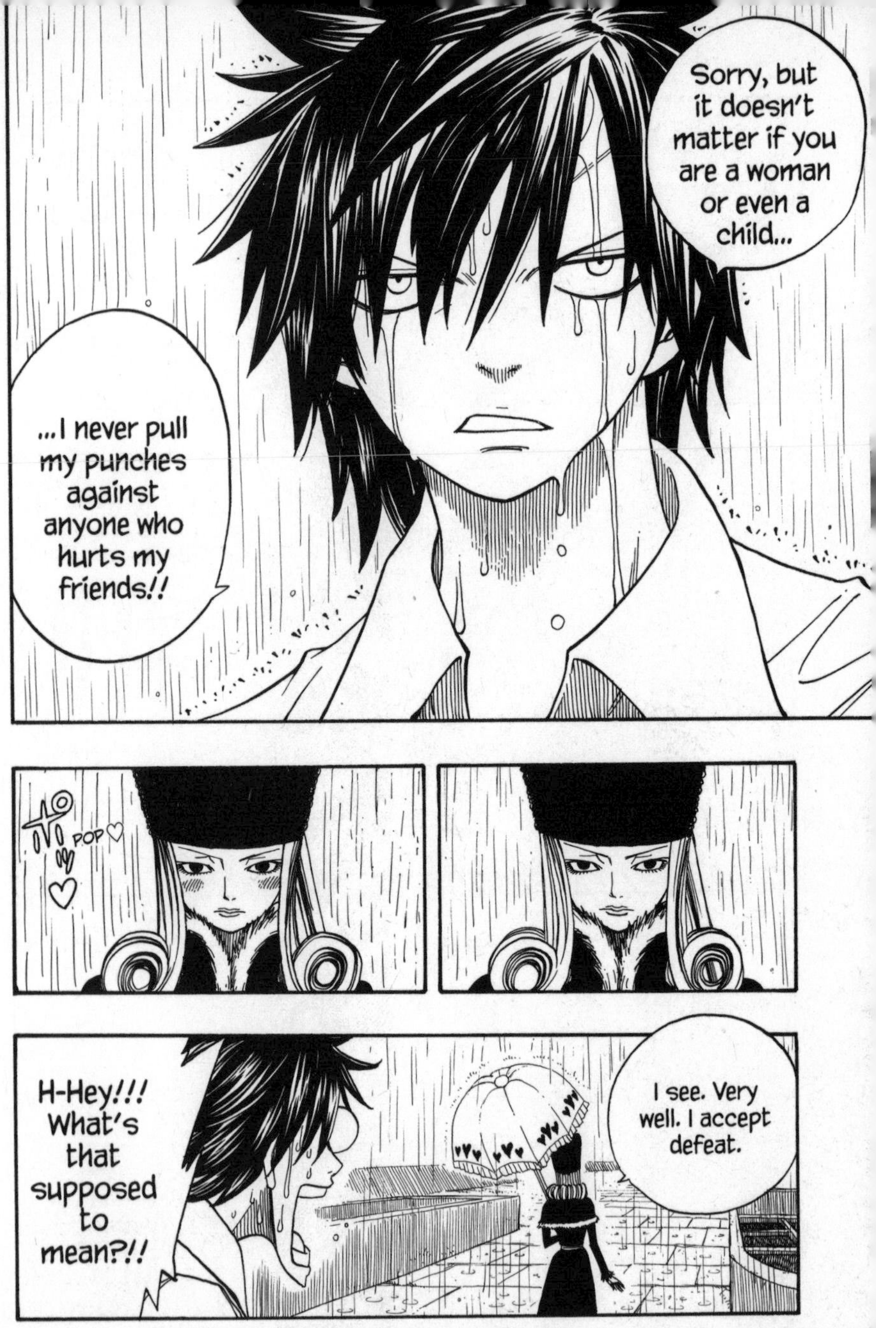
Sorry, but it doesn't matter if you are a woman or even a child...
...I never pull my punches against anyone who hurts my friends!!
POP
I see. Very well. I accept defeat.
H-Hey!!! What's that supposed to mean?!!

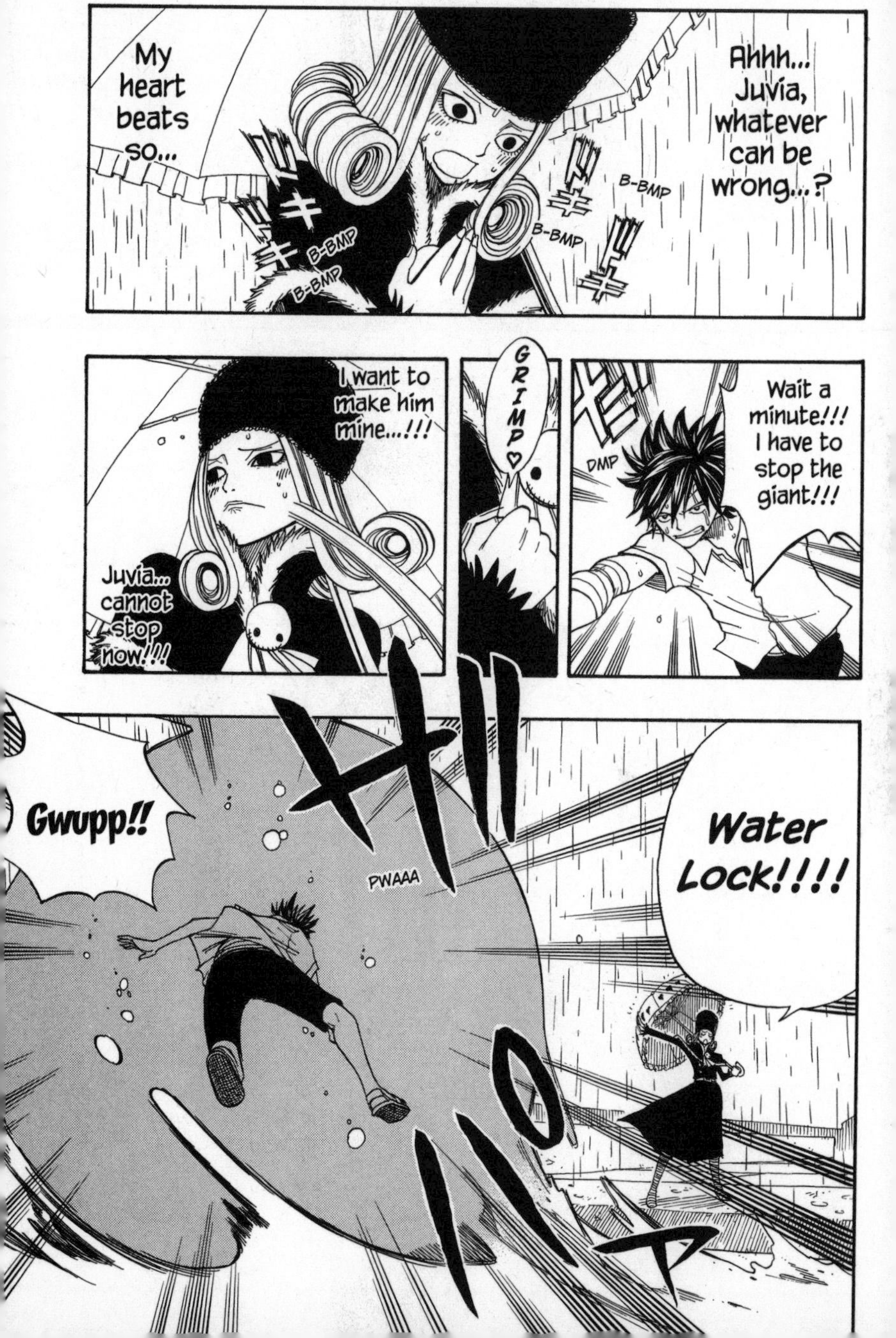
Ahhh... Juvia, whatever can be wrong...?
B-BMP
B-BMP
My heart beats so...
B-BMP
B-BMP
Wait a minute!!! I have to stop the giant!!!
DMP
GRIMP♡
I want to make him mine...!!!
Juvia... cannot stop now!!!
Water Lock!!!!
PWAAA
Gwupp!!

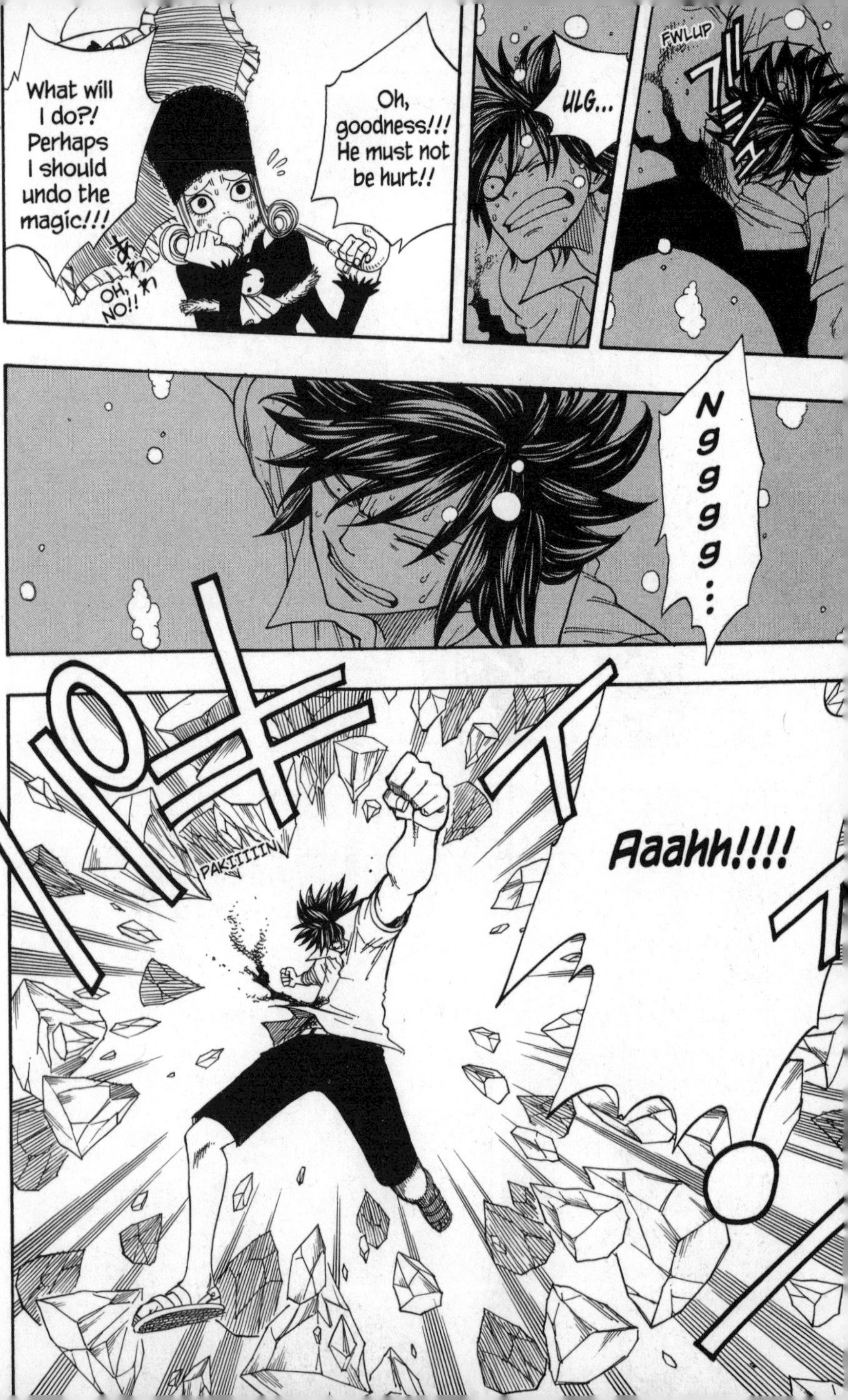
FWLUP
ULG...
Oh, goodness!!! He must not be hurt!!
What will I do?! Perhaps I should undo the magic!!!
あわわ
OH, NO!!
Ngggg...
Aaahh!!!!
PAKIIIIIN

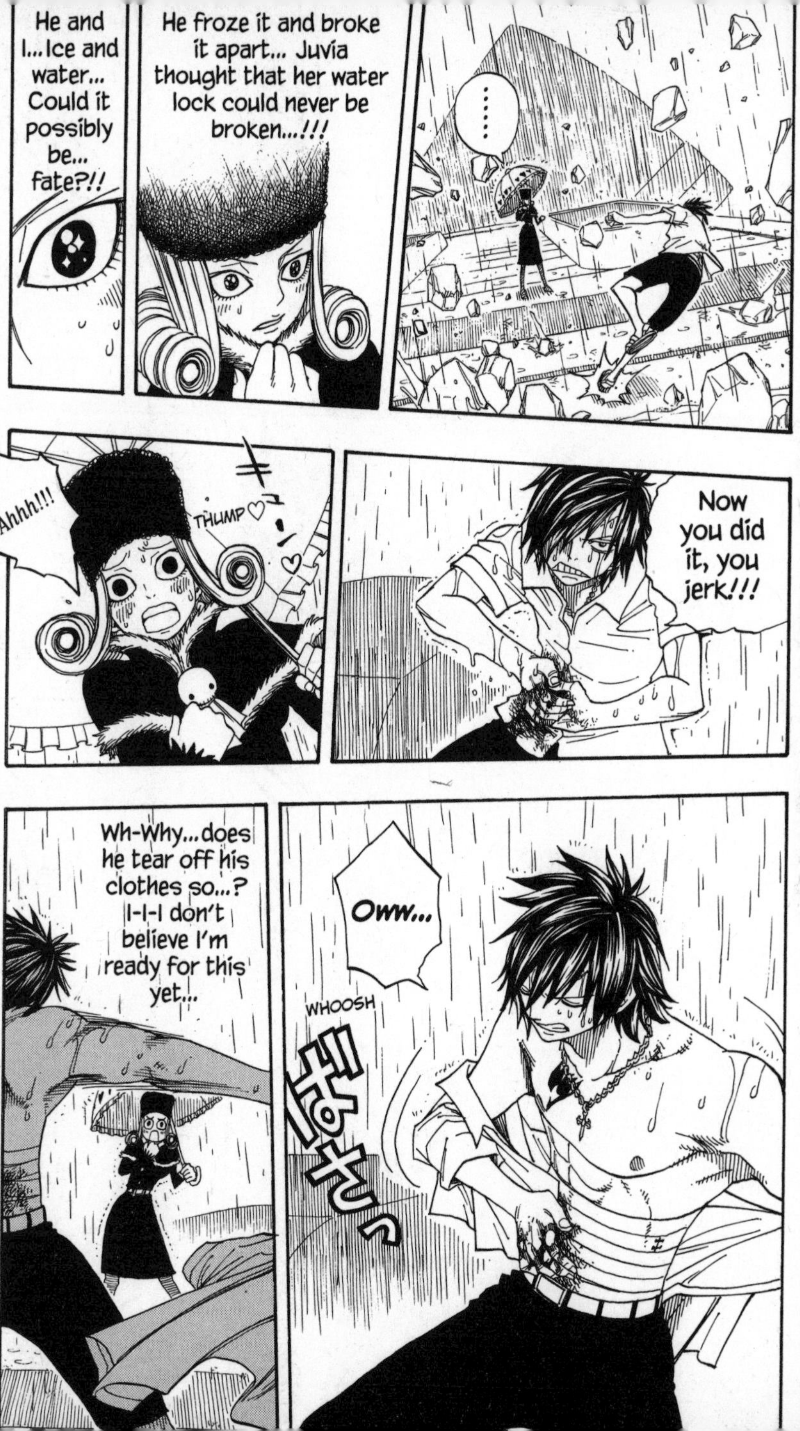
......
He froze it and broke it apart... Juvia thought that her water lock could never be broken...!!!
He and I...Ice and water... Could it possibly be... fate?!!
Now you did it, you jerk!!!
THUMP♡
Ahhh!!!
Oww...
WHOOSH
Wh-Why...does he tear off his clothes so...? I-I-I don't believe I'm ready for this yet...

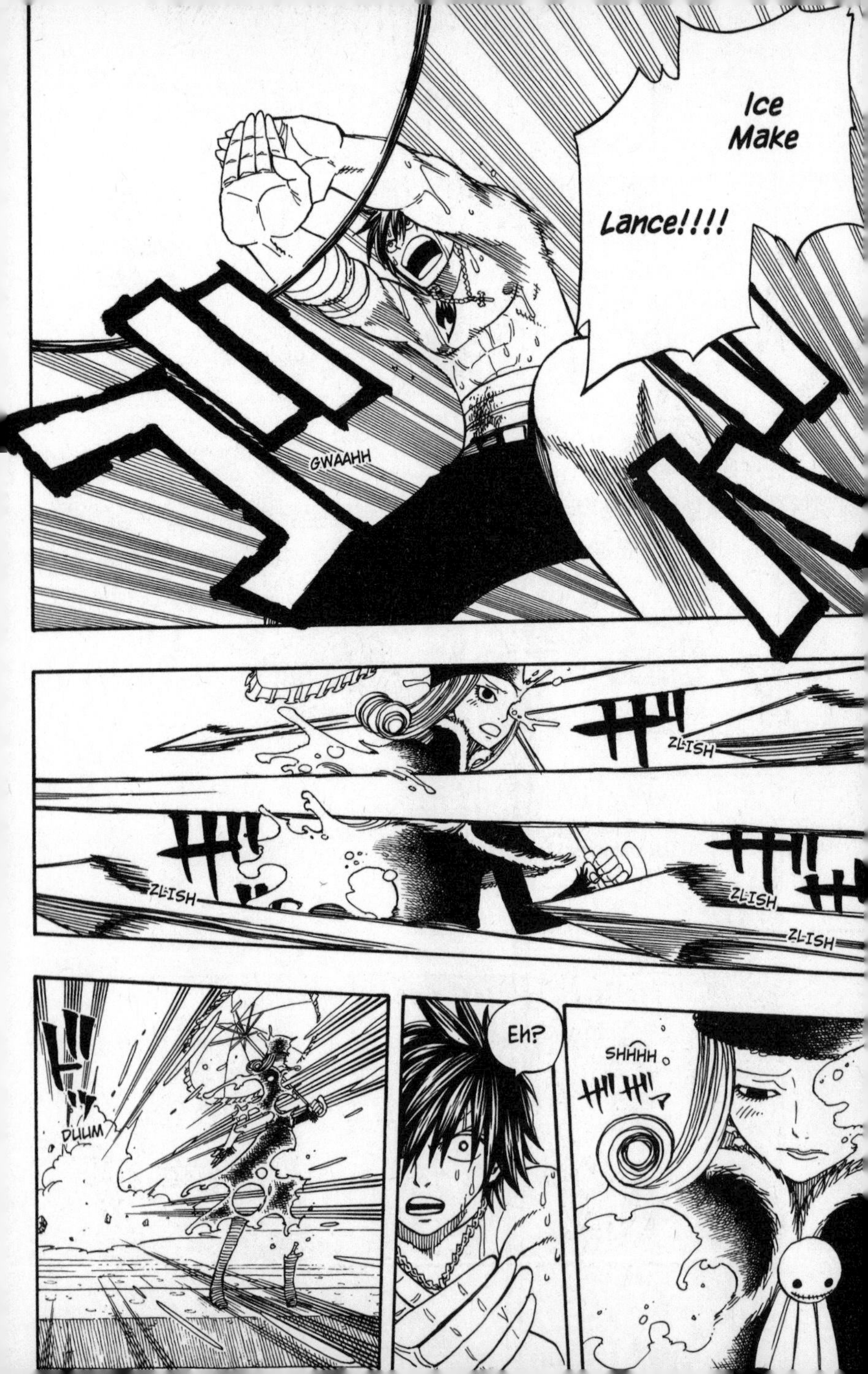
Ice Make
Lance!!!!
GWAAHH
ZL-ISH
ZL-ISH
ZL-ISH
ZL-ISH
SHHHH
Eh?
DUUM

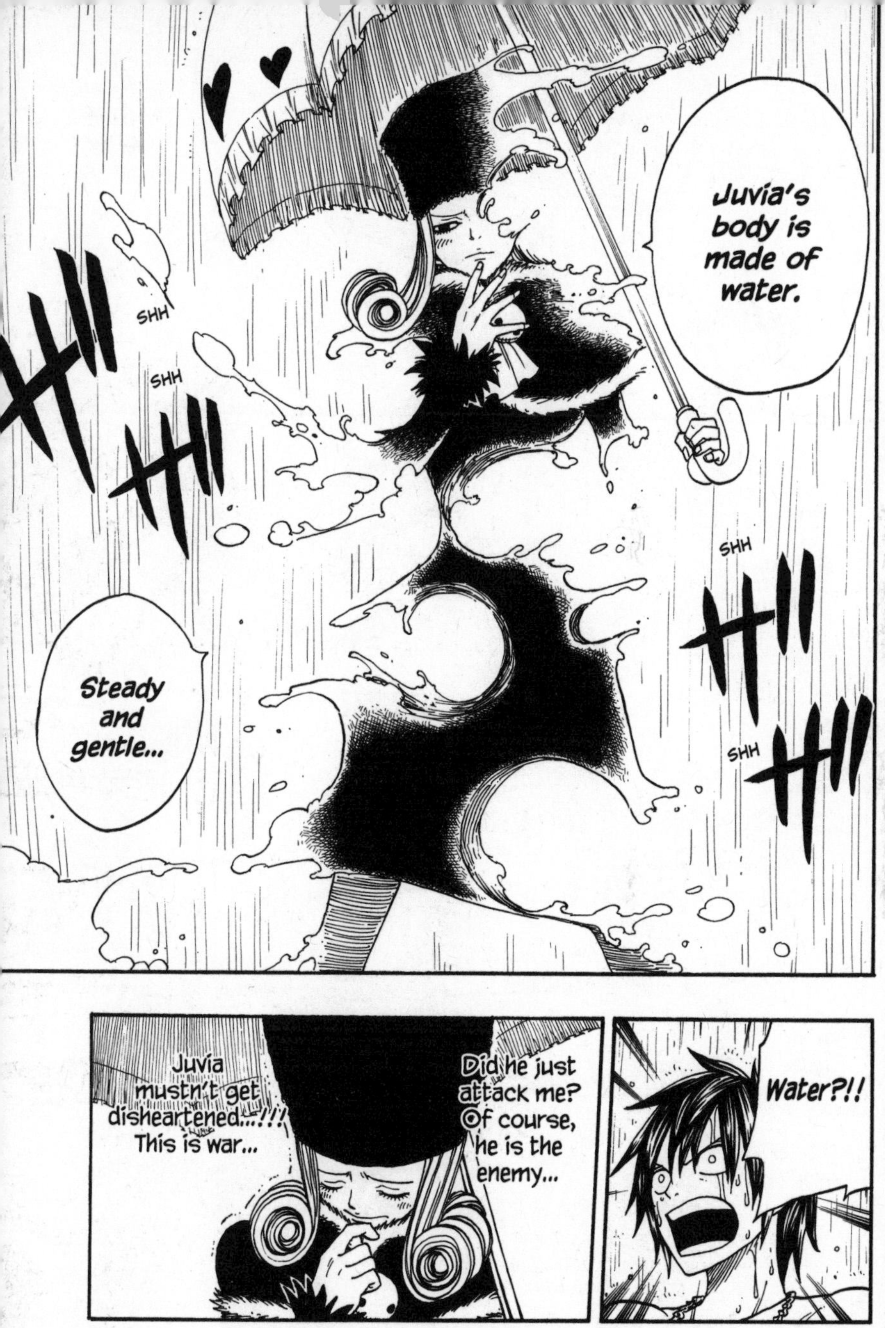
Juvia's body is made of water.
SHH
SHH
SHH
SHH
Steady and gentle...
Water?!!
Did he just attack me? Of course, he is the enemy...
Juvia mustn't get disheartened...!!! This is war...

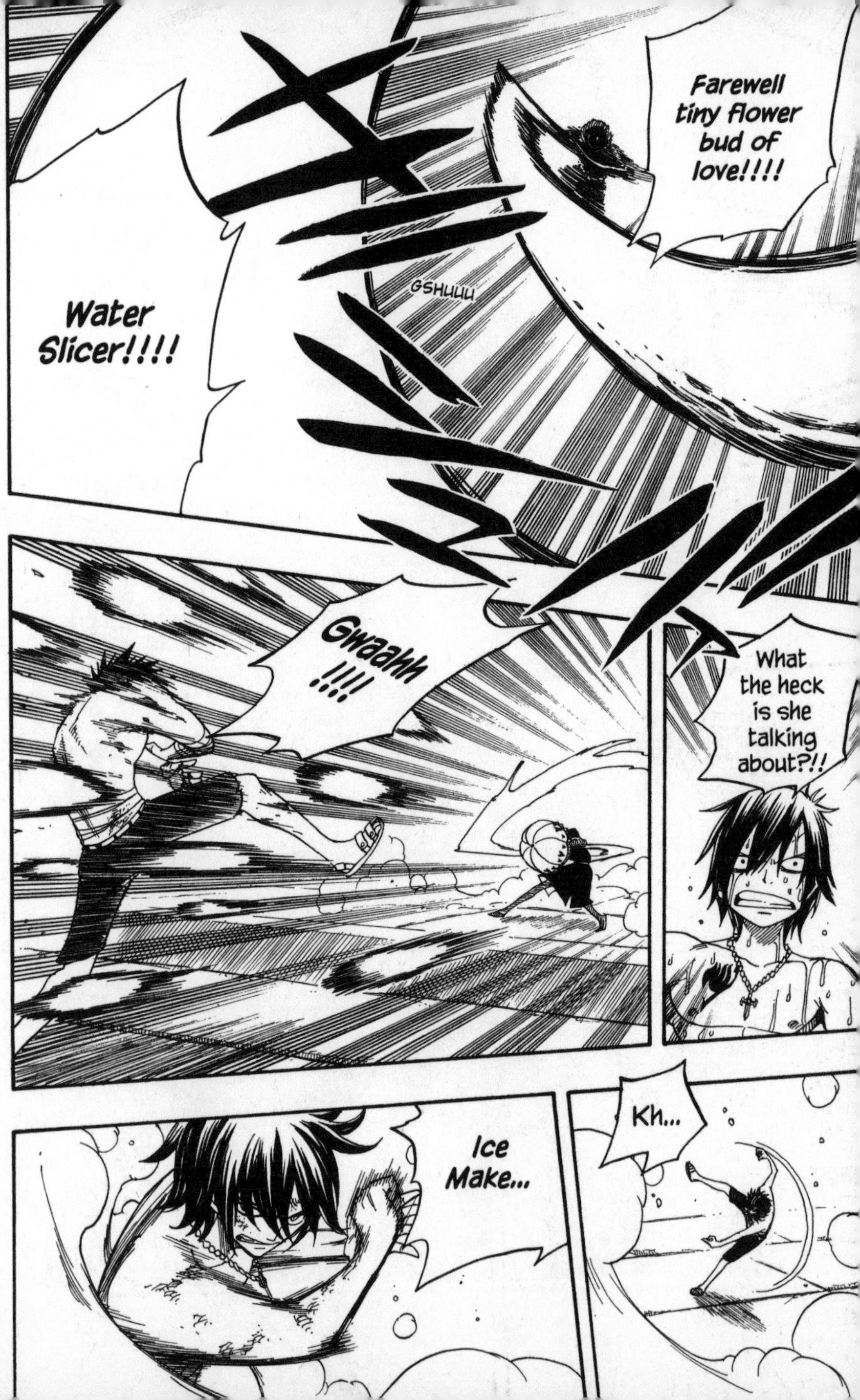
Farewell tiny flower bud of love!!!!
GSHUUU
Water Slicer!!!!
What the heck is she talking about?!!
Gwaaahh !!!!
Kh...
Ice Make...

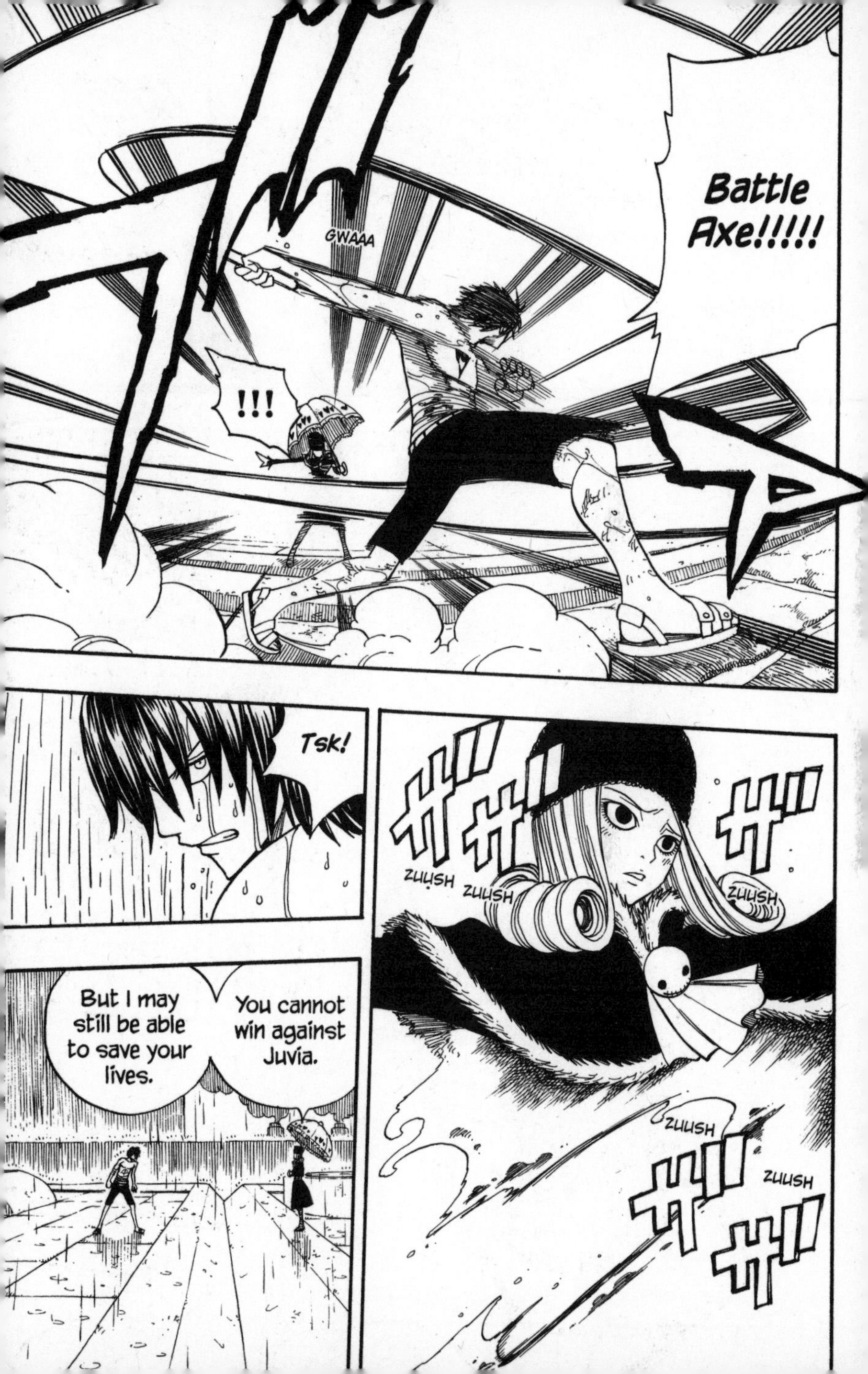

Battle Axe!!!!!
GWAAA
!!!
ZUUSH
ZUUSH
ZUUSH
ZUUSH
ZUUSH
Tsk!
You cannot win against Juvia.
But I may still be able to save your lives.

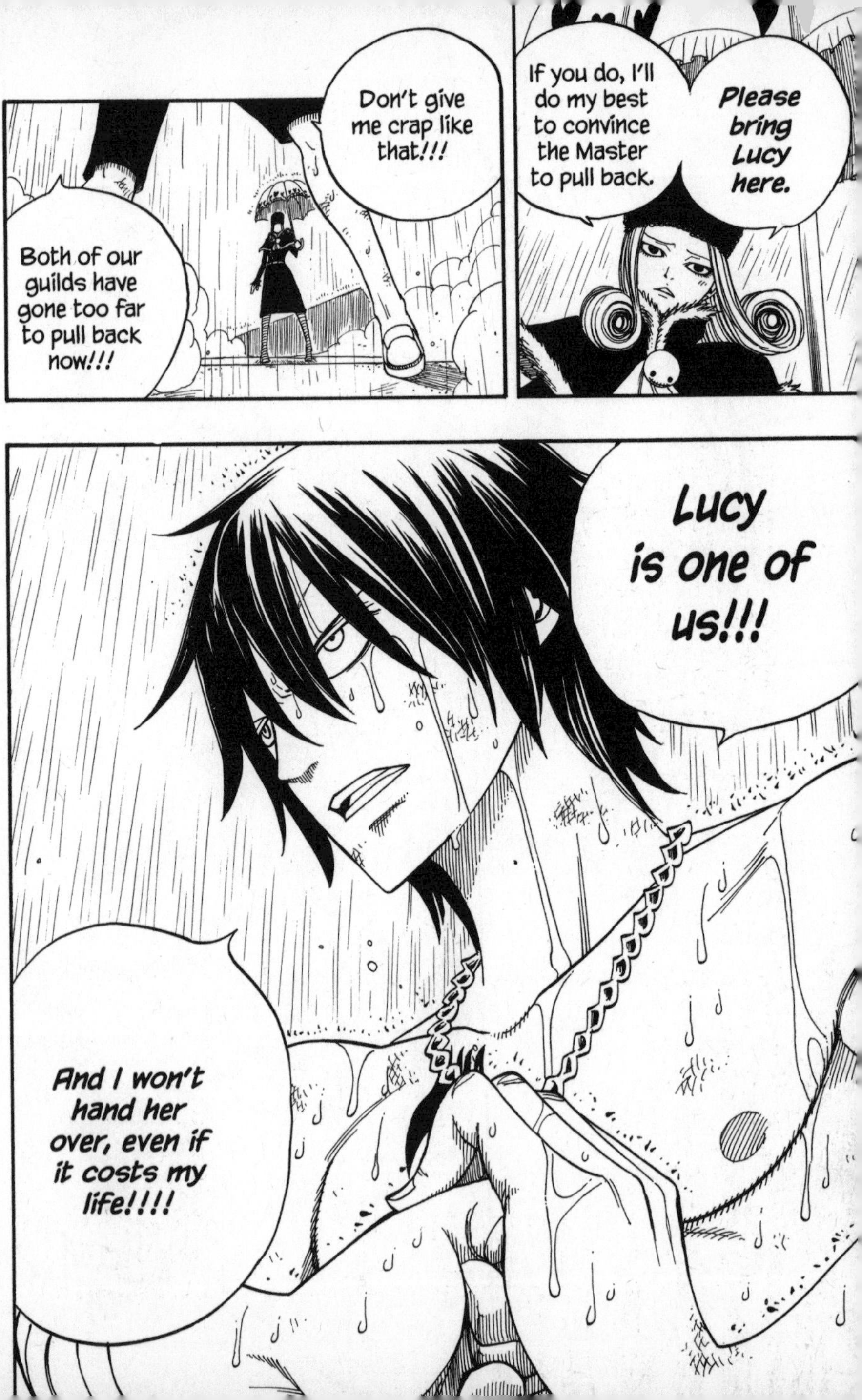
Please bring Lucy here.
If you do, I'll do my best to convince the Master to pull back.
Don't give me crap like that!!!
Both of our guilds have gone too far to pull back now!!!
Lucy is one of us!!!
And I won't hand her over, even if it costs my life!!!!

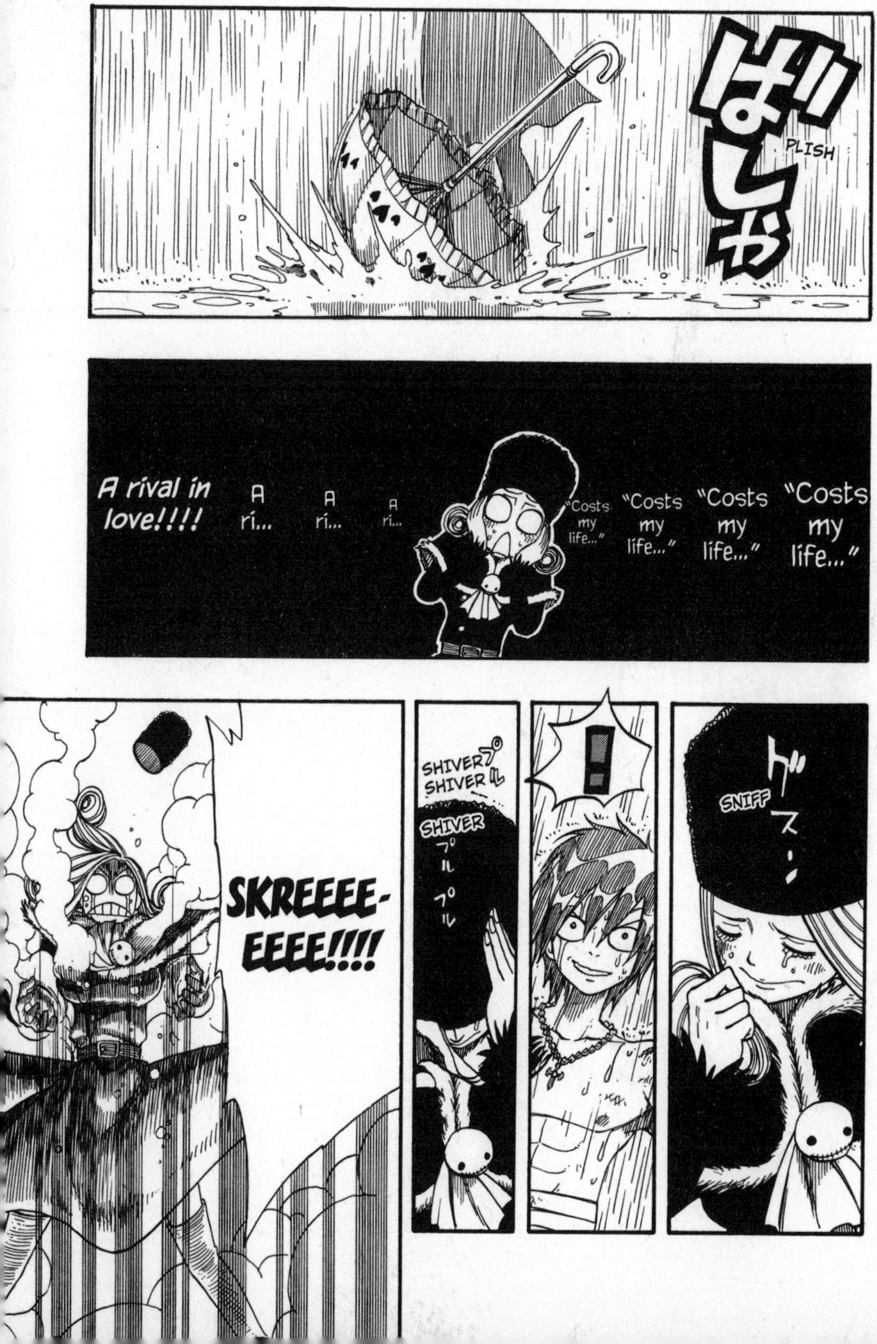
ぱしゃ
PLISH
"Costs my life..."
"Costs my life..."
"Costs my life..."
"Costs my life..."
A ri...
A ri...
A ri...
A rival in love!!!!
SNIFF
!
SHIVER SHIVER
SHIVER
プルプル
SKREEEEE-EEEE!!!!

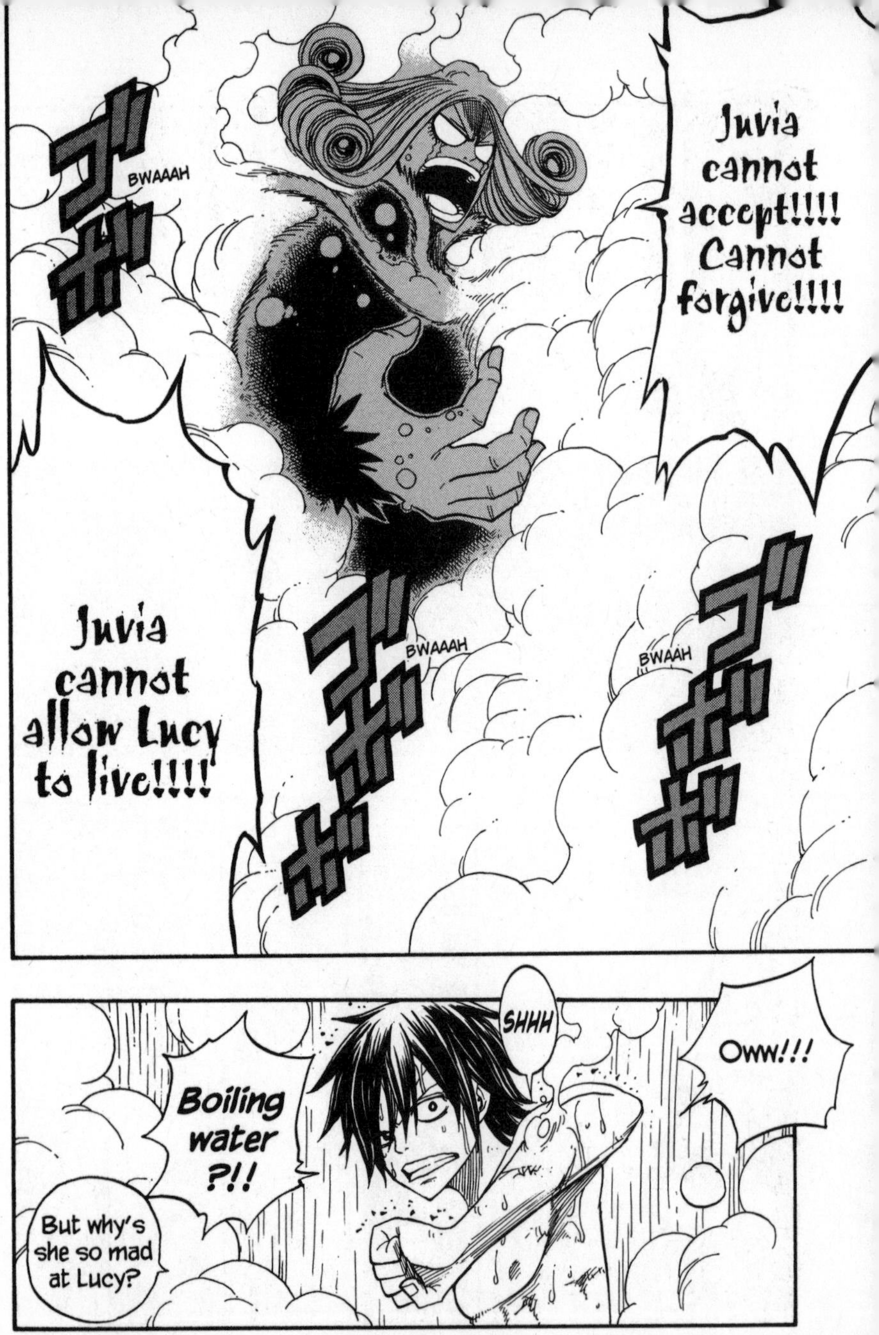
Juvia cannot accept!!!! Cannot forgive!!!!
BWAAAH
BWAAH
BWAAAH
Juvia cannot allow Lucy to live!!!!
Oww!!!
SHHH
Boiling water?!!
But why's she so mad at Lucy?

TO BE CONTINUED

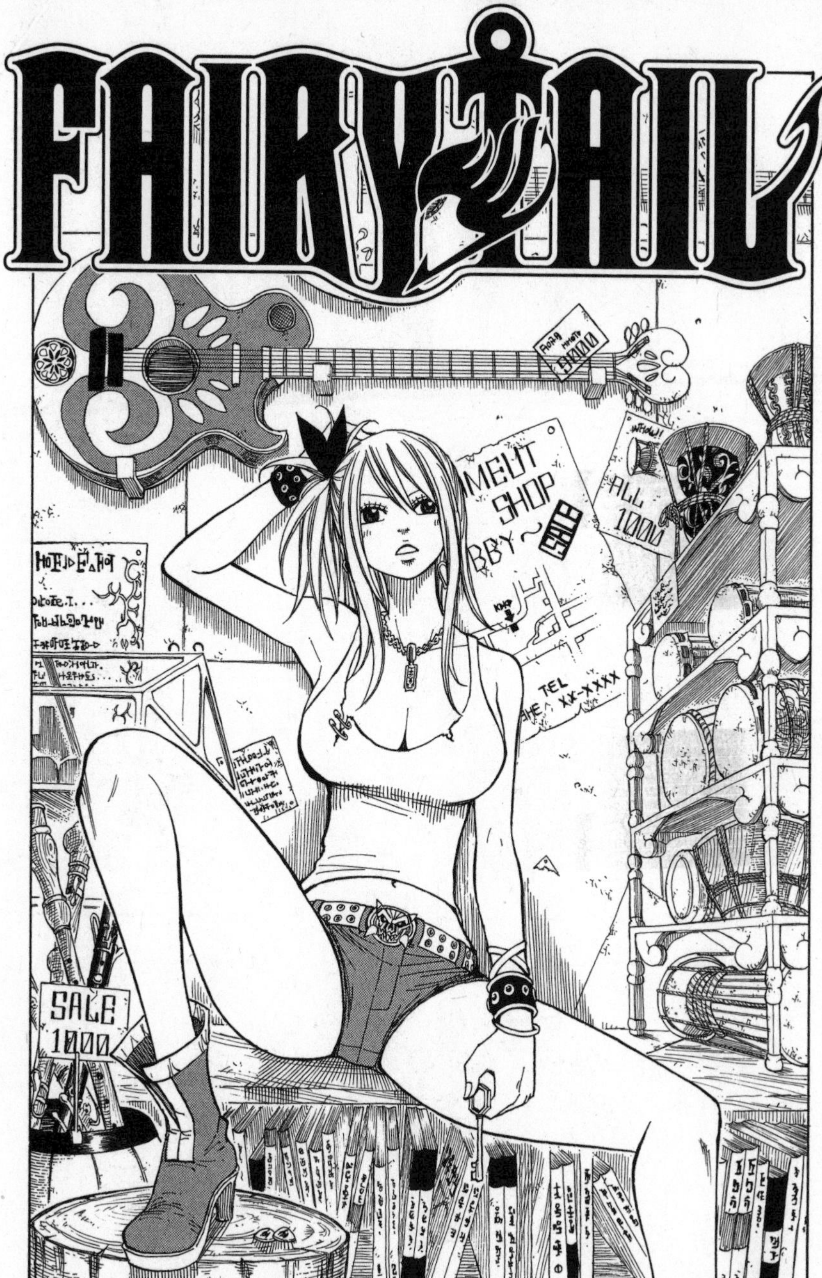
FAIRY TAIL
MEUT SHOP
SALE
TEL XX-XXXX
ALL 1000
SALE 1000

BONUS PAGES

TAIL D'ART

The *Fairy Tail* Guild d'Art is an explosion of fan art! Please send in your black-and-white art on large postcard stock!! Those chosen to be published will get a signed mini poster! ♪ Make sure you write your real name and address on the back of your postcard!

▼ Well... Let's just leave it at that. (laughs)

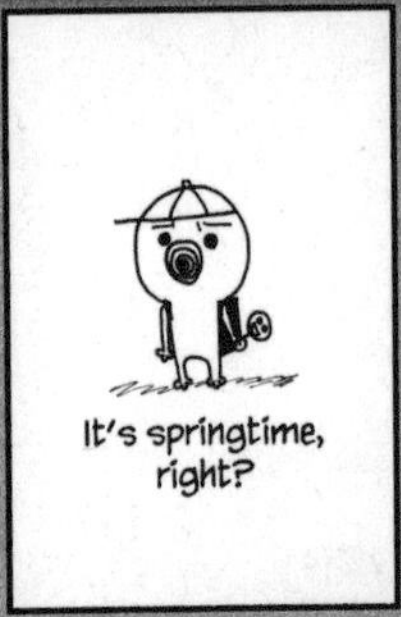
It's springtime, right?

Fukushima Prefecture, Kai

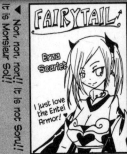

▼ Maybe the "Entei" (Fire Empress) armor will come some time later in the manga... (sweat, sweat)

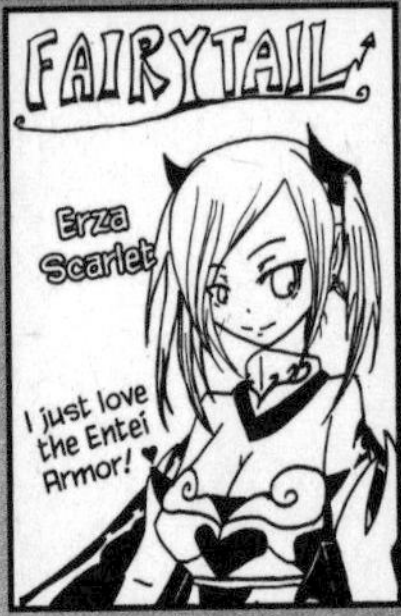
FAIRYTAIL
Erza Scarlet
I just love the Entei Armor! ♥

Chiba Prefecture, Jelly

▼ Non, non, non!! It is not Soru!! It is Monsieur Sol!!

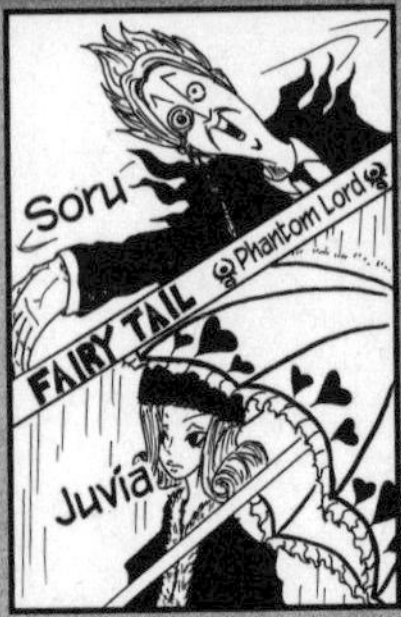
Soru
Phantom Lord
FAIRY TAIL
Juvia

Fukushima Prefecture, Narumi

▼ Everybody knows that the Palace of the Water Bearer refers to the star sign Aquarius, right?

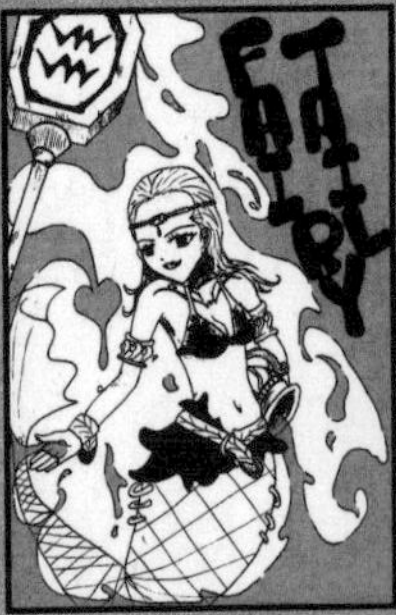

Kanagawa Prefecture, Kaoringo

▼ Everybody cheer!!! Hurray! Hurray! Ma-shi-ma!!

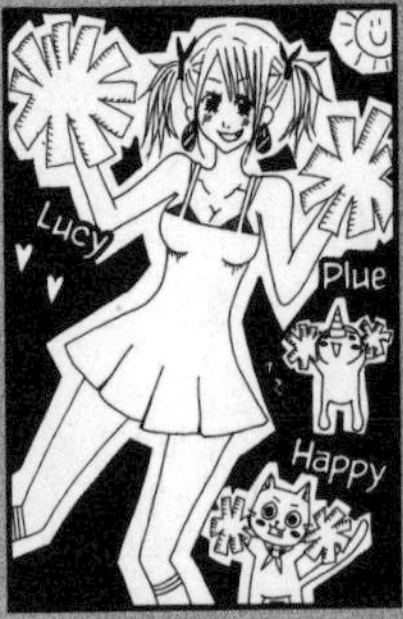
Lucy
Plue
Happy

Osaka, Haruna

▼ Elfman's popularity is really on the rise!! What did you think of his part in this volume?

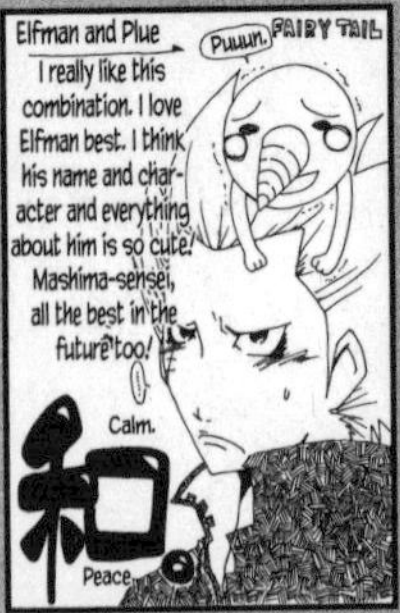
Elfman and Plue
Puuun.
FAIRY TAIL
I really like this combination. I love Elfman best. I think his name and character and everything about him is so cute! Mashima-sensei, all the best in the future too!
Calm.
和。
Peace.

Okayama Prefecture, Ikuma

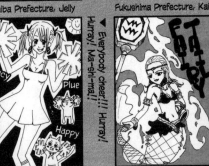

▼ Wow!! So cute!! I wonder what kind of dream she's having!

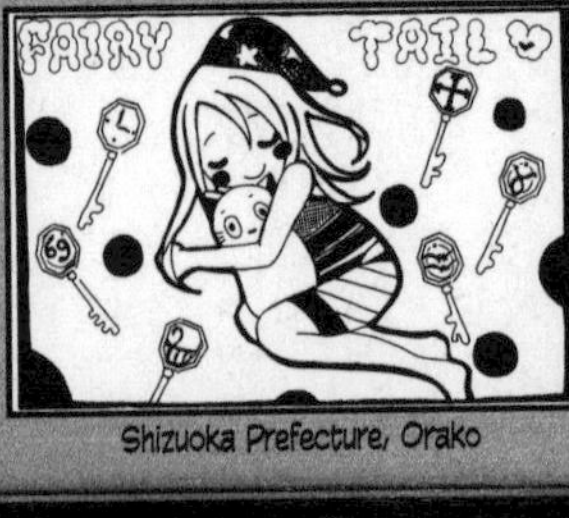
FAIRY TAIL ♥

Shizuoka Prefecture, Orako

▼ Will these two fight out their ultimate battle?!! What will the outcome be?!!

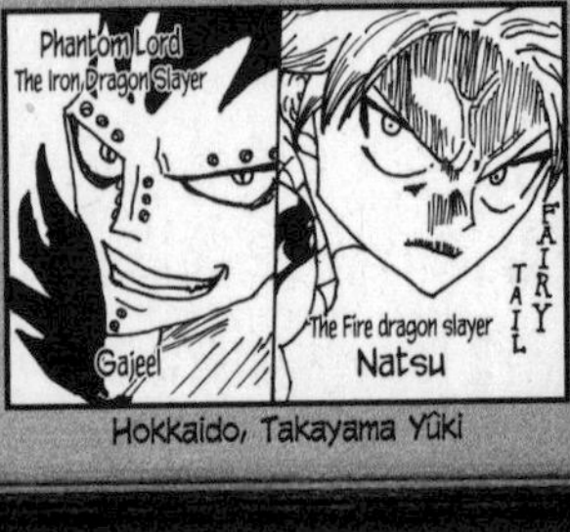
Phantom Lord
The Iron Dragon Slayer
FAIRY TAIL
The Fire dragon slayer
Natsu
Gajeel

Hokkaido, Takayama Yûki

Send to Hiro Mashima, Kodansha Comics
451 Park Ave. South, 7th Floor New York, NY 10016

FAIRY GUILD

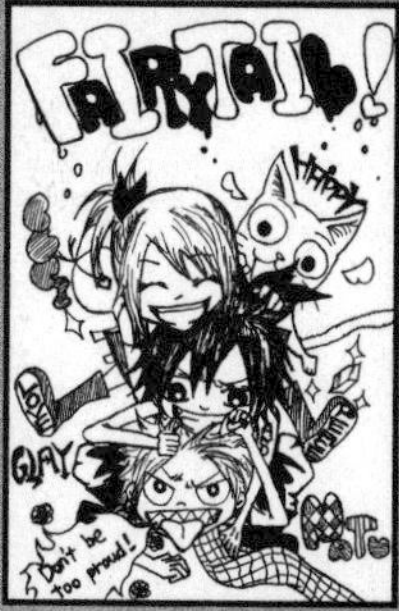
FAIRY TAIL!
Don't be too proud!
Nagano Prefecture, Getta

▼ Everyone looks like they're having so much fun!! Great facial expressions!

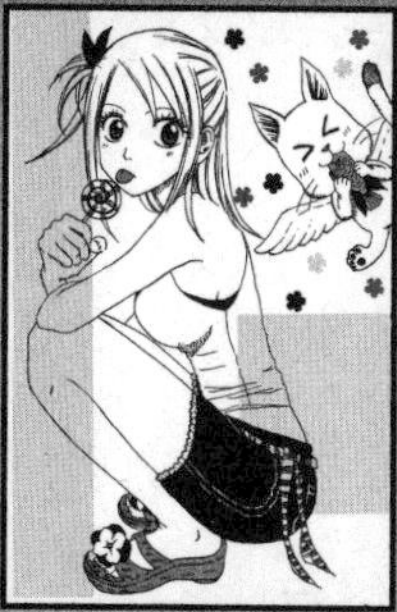
Oita Prefecture, Kazaneko

▼ So well drawn!!! This person must be experienced in drawing the human form.

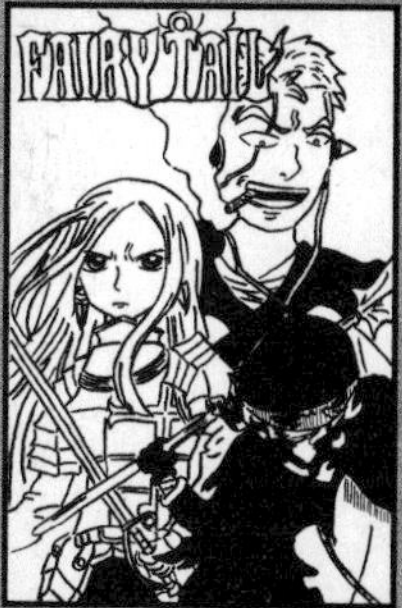
FAIRY TAIL
Shimane Prefecture, Iruka

▼ The top three of Fairy Tail! (Probably.)

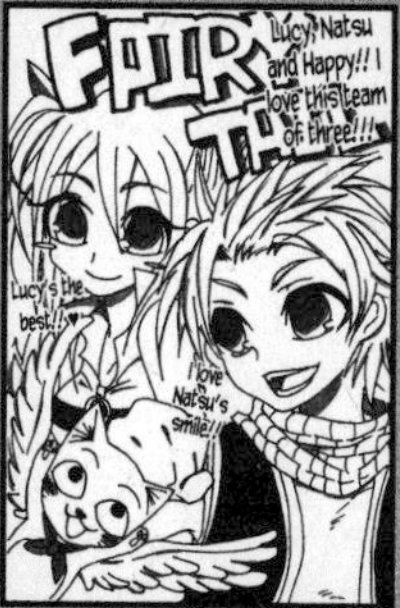
FAIRY TAIL
Lucy, Natsu and Happy!! I love this team of three!!!
Lucy's the best!!
I love Natsu's smile!
Nara Prefecture, Sorano Yukimi

▼ She says she loves this team of three!! Thank you!!!

Any letters and postcards you send with your personal information, such as your name, address, postal code, and other information, will be handed over, as is, to the author. When you send mail, please keep that in mind.

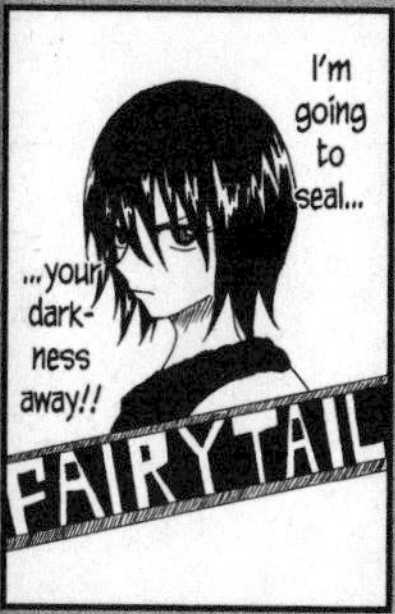
I'm going to seal...
...your darkness away!!
FAIRY TAIL
Hiroshima Prefecture, Iwamori Yûka

▼ Ur...She's so cool, huh?! All my best to Ultear, her daughter too!

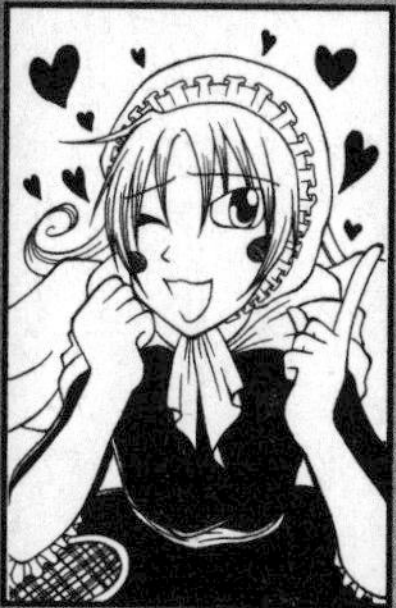
Fukushima Prefecture, Kasuga Hikari

▼ Oh ho!! An unusual character makes her appearance!!

Rejection Corner

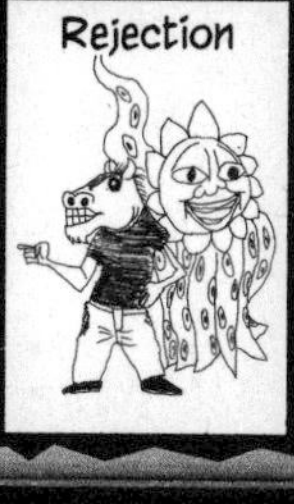
Rejection

◀ All right... Exactly as you wish...
Tôyama Prefecture, Impact Absorber

GUILD D'ART, STAFF EDITION!!

A bit of artwork that got caught up in the confusion.

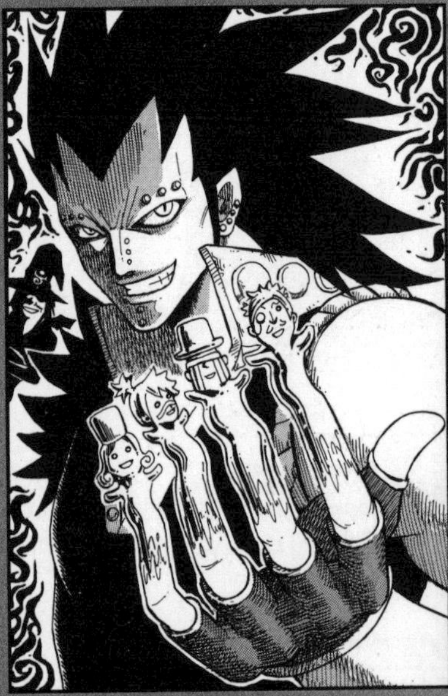

Bozu

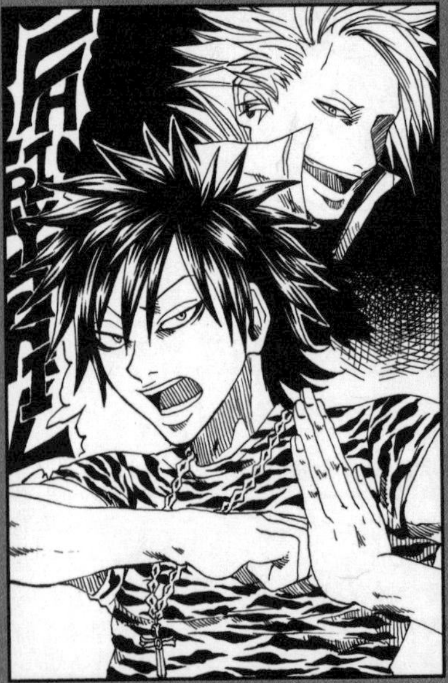

Nakamura Shô

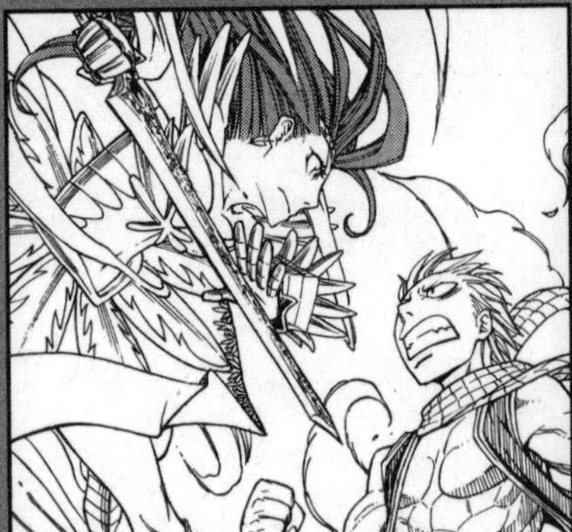

Bobby Ôsawa

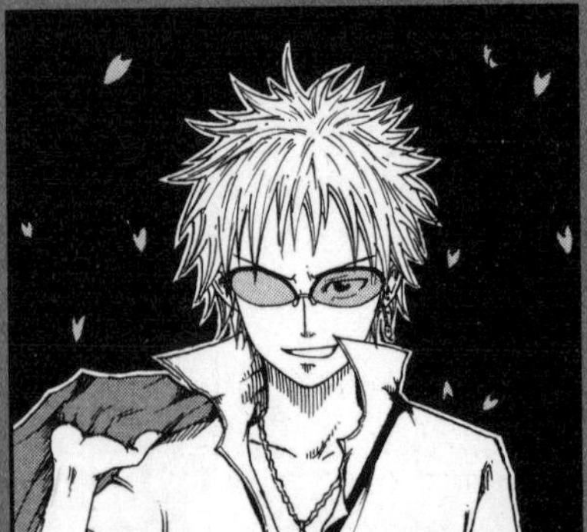

Ueda Yui

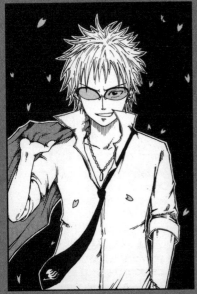

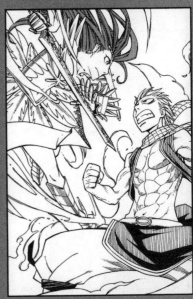

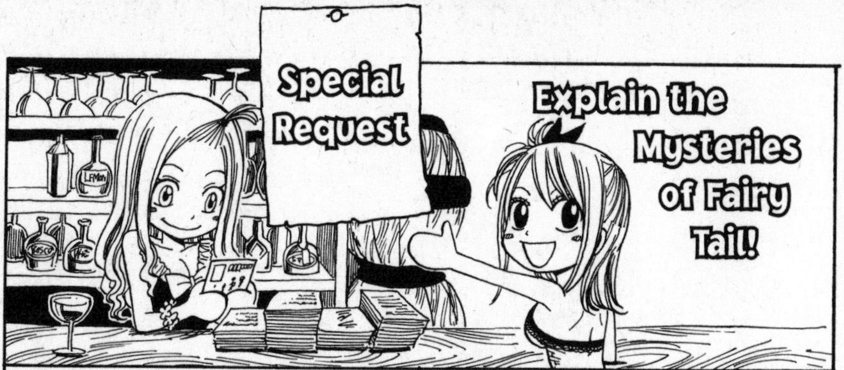
Special Request
Explain the Mysteries of Fairy Tail!

From the Fairy Tail Bar

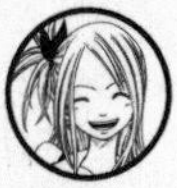
: Hello there!! I'm Lucy, the cute and sexy manager of Fairy Tail!!

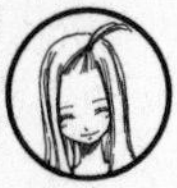
: The author just loves to draw Lucy, doesn't he... Heh heh.

Lucy: Oh, he's just a lecher!! Really!! All he ever thinks about is sex!!
Mira: Let's get started. We've received a bunch of questions after people read volume 6.

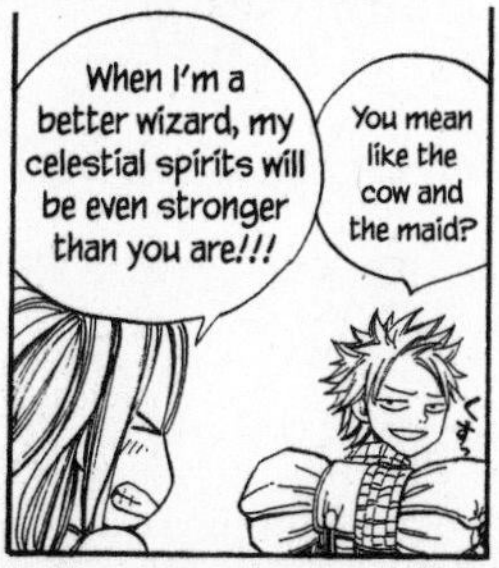
When I'm a better wizard, my celestial spirits will be even stronger than you are!!!
You mean like the cow and the maid?

Does the strength of the celestial spirits change according to the magical power of the wizard using them?
Lucy: That's right.
Mira: ....
Lucy: ....
Mira: Is that all?
Lucy: I know what you want to say!! That the keys I have to the Twelve Golden Gates are wasted on me, right?
Mira: You knew exactly what I wanted to say.
Lucy: ***Ow!!*** That knife in my back hurts!! Sniff...
Mira: But we don't know what the future holds. When Lucy trains herself up to be a powerful wizard, I'd like to see what that bull looks like!
Lucy: Oh, Mira-san!! Sniff...
Mira: Just think of the T-bone barbecue we'll have then!!

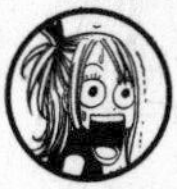
: You can't eat him!!!!

Mira: Now on to the next question.

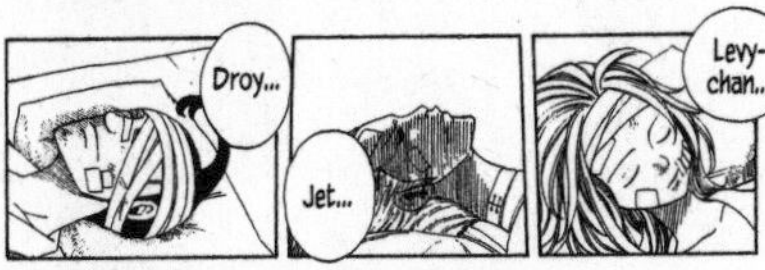
Levy-chan...
Jet...
Droy...

Is Levy-chan still alive?
Lucy: Of course she is!!
Mira: Don't worry. Jet and Droy are alive and kicking too.

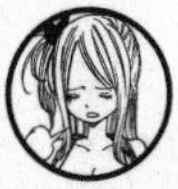
: But with the author's previous work, leading characters died off, one after the other.

Continued on the next page

I can see why everyone would be nervous.

Mira: That's true. Sometimes the Master says, "I wonder if I'm the next to die!" and "It seems like a real possibility" and "I could just cry!" He seems really worried about it.

Lucy: Oh, dear... (sweat, sweat)

Mira: Let's go to the next question, shall we?

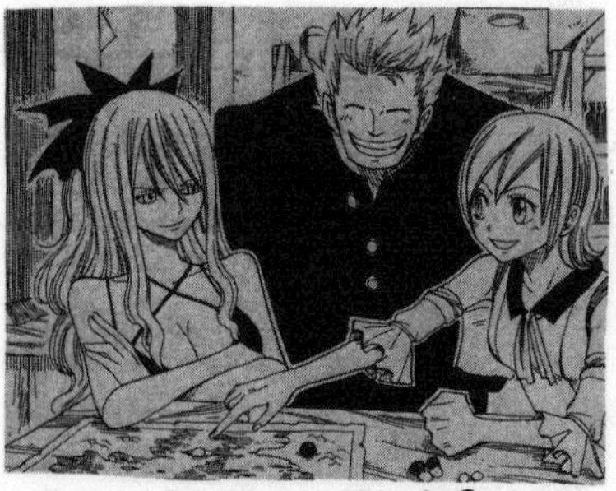

I-Is the one on the left... really...M-Mira-chan?

Shudder, shudder!

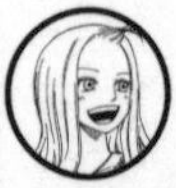
: Eh? Why would anyone bother to ask such an obvious question?

Lucy: B-But there's something about the girl in the picture that doesn't seem like you!

Mira: You think so? Well, I ***was*** quite young.♡

Lucy: A-And scary...

Mira: It was a fun time!! Elfman was a loose cannon who I always had to keep my eye on. But we'd go taking Lisanna with us...

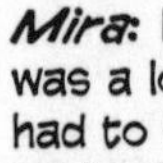
: Mira-san...

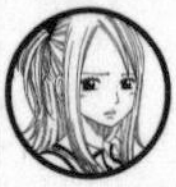
: And we'd get into all sorts of brawls with Erza or Natsu and the gang...

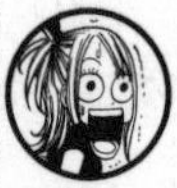
: ***Ehhhhh?!!!***

Mira: That's what it means to be young, Lucy! Everybody does it, don't they?

Lucy: Normally, girls don't get into that kind of stuff...

Mira: And now on to our last question.

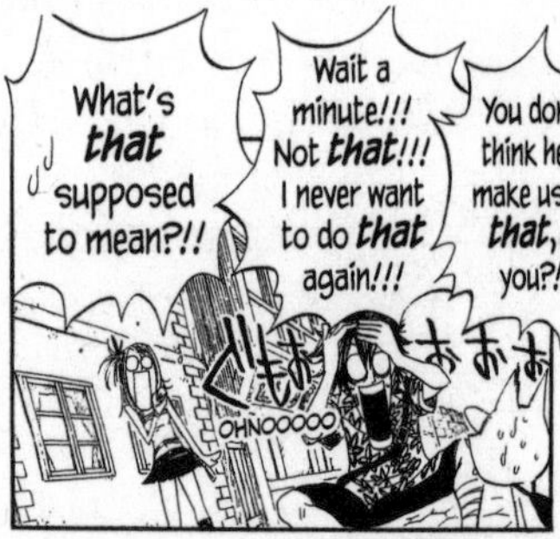
You don't think he'd make us do **that**, do you?!!
Wait a minute!!! Not **that**!!! I never want to do **that** again!!!
What's **that** supposed to mean?!!
OHNOOOOO

So what exactly is "that"?

Lucy: Urk! That's right!! I never did find out!!

Mira: Heh heh... Oh, of course, "that"!

Lucy: ?

Mira: We're still keeping it a secret.♥

Lucy: ***What the heck is "that"?!!***

We're collecting questions about *Fairy Tail*! Send them to the address below!

↓

Hiro Mashima
Kodansha Comics
451 Park Ave. South, 7th Floor
New York, NY 10016

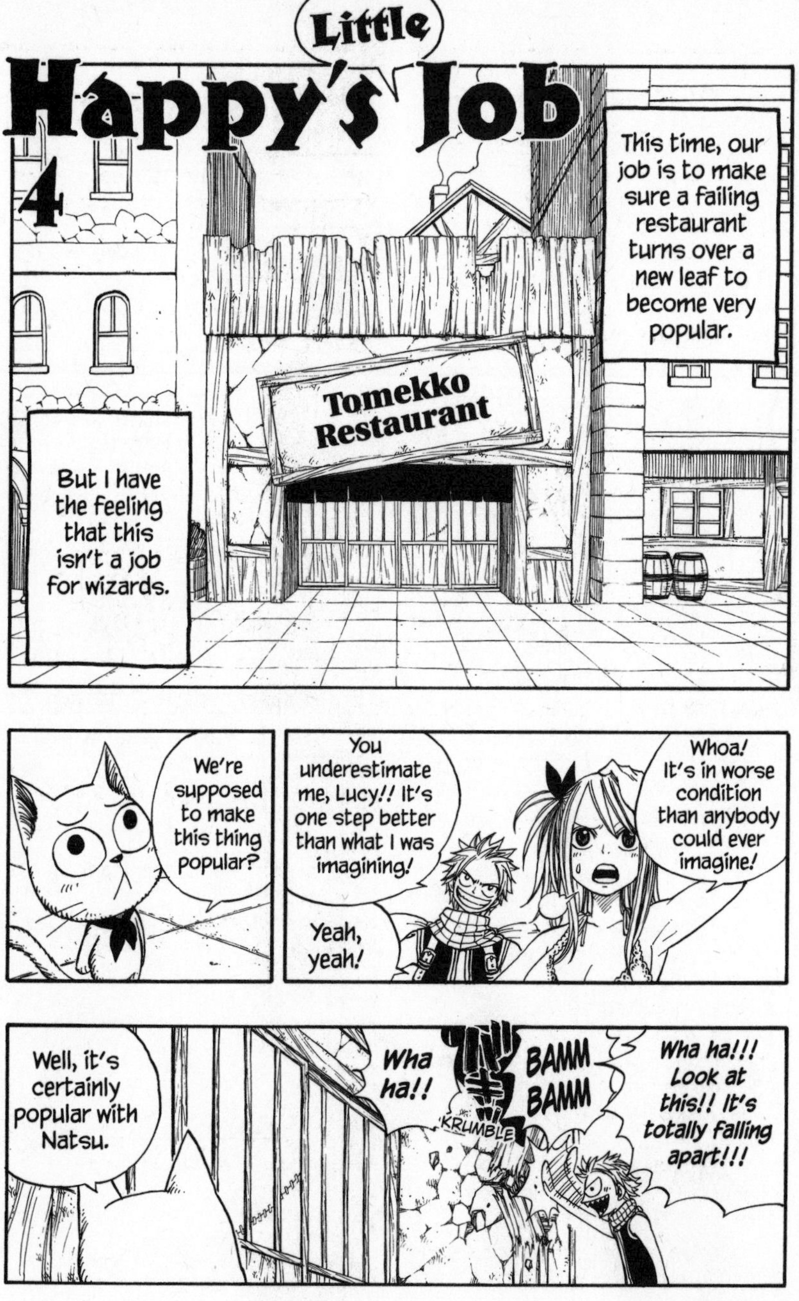
Little
Happy's Job
4
This time, our job is to make sure a failing restaurant turns over a new leaf to become very popular.
Tomekko Restaurant
But I have the feeling that this isn't a job for wizards.
Whoa! It's in worse condition than anybody could ever imagine!
You underestimate me, Lucy!! It's one step better than what I was imagining!
Yeah, yeah!
We're supposed to make this thing popular?
Wha ha!!! Look at this!! It's totally falling apart!!!
BAMM BAMM
KRUMBLE
Wha ha!!
Well, it's certainly popular with Natsu.

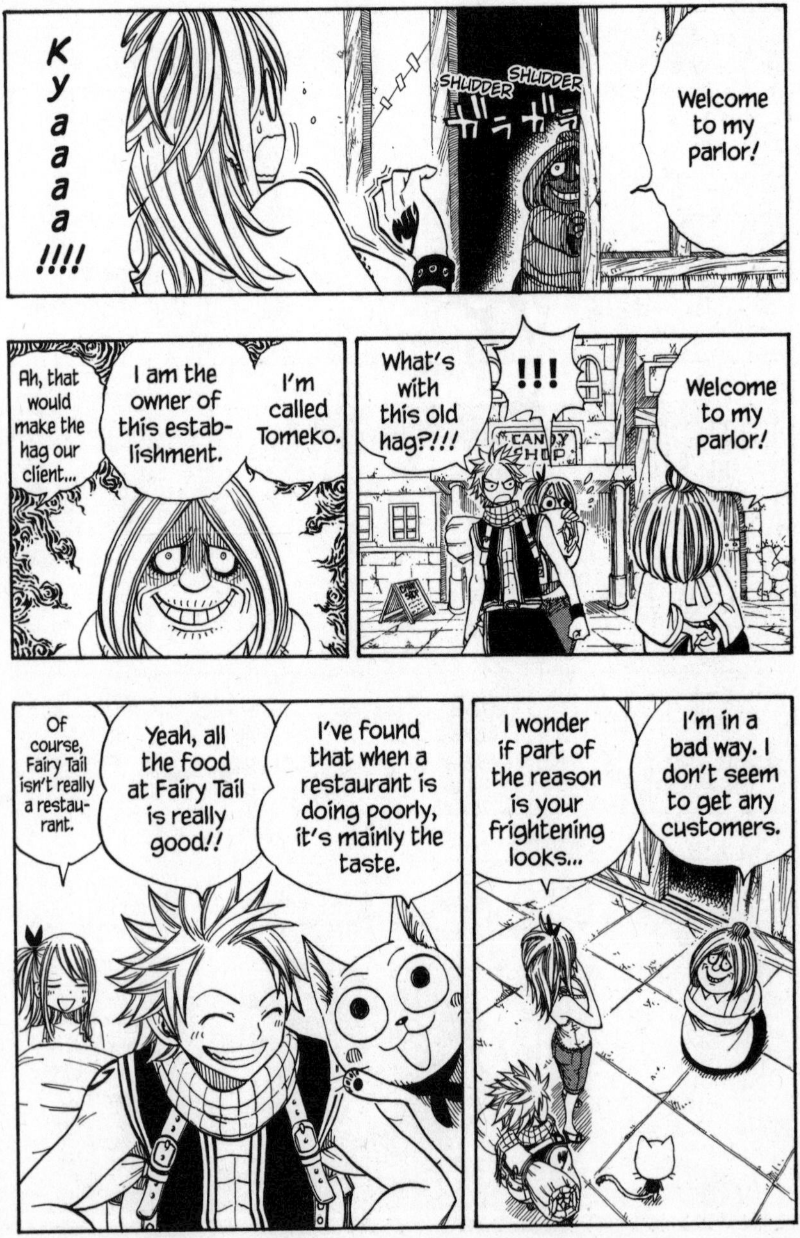
Welcome to my parlor!
SHUDDER SHUDDER
Kyaaaa!!!!
Welcome to my parlor!
!!!
What's with this old hag?!!!
I'm called Tomeko.
I am the owner of this establishment.
Ah, that would make the hag our client...
I'm in a bad way. I don't seem to get any customers.
I wonder if part of the reason is your frightening looks...
I've found that when a restaurant is doing poorly, it's mainly the taste.
Yeah, all the food at Fairy Tail is really good!!
Of course, Fairy Tail isn't really a restaurant.

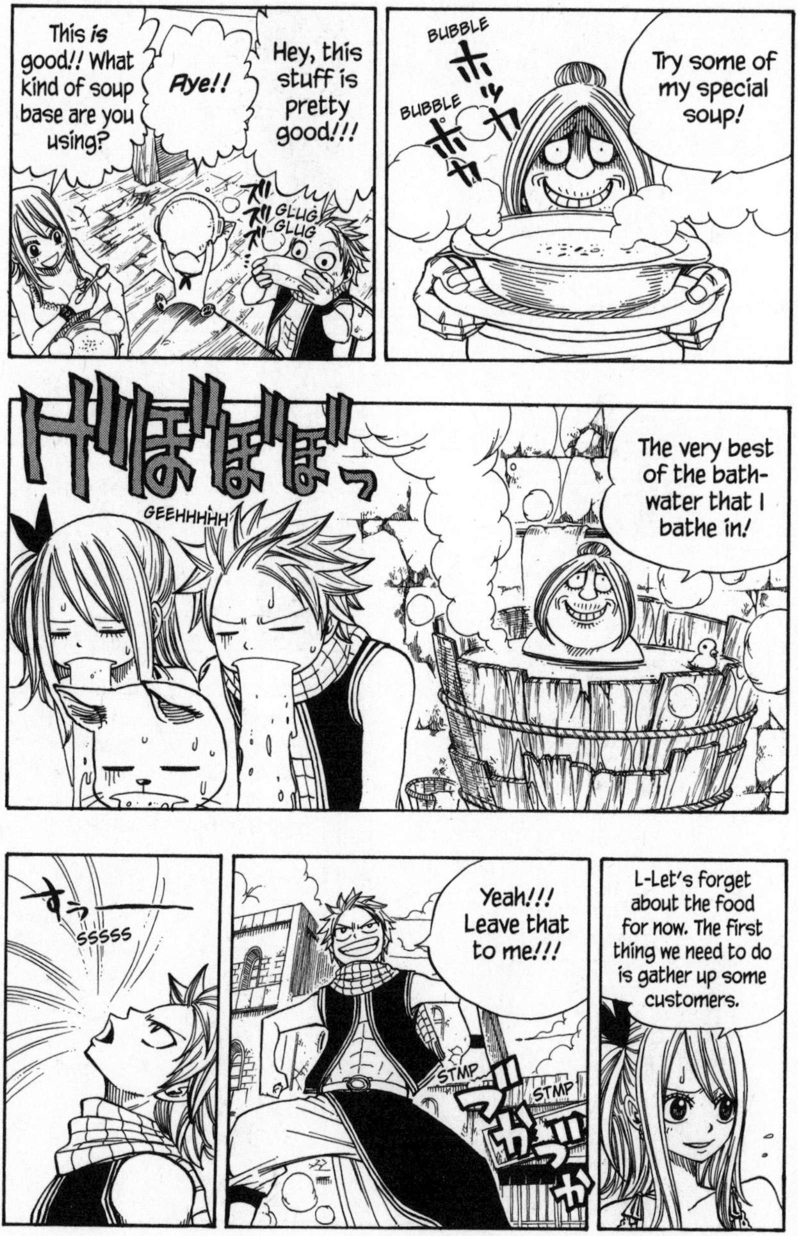
BUBBLE
BUBBLE
Try some of my special soup!
Hey, this stuff is pretty good!!!
Aye!!
This *is* good!! What kind of soup base are you using?
GLUG GLUG
The very best of the bath-water that I bathe in!
GEEHHHHHH
L-Let's forget about the food for now. The first thing we need to do is gather up some customers.
Yeah!!! Leave that to me!!!
STMP
STMP
SSSSS

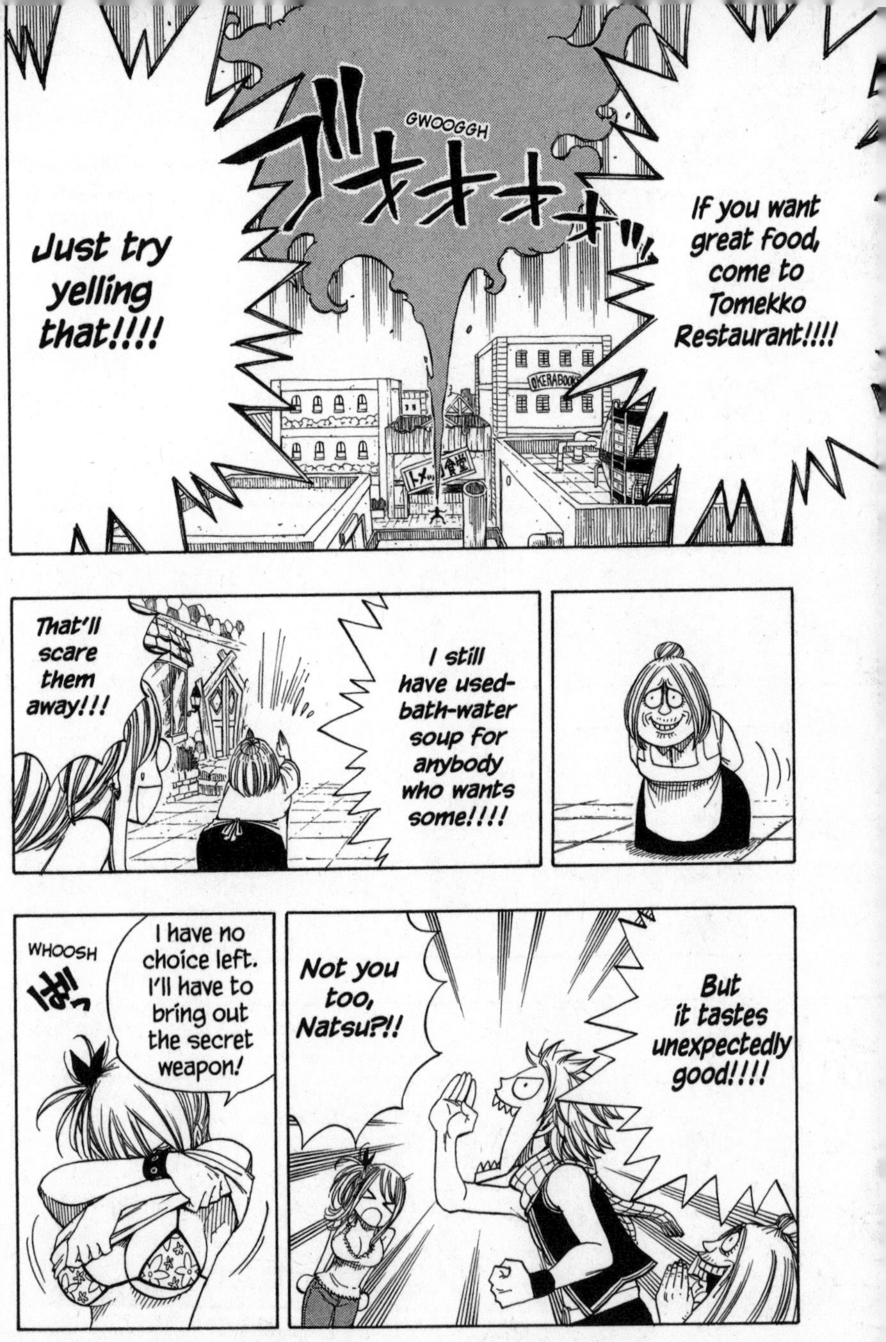
GWOOGGH
If you want great food, come to Tomekko Restaurant!!!!
Just try yelling that!!!!
OKERABOOKS
I still have used-bath-water soup for anybody who wants some!!!!
That'll scare them away!!!
But it tastes unexpectedly good!!!!
Not you too, Natsu?!!
I have no choice left. I'll have to bring out the secret weapon!
WHOOSH

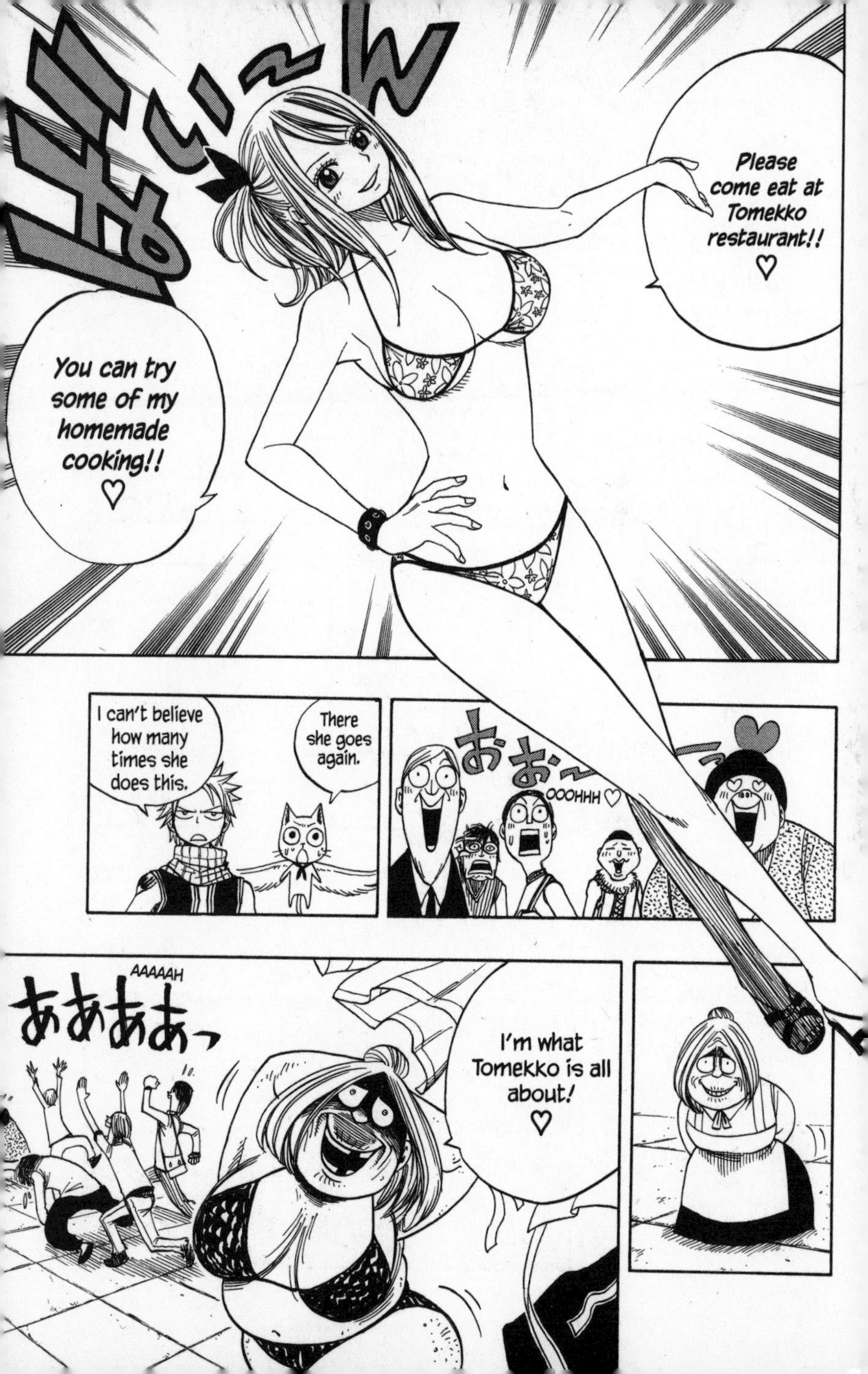
Please come eat at Tomekko restaurant!! ♡
ぱい～ん
You can try some of my homemade cooking!! ♡
おお～
OOOHHH ♡
There she goes again.
I can't believe how many times she does this.
I'm what Tomekko is all about! ♡
ああああっ
AAAAAH

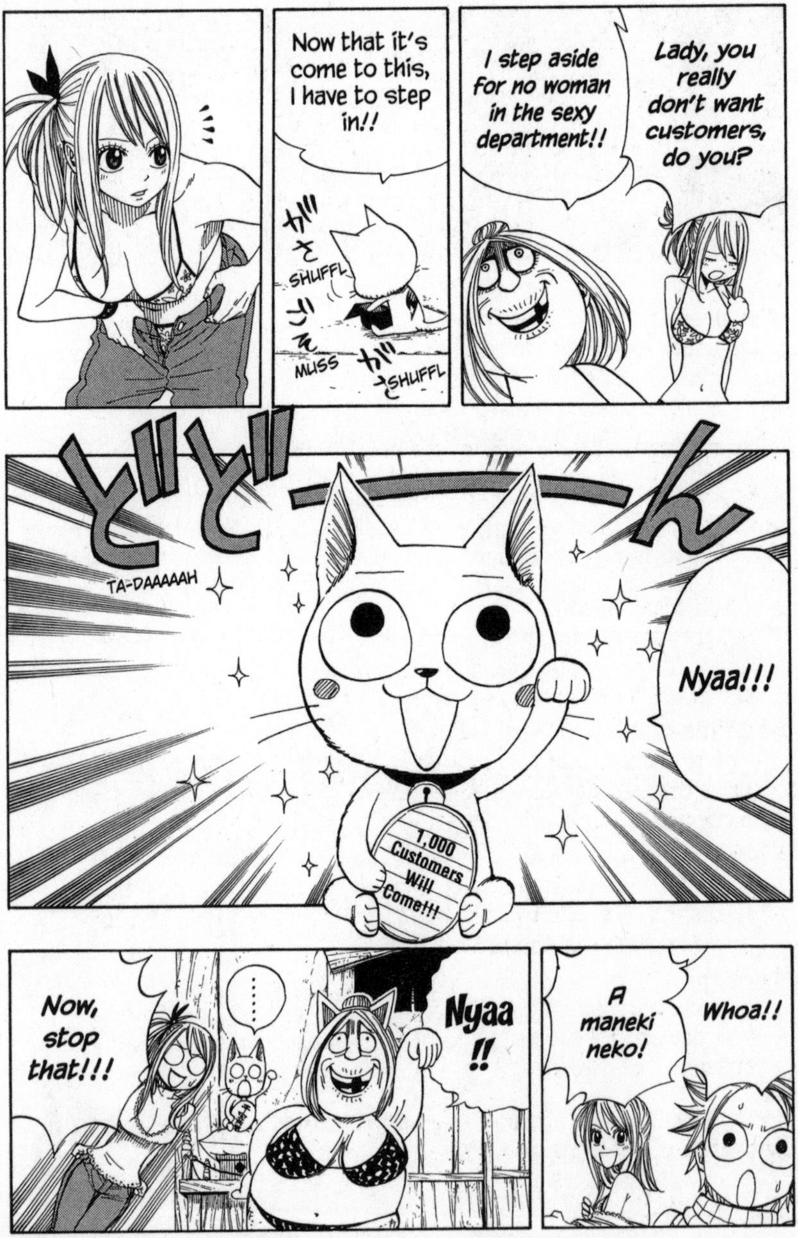
Lady, you really don't want customers, do you?
I step aside for no woman in the sexy department!!
Now that it's come to this, I have to step in!!
SHUFFL
MUSS
SHUFFL
Nyaa!!!
TA-DAAAAAH
1,000 Customers Will Come!!!
Whoa!!
A maneki neko!
Nyaa!!
......
Now, stop that!!!

THE END

AFTERWORD

I'm sleepy!!! The seasons change, and I just can't keep my eyes open!! (Right now, the season is changing from summer to fall.) Long ago, I could get only a couple of hours sleep and still have lots of energy, but as I get older, that has slowly changed. Even so, I usually get about seven hours of sleep a night, and the other manga authors keep saying things like, "Wow, that's a lot!! I'm jealous!!" But even so, when I get sleepy, I get really sleepy. And with that, and the fact that I do work that takes long hours, I've figured out ways to deal with my sleepiness while I'm drawing my manga!

1 · I talk with the staff.
   It depends on how much people are into the conversation, of course, but it can really charge my batteries back up! There are a lot of times when I even forget how sleepy I was! O

2 · Coffee and Cigarettes.
   I go to the veranda and smoke one cigarette and come back to life! I have the feeling that coffee doesn't work on me anymore, so I use it more as a comfort drink. △

3 · Play.
   I watch DVDs, play games, go outside for a bit, and come back refreshed!! But while I'm doing it, I can get absorbed, and the manga doesn't get drawn! △

4 · Sleep.
   You know, just stop fighting it and get some sleep! And when you do, you don't just get rid of the sleepiness, you also get your strength back. O

Yeah, I know!! When you're sleepy, you should sleep! And to take my own advice...Good night, everybody!!

About the Creator

HIRO MASHIMA was born May 3, 1977, in the Nagano prefecture. His series *Rave Master* has made him one of the most popular manga artists in America. *Fairy Tail*, currently being serialized in *Weekly Shonen Magazine*, is his latest creation.

Translation Notes

Japanese is a tricky language for most Westerners, and translation is often more art than science. For your edification and reading pleasure, here are notes on some of the places where we could have gone in a different direction in our translation of the work, or where a Japanese cultural reference is used.

General Notes:
Wizard

In the original Japanese version of *Fairy Tail*, you'll find panels in which the English word "wizard" is part of the original illustration. So this translation has taken that as its inspiration and translated the word *madôshi* as "wizard." But *madôshi*'s meaning is similar to certain Japanese words that have been borrowed by the English language, such as judo (the soft way) and kendo (the way of the sword). *Madô* is the way of magic, and *madôshi* are those who follow the way of magic. So although the word "wizard" is used in the original dialogue, a Japanese reader would be likely to think not of traditional Western wizards such as Merlin or Gandalf, but of martial artists.

Names

Hiro Mashima has graciously agreed to provide official English spellings for just about all of the characters in *Fairy Tail*. Because this version of *Fairy Tail* is the first publication of most of these spellings, there will inevitably be differences between these spellings and some of the fan interpretations that may have spread throughout the Web or in other fan circles. Rest assured that the spellings contained in this book are the spellings that Mashima-sensei wanted for *Fairy Tail*.

The Moon Can Be Hidden by Clouds, page 3

"The Moon Can Be Hidden by Clouds; Flowers Can Be Scattered by the Wind," is a Japanese proverb (*kotowaza*) that means that nothing in this world is certain.

The young debutant of the Heartfilia Konzern, Miss Lucy-sama!!!

Konzern, page 36

Konzern is a German word that Japanese sometimes borrows to refer to a business empire.

Lacrima, page 59

Lacrima is Latin for "tear," and the word has been used in Japanese to describe certain types of crystals and beads. The Fairy Tail universe seems to use the word for magical crystals.

This time, I'm taking all of my exploding lacrima crystals with me!!!

You have no final ace to play.

Final ace, page 80

This is an approximate translation. In Japanese, Jose said, "You will never have your triumphal song." That doesn't really come across in English as well as I wanted it to, so I changed the reference to playing aces in cards, which conveyed the same feeling without the unusual concept.

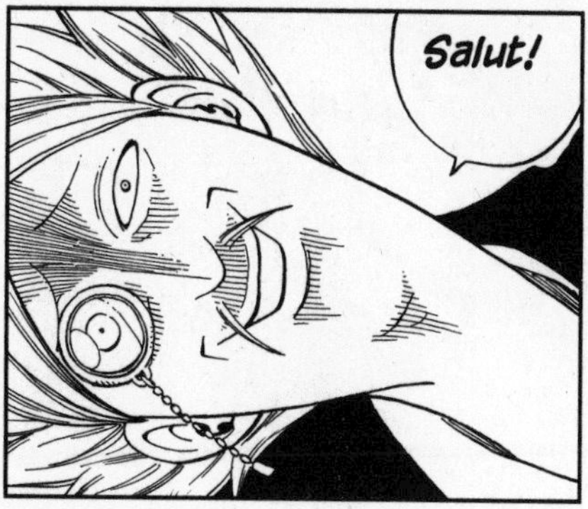
Salut!

Salut, page 132

Salut is French for "greetings."

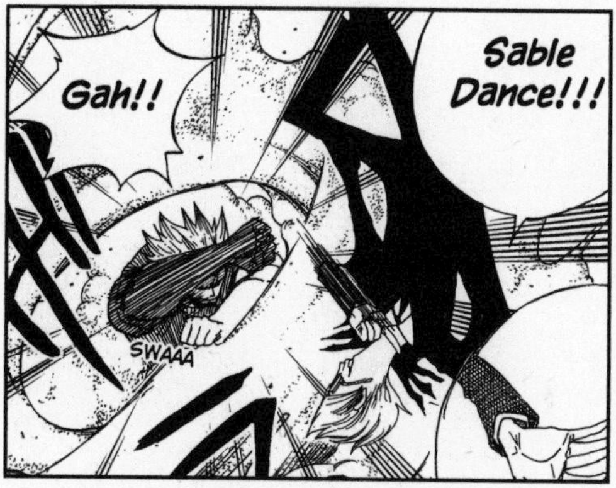
Sable Dance!!!
Gah!!
SWAAA

Sable Dance, page 137

Sable is French for "sand."

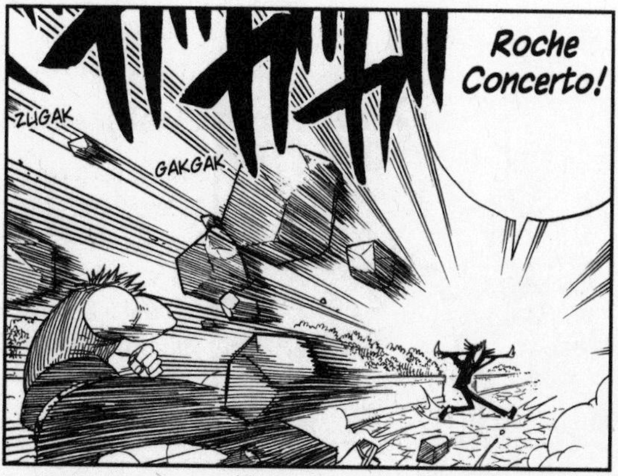
Roche Concerto!
GAKGAK
ZUGAK

Roche Concerto, page 138

Roche is French for "rock."

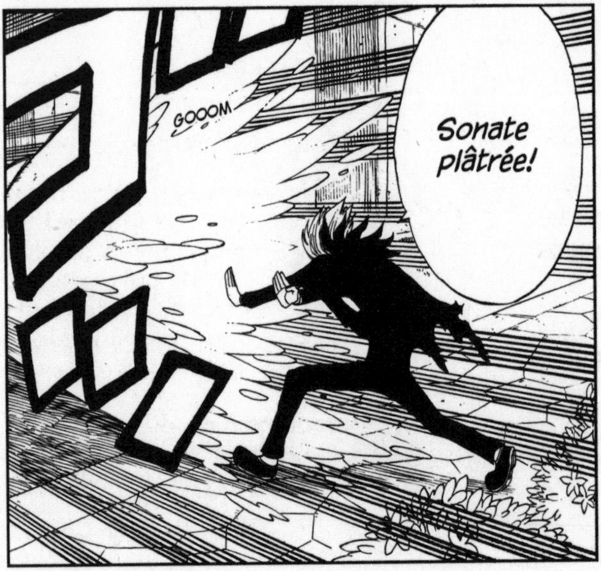
Sonate plâtrée!
GOOOM

***Sonate plâtrée*, page 142**

Sonate plâtrée is French for "Plaster sonata."

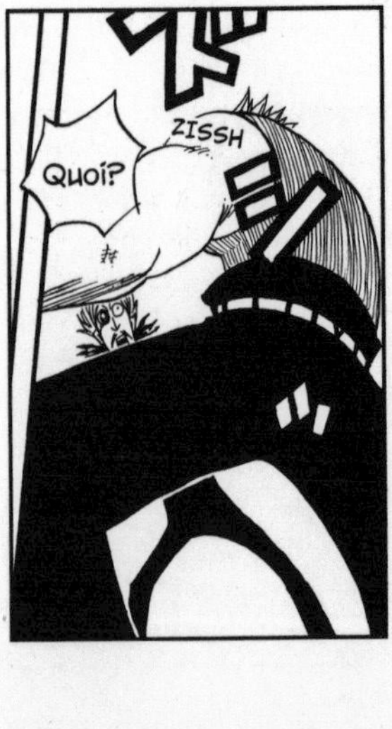
ZISSH
Quoi?

***Quoi?*, page 146**

Of course, *quoi* means "what" in French.

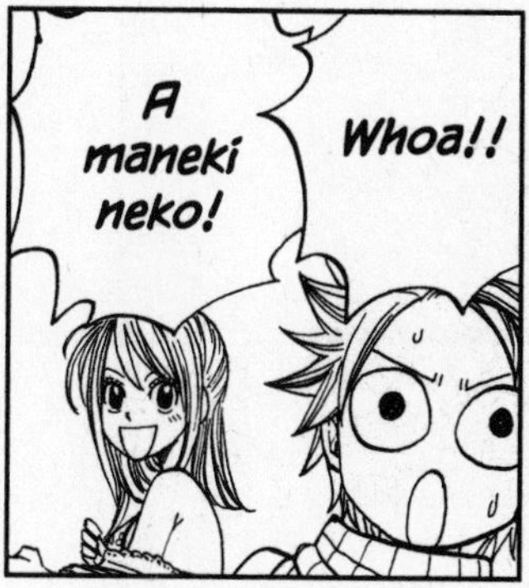
Whoa!!
A maneki neko!

maneki neko, page 190

Most Japanese businesses have a ceramic cat figure with one paw raised in a "come here"-like invitation and a traditional-style gold coin held close to its body. It is a good-luck charm made especially for businesses (but other establishments may also use it). The raised paw is an invitation for customers to come and the gold coin represents financial success.

Circles/triangles/X-marks, page 191

After Mashima-sensei describes his methods for staying awake, he gives them a rating. This rating is very common among Japanese. The circle ○ represents a yes vote, or a stamp of approval. The triangle △ represents a flawed answer that may have good points, but doesn't really cut it. The no vote, or an answer that is completely wrong, is represented by an X-mark, X.

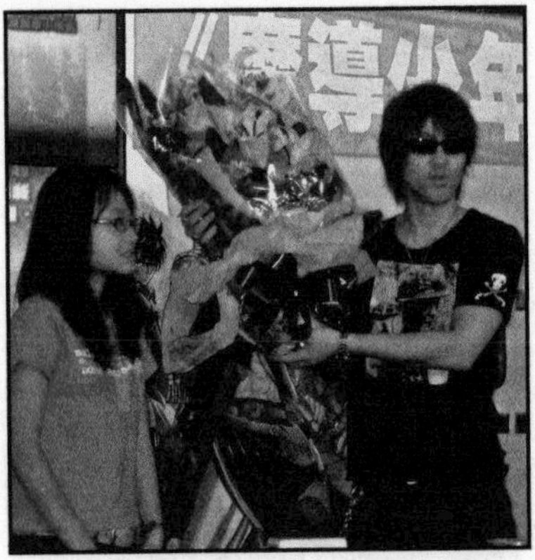
魔導少年

I went to a signing in Taiwan!! They gave me such a warm and passionate welcome! Some of the fans even brought me bouquets of flowers! Really! I was so happy to be able to have such close contact with the fans! I got carried away and shouted, "Everybody!! I love you all!" For some reason, that got printed in the local newspapers.

—Hiro Mashima

Preview of Volume 8

We're pleased to present you with a preview from volume 8, now available from Kodansha Comics. Check out our Web site (www.kodanshacomics.com) for more details!

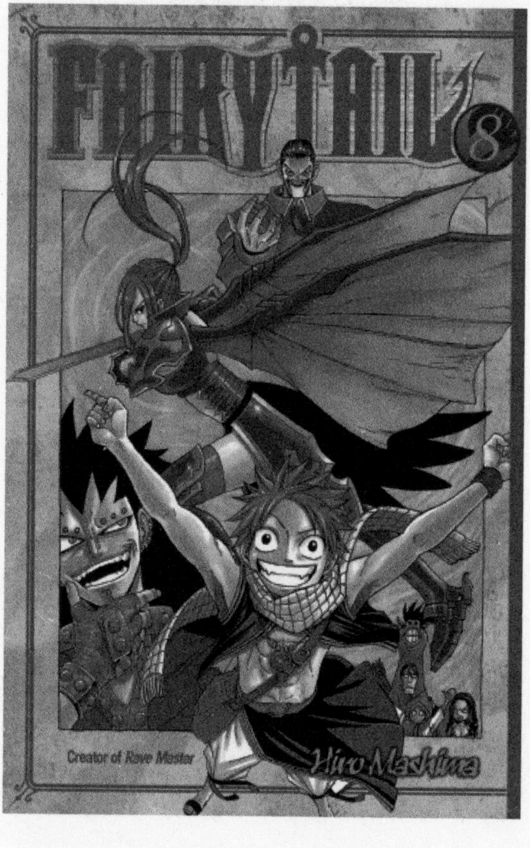
FAIRY TAIL
8
Creator of Rave Master
Hiro Mashima

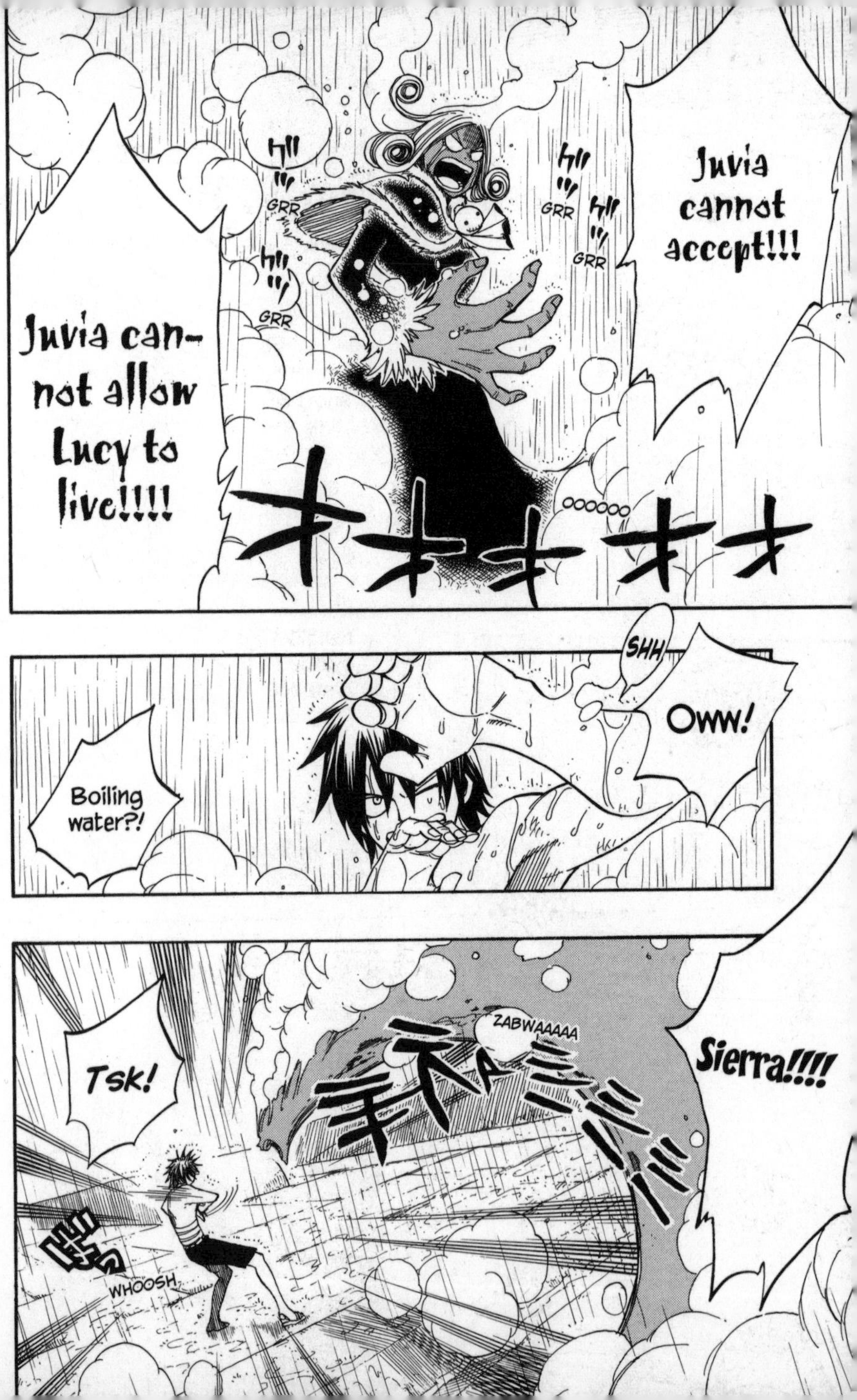
Juvia cannot accept!!!
GRR
GRR
GRR
GRR
Juvia cannot allow Lucy to live!!!!
OOOOOO
SHH
Oww!
Boiling water?!
Sierra!!!!
ZABWAAAAA
Tsk!
WHOOSH

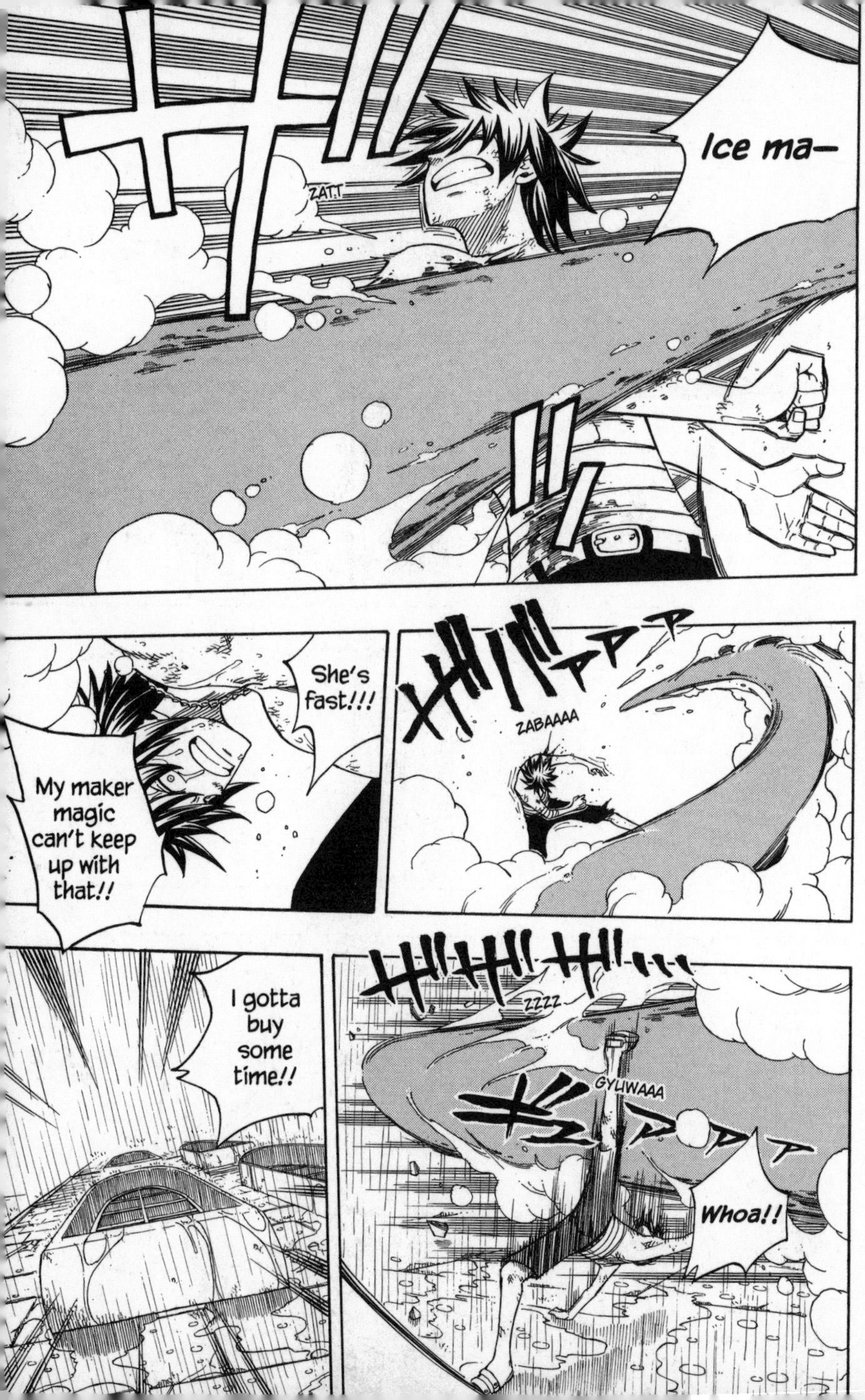
ZATT
Ice ma–
ZABAAAA
She's fast!!!
My maker magic can't keep up with that!!
ZZZZ
GYUWAAA
Whoa!!
I gotta buy some time!!

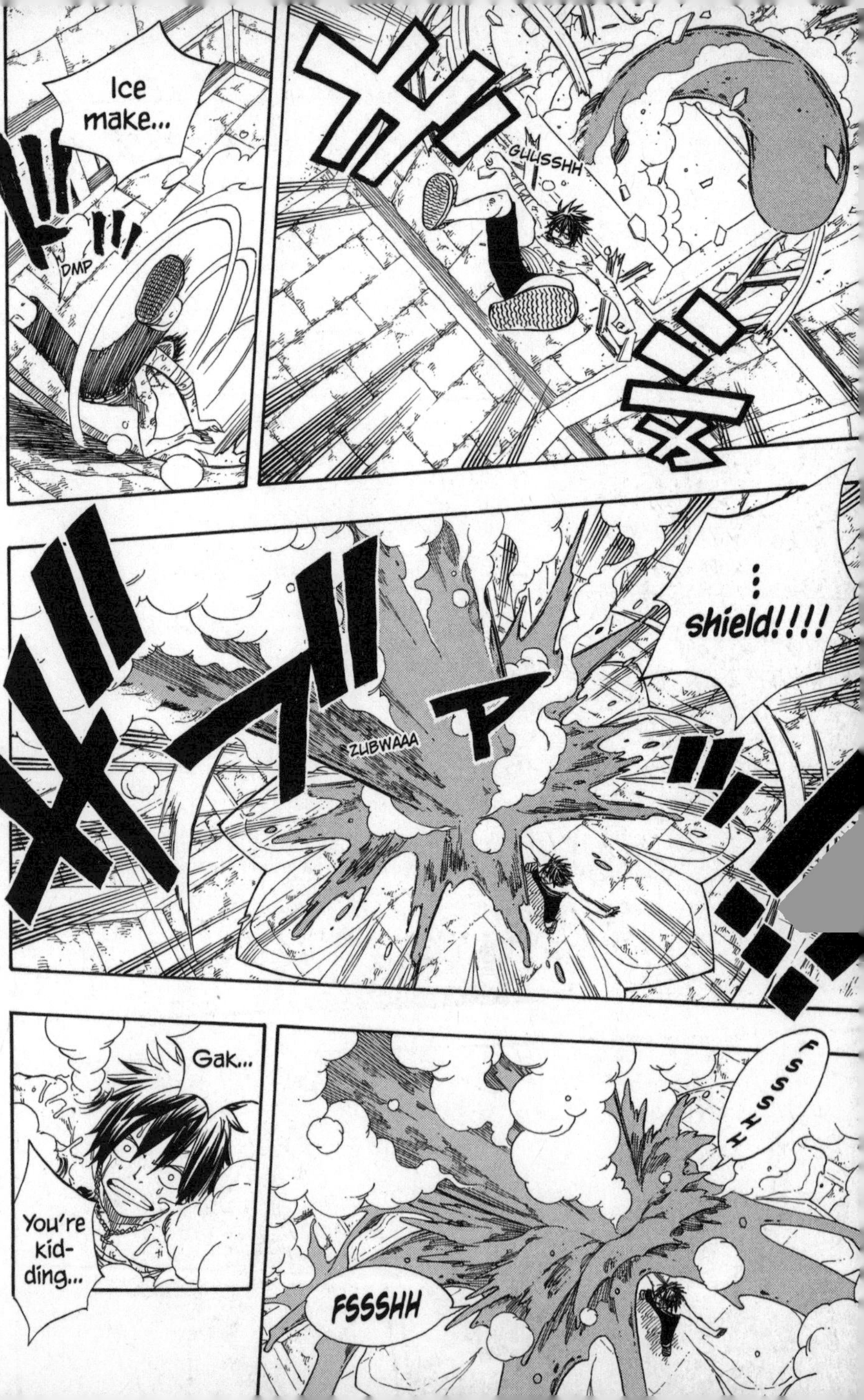
GUUSSHH
Ice make...
DMP
...
shield!!!!
ZUBWAAA
FSSSHH
FSSSHH
Gak...
You're kid-ding...

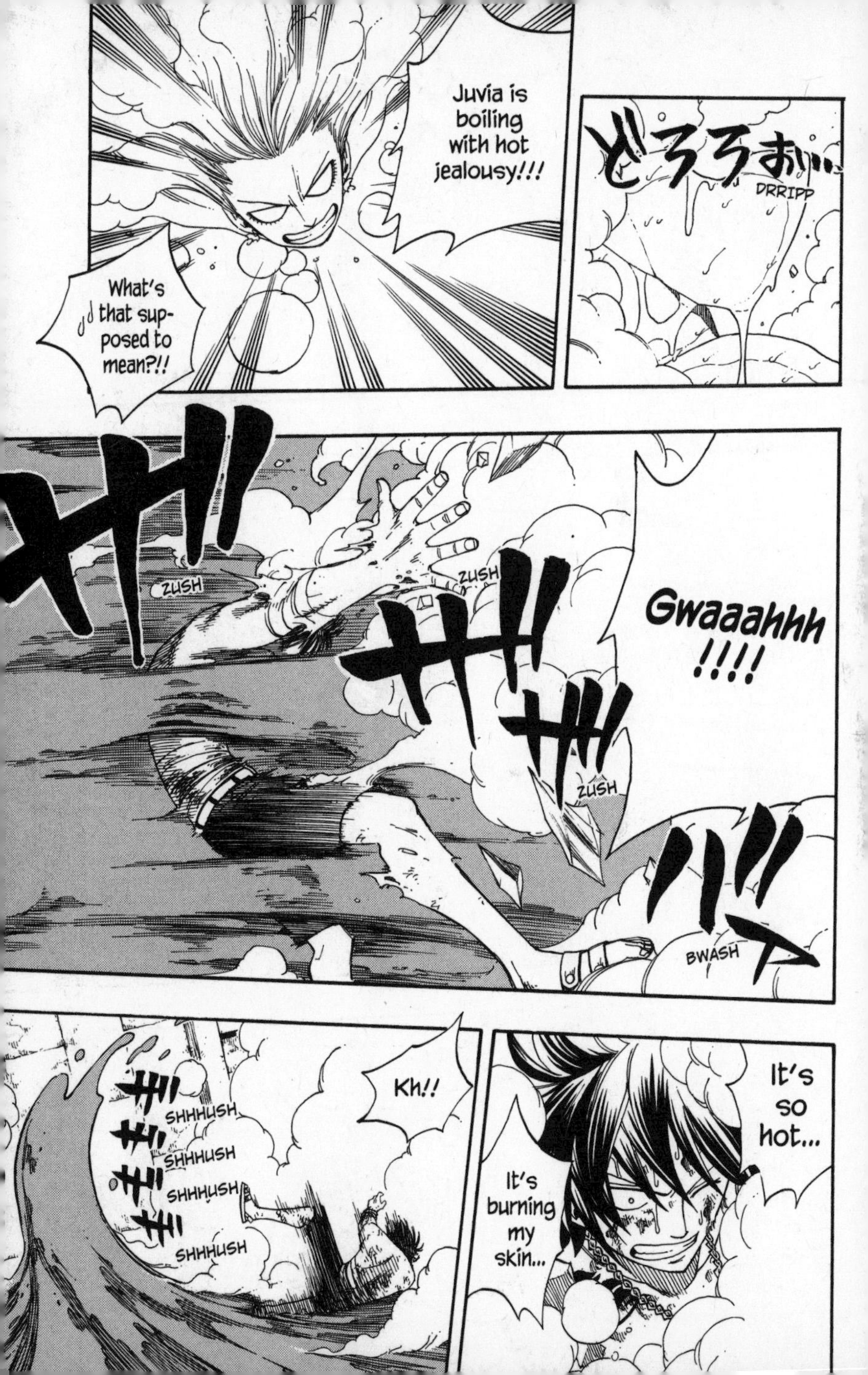
DRRIPP
Juvia is boiling with hot jealousy!!!
What's that sup-posed to mean?!!
Gwaaahhh !!!!
ZUSH
ZUSH
ZUSH
BWASH
It's so hot...
It's burning my skin...
Kh!!
SHHHUSH
SHHHUSH
SHHHUSH
SHHHUSH

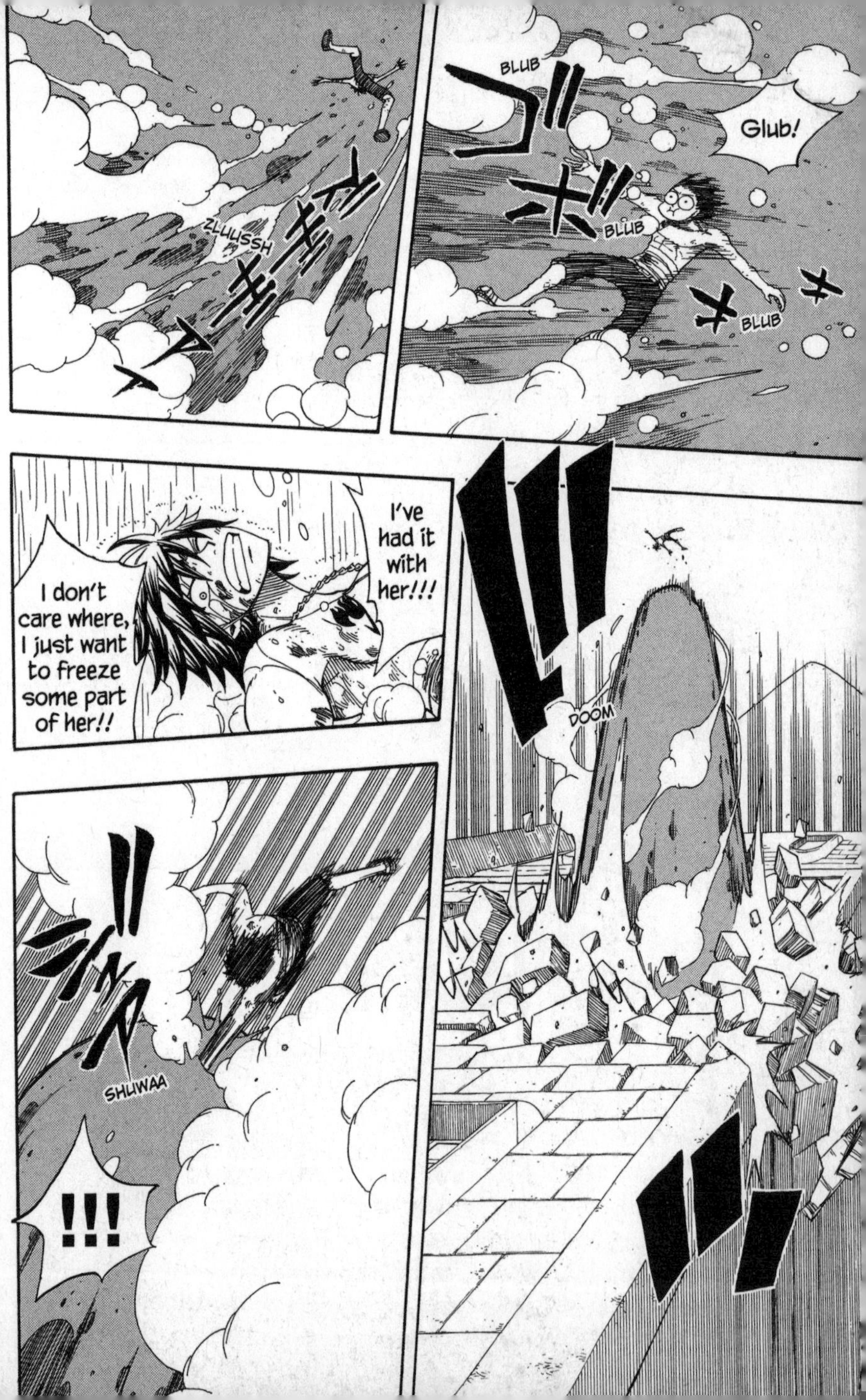
Glub!
BLUB
BLUB
BLUB
ZLUUSSH
DOOM
I've had it with her!!!
I don't care where, I just want to freeze some part of her!!
SHUWAA
!!!

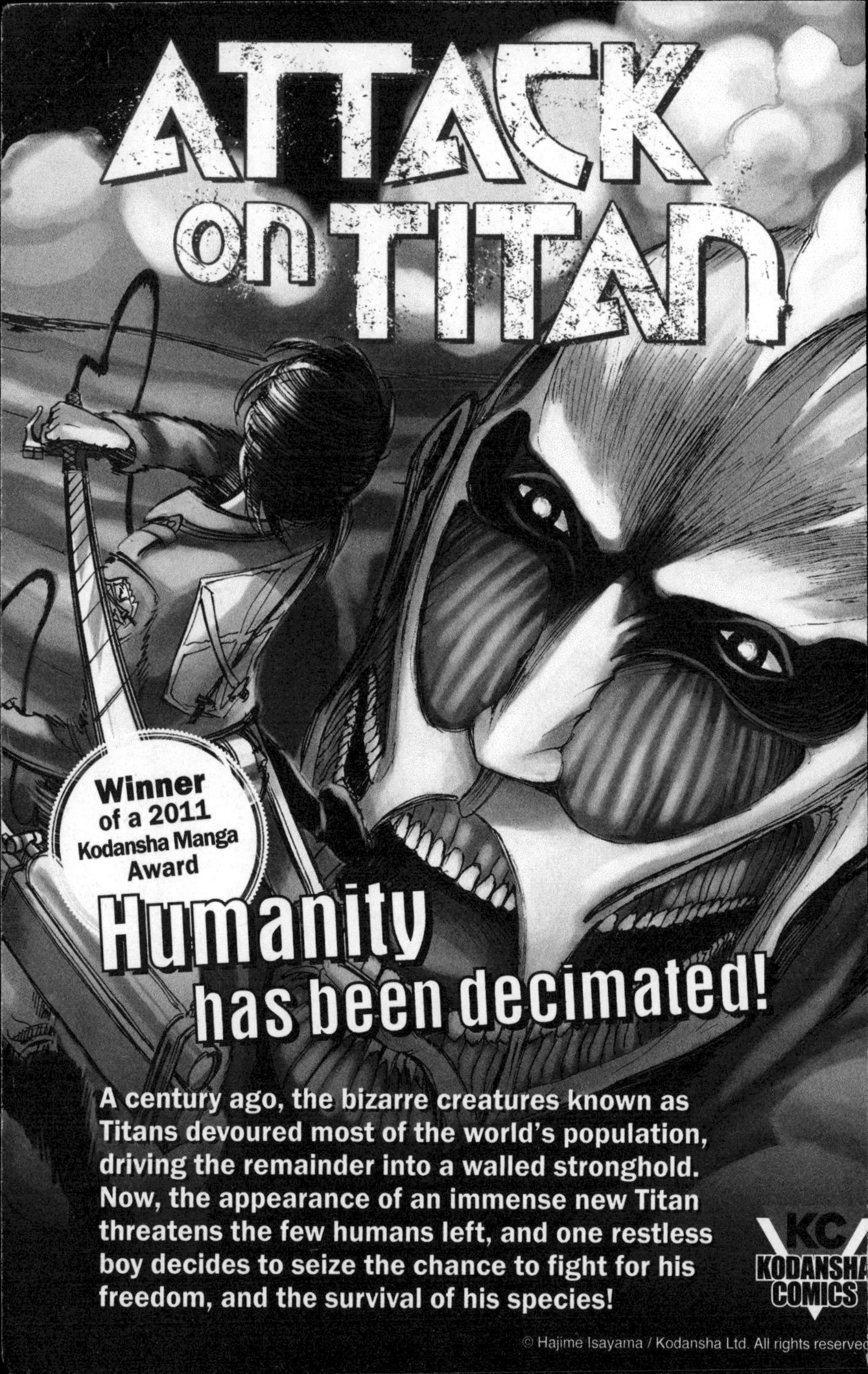
ATTACK ON TITAN
Winner of a 2011 Kodansha Manga Award
Humanity has been decimated!
A century ago, the bizarre creatures known as Titans devoured most of the world's population, driving the remainder into a walled stronghold. Now, the appearance of an immense new Titan threatens the few humans left, and one restless boy decides to seize the chance to fight for his freedom, and the survival of his species!
KC KODANSHA COMICS
© Hajime Isayama / Kodansha Ltd. All rights reserved